CW00690466

# ETHNIC AND LINGUISTIC
# CONTEXT OF IDENTITY:

# FINNO-UGRIC MINORITIES

Uralica
Helsingiensia 5

# Ethnic and Linguistic Context of Identity:

# Finno-Ugric Minorities

EDITED BY
RIHO GRÜNTHAL & 
MAGDOLNA KOVÁCS

HELSINKI 2011

Riho Grünthal, Magdolna Kovács (eds):
*Ethnic and Linguistic Context of Identity: Finno-Ugric Minorities.*
Uralica Helsingiensia 5.

The articles in this publication are based on presentations given at the symposium *"Ethnic and Linguistic Context of Identity: Finno-Ugric Minorities"* held at the University of Helsinki in March, 2009.

Layout, cover Anna Kurvinen
Cover photographs Riho Grünthal
Map on page 269 Arttu Paarlahti
Maps on pages 280, 296, and 297 Anna Kurvinen

ISBN 978-952-5667-28-8
ISSN 1797-3945

Vammalan Kirjapaino Oy
Sastamala 2011

**Orders · Tilaukset**

Tiedekirja            www.tiedekirja.fi
Kirkkokatu 14         tiedekirja@tsv.fi
FI-00170 Helsinki     fax +358 9 635 017

## Uralica Helsingiensia

Uralica Helsingiensia is a series published jointly by the University of Helsinki Finno-Ugric Language Section and the Finno-Ugrian Society. It features monographs and thematic collections of articles with a research focus on Uralic languages, and it also covers the linguistic and cultural aspects of Estonian, Hungarian and Saami studies at the University of Helsinki.

The series has a peer review system, i.e. the manuscripts of all articles and monographs submitted for publication will be refereed by two anonymous reviewers before binding decisions are made concerning the publication of the material.

Uralica Helsingiensia on Helsingin yliopiston suomalais-ugrilaisten kieliaineiden yhdessä Suomalais-Ugrilaisen Seuran kanssa julkaisema sarja, jossa ilmestyy monografioita ja temaattisia artikkelikokoelmia. Niiden aihepiiri liittyy uralilaisten kielten tutkimukseen ja kattaa myös Helsingin yliopistossa tehtävän Viron kielen ja kulttuurin, Unkarin kielen ja kulttuurin sekä saamentutkimuksen.

Sarjassa noudatetaan refereekäytäntöä, eli julkaistavaksi esitettävien tutkimusten käsikirjoitus annetaan kahden nimettömän asiantuntijan arvioitavaksi ennen kuin lopullinen julkaisupäätös tehdään.

Publishers · Julkaisijat
        University of Helsinki: Department of Finnish, Finno-Ugrian and Scandinavian Studies ·
        Helsingin yliopisto: Suomen kielen, suomalais-ugrilaisten ja pohjoismaisten kielten ja kirjallisuuksien laitos
        Finno-Ugrian Society · Suomalais-Ugrilainen Seura

Editors · Päätoimittajat
        Ulla-Maija Forsberg, Riho Grünthal

Editorial board · Toimitusneuvosto
        Márta Csepregi, Cornelius Hasselblatt, Magdolna Kovács, Johanna Laakso, Helle Metslang, Matti Miestamo, Irma Mullonen, Karl Pajusalu, Janne Saarikivi, Anneli Sarhimaa, Elena Skribnik
        www.sgr.fi/uh

The publications are indexed in ARTO data base with the index Urbis.
Julkaisut luetteloidaan ja indeksoidaan ARTO-tietokantaan tunnuksella Urbis.

# Contents

Riho Grünthal & Magdolna Kovács
Introduction     7

Johanna Laakso
Being Finno-Ugrian, Being in the Minority
– Reflections on Linguistic and Other Criteria     13

Irja Seurujärvi-Kari
"We Took Our Language Back"
– The Formation of a Sámi Identity within the Sámi
Movement and the Role of the Sámi Language
from the 1960s until 2008     37

Elisabeth Scheller
The Sámi Language Situation
in Russia     79

Vilmos Tánczos
The Moldavian Csángós – Questions of Demography
and Linguistic Assimilation     97

Magdolna Kovács
Ethnic and linguistic identities of Hungarians
and their descendants in Finland     121

Boglárka Straszer
Language and Identity among Hungarians in Sweden     161

Raimo Raag
I'm Estonian – What Is Your Excuse?
– Ethnic and Linguistic Aspects of the Identity
of Estonians in Sweden     197

Kristiina Praakli
The New Estonian Community
in Finland     217

Kadri Koreinik
Language Ideologies and Identity-building
in the Public Discourse of South Estonian     247

Riho Grünthal
Population decline and the Erosion
of the Veps Language Community 267

Larisa Shirobokova
Ethnic Identity and Udmurt people 295

Outi Tánczos
Identity Construction in an Udmurt Daily Newspaper 321

Márta Csepregi & Sofia Onina
Observations of Khanty Identity: the Synya and Surgut Khanty 341

Zoltán Nagy
The Invisible "Ostyaks": The Khanty people
in the Tomsk Oblast 359

Sándor Szeverényi & Beáta Wagner-Nagy
Visiting the Nganasans in Ust-Avam 385

List of Contributors 405

RIHO GRÜNTHAL & MAGDOLNA KOVÁCS

# Introduction

| | |
|---|---|
| *Sámegiella, gollegiella* | *Sámi language, golden language,* |
| *manne oađát šlundadat?* | *why is it you sleep and brood?* |
| *Ale jaskkot eatnigiella,* | *Do not yet fall silent* |
| *dasgo vieris gielat, mielat dutnje* | *while foreign minds and tongues* |
| *juo hávddi goivvodit,* | *dig for you a grave,* |
| *vaikke it leat vel liđđon,* | *although you have as yet not blossomed,* |
| *eaige urbbit rahpasan.* | *or opened out your buds.* |
| (Hans Aslak Guttorm 1934) | |

Language never stops changing, nor do the societies in which languages are spoken. The 20th century brought about an enormous change in relationships between languages, speech communities and geographical areas. Distances that could be measured in miles or days spent on a boat, in a sleigh or horse-drawn carriage were replaced by free mobility, air travel and the hours it took to pass from one distinctive part of the world to another. Moors, forests, rivers and seas no longer corresponded to language borders.

From a linguistic viewpoint, one of the most significant results of the accessibility of distinct areas is an invigorated discussion on the differences between majority and minority languages. Because a majority language is often the basic communication tool in society, minority language speakers have to constantly adopt new means and linguistic strategies. During the 20th century and at the beginning of 21st, economic conditions, educational systems and legislative aims have seldom favoured the sustainability of minority language communities and the identity of their speakers. While new minority communities arise all the time, numerous old unique ones have ceased to exist or are on the verge of being irreversibly lost. The documenting, explaining and understanding of what is currently going on in

*Ethnic and Linguistic Context of Identity: Finno-Ugric Minorities.* 7–12.
Uralica Helsingiensia 5. Helsinki 2011.

language communities constitute a major challenge for modern linguistics and societies.

The current volume focuses on the language and language identity of individual speakers and communities among the Finno-Ugric minorities. The Finno-Ugric minorities live in a world in which borders can easily be crossed. These people have different histories, their political and economic circumstances are far from uniform, and they are different from the majority language groups in many ways. Every language community has its own special characteristics, but in general, there is considerable liaison between different minorities and these languages can well be studied within the same type of framework. The Finno-Ugric minority languages considered in this book illustrate the fate of language minorities in more general terms.

The more evident the language shift and loss of cultures have become the more important it has become to describe the state-of-art of the minority languages and the linguistic identity of their speakers. An understanding of the minority language situation starts with an explanation of the historical background and the emergence of minority language status. In the case of those Finno-Ugric minorities that are the topic of the present book, some examples represent autochtonous languages, whereas in other cases migration has brought people into new linguistic and cultural environments. Hungarian, for instance, has a long history as the main language of a modern European country, but those varieties spoken outside of Hungary represent local minority languages with very different profiles. Although many Hungarians do live in those countries neighbouring Hungary, there are also smaller groups of migrants in more distant locations, such as Finland and Sweden.

One of the most dramatic changes on the linguistic map of the modern world concerns the use of language. The possibility of using a minority language depends on population size, cultural context, language rights and, last but not least, awareness of linguistic identity by individual speakers. Their active command of the language is crucial for language vitality and intergenerational transmission. Social, economic and political changes that have affected language communities also affect the domains in which a given language is used. It is very common for new domains and a different cultural context to trigger language shift, and bilingual or multilingual speakers choose the language that better fits a given situation. Bilingualism and the imbalance between majority and minority languages are not focused on in this book. However, these aspects are inherently embedded in the debate about minority languages. Without a majority there is no minority.

The parallel existence of different cultural environments in which different languages are used means that the concept of language is far from unambiguous. Both in eroding communities and migrant societies minority language is often related to the individual. Speaking a minority language is an individual experience to a very large extent. The result of a partial or only a loose collective experience is that the perception of language varies among language speakers.

Although geographical adjacency and genetic affinity are not very important in sociolinguistic analyses, the selection of articles in this book reflects some areal viewpoints, too. Geographical location, economic conditions and political systems certainly affect the state of minority languages.

The articles intertwine several thematic viewpoints. The Sámi languages represent autochtonous northern European languages, both of Scandinavia and north-western Russia. Hungarian outside of Hungary and Estonian outside of Estonia represent vigorous modern languages that have a different status as autochtonous or migrant languages outside of these two countries. The Baltic Sea area is strongly represented both in the form of old minority languages, such as South Estonian and Veps, and migrant groups such as Estonian and Hungarian in Finland. Most Finno-Ugric minority languages are spoken in Russia. The Udmurts, illustrating a partly urbanised minority, live in the European part of Russia, whereas some others, namely the Khanty and the Nganasans, represent small indigenous minorities in Siberia that have very lately been forced into contact with urban centres and their structures.

Numerous details distinguish languages from one another. Minority languages and their cultural environments diverge. The aim of this volume is not to find similarities and dissimilarities between individual groups: the main point is to illustrate the diversity of Finno-Ugric minorities in various countries, societies, cultural and geographical environments.

The authors of the articles were asked to present available information concerning the population size of the minority under research and briefly comment on the historical background of the investigated group. This should make the articles and the minorities easy to compare. The methodologies applied and the empirical parts of the articles, in turn, depend much more on the chosen perspective. Their main points are characteristically case specific. In most cases the authors approach the crucial importance of language for individual speakers and entire groups from different viewpoints.

Although the genetic affinity between the Finno-Ugric languages and their geographical distribution play only a marginal role in the discussion concerning the current state of minority languages, the book is organised in such a way that the articles reflect different areal perspectives.

A general overview of the Finno-Ugric minority languages and their research perspectives is provided by Johanna **Laakso** (University of Vienna). She also reflects on the ambiguity of talking about the Finno-Ugric language family and minority languages within the same framework. Besides academic issues, there are certain moments during which genetic affinity is applied as an identity strengthening resource.

Two articles show the dissimilarities between Sámi groups. Irja **Seurujärvi-Kari** (University of Helsinki), a native speaker of North Sámi herself and lecturer in Sámi languages, describes the successful revitalisation of the North Sámi language and recognition of Sámi identity within the Sámi movement. The change that brought an end to language shift and the assimilation of the Sámi people occurred more than thirty years ago. The state-of-the-art of the Sámi languages in the Kola Peninsula, in the north-western corner of Russia, is much more serious. Elisabeth **Scheller** (University of Tromsø) illuminates the multiplicity of Sámi identity in this context.

In Hungarian ethnography the Csángós are often characterised as a most special group living far from modern Hungary. The sociolinguistic situation of this particular group, the Moldavian Csángós, is discussed by Vilmos **Tánczos** (Babeş-Bolyai University, Cluj / Kolozsvár). Two other articles deal with the Hungarian minorities in northern Europe. Magdolna **Kovács** (University of Helsinki) and

Boglárka **Straszer** (Uppsala University) approach the diversity of Hungarian minorities from the viewpoint of sustaining Hungarian identity and fostering the language in Finland (Kovács) and Sweden (Straszer). Both communities were formed gradually during the second half of the 20th century.

In the case of Estonian, the post-war period has been characterised by strong alternations in population mobility and new settlements. Raimo **Raag** (Uppsala University), himself a descendant of Estonian refugees from World War II, discusses the arrival, settling and finally integration of the Estonian minority in Sweden after World War II and during the following decades. For political reasons, there was no parallel group in Finland, as Kristiina **Praakli** (University of Tartu) shows. Nevertheless, the past two decades have been marked by a period of intensive contact between these closely related languages following the arrival of numerous Estonians in Finland. The multiplicity of migrant groups is illustrated in the varying linguistic identity of Estonians in Finland. Kadri **Koreinik** (University of Tartu), in turn, considers the manifestations of minority groups in southern Estonia, most notably the role of newspaper texts published in the Võru language in constructing and deconstructing local identity.

One of the smallest autochtonous minorities in the Baltic Sea region, the Veps, has suffered from a constant population decline since the 1930s. Even so, the Veps example shows the inadequacy of relying on official data when considering the actual language situation as Riho **Grünthal** (University of Helsinki) writes. In general, urbanisation and an abrupt change of life style have strongly influenced the Finno-Ugric minorities in Russia. Larisa **Shirobokova** (ELTE University, Budapest), representing young Udmurt adults like herself, and Outi **Tánczos** (University of Helsinki) both discuss the changing identity of the Udmurts. Shirobokova discusses young Udmurt adults living in towns, Tánczos evidence from newspaper texts. The way in which assumed ethnic identity and actual perception of the Udmurt language diverge is illustrated by means of the critical discourse analysis that Tánczos applies to her study.

Finally, three papers focus on the cultural and linguistic erosion of the Siberian minorities, two on Khanty and one on Nganasan

Samoyeds. Márta **Csepregi** (University of Budapest) and Sofia **Onina** (Yugra State University, Khanty-Mansiysk) discuss the sociolinguistic differences between two distinct Khanty groups, the eastern Surgut Khanty and the northern Synya Khanty, the group in which Onina was herself born. Regardless of a relatively small population there are very different ways in which modern Khants use their language and transfer it to the next generation – or change to Russian. The last focus group, the Nganasans, live in three settlements in which they belong to the periphery of modern urban centres but without having any real possibility of continuing their traditional way of life either, as reported by Sándor **Szeverényi** (University of Szeged) and Beáta **Wagner-Nagy** (University of Hamburg).

Most of the languages included in the examples of Finno-Ugric minorities are linguistically relatively well documented. With the exception of Nganasan there are dictionaries, grammatical overviews and texts that illustrate at least on a rudimentary level what the languages look like. Since the summaries are presented in the investigated languages, such as North Sámi, Kildin Sámi, Estonian, Veps, Udmurt, Hungarian etc., we have tried to make this fact visible in this book as well, at the end of individual articles. Alternatively, the summary is published in the dominant language that is important for the given case study.

However, there is much less information on how and why the ascribed language populace became communities of minority language speakers, what it means for people to be bilingual or even multilingual and how this affects the mutual connections between various groups and everyday life. Hopefully, this volume will contribute to this difficult and recurrent topic, and increase the reader's interest in minority languages.

JOHANNA LAAKSO

# Being Finno-Ugrian,
# Being in the Minority
# – Reflections on Linguistic
# and Other Criteria

## Abstract

Of the 20 to 40 Finno-Ugrian languages, all but three are spoken only by ethnic minorities, and minorities constitute perhaps even one third of the speakers of all Finno-Ugrian languages in sum. Today, being in minority implies a practical multilingualism. However, the traditions of Finno-Ugrian studies, departing from a monolingual view in the spirit of Romantic Nationalism, tended to overlook this reality of multilingualism and idealise "pure", monolingual speakers and communities. This tendency was compounded by political circumstances, purism in language planning and the Positivist ideologies in linguistics. Thus, the concepts of "Finno-Ugrianness", minorityhood and multilingualism have hardly been dealt with together. Yet, there are numerous ways in which minority research and Finno-Ugrian studies could benefit each other, and the minority perspective on Finno-Ugrian languages inevitably leads to fundamental questions of knowledge, explanation, and research ethics.

*Ethnic and Linguistic Context of Identity: Finno-Ugric Minorities.* 13–36.
Uralica Helsingiensia 5. Helsinki 2011.

## 1. Finno-Ugrian Minorities

Of the 20 to 40 (depending on the criteria used) Finno-Ugrian languages, all but three are minority languages wherever they are spoken. Although most speakers of Finno-Ugrian languages in European Russia have their own titular republics with national institutions and language laws, these languages live under the strong dominance of Russian and their speakers are a minority everywhere, except, perhaps, at the lowest level of local administration. In addition, the three "major" Finno-Ugrian languages are also spoken by large minority groups outside the nation-states of Hungary, Finland and Estonia.

As shown in Table 1 (largely based on statistics published by Tapani Salminen and the information centre SURI on their websites[1]), more than one fourth, maybe even one third, of the speakers of Finno-Ugrian languages belong to minorities. Note that the numbers given below are extremely crude approximations. In fact, not only are the statistical data often unreliable, outdated or even unavailable, it is also the controversial character of minority identity that often makes determining the numbers of modern minorities practically impossible. In particular, the relationship between ethnic and linguistic identity is often problematic. Ethnic identities in the Soviet Union and Russia are officially independent of language, and census data on mother tongues and even the definitions of "mother tongue" may be questionable or controversial.

---

1. <http://www.suri.ee/uralic.html>, <http://www.helsinki.fi/~tasalmin/fu.html>. I have also used the homepages of the national institutes for statistics in Estonia and Finland (<http://www.stat.ee>, <http://www.stat.fi>) and information from a number of colleagues; all inaccuracies and errors, of course, are my own – but once again, I would like to emphasise that looking for exact figures and completely reliable statistics is meaningless. For a more detailed evaluation of the number of the Finno-Ugrian populations in the Soviet Union and Russia, see Lallukka 1990, 2001, 2005.

| Language | Speakers in Sum | Minority Speakers | Speakers of State Language |
|---|---|---|---|
| Sámi languages | 35,000 | 35,000 | |
| Finnish | 5,400,000 | 600,000 | 4,800,000 |
| Meänkieli (Tornedal Finnish), Kven | 35,000 | 35,000 | |
| Karelian, Lude | 60,000 | 60,000 | |
| Veps | 5,000 | 5,000 | |
| Ingrian | 200 | 200 | |
| Vote | 5 | 5 | |
| Estonian | 1,000,000 | 90,000 | 910,000 |
| Võro-Seto (Southeast Estonian) | 50,000 | 50,000 | |
| Livonian | ? | | |
| Mordvin (Erzya, Moksha) | 600,000 | 600,000 | |
| Mari (Western, Eastern) | 500,000 | 500,000 | |
| Udmurt | 450,000 | 450,000 | |
| Komi (Zyryan), Komi Permyak | 300,000 | 300,000 | |
| Hungarian | 13,500,000 | 3,500,000 | 10,000,000 |
| Mansi | 2,500 | 2,500 | |
| Khanty | 13,000 | 13,000 | |
| Nenets (Tundra/Forest) | 26,000 | 26,000 | |
| Enets | 40 | 40 | |
| Nganasan | 500 | 500 | |
| Selkup | 1,100 | 1,100 | |
| In sum | 21,978,370 | 6,233,370 | 15,710,000 |

Table 1. The estimated number of the speakers of the Finno-Ugrian languages (Salminen 2009, SURI 2010).

The fact that such a large proportion of linguistically (how else?) definable "Finno-Ugrians" are in a minority position is a result of clear and well-known historical reasons. First of all, the expansion of East Slavs and the genesis of the Russian empire, together with large-scale assimilation and migration processes, led to a situation in which the kind of nationalism and nation-state projects seen in Western Europe were completely unthinkable for most minorities of Russia. Finally, geographical and social fragmentation and assimilation were accelerated by the upheavals of the 20th century: Stalinism, World War II, urbanisation and industrialisation. Similar assimilation and fragmentation also took place in Latvia and ended with the extinction of Livonian (at least in the form spoken in traditional Livonian speaker communities).

West of Russia, the Nordic nation-states were established, and since gaining independence in 1917 Finland has also identified itself with this group. For a long time, the Nordic ideals of democracy did not specifically include linguistic human rights for minorities (such as the Sámi, the Finns in Norway and Sweden, and the Karelians in Finland); on the contrary, assimilation of minorities was encouraged. In Central Europe, national controversies within the state of Hungary, an even more clearly "national" state with many minorities and itself part of a multinational empire, gradually increased, culminating in the peace treaty of Trianon following World War I. This treaty, which has been a national trauma for Hungarians ever since, left large Hungarian minorities in the new neighbouring states, and the nationalist ideologies prevailing in this whole area have been a constant source of problems.

Finally, political and social upheavals during and after World War II created new diaspora groups: Estonians (mostly in 1944) and Hungarians (especially after 1956) fleeing from the terror of Soviet(-controlled) regimes, and the baby-boom generations migrating *en masse* from Finland to Sweden in search of better job opportunities and a higher standard of living. On a smaller scale, these migration processes still continue in a more individualistic form of through the "EU mobility" of students and professionals. Considering the changing opinions on multilingualism, the relatively high level of education among modern migrants and the new perspectives opened by modern technology, it may be that the linguistic consequences of this modern mobility are different from those investigated in connection with traditional migrant groups. Modern mobility might even challenge the traditional research on language contacts and minority languages.

## 2. "National Finno-Ugrianness"

*... I noticed a sign on the bathroom wall: "Incredible but true, even men can pee sitting down." Incredible but true, I thought: this is how Red-Green Germany attempts to force unnatural practices on a straight, middle-class, Finno-Ugrian male. [...] The plenary meeting ended some time around 11 o'clock in the evening. I was planning to stay in the commune overnight, but being hungry, I was compelled to make the decision of a straight, middle-class, Finno-Ugrian male: I drove off towards the nearby city of Kassel to find a McDonald's.*
(Heikki Aittokoski in his book *Lihavan kotkan maa* ['The Land of the Fat Eagle', WSOY 1999] describes his visit to a community of alternative Green Socialists in Germany. Translation JL.)

Following the discovery of the relatedness of Finno-Ugrian languages, the institutionalisation of comparative Finno-Ugrian Studies roughly coincided with Romantic Nationalism, national awakening and national language reforms. In Hungary, these processes already began at the turn of the 19th century (thus being earlier and less clearly connected to the "kindred peoples" ideology), in Finland during the 19th century and in Estonia, where the political circumstances were less favourable, even later. In Finland, in particular, research into the relatedness of Finno-Ugrian languages was regarded as a national cause, the nation's search for its roots and identity. This national(ist) viewpoint was facilitated by the fact that many Finno-Ugrists up to the present day have been "ethnic Finno-Ugrians" whose work was also motivated by an honest nationalist tendency to place their own nation on the linguistic and ethnic map of the world.

In Finland, being "Finno-Ugrian" was thus understood to be a synonym for being a genuine, authentic, typical Finn – something at the heart of the Finnish identity. Seen the other way round, Finns considered themselves to be the purest representatives of Finno-Ugrianness (cf. Fewster 2006, Kemiläinen 1998), in the same way as Swedes, for instance, have wanted to see themselves as the purest and most original Germanic stock, the heart of the Nordic race (Hagerman 2006). Even today, "Finno-Ugrian" is often used as a jocular synonym for "a typical, genuine Finn", in particular when Finnishness is contrasted with characteristics of other European nations (as in Heikki Aittokoski's sarcastic book about Germany quoted at the beginning of this chapter).

Strangely enough, this interpretation of Finno-Ugrianness also implied that there could be no Finno-Ugrian minorities in Finland. According to the traditional colonialist view, the Sámi were "others" (in linguistics, this was manifested in the so-called "Proto-Lapp hypothesis", recently reevaluated by Aikio 2004), foreigners who had switched to speaking a Finno-Ugrian language but who still belonged to the other side of a racial border (cf. Isaksson 2001). The Karelians, as the source of symbolic cultural values such as the national epic *Kalevala,* were reinterpreted as part of the Finnish nation, at least at the level of symbols and ideals, even if attitudes towards flesh-and-blood Karelians could be hostile, condescending and influenced by a general Russophobia. A similar role – national at the level of national symbols, strange and foreign in everyday contacts – has been played by the Setu in Estonian culture (Hagu 2002: 435; cf. also Koreinik's paper in this volume) and the eastern Székely and Csángó minorities in Hungarian culture (Kapitány & Kapitány 2002: 23).

This reveals an interesting paradox. The Finns (and, at least to some extent, the Estonians and Hungarians as well), mainly emphasised their Finno-Ugrianness because they felt "different" among the great nations of Europe: We are strange and foreign in European culture, our language is unintelligible to all outsiders and our roots are somewhere in the primeval darkness of the East. On the other hand, their "exotic" Finno-Ugrianness was the cornerstone of a monistic, monolingual nation-state project, which acknowledged no minorities, no "others". The idea of a Finno-Ugrian minority identity was either forgotten and suppressed or defined as something negative: being in a minority (as opposed to the ethnicity of a "pure" and authentic imagined community) means being endangered. Minorities, having lost their purity, are on their way to fatal assimilation.

## 3. Ideals of Research vs Everyday Life of a Language

*Such a pity that you could not bring a Vogul with you! What with us here already waiting for a Vogul steak with watering mouths! [...] One should really get hold of both an Ostyak and a Vogul to be brought here later on, because we really need them for our investigations.*
(E. N. Setälä to Artturi Kannisto 1907, quoted in Salminen 2008: 75, translation JL.)

*... Prof. Ilminski left all his Votyaks (20 in sum) completely at my disposal.*
(Yrjö Wichmann's field report, quoted in Salminen 2008: 33, translation JL.)

That many minorities are endangered is, of course, sad reality. Field linguists among the Finno-Ugrian minorities already saw this reality – alcoholism, poverty and apathy – with their own eyes more than a hundred years ago. Their letters and field reports often express genuine sorrow and pity – or chastise the ruthlessness of Russian civil servants and the greed of Russian merchants. However, often the only thing that Finno-Ugrists in the field could do was to record language and collect objects of ethnographic value; memories of a world which would soon belong to the past. Heikki Paasonen, perhaps the most eminent researcher of the Mordvin language, believed that it was not worth while trying to save the Mordvin nation, 'that half-dead carcass'. However, in his opinion, the Komi and the Udmurt peoples still had some vitality. (Salminen 2008: 93.)

The heroes of the golden era of Finno-Ugrian fieldwork led a simple and modest life side by side with their research subjects, facing cold, hunger and illness, and it would be unjust and anachronistic to regard them as colonialist oppressors or criticise their lack of activism in minority rights. True, a modern reader is shocked by many statements quoted by Salminen (2008) in his history of the Finno-Ugrian Society, the most important force behind this epochal fieldwork project. Subjects were treated in a friendly way, of course, but also in a condescending and paternalist way, they were threatened with punishments for laziness or excessive drinking, and they could be "ordered" (from local authorities, priests or teachers), in so and so many "exemplars". However, these attitudes cannot be dismissed as merely naïve and racist, they simply reflect what was perceived as normal and correct in Western European culture at the time. The field researchers were not only children of their time but also representatives of the academic ideals of the era.

The ideas of scientific or scholarly inquiry of the day included a rigid Positivist view of truth, and the idealisation of scientific objectivity and historicity. The object of research according to those ideas was a supra-individual abstraction, an idealised authentic language or tradition. Speakers and carriers of traditions – no matter whether the researcher saw them as nice, intelligent people or stupid drunkards – were not independent agents, but passive vessels carrying the language to the researcher's desk or manifesting the national culture, mentality and *Volksgeist*. Researchers were not supposed to ask themselves how they could help endangered minorities revitalise their languages and cultures. They were not supposed to investigate the ways in which an individual Nenets speaker in discourse constructs his/her Nenets identity. They were supposed to collect material in order to shed light on the essence of the language in question, its history – and, in the case of Finnish field linguists, on the prehistory of the Finnish language.

Idealising the pure and authentic language of the past was merely one form of the so-called classical fallacy, one way of confusing reality with the abstractions and idealisations that are essential in research. As pointed out by many critics in the late 20th century (see e.g. Milroy 1987: 9; Hakulinen 1991), this same classical fallacy took on new guises in 20th-century mainstream linguistics: the perfect authentic system was no longer localised in the past but in the reality of a postulated, genetically conditioned language facility. In effect, language as a system was reified: the linguist wants to see his abstraction as something which really exists (or has existed). (Note: this does not mean that proto-languages never existed. It is ontologically impossible to explain language relatedness in any other way. This simply means that the reconstruction as an image of a real language is a crude image only, inevitably flawed and imperfect.) How-ever, as pointed out, for example, by Croft (2000: 1–2), a language system has no spatiotemporal reality: it does not exist in space and time (only individual speakers' individual grammars and the com-munities consisting of individual speakers do). This brings us to deep philosophical questions of explanation in linguistics. But it also poses questions of ethics: by what right does the researcher choose his/her subject and his/her perspective?

In his pamphlet *The rise and fall of languages,* the Australian linguist R. M. W. Dixon (1997) accused general linguistics of a dan-gerous theoretical bias, of considering the work done by the "theoreti-cians" "more difficult, more important, more intellectual, altogether on a higher plane than the basic work undertaken by the descriptiv-ists." (Dixon 1997: 134.) He challenged linguists to leave their ivory towers and descend to the reality of endangered languages – as long as they exist. It is as painfully as undeniably true that both theoreti-cal ambition and practical difficulties prevent armchair linguists from setting off to describe less accessible exotic languages. (Besides, even concerning the recruitment of students, minor languages have far less promising professional prospects to offer than major European lan-guages.) This has led to the bizarre situation where there is probably much more ambitious linguistic work being done on the English spo-ken by the Teletubbies[2] or on fantasy languages such as Klingon than on thousands of "real" endangered languages.

## 4. The Multilingual Life of Minorities

In addition to general issues of research policy and the sociology of science, there were particular obstacles for the research of Finno-Ugrian minorities in the Soviet Union (i.e. the majority of Finno-Ugrian minorities). Western researchers very seldom had access to native speakers, although there were some brilliant exceptions such as Pertti Virtaranta's fieldwork with the Karelians and Gábor Bereczki's travels to the minorities of the Volga region. Some subjects could be

2. This topic was discussed on the LINGUIST mailing list in July 2000; see
<http://listserv.linguistlist.org/cgi-bin/wa?A2=ind0007D&L=linguist&P=R2630>.

reached in cities open to Western tourists (for instance, the peoples of the Russian Far North at the Herzen Institute in Leningrad or the last Livonians in Riga), but for the most part, Finno-Ugrian Studies in the West was based on researching and editing the material collected before World War I. This situation has changed with the collapse of the Soviet Union, although the political situation in Russia still (or again) has its peculiar problems. Still, this means a completely new perspective on the life of Finno-Ugrian minority languages.

At the same time, approaches and theories are changing in linguistics too. For quite a few decades, there has been very active work in "connectionist" linguistics, i.e. in the border between linguistics and research on society, culture and human behaviour. The classical traditions of historical-comparative Finno-Ugrian studies (for instance, questions of proto-language reconstruction or etymology) are still a central area of active cutting-edge linguistic research. However, there are also important areas of linguistic inquiry originating not from language as an abstract, idealised system, but from the multitude of diverse, contacting and intertwining language varieties. This implies an emphasis on the active agency of the speakers and a shift from monism to pluralism.

The political and ideological background of this shift can be found in the emancipation of linguistic minorities, both indigenous/autochthonous groups and the new minorities formed by immigration to Western countries. This emancipation process has led to the insight that identity is not an organic part of ethnicity based on "race" and origin: identities are constructions and one person can have multiple, different or partly overlapping identities. We all belong to various different reference framework groups – based on family and relatedness, studying, work, hobbies etc. – which may imply different identities and also different ways of using language. In the same way, today's Sámi can simultaneously identify themselves with the Sámi as a cross-border nation and with Finns, Swedes or Norwegians, or a present-day Komi can describe him/herself as both Komi and Russian (or: *Rossiyanin,* citizen of the multiethnic Russian state).

It must be noted, however, that there are essential differences between minorities and their development. Toivanen (2004) claims that the pressure of essentialising and homogenising Sámi policies in the Nordic countries is driving the Sámi emancipation movement towards a more and more nation-state-like idea of Sáminess, which would mean that it is increasingly difficult for present-day Sámi activists to maintain parallel ethnic-national identities such as "Sámi *and* Finnish". The comparison of cross-border Hungarian minorities also reveals great differences between conscious "hyphenated Hungarianness" and very vague self-identification. In Austria, according to the census of 2001, there are more than 40,000 Hungarians, and a little more than a half of them mention Hungarian as their language (or one of their languages) of everyday spoken communication (*Umgangssprache*). However, according to a study in 2005[3], more than 90,000 Austrians can speak Hungarian, and most of them probably have a Hungarian ethnic background (*Jelentés* 2006). Obviously for many people of Hungarian descent in Austria their heritage language does not suffice to identify them as "Hungarians".

In any case, modern minorities are typically bi- or multilingual. Knowledge of the state/majority language is often already acquired at pre-school age, and even within families there is wide-ranging multilingualism due to migration and mixed marriages. For instance, Hungarian speakers in Austria may be children of mixed marriages with one parent speaking Hungarian and the other German or some other language, they may be second-generation immigrants who grow up with German as their primary language, or they may be immigrants from an ethnically mixed area, whose ethnolingual background includes both Hungarian and another language such as Serbian, Slovak or Romanian – or they may represent all three of these alternatives simultaneously! How these people define their linguistic and ethnic identity can be an extremely complicated question.

There is no return to the world of historical language atlases, where different colours represented different areas populated by homogeneous communities of illiterate, non-mobile, monolingual peasants. Of course, this was already a naïve interpretation before World War I and the ethnic upheavals of the 20th century. Among many Finno-Ugrian minorities, knowledge of the local majority lan-

---

3. Most probably, this means the Eurobarometer study "Europeans and their languages"; however, the full report published at <http://ec.europa.eu/public_opinion/archives/eb_special_260_240_en.htm> does not give any precise figures.

guage, or even more than one, (for the Sámi for instance, Finnish *and* Swedish or Norwegian) was already relatively widespread in the 19th century, although there were intra-community differences (for example, men, due to their greater mobility, were often better versed in other languages).

In fact, the crucial issues for modern multilingual minorities do not pertain to the role of language as a carrier of information. It is, perhaps, not so vital for them to have all official announcements, laws, news and street signs in their own language or to provide them with interpreter services. In many cases, the majority language is completely accessible to them and part of their everyday life together with their heritage language. As the young Inari Sámi writer Petter Morottaja states in his recent article, "the coexistence of Inari Sámi and Finnish means that the use of Inari Sámi does not merely concern the level of conveying information. For example, it is almost meaningless to offer news services in Inari Sámi, because the media in other languages has far more resources." (Morottaja 2009: 72; translation JL.) What is essential is not information, but the cultural, social and symbolic capital carried and represented by the language. This makes the central question of language planning even more vital: *whose* language?

## 5.  Whose language?

*ott vót az alsóőri tanárnő (--) az egyátalán (.) nem hagyta hogy*
*valamit a: a dialektusba beszéljé. tehát (--) örűtem hogy tudok*
*magyarul (.) na hogy (--) és mindent kijavított. mondta hogy*
*nincs ZSÖMle. nincs ruhaakasztó. (--) meg (--) mittudom (.) én.*
*tehát azokat a szavakat amit otthon hasznátá [...] mondta MI*
*röndösen tanulunk magyarul irodalmilag. mondom a nagyma-*
*mám így MONdta ez egy ZSÖMle egy vajaszsömle akkor ezt így is*
*MONdjuk. hogyha tíz évig azt hallod (1.0) tehát az nagyon bántott.*

'There was that teacher from Unterwart, she didn't allow us at
all to say something in the dialect. I mean, I was so happy that
I knew Hungarian, and then, she corrected everything. She
said that there is no such thing as *zsömle* [wheat roll]. There's
no *ruhaakasztó* [clothes hanger]. And, whatever. I mean, those
words you used at home. [...] She said that WE would learn
proper Hungarian, literary language. I said, my grandmother
said so, that's a *zsömle, a zsömle* with butter, so this is what we
call it. If you have to listen to this for ten years... I mean, that
really hurt.' (Hungarian speaker from Burgenland, Austria,
reminiscing on the teaching of Hungarian at school; quoted in
Dávid 2008: 170, translation JL).

As mentioned above, defining ethnolinguistic identity and displaying it
in statistics can be very problematic. Anybody familiar with situations
involving linguistic minorities, multilingualism and language contact
will know how difficult it can be to define concepts such as "first language" or "native speaker". Is the mother tongue or the first language
the language we learn first in early childhood (and if we acquire two
or more languages, which of these?), is it the language we have the
best command of (in what sense, on what criteria, in speech or in writing?), the language we use the most in our everyday life or the heritage
language of the community with which we want to identify ourselves?

Statistics, if based on reliable and well-planned research, may
reflect the numbers of people who *consider* a certain language to be
their mother tongue. However, statistics and census data are often
unreliable. We do not know for certain how people interpret concepts

such as "first language", "home language" or "the language I know best", and if only one language is accepted as an answer, members of multilingual families often cannot give an unequivocal answer. Many field linguists working on endangered languages have observed that speakers tend to overestimate their knowledge and range of use of the language, confusing their (or the linguist's) wishful thinking with reality. We also know that census data are not always to be trusted. In the former Soviet Union, the choice of ethnicity and mother tongue (both of which were registered for every Soviet citizen) could be dependent on the caprices of the authorities, as shown by the statistical increase of ethnic Vepsians in the last years of *Perestroika*. What had changed was not the number of Vepsians, or their identity, but the attitude of the authorities towards allowing "Vepsian" as an official designation marked on the passport. On the other hand, there are countries where collecting and storing information about the mother tongue or ethnicity of individual persons is explicitly forbidden; for this reason, there are only estimates on size of linguistic minorities in Sweden.

Parallel or multiple identities make it difficult or impossible to determine "the" first language. This is normal for people living in multilingual families and for diaspora minorities. On the website of the Finnish Migration Institute, the number of expatriate Finns is estimated to be more than 600,000 (expatriate Finns by this definition are first-generation emigrants and their children; Korkiasaari 2003); the estimated number of Hungarians outside Hungary can range up to five million, at least if both the old Hungarian minorities and the more recent diaspora groups are included. But these numbers cannot be directly transformed into speaker statistics, given that there are already large differences in language maintenance between first generation emigrants. According to my own experiences of second-generation expatriate Finns and Hungarians, their knowledge of their heritage language can range from practically perfect to virtually non-existent (and even in the latter group there are probably differences between those who lack any exposure to their heritage language and "latent speakers" – cf. Basham & Fathman 2008). Language attrition and language loss typically arouse strong negative emotions, and representatives of minority groups (as well as some politicians in the homelands of expatriate minorities) are often reluctant to acknowledge the sad reality of language loss. On the other hand, considering the problems of defining "native speakerhood" and the general unreliability of speaker statistics, it is more than understandable that certain minorities simply refuse to "play with numbers" and produce statistical data.

But it is not only the concept of "speakerhood" that is problematic, there are also problems with the concept of "languageness" (cf. Garner 2004). Determining whether closely related varieties are separate languages or dialects of one language is notoriously difficult, and the last few decades have seen various European language varieties emancipated and their status raised to that of separate languages. Within the Finnic group, there are three fine examples: *Meänkieli* (Tornedal Finnish) in Sweden, Kven (Finnmark Finnish) in Norway and Võro-Seto in Southeast Estonia. In all these cases, the speakers do not want to see their language as "just a dialect" of a "foreign language" – a standard language with which the speakers, for political or ethnocultural reasons, do not want to identify themselves.

However, there may also be discrepancies between the opinions of speakers and outsiders. The two Mordvin languages, Erzya and Moksha, are very closely related, and many linguists – outsiders in particular – still plead for a common standard Mordvin language (e.g. Mosin 2005; Zaicz 2005). At the same time, many Mordvin activists themselves strongly resent the idea of a common Mordvin identity: they do not regard themselves as "Mordvin" but as Erzya or Moksha. In Finnish population statistics – at least in the 1990's – many people were recorded as being speakers of "Ingrian" (*inkeri*), a language unknown to Finnic linguistics, in which the languages of (immigrant Lutheran) Ingrian Finns and (indigenous Orthodox) Izhorians[4] are

---

4. Ingria, the region south and east of the eastern end of the Gulf of Finland, around the site where St. Petersburg was founded at the beginning of the 18th century, was inhabited by two autochthonous Finnic peoples, the Izhorians or Ingrians and the Votes. In the 17th century, when Ingria belonged to the Swedish empire, many old inhabitants resenting the new régime emigrated to Russia, and a massive exodus from Finland took place. Izhorians and Ingrian Finns lived side by side but separated by a clear boundary (marked by different religions) until the terror of the Stalin era and World War II. After World War II, most surviving Ingrian Finns lived scattered in Estonia, in Russian Karelia and other parts of the Soviet Union, and quite a few were "repatriated" to Finland from the 1980's on. In linguistics, the Finnish dialect of Ingrian Finns and the language of the Izhorians (sometimes called *inkeroismurteet*, "Ingrian/ Izhorian dialects" in Finnish, because of its unclear taxonomical status) are seen as two clearly different language varieties, but most laymen know nothing about this.

seen as two strictly separate varieties. Research on the identity of "Karelians" in Finland has shown that today's Finns have very vague ideas of what is meant by the Karelian language and by the so-called Karelian dialects of Finnish proper (Palander & Nupponen 2005). Defining minority languages and minority speaker communities can be problematic for both the minorities themselves and the majority.

Problematic issues of speakerhood and languageness meet in those cases where the language use of a minority group clashes with norms and standards, with "language correctness". Small speaker communities may find it particularly difficult to accept standards created by outsiders; on the other hand, diaspora varieties may be stigmatised in the "motherland". For example, the Hungarians in Burgenland, Austria, sometimes report unpleasant experiences concerning the attitude of Hungarian nationals towards their dialect. How this is realised in the teaching of Hungarian in school (the teachers are often first-generation immigrants from Hungary) is exemplified in the quotation at the beginning of this chapter. Saving the minority language from stigmatisation and decreasing use may require one of two strategies: either emancipation to the status of an independent language (as in the case of Meänkieli) or a more pluricentric view of language planning in the motherland. In the Hungarian-speaking area, a project of "de-Trianonisation" *(határtalanítás,* "de-bordering") has been launched recently. The goal is to include words and expressions used by cross-border Hungarian minorities in dictionaries of Standard Hungarian, in order to show that these words also belong to the Hungarian language and that the language varieties spoken by Hungarian minorities are no "less Hungarian" or less valuable than the motherland standard.

## 6. The Responsibility of Finno-Ugrian Studies

*Es gibt vier Sprachen, die du nur kraft der Muttermilch hin-*
*kriegst, aber niemals erlernen kannst: Ungarisch, Finnisch,*
*Lustenauerisch und die Schnalzsprache der Zulus.*
Helmut A. Gansterer in the Austrian weekly magazine *Profil*
(12/40, 16 March 2009) illustrates the character of the Vorarl-
berg dialect by comparing it with other exotic and unlearnable
languages.

A final question for professional linguists remains: how should Finno-
Ugrian language studies respond to the challenges posed by the situation of today's minority languages? As seen above, hard-core Finno-
Ugrists traditionally had a Positivist, objectifying approach to the
languages under study. The linguist had the right to draw the borders
of the language variety s/he was studying, to define what was authentic and what was more recent or contact-induced – and who, i.e. what
kind of subjects, spoke the language in the form that was to be investigated. A particularly impressive example is Wolfgang Schlachter's
study on consonant gradation in Malå Sámi and how the gradation system "deteriorates" (for a detailed review see Terho Itkonen
1993). The linguist analyses incredibly complicated phonological and
morphophonological phenomena relying merely on his own perception, and he also draws far-reaching conclusions about which phenomena result from internal developments or from external influence, and
by what right he can take the idiolect of his subject as representative
of the language as a whole.

Classical Finno-Ugrian studies in the golden era of fieldwork
before World War I (and also partly afterwards) preferred speakers
of so-called "pure" language. Subjects were selected from the oldest generations, as monolingual and non-mobile as possible, and the
language samples they produced were "edited" (which could even
involve replacing foreign words or expressions with authentic ones).
Research constructed its own object (cf. Sarhimaa 2000). In the theoretical framework of those times, this was understandable, but it also
led to a kind of unholy alliance. According to both positivist empirical linguistics and folk-linguistic ideas of language planning based

on prejudices and purism, the correct or authentic language was seen as the one and only, clearly delimitable and problem-free system, and arguments of empirical linguistics (such as "authenticity" or "originality") could be used as political legitimation for puristic language planning.

In the Finno-Ugrian nation states, this puristic language planning was combined with nationalism and the nation state project as a whole. Minorities were left outside, in a kind of a pre-modern limbo, leaving only two possibilities: assimilation or the creation of a monolingual mini-nation according to the ideals of Romantic Nationalism. These ideals were unaccessible to most Finno-Ugrian minorities, but today they may seem more and more impossible even for the majorities of non-English-language nation states. The diglossia of English and the national language is spreading in Europe. In Finland, knowledge of English is often taken for granted, and a Finn in his homeland may face a situation where customer service is only available in English.

Research into language contacts and the coexistence of languages is nothing new in Finno-Ugrian studies. On the contrary, language contact and multilingualism have been dealt with by Finno-Ugrists as long as scholarly Finno-Ugrian studies have existed. The difference is merely in the choice of focus or perspective: in Finno-Ugrian contact linguistics, language contact is no longer the basis of opportunistic explanations (almost anything that lacks an internal explanation can be explained by language contact) but the explanandum, the main object of study. However, unlike historical-comparative linguistics, where the Finno-Ugrian perspective has considerably contributed to our knowledge of the linguistic prehistory of Eurasia and to language change in general, there are no easy generalisations to be expected from Finno-Ugrian contact linguistics – in fact, nothing that could be labelled "Finno-Ugrian".

Language contact phenomena are notoriously messy, and the outcomes of language contact situations are very difficult to predict. What happens in language contact and situations involving multiple identities is also only very loosely connected to the structure and substance of language, to its history and background – that is to issues traditionally central to Finno-Ugrian studies. How representatives of minorities regard their language as a factor for constructing their identity, how they use their language or fail to use it, or how the majorities see the minority language are questions that have practically nothing to do with the genetic affiliation of the language. It is also clear that Finno-Ugrian minorities cover practically the whole spectrum of minorityhood, from cultivated, strong, officially acknowledged languages to endangered, almost extinct, even "virtual" languages (this is how we could perhaps describe languages like Livonian, where all present-day users are "revitalised" – often well-educated, urban people who have consciously studied and learnt the language in adolescence or adulthood). It is hard to see a common core of Finno-Ugrian minorityhood. Is there any sense in calling minority language studies "Finno-Ugrian"?

The researching of each Finno-Ugric speaking minority is, of course, the responsibility of Finno-Ugrian studies; it is in Finno-Ugrian circles that the deepest theoretical knowledge of Livonian, Skolt Sámi, Mari, Csángó Hungarian or Enets is to be found, or at least should be. However, is there a further reason for organising, for instance, conferences on Finno-Ugrian minorities independently of Scandinavian, Slavic or Turkic studies? I will conclude by claiming that there are three possible reasons: one of them is questionable, the second somewhat banal, the third tenuous but interesting.

The construction of the national identity of many Finno-Ugrian nations has included the concept of Finno-Ugrianness, which – outside the well-defined areas of language relatedness and historical linguistics – is almost completely empty and thus lends itself to all kinds of symbolic uses (recall the " straight, middle-class, Finno-Ugrian male" mentioned above). There have also been attempts to fill it with relativist content in the spirit of strategic essentialism (as characteristic also of certain schools of post-colonial or feminist philosophy). Ethnofuturism, the post-modern school of art and art philosophy that came into being in Estonia in the last years of the Soviet system, attempts to create a modern Finno-Ugrian identity in a way which expresses a typically post-modern opportunistic attitude to facts and empirical questions. Some Ethnofuturist texts explicitly express a firm belief in a Finno-Ugrian way of thinking or a Finno-Ugrian philosophy based on linguistic Finno-Ugrianness. However, none of the authors of these

31

texts is a researcher of Finno-Ugrian languages, nor an expert on the present state of the Finno-Ugrian minorities. The loudest proponents of a postulated Finno-Ugrian *Weltanschauung,* the Finnish literature scholar Kari Sallamaa (see e.g. Sallamaa 2001) and a Hungarian music teacher working in Finland, György Kádár (see e.g. Kádár 2008), have very little to do with Finno-Ugrian studies proper.

The other possible basis for the concept of Finno-Ugrian minority research is an opportunistic one. The term "The Finno-Ugrian World" is often used in contexts where Uralic languages, their speakers and the cultures of these peoples are dealt with as a group. Although Finno-Ugrianness from the point of view of minority studies is a void concept, it is an established concept connected to certain institutions of research and academic teaching, international cooperation, conferences and publications. Even politicians from Finland, Estonia and Hungary may refer to a possible "Finno-Ugrian lobby" in the organs of the EU. Why not exploit these existing connections? Could not research on Csángó Hungarians be as interesting for Sámi researchers as Basque or Breton speakers?

Finally, the tenuous but interesting strand that could be followed in future research. There really is an aspect of Finno-Ugrian minorityhood, although not only characteristic of Uralic peoples and unable to exhaustively determine everything connected with Finno-Ugrianness, but yet, worth, perhaps, elaborating on. By this I mean a *difference* based on linguistic "otherness".

Most language communities and all so-called major languages in today's Europe are flanked by languages which are related to them in a way that is obvious even to the layman, i.e. other Germanic, Romance or Slavic languages. The Finno-Ugrian languages, in contrast, are essentially strange, and their otherness is not connected to such images of "decayed", "mixed", "more archaic" or "more primitive" language that, for instance, the French may associate with Provençal or the Swedes with Danish – they are simply separated from the rest of Europe by a barrier of mystified otherness. The myth of Finnish or Hungarian as "languages impossible to learn" is still being transmitted. Could it be that a minority speaking a completely unknown and unintelligible language is treated in a different way to a minority whose language is "somewhat like ours but sounds funny"?

For example: why is it that all Finnic and – at least partly – Sámi peoples are connected in the traditions of their Indo-European neighbours with magic and sorcery? Is it only because European Christianity, with its social and cultural institutions, reached the peripheral peoples much later than the majorities closer to the cultural and political centres, or is it because the *unintelligible word* had a strange power over the Pre-Modern human mind? Or do the ideas of complete strangeness and unlearnability still influence language policies and language planning as concerns the Finno-Ugric minorities?

There is no single, unified Finno-Ugrian minorityhood, but there are numerous feasible approaches to Finno-Ugrian minorities, both inside traditional hard-core Finno-Ugrian studies and outside it. As I hope to have shown in my article, research into Finno-Ugrian minorities also leads us towards basic questions of knowledge, explanation and research ethics in the humanities.

## References

Aikio, Ante 2004: An essay on substrate studies and the origin of Saami. – Irma Hyvärinen, Petri Kallio & Jarmo Korhonen (eds), *Etymologie, Entlehnungen und Entwicklungen: Festschrift für Jorma Koivulehto zum 70. Geburtstag.* Mémoires de la Société Néophilologique de Helsinki 63. Helsinki: Société Néophilologique. 5–34.

Basham, Charlotte & Fathman, Ann K. 2008: The Latent Speaker: Attaining Adult Fluency in an Endangered Language. – *International Journal of Bilingual Education and Bilingualism* 11/5. 577–597.

Croft, William 2000: *Explaining language change: an evolutionary approach.* London: Pearson Education.

Dávid, Ágnes 2008: Ungarisch in Österreich: Eine neue Sprechergeneration des Ungarischen. – Johanna Laakso (ed.), *Ungarischunterricht in Österreich = Teaching Hungarian in Austria.* Finno-Ugrian Studies in Austria 6. Wien: LIT Verlag. 154–178.

Dixon, Robert M. W. 1997: *The rise and fall of languages.* Cambridge: Cambridge University Press.

Fewster, Derek 2006: *Visions of Past Glory: Nationalism and the Construction of Early Finnish History.* Studia Fennica Historica 11. Helsinki: Suomalaisen Kirjallisuuden Seura.

Garner, Mark 2004: *Language: an ecological view.* Contemporary Studies in Descriptive Linguistics, vol. 1. Bern: Peter Lang.

Hagerman, Maja 2006: *Det rena landet: om konsten att uppfinna sina förfäder.* Stockholm: Prisma.

Hagu, Paul 2002: Epic works of the Setu singer Anne Vabarna. – Lauri Honko (ed.), *The Kalevala and the world's traditional epics.* Studia Fennica Folkloristica 12. Helsinki: Suomalaisen Kirjallisuuden Seura. 433–463.

Hakulinen, Auli 1991: Kielentutkimus ja arvot. – *Virittäjä* 95: 409–416.

Isaksson, Pekka 2001: *Kumma kuvajainen. Rasismi rotututkimuksessa, rotuteorioiden saamelaiset ja suomalainen fyysinen antropologia.* Pohjoiset historiat 1. Inari: Kustannus Puntsi.

Itkonen, Terho 1993: Eine ertragreiche Monographie zum lappischen Stufenwechsel (Schlachter, Wolfgang: Stufenwechselstörungen im Malålappischen. Aufbau oder Abbau eines Systems?) – *Finnisch-Ugrische Forschungen* 51. 244–272.

*Jelentés 2006* = 2006. évi jelentés az ausztriai magyarok helyzetéről. – <http://www.hhrf.org/htmh/?menuid=060202> 29.3.2009.

Kádár György 2008: *Egy lehetséges uráli filozófia.* Budapest: Püski kiadó.

Kapitány Ágnes & Kapitány Gábor 2002: *Magyarságszimbólumok.* Budapest: Európai Folklór Intézet.

Kemiläinen, Aira 1998: *Finns in the Shadow of the "Aryans": Race Theories and Racism.* Studia Historica 59. Helsinki: Finnish Historical Society.

Korkiasaari, Jouni 2003: Suomalaiset maailmalla. – <http://www.migrationinstitute.fi/db/articles/art.php?artid=3> 10.3.2009.

Lallukka, Seppo 1990: *The East Finnic Minorities in the Soviet Union. An Appraisal of the Erosive Trends.* Suomalaisen Tiedeakatemian Toimituksia B 252. Helsinki: Suomalainen Tiedeakatemia.

—— 2001: Finno-Ugrians of Russia: Vanishing Cultural Communities? – *Nationalities Papers* 29. 9–39.

—— 2005: Venäjän suomalais-ugrilaiset: väestölaskentojen kertomaa. – *Castrenianumin toimitteita* 64. Helsinki: Suomalais-Ugrilainen Seura ja Helsingin yliopiston Castrenianumin laitokset. 28–46.

Milroy, Lesley 1987: *Observing and analysing natural language: a critical account of sociolinguistic method.* Oxford: Blackwell.

Morottaja, Petter 2009: Inarinsaamelaisen kirjallisuuden ensiaskel ja askel sen jälkeen. – Klaas Ruppel (ed.), *Omin sanoin. Kirjoituksia vähemmistökielten kirjallistumisesta.* Kotimaisten kielten tutkimuskeskuksen verkkojulkaisuja 6. – <http://scripta.kotus.fi/www/verkkojulkaisut/julk6> 8.3.2009.

Mosin, Mihail 2005: Zweisprachigkeit und ethnische Identität in der Republik Mordwinien. – Eugen Helimski, Ulrike Kahrs & Monika Schötschel (eds): *Mari und Mordwinen im heutigen Russland: Sprache, Kultur, Identität.* Veröffentlichungen der Societas Uralo-Altaica 66. Wiesbaden: Harrassowitz. 39–53.

Palander, Marjatta & Anne-Maria Nupponen (eds) 2005: *Monenlaiset karjalaiset. Suomen karjalaisten kielellinen identiteetti.* Studia Carelica Humanistica 20. Joensuu.

Sallamaa, Kari 2001: Ethnofuturism and cosmofuturism. About the forth-developing of our philosophy. – <http://www.suri.ee/etnofutu/4/cosmo-en.html> 10.3.2009.

Salminen, Timo 2008: *Aatteen tiede. Suomalais-Ugrilainen Seura 1883–2008.* Helsinki: Suomalaisuuden Kirjallisuuden Seura.

Sarhimaa, Anneli 2000: Neighbours getting together in Karelia. – Johanna Laakso (ed.), *Facing Finnic.* Castrenianumin toimitteita 59. Helsinki: Suomalais-Ugrilainen Seura ja Helsingin yliopiston Castrenianumin laitokset. 185–209.

Toivanen, Reetta 2004: The development of Sámi civil societies. – Jurij Kusmenko (ed.): *The Sámi and the Scandinavians: aspects of 2000 years of contact.* Schriften zur Kulturwissenschaft 55. Hamburg: Dr. Kovač. 129–139.

Zaicz, Gábor 2005: Aktuelle Fragen der Entwicklung der mordwinischen Schriftsprachen. – Eugen Helimski, Ulrike Kahrs & Monika Schötschel (eds): *Mari und Mordwinen im heutigen Russland: Sprache, Kultur, Identität.* Veröffentlichungen der Societas Uralo-Altaica 66. Wiesbaden: Harrassowitz. 55–74.

# Suomalais-ugrilaiset vähemmistössä: kielellisten ja muiden kriteerien pohdintaa

*Johanna Laakso*

Suomalais-ugrilaisten kielten puhujista suuri osa, kenties jopa kolmannes, kuuluu vähemmistöihin – joko "katottomiin" vähemmistöryhmiin, joiden kieli ei missään ole enemmistö- tai valtakielenä, tai kolmen suomalais-ugrilaisen kansallisvaltiokielen rajantakaisiin puhujaryhmiin. Viimeksi mainituissa on sekä ns. vanhoja vähemmistöjä että myöhempien maastamuuttoaaltojen synnyttämiä ryhmiä. Tyypistä riippumatta kaikki nämä vähemmistöt ovat nykyään lähes sataprosenttisesti kaksi- tai monikielisiä. Fennougristiikan perinteessä monikielisyyttä ilmiönä on kuitenkin viime vuosikymmeniin saakka tutkittu yllättävän vähän, vaikka kielikontaktien (etenkin lainasanojen) tutkimuksella onkin pitkät perinteet. Klassinen fennougristiikka asetti etusijalle idealisoidut "puhtaat" kieliyhteisöt ja kielimuodot – ja samalla kun esimerkiksi suomalaisuus nähtiin puhtaana ja tyypillisenä suomalais-ugrilaisuutena, Suomen saamelainen ja karjalainen vähemmistö unohtuivat suomalais-ugrilaisuuden imagosta tykkänään. Tieteessä nämä aatehistorialliset virtaukset osuivat yhteen kieltä reifioivan, "esineistävän" positivismin kanssa.

Onko nykyään mieltä puhua vähemmistötutkimuksesta ja fennougristiikasta yhdessä, onko olemassa suomalais-ugrilaista vähemmistöyttä? Ankarasti ottaen kielisukulaisuus (yhteisestä kantakielestä polveutuminen) ja kielen asema yhteisössä ja maailmassa ovat yhteensopimattomia käsitteitä. Suomalais-ugrilaisen vähemmistöyden pohdinta on kuitenkin mielekästä jo siksi, että se vie sekä tieteellisen selittämisen että tutkimusetiikan peruskysymysten äärelle.

IRJA SEURUJÄRVI-KARI

# "We Took Our Language Back" – The Formation of a Sámi Identity within the Sámi Movement and the Role of the Sámi Language from the 1960s until 2008

## Abstract

In this article, I discuss the role of the Sámi language, especially the role of the North Sámi language, in constructing a collective identity during the period 1960–2008. I focus on the relationship between the identity policies of the Sámi movement, language, revitalisation and ethnicity at the level of the Sámi community from a transnational and ethnopolitical viewpoint. The ideological basis for revitalisation is what all of the practical revitalisation activities that follow it are built upon. The revitalisation of a language is visible to society when the language once again takes its place in schools and day-care centers, when it starts to be used in the media and in literature and the arts. Language is one of the most important ethnic symbols and one of the strongest factors defining the uniformity and solidarity of the Sámi movement alongside certain other joint representative traditions. Language is also the factor that provides the Sámi with a voice that fortifies the Sámi community and enables them to identify with their national identity wherever they live.

*Ethnic and Linguistic Context of Identity: Finno-Ugric Minorities.* 37–78.
Uralica Helsingiensia 5. Helsinki 2011.

## 1. Introduction

In this article, I discuss the role of the Sámi languages in constructing a collective identity during the period 1960–2008. I focus on the relationship between the identity policies of the Sámi movement, language, revitalisation and ethnicity at the level of the Sámi community from a transnational and ethnopolitical viewpoint.

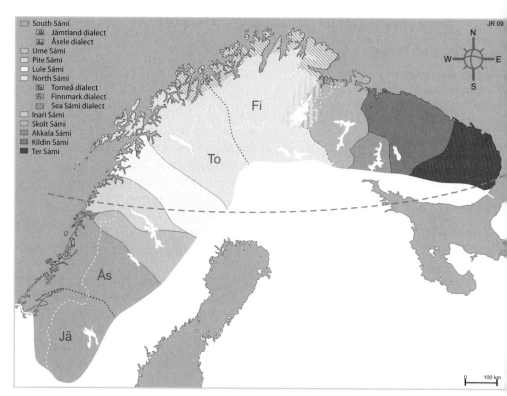

Map. The group of Sámi languages.

Traditionally ten Sámi languages are distinguished, South Sámi, Ume Sámi, Pite Sámi, Lule Sámi, North Sámi, Inari Sámi, Skolt Sámi, Kildin Sámi, Ter Sámi and Akkala Sámi (see the map). They do not have any deep linguistic boundaries because, in particular, the neighboring languages and dialects on the language boundaries are generally close to each other. In this article when I generally discuss Sámi language issues, I refer to them in the singular. However, the North Sámi language, which is the most widely spoken Sámi language, is the language mainly used in the context of the Sámi movement. In the current Sámi language acts of Finland, Norway and Sweden the singular form is also used when referring to the Sámi languages spoken in Finland, Sweden and Norway – North Sámi, Lule Sámi, South Sámi, Inari Sámi, Skolt. (Kulonen et al. 2005: 176, 177–180.)

In addition to those five Sámi languages, there are two more Sámi languages, Kildin and Ter Sámi, still spoken in Russia. A third Sámi language, Akkala Sámi once spoken in Russia, has recently become extinct (Kulonen et al. 2005: 88–89). A few years ago, in 2003, the last remaining speaker of Akkala Sámi, Marija Sergina ig. Osipova of the municipality of Kovdor on the Kola Peninsula died (Rantala & Sergina 2009: 73). In addition, the writing system of Ume Sámi has been lately renewed and the use and teaching of this language has been revitalised to some extent. Pite Sámi is no longer in use, but recently there have been some efforts to revitalise this language as well. At least two Sámi languages become extinct a long time ago. They are Kemi Sámi (used until the end of 18th century in the southern part of Lapland in Finland) and Kainuu Sámi (used until 16th–18th century in the area of the Forest Sámi people in central Finland and in the Republic of Karelia).

The death of even a single language goes against humanity and human rights for much rich cultural heritage becomes lost when a language dies. Furthermore, as an indigenous people, linguistic diversity is as natural for the Sámi as ecological diversity, since they have always lived amongst other peoples and accepted the fact that various dialects and languages are spoken around them. It is also a question of linguistic human rights, the right to one's own language and the right to an education in one's own language (Skutnabb-Kangas and Phillipson 1989, Skutnabb-Kangas 1999). Only a small number of speakers of the world's 6000 languages have these rights, and most of the world's languages, some 4000–5000, without linguistic human rights, are indigenous languages (Huss 1999: 20).

The present number of speakers (based mostly on Kulonen et al. 2005: 89,146, 176, 205, 248, 272, 396, 405, 421) can only be estimated:

- North Sámi: around 30,000
- South Sámi: 1,000
- Ume Sámi: very few under the age of 70 years
- Pite Sámi: very few
- Lule Sámi: around 2,000
- Inari Sámi: around 350
- Skolt Sámi: around 300, very few in Russia
- Akkala Sámi: 0 (Rantala & Sergina 2009: 71)
- Ter Sámi: very few
- Kildin Sámi: around 700

My objective is to show how the identity strategies of organisations arising in the 1960s and the revitalisation movement headed by the Sámi from the 1970s fought against linguistic assimilation and discrimination by society. How did the Sámi associations redefine what it meant to be Sámi and how did they oppose those negative aspects associated with the Sámi culture and languages as a result of assimilation? How were the languages used as a driving force during the construction of the Sámi identity? What kinds of social and cultural creativity did the organisations and their representatives use to achieve this? The redefinition and reconstruction of an ethnic group's identity is often part of a process where that group becomes more confident. In particular, language may be the culturally specific feature that is reassessed. The current renaissance of small languages all over the world is a phenomenon that started to occur as globalisation accelerated (Wright 2004: 14).

Indeed, language is one of the strongest factors defining the uniformity and solidarity of the Sámi movement alongside certain other joint representative traditions. In my opinion, this boils down to the fact that the Sámi worked together without regard for national borders, and, therefore, their identity strategies had the greatest impact on the revitalisation of the Sámi languages. When a language is undervalued and stigmatised, its speakers switch over to the majority language, but when it is better valued and its status improves, its speakers want to show that they know that language in order to show that they belong to that particular group. (Hyltenstam & Stroud 1991: 67.)

The status of languages reflects the status of their speakers; this can be seen in the correlation between the colonial past and the annihilation of languages amongst the Sámi and other indigenous peoples. Indeed, the primary goal of the revitalisation and Sámi movements was for them to reclaim their languages, to safeguard them and promote them. The significance of a language previously undervalued and scorned must be reassessed if the goal is to revitalise it. Its speakers must ask themselves:

– Why is our language dying out?
– What do we want to do or what can they do?
  Why is it important to protect and preserve our language?
– What can we do to preserve the language and to prevent it from dying out?

This ideological basis for revitalisation, e.i. the consciousness-raising of the importance of revitalisation and unity-building of people, which Joshua Fishman (1991) calls 'ideological clarification' is what all of the practical revitalisation activities that follow it are built upon. Revitalisation movements are crucially important for many minorities and indigenous peoples to start building a new identity and a positive tendency towards one's own language which has been stigmatised for a long time. The revitalisation of a language is visible to society when the language once again takes its place in schools and day-care centers, when it starts to be used in the media, on the radio, on TV, in other electronic communication media and in the arts. (Huss 1999: 15, 29.)

The revitalisation process of a traditional culture within a modern context means that latent cultural symbols and practices are revived. A revitalised culture, however, is always different from original. Revitalisation movements are traditional in that they try to place relevant traditions, such as language, in new contexts that are modern but no longer traditional (Eriksen 2001 [1995]: 289).

When ethnic identity and language are discussed, two central concepts, ethnicity and identity, must first be discussed in order to understand why minority languages are not valued in the modern world. For this reason, I start with ethnicity and the relationship between linguistic and ethnic identity in the Sámi community. After that, I focus on the ethnopolitical activities of the Sámi and the lin-

41

guistic revitalisation that arose from these activities. I focus on three periods of time: the 1960s and the 1970s when the Sámi-run revitalisation movement arose and the Sámi cultural renaissance commenced; the 1980s, when the Alta Controversy saw the Sámi rise up against the Norwegian government and brave the consequences of so doing. Finally, I look at topical issues related to language policies.

## 2. Ethnicity Discourse

Ethnicity has become more important these days. It is considered to be socially and politically constructed, even though it is often considered to be a regressive and primitive phenomenon mobilised by particular groups in order to achieve their own political ends. In specific, ethnicity was only used to describe a minority in contrast to the majority. In this way, the associations of 'ethnic' and 'minority' reflected the pejorative construction of an ethnic group compared to the nation state and to what is modern. (May 2001: 26). The term 'ethnic group' has, however, become nearer a concept of 'a people', since ethnicity today is also used to describe the majority.

Ethnicity sheds light on both the similarities and differences between social contexts and historical circumstances. (Eriksen 2002 [1993]: 11–12.) Nowadays, ethnicity is considered to be constructed through the symbolic, such as linguistic and informational indicators instead of external cultural characteristics. Language is a significant ethnic symbol and that's why "language and ethnic identity appear to be reciprocally related: Language use influences the formation of group identity, and group identity influences patterns of language attitudes and usage" (Liebkind 1999: 144).

B. Anderson (1983: 6) defines a nation as an "imagined political community". Like ethnicity, an "imagined community" is one of the fundamental features of the contemporary world (Smith (1994) 2002: 721). The community is conjured up in the minds of people through the use of images that are expressed in print; it is possible to create and conceive of some of their traditions in a way that rules and rituals and other repetitive practices can be used to entrench values and norms that signify continuity from the past to present in the minds of people.

(Anderson 1983, 1991: 1–7, 9–36; Hobsbawm and Ranger 1984 [1983]: 1–14, 263–307.) In the opinion of constructionists, it is essential that people imagine the nation to be a certain type of nation, even if it were not real (Anderson 1983: 6). The national culture is a discourse – a way to construct meaning to help us direct and organise our activities and our ideas about ourselves. National cultures construct identities by creating meaning out of the "people" that we can identify with. These are included in stories that are told about the nation, memories that connect the nation's present to its past. Language is an especially important ethnic marker and also one way of differentiating between ethnic groups.

## 3. National concepts

The ethnopolitical activities of the Sámi have given rise to the construct of *sámi álbmot* 'the Sami people', who live in a territory stretched across four different countries. The concept of a transnational 'Sámi people' has been reinforced at the joint Sámi Conferences where political and cultural programs have been initiated (1971, 1980 and 1986) and national symbols have been created. These national symbols are their own flag (approved at the 13th Nordic Sámi conference in Åre in 1986), a Sámi National Day on February 6th (approved at the 15th Sámi conference in Helsinki in 1992), and the national anthem *Sámi Soga Lávlla* (Song of the Sami People (its text was approved at the 13th Nordic Sámi conference in Åre in 1986, and its composition at the 15th Sámi conference in Helsinki in 1992). *Sámi Soga Lávlla* was written by Isak Saba (1875–1921), and published in 1906 in the Sámi language periodical *Sagai Muittalaegje* (1904–11). Arne Sørlie is the composer of the song. It has been translated into six Sámi languages and into other languages as well.

The expression 'the Sámi people' can be used to refer to the inhabitants of a specific geographical area as well as to all of its inhabitants in the same way that we can refer to 'the Finnish people', 'the Norwegian people' and 'the Swedish people', terms which are used to refer to the nation-state and its citizens. Professor Martin Scheinin, however, states that the significance of the concept 'a people' "may be symbolic" (Scheinin 2006: 40).

In law the Sámi people are nowadays recognised as 'an indigenous people', who have their cultural self-government. Current Finnish legislation pertaining to the Sámi, such as sections 17(3) and 121(4) of the Constitution of Finland and the Act on the Sami Parliament (974/1995, amended in 1279/2002, etc.) do not, however, use the term 'the Sámi people', but refer to the Sámi as an 'indigenous people' who have the right to preserve and develop their language and culture. Let it be noted, however, that the indigenous peoples of the USA and Canada have been referring to themselves as 'First Nations' since the 1960s. It can thus be considered quite self-evident that the term 'a people' can be used to refer to an ethnic group that has no nation-state of its own and that resides in a pre-existing country or countries.

Article 3 of the Nordic Sámi Convention of 2005 (Pohjoismainen saamelaissopimus. Suomalais-norjalais-ruotsalais-saamelaisen asiantuntijatyöryhmän 27. lokakuuta 2005 luovuttama luonnos. Oslo. 2005) states (underlining added by the author):

> *As a people, the Saami have the right of self-determination in accordance with the rules and provisions of international law and of this Convention. In so far as it follows from these rules and provisions, the Saami people have the right to determine their own economic, social and cultural development and their own natural resources, which they can dispose of to their own benefit.*

Under international law and in accordance with human rights instruments, *a people* (in this case, the Sámi people) must be considered to possess the right to self-determination (Henriksen et al. 2005: 267.) The right of the Sámi people to self-determination has manifested itself in Norway, Sweden and Finland as ethnopolitical cultural autonomy run by the Sámi Parliaments in each of the three countries. The right of these people to self-determination especially means their fundamental right to the Sámi language and culture, for instance the clause 17.3 of the Constitution of Finland states:

> *The Sámi, as an indigenous people, as well as the Roma and other groups, have the right to maintain and develop their own language and culture.*

In Finland the provisions of the acts concerning the Sámi apply in the Sámi homeland. The Sámi homeland (Act on the Sámi Parliament 974/95, 4 §) comprises the three northernmost municipalities of Finland (Utsjoki, Inari and Enontekiö) and the area of the Lapland Reindeer Herding Association in the municipality of Sodankylä. However, nowadays over a half of Sámi people in Finland live outside this Sámi homeland. In Norway and Sweden there are no similar territories, but separate administrative areas were established by language laws designating the municipalities where an individual has the right to use Sámi in both speech and writing, in both private and public, and where the authorities are obliged to serve Sámi speakers in their own language.

## 4. Language, ethnic identity and the Sámi community

From a constructionist point of view, language does not just reflect reality, it also constructs it. In modern ethnopolitics, language has become the main symbol of a culture. It is usually considered to be the most significant cultural feature and criterion of ethnic groups. In this way, language indicates who belongs to the group. Furthermore, language has been used to construct the national identity of many European countries, which has allowed languages to be converted into symbols of national interest. (Johansson and Pyykkö 2005: 12–13.)

Language has an important communicational function: if two people can communicate with each other in their mother tongue, it is a cogent marker of community, and there is no need to separately construct an identity based on it. When you speak a language, you become placed in a specific speech community. A common language helps to give people a cultural identity. However, Sámi speakers are bi- or multilingual and the aim of the Sámi education system is bi- and multilingualism, however, to become fully bilingual one has to learn one's own language perfectly.

Nowadays Sámi children can usually study Sámi at school, mainly in the Sámi homeland, as a mother tongue, a second language or a foreign language or their whole education is in the Sámi language. However, in Finland, education in Sámi regularly takes place only at primary school, but not at secondary school because of the shortage of teachers of different school subjects. At the end of secondary education Sámi students are allowed to choose both the Finnish and Sámi exams for their mother tongue exams but they usually choose the Finnish exam as their mother tongue exam and sit the Sámi exam as a foreign language.

The members of a certain speech community share the same values, customs and traditions, even when they do not approve of or use them all. Like culture, language is learned and communicated, it is a continual discourse. (Hall 2003: 90.) Language and other cultural characteristics also vary according to the definition of ethnicity at various times (May 2001: 129).

The modern peoples and ethnic communities of this era always have a particularly ethnic background, an "ethnic core" comprised of common historical myths, memories and cultural characteristics such as language and a presumed point of origin. One of the main cultural characteristics of ethnic communities is language, through which a mutual connection and the idea of solidarity are created. (Smith (1994) 2002: 724.) The role of politics and ideology has been evident in the construction process of ethnic groups and their languages (Hobsbawm 1994: 57–64, 109). The opening words of the Sámi political program (adopted 1980, renewed 1986) state the attributes unique to the Sámi and the criteria for a Sámi identity (Sámepolitihkkálaš prográmma 1989):

> *We Sámi are one people and national borders cannot be allowed to destroy the connection between us. We have our history and traditions, our own culture and our own language.*

According to that definition, ethnic identity provides people with a reassuring and immutable concept of solidarity and continuity. Ethnic symbolism points to the past, i.e., an ancient language, but also to a custom, lifestyle or kinship system that plays an important role in maintaining ethnic identity. Thus the role of language is very important in generating imagined communities and in building solidarity.

Even though language is no longer usually considered a primordial (or given, essentialist) feature, when "you've been born into a specific ethnic group, this circumstance decides what your mother tongue (or tongues, if your parents speak different languages) will initially be", as Skutnabb-Kangas states (1999: 55). In addition, the Sámi have a special relationship to their mother tongue. First and foremost, a 'mother tongue' refers to the particular language and parlance learned in childhood. A mother tongue can, however, refer to a language learned after childhood or people can have more than one mother tongue, which thus reaches back into one's past time and personal history.

The following examples can show how strong the relationship between Sámi ethnicity and language can be and how language can be a very positive force in peoples' lives:

*Giella lea olmmoščeardda heaggasuotna. Go dat nohká, ja vajáldahttojuvvo, de nohká maiddái olmmoščearda.*
'Language is the lifeblood of mankind. When it is no longer and lies forgotten, so shall mankind.' (Anders Larsen in Sagai Muittalægje, July 1st, 1905 (Solbakk 2006).)

*Jos sámit ráhkistit sin máttarvánhemiid ja sin giela, de leat sii sápmelaččat, lehkos sis gákti dehe fráhkka badjelis.*
'If the Sámi love their forefathers and their language, then they are Sámi whether they are wearing the traditional Sámi gákti or a white tie.' (Larsen, Anders, Sagai Muittalægje, February 1st, 1905.)

*Giella lea váimmu dulka, sielu govva.*                      .
'Language is the interpreter of the heart, an image of the soul.' (Per Fokstad in Sabmelaš, August 19th, 1940 (Solbakk 2006).)

This article is a part of my research into the construction of identity in the Sámi movement in the context of the international indigenous movement during the period 1960–2008. My method is based on fieldwork. My fieldwork methods involved interviews and observation of participants. I carried out my interviews during 2005–2007 in the capitals of Helsinki and Oslo and in northern Finland and northern Norway. To guarantee the objectivity of my study I interviewed people of both genders, of different ages, and from different places. The fact that most of those interviewees have sometimes been active in Sámi organisations does not make them unreliable. On the contrary, they have become more conscious of the real situation of the language. In addition, my research material includes the minutes of Sámi organisations, the Sámi Council and the Nordic language board, which also helps to give better perspectives on the development of Sámi issues. The objective of the fieldwork was to understand the attitudes and viewpoints held by, in particular, those Sámi who have been involved in the Sámi movement and associations, and thus to clarify the cultural contexts within which these occur. This material has subsequently enabled the interpretation of culture, and even the construction of theoretical concepts, which will undoubtedly be used to achieve a deeper perspective on the issue dealt with in this article and will affect the results in the form of individual opinions.

I asked my interviewees what the distinguishing features of Sáminess were. They often listed several features, the most important of which were language, family, the place where they were from, 'a sense of place', traditional livelihoods and way of life, as Berit, who was temporarily living in a city, says:

> *Sámivuođa dovdomearkkat, kriterat, dat lea gal váttes gažaladat. Olu olbmuin leat iešguđet dovdomearkkat. Sámevuohta lea viiddis gažaldat: dat lea vuos giella, kultuvra, eallinvuohki... Mu máttut leat maid boazodoalus. Gal dat dohkke dáppe Oslos orrut, go dieđán ahte leat doppe olbmot geat fievrridit dien eallinvuogi. Danin jurddašan dain, geat dáppe orrot, dat vuosttas ja nubbi soahkabuolva, lea sámevuohta čadnon sámeguvlui ja sámi eallinvuohkái, dasa mo sámit leat eallán sámeguovllus. Dáppe giela doalahit, muđui gal geat dáppe orrot šaddet eallit sullii seammaláhkai go eará olbmotge. Árvvut, fuolkevuohta, dat árvvut mat sšmiin lea ... lea maid daid olbmuid.* (Berit, born in 1947, a city dweller; interviewed in February 2006.)

'What makes a Sámi, that's a difficult question to answer. Everyone has their own criteria. What it means to be Sámi is a broad question: first off language, culture, way of life... My roots are in reindeer herding. It's ok to live in Oslo, too, since

I know that there are still people who are engaged in it. That's why I think that for the people living here, the first and second generations, Sáminess is bound up with the Sámi territory and way of life, the way the Sámi have lived in the Sámi territory. Here we try to maintain our language, but we have to live pretty much like everyone else here. Values, kinship, the values the Sámi have... are also part of these people.'

Language is also a significant symbol for the Sámi living in the diaspora, outside the central Sámi area, especially in the capitals, even when they no longer speak it. They identify with the speakers of a specific language and want to maintain that identification, and so this shows very well why language and ethnic identity are recipro- cally related and how language use influences the formation of group identity (Liebkind 1999: 144). The Sámi often stress that even though they might have lived a long time outside the traditional Sámi terri- tory, they do not lose their language. Many people want to show that they know Sámi and thus are 'real' Sámi by using it in different situ- ations in public. Sámi who have lost their language, however, stress that they want to learn Sámi so that "Sápmi... is yours, mine", as the Sámi author Anna Stina Svakko wrote about the experiences of the younger generation when learning Sámi and rediscovering their roots (Svakko 1991). How to go about being a 'real Sámi' is an idea that has arisen during various types of interaction between people.

The bond between language and ideology is thus strong. When a language is lost or it is not transmitted from one generation to the next, then the traditional and spiritual knowledge transmitted by the language is also lost (the author's own notes from the 2008 session of the United Nations Permanent Forum on Indigenous Issues, New York, Wright 2004: 220–221). In indigenous movements it is stressed that the loss of an indigenous language is more than just the loss of traditional knowledge, as cultural diversity and spirituality are also lost in the process. In the spring 2008 session of the UN Permanent *Forum* on *Indigenous* Issues, it was stressed that biological, linguistic and cultural diversity are inseparable and mutually reinforcing; lan- guage maintenance is, therefore, also tied to various environmental challenges. That is why 'Mother Earth' is very central to indigenous discourse and in philosophy throughout the world (the author's own notes from the 2008 session of the United Nations Permanent Forum on Indigenous Issues, New York). However, more than just being knowledge about nature and livelihoods, traditional knowledge also includes folklore and other spiritual culture tied to language. The spiritual culture of the indigenous peoples is particularly rich and original, since the dominant culture has not yet had a chance to squash it.

It seems a good idea to use biological and evolutionist metaphors to describe the distress of languages today as these metaphors focus on the death of languages and the gravity of the consequences of their deaths. On the other hand, the use of biological metaphors can be criticised since they emphasise the widely accepted Darwinian viewpoint, often articulated by speakers of the dominant language, that language loss is an inevitable part of social and linguistic evolution (May 2001: 3). That is not the case.

Language also plays a political role in the construction and maintenance of the group identity of an ethnic group, especially at that point in time when the collective bond is being constructed and the group wants to make the difference between 'Us and Them'. In Barth's opinion, cultural attributes such as the language of an ethnic group are not in their own right significant and that their significance actually lies in their usefulness in preserving the boundaries between groups. Cultural attributes thus become important and a marker of ethnic identity once the group itself feels that they are necessary. The significance of cultural boundaries grows the more those boundaries are encroached upon or threatened. (Barth 1969, May 2001: 129.)

In their own language the Sámi have always differentiated between the concepts of *sámit* 'the Sámis' and *láttit* 'the Lapps'. The polarity of these two terms is closely related to the idea of one's own language separate from other languages. Language can also act as a dividing factor between the Sámi and the majority (Collinder 1957: 191).

In the 1990s in northern Finland, the topic of the day was the so-called *lappalaisilmiö* 'the Lapp phenomenon', which pertained to the issue of determining who was Sámi. Local non-Sámi started to object to the proposed amendments to legislation that would provide the Sámi with augmented rights and the proposed Act on Cultural Autonomy for the Sámi. The discussion particularly revolved around the definition of Sámi identification, e.g., who is a Sámi and does having ancestors identified as a 'Lapp' in historical land, taxation or population registers many generations ago really give someone the right to be recorded in the Sámi register. This discussion, which started out being about the rights of the Sámi, culminated in an argument among ethnic groups, the local Finns, and the Sámi. The Sámi movement did not want to accept people to be included on the electoral roll for the Sámi Parliament who did not have a close relationship with the language and culture, and the reason for that was that the primary objectives of the movement were especially to safeguard the language and culture and not to assimilate them into mainstream society. In its decision of September 22nd, 1999, the Supreme Administrative Court of Finland concurred with the Sámi Parliament when it stated that the argument for the inclusion of the Sámi language in the definition of who is eligible to vote was acceptable and that anyone registering solely based on descent cannot receive more privilege than those registering on the basis of linguistic criteria, with the cutoff set at having a grandparent who was Sámi. (Press release of the Supreme Administrative Court of Finland from September 22nd, 1999, Seurujärvi-Kari 2000: 11.)

## 5. The Sámi revitalisation movement and ethnopolitical activities

### 5.1. The rise of the revitalisation movement and its objectives from the 1960s to the 1970s

The more than one hundred years of assimilation policies by the nation-states in which the Sámi lived resulted in a dramatic language shift. Many managed to switch their language and become Swedes, Finns or Norwegians in a single generation. (Collinder 1957: 184–198.) The minority had to capitulate to the decisions and authority of the majority in the name of state assimilation politics. Their rights as individuals or, in particular, as group members were not officially taken into consideration. This situation gave rise to an asymmetric situation between the various ethnic groups. During this process, the nation states did not recognise the Sámi as an ethnic minority, which resulted in them becoming a part of society with no constitutional status, either as individuals or as a group: without any official right to their own language, culture or territory. (Eidheim 1985: 158–159.)

Assimilation particularly targeted languages, which led to them being undervalued and excluded from public use. They were turned into informal, outmoded languages since they were not used in schools. Assimilation also influenced attitudes: parents started to be ashamed of their language, since they had been led to believe that minority languages are not as valuable as dominant languages. Once the language had been stigmatised, parents no longer spoke it to their children, which in turn made it unlikely that the language would be transmitted to the next generation. This resulted in the partial or complete loss of people's own mother tongue. Thus linguistic assimilation has had far-reaching implications and the Sámi people have been depressed for decades. (Seurujärvi-Kari 2005b: 24– 25.) Of course, we have also heard other lamentable stories of language loss from around the world (e.g. May 2001: 2, Nettle & Romaine 2000: 8–10, Romaine 2006: 441).

The school system, with its boarding schools, was a symbol of state control. The boarding school system in the Sámi territory took on a special meaning. The dormitory founded in South Varanger, Norway, in 1905, marked the beginning of the entire system, which spread throughout the Sámi territory all the way to Snåsa, where the Southern Sámi lived, "[T]his initiated a 50-year period during which boarding schools were built and during which these schools from Sámi areas to Snåsa were under the supervision of municipalities and the state". This was a time of an intense policy of assimilation. (NOU 1980: 20.) Children lived in the non-Sámi environment of the dormitory. Sámi people felt the goal of the boarding school and school systems was the transformation of the Sámi into Norwegians, Finns and Swedes. (Seurujärvi-Kari 2005b: 24–25, Todal 2002: 215.) In the race to achieve that objective, "the Sámi language and culture were considered to be distracting factors that prevented their users from being educated" (NOU 1980: 20).

The first step the Sámi movement took in rebuilding the Sámi identity was to deconstruct the linguistic asymmetry that was used to classify the majority or minority on the basis of certain languages. Under this linguistic asymmetry only the language of the majority was important for identity and good of the nation. The minority language was stigmatised as being less valuable. This set the boundaries between the different dichotomies such as 'majority' and 'minority', 'Us' and 'Them', 'modern' and 'tradition'. (Eriksen 2002 [1993]: 11.)

It became important for some young people, in particular, for those attending upper secondary school or university, to find ways of becoming Sámi, of being Sámi and of restoring and reclaiming the language. For some, this was natural, while for others it was more difficult, especially since it was a matter of drumming up the courage to find the right strategies to restore their own self-esteem and identity. Traditional knowledge of Sámi was dwindling away due to the language and culture no longer being taught. A small group of young people started fervently to look for their roots by studying history. These same people stressed their Sáminess by putting emphasis on traits and symbols characteristic of the Sámi, such as the Sámi language and the use of traditional clothing. They felt that it was their responsibility to do so and that they had to do something to restore their language. They started to participate in and arrange courses. As one interviewee, JE from Karasjok, Norway, said: "we were strong". Of course, some people, especially older people, did not agree on everything with their young people on what the young people were doing because they thought it is of no use to restore Sámi language. They wanted their children to learn only the dominant language at school because they thought that is how their children will succeed in life better than they themselves had done. I was told by some interviewees they had to meet secretly, away from their parents in the beginning.

By the mid 1960s, there were already dozens of local Sámi organisations. These arose due to "the dominant society and majority parties not taking the Sámi and our needs into consideration, and many Sámi felt that Sáminess should be made visible ...". Sámi activities started to spread from the capital regions to the local level and closer to the Sámi themselves (Ruong 1969: 31). At that point in time, the Sámi were still quite politically and culturally dispersed. For this reason, the next objective was to bring together under one roof Sámi from different regions, Sámi who spoke different languages and represented various professions, thus creating legitimate organisations that only the Sámi could be members of and that could then represent the Sámi

53

in the Nordic Countries and worldwide. This "grouping" took place pretty much along the same lines in Norway, Sweden and Finland; local organisations merged to form central organisations that then participated in Nordic conferences where a common political viewpoint was created. The delegates to the conferences were named by various central organisations: *the Central Organisation of the Sweden Sámi, the Association of Reindeer Herders* (1950), *Same-Ätnam, the Central Organisation of Cultural Sámi* (1944), *the Central Organisation of Norwegian Reindeer Herding Sámi* (1947), *the Central Organisation of Norwegian Sámi* (1968), and *the Delegation for Sámi Affairs from Finland* (1973). The delegation in Finland was the first elected political body for the Sámi. In this way, the start of an organisational pyramid was created. (Seurujärvi-Kari 2005g: 349–350.)

The ideological work begun by a small group of Sámi young in the 1960s was still being carried out in the 1970s. The ideological strategies of the 1970s included joint declarations and programs drafted and approved at the Sámi Conferences held every three years. Their objectives started to be swiftly implemented with the building of a Sámi administration, a cultural institution and the revitalisation of the Sámi culture. These ideological activities, spanning the course of twenty years, set the foundation for future practical revitalisation work and their main message can be seen in the already familiar foreword to the politico-cultural program (Sámiid kulturpolitii'ka 1974) adopted in 1971 at the Sámi Conference held in Gällivare:

*Mii leat sámit ja háliidit leat sámit, eat daðe eanet, dahje unnit go máilmmi eará álbmogat. Mii leat okta álbmot, mis lea min iehčamet ássanguovllut, min iehčamet giella ja min iehčamet kultur- ja servodatráhkadus. Áiggiid mielde mii leat skáhppon áigáiboaðu ja eallán Sámieatnamis ja mis lea kultuvra, man mii doaivut ovdánit ja eallit viidáseappot.*

'We are Sámi and we want to be Sámi. We don't want anything more or less than any of the other people of the world. We are one nation; we have our own land, our own language, our own cultural and societal structure. Over time, we have made a living and we have lived in Sápmi. We have our own culture that we hope to see being developed and thriving in the future'.

## The Sámi organisations and administration in the 1960s and 1970s

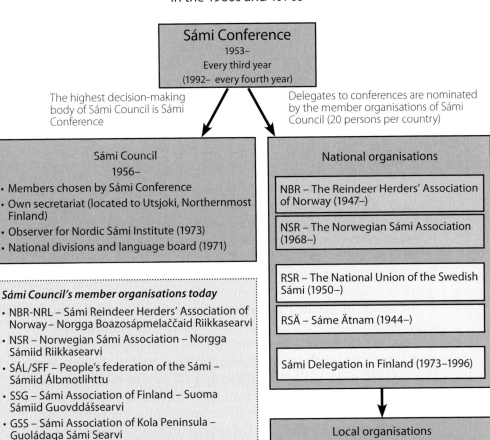

Figure 1. Sámi organisations and administration by the 1970s.

## 5.2. Linguistic and cultural renaissance in the 1970s

## 5.2.1. The language enters the school building

The Sámi youth started to reclaim their language collectively, through organisations. According to the resolutions of the Sámi Conferences, schools had to create a sense of safety for children by educating them in more depth about the Sámi language, culture, history and way of life. The Sámi understood that education and learning about one's own language is not enough, that bilingualism as an educational objective is an incredibly important factor in constructing a nation. Solid information about one's own people and its culture was needed, but at the same time, they needed to learn to play by the rules of the dominant society. Educational issues were key points in the objectives of the Sámi's own organisations right from the beginning (Saba and Fokstad's educational programs at the beginning of the 1900s).

In the 1960s, the local organisations and Nordic cooperation had particularly success in bringing the North Sámi language into the school building. It is worth mentioning that the teaching of the South Sámi was initiated a decade before in the Snåsa Sámi school (established in 1953). By the end of the 1960s, Norway even granted the possibility of learning in North Sámi and a Sámi upper secondary school was built in Karasjok. A Sámi Folk High School was founded in Jokkmokk and a junior high school in Gällivare. In Inari, Finland, a Sámi Christian Folk High School had already been up and running for some time. These institutions also served as the heart of the Sámi revolution and a place for the youth to meet up. Sámi-language education commenced at the Universities of Oslo and Uppsala and at the Tromsø Teacher College. At the beginning of the next decade, a teachers' training institute had been founded in Alta, Norway; a Sámi department was also established there. This department started to be criticised, however, soon after its founding by Sámi organisations for being too Norwegian (NRS-dieđáhusat 1974: 6).

The dominant languages still occupied center stage and Sámi was relegated to the role of backup language. As a language, Sámi was still strongly integrated into the national educational system in respect to content, organisation and administration. (NOU 1980: 21.)

Since the 1980s, bilingualism has become the main principle of Sámi education, which has also afforded Sámi the status of an official school subject. (NOU 1985: 18, Linnankivi 1993: 5.)

It is significant that thanks to the politico-cultural program of the Sámi, their academic campaigning and the Sámi movement resulted in a Nordic Sámi Institute, *Sámi instituhtta*, was founded in Kautokeino, Norway in 1973. The institute started operations the next year. Since then *Sámi instituhtta* and the Sámi University College, *Sámi allaskuvla* (1989) have joined forces to serve and improve Sámi research and education. The goal of this reorganisation is to create a new fertile information environment, *diehtosiida*, an academy for the Sámi.

## 5.2.2. Standardising the North Sámi language

From the very first Sámi organisation, there have been ideas floating around about standardising the Sámi languages, as their orthographies had been shaped to conform to the orthographies of the dominant languages of the countries they were in. This caused them to grow apart from the language spoken by the people themselves, making it difficult for people to learn the written form. At a conference of Sámi teachers held in Máze at the end of the 1960s, the representatives concurred with the idea of the Sámi Council and the demands of the 5th Sámi Conference on expanding the Cultural Word Board created as part of the Sámi Council into a Nordic Sámi Language Board. According to the decision of the Sámi teacher conference, it was intended to be, perhaps the Sámi Institute. (Minutes. 1966; see also Aikio 1987, Bergsland 1952, Itkonen 1951, Korhonen 1981: 53–75.)

At the 1971 Sámi Conference held in Gällivare, *Sámi giellalávdegoddi*, a Sámi Language Board was established. Nine representatives of various Sámi languages, including South Sámi, Lule Sámi, North Sámi and Skolt Sámi, were elected to serve on the board. The goal of the Language Board was to create a unified literary language in order to provide the Sámi with education in their own language and to provide the Sámi with a tool to express themselves in writing. A solid, strong literary language was necessary for Sámi education and promoting the Sámi language.

The revision of the North Sámi orthography proved to be quite an arduous job. Linguistic work commenced in 1973 (Magga 1985: 45). The original plan was for the Lule Sámi orthography to follow that of Northern Sámi, or even for all the Sámi languages to have orthographies close to one another. In the end, however, the various languages broke off from each other, each with its own orthography. The reason for this break was that the representatives of each language group emphasised the difference between various their languages, and that they were afraid of losing their identity traditionally based on certain language. Thus the aim of the Sámi movement to create a common national language failed, but this fact didn't wither the unity of the people. In the Sámi movement it is customary and strategically right, when discussing the Sámi language issues to refer to these languages in the singular form as mentioned in the introductory chapter of this article.

At the beginning of the project, the Language Board adopted two main principles: ease and simplicity. For this reason, a decision was made not to use letters from the languages of the dominant cultures as this would further bind the Sámi languages to the dominant languages, which was not in accordance with for the Sámi standardisation objective of the Sámi movements or for working up literary strength. The orthography also had to be as accurate as possible. "Pedagogicalness" and a close connection with the spoken language were the two common starting points for the revision so that normal people would be able to learn and reclaim their language more easily than before. Sámi teachers participated in the various stages of the revision work, as did the Sámi Council, the Sámi Conference, many organisations and private individuals.

At the Sámi Conference in 1978, the new unified orthography for North Sámi was approved. The Sámi Council launched the new orthography on July 1st, 1979, after which the Norwegian Ministry of Church and Education approved it on September 10th, 1979. During the entire period, *Sámi Instituhtta*, The Nordic Sámi Institute (the Sámi research institute) served as the language board's expert. The Research Institute for the Languages of Finland approved the orthography for general use and it was launched in Sweden, as well. The new orthography was created rather quickly once the language board started its actual work in 1973. (Magga 1985: 62.)

The revitalisation of written Northern Sámi had commenced. Later on, improved orthographies for Lule Sámi, Inari Sámi, Skolt Sámi, Southern Sámi and Kildin Sámi were also approved. Kildin Sámi, which is spoken on the Kola Peninsula in Russia, uses Cyrillic as the basis of its orthography.

National literary languages are artificial, practically contrived. Modern nations were created mainly around a common written language. According to Anderson (1983, 1991) and Hobsbawm (1994: 64–65), it is a written language that is essential when creating and concocting an "imagined community". Furthermore, the role politics and ideology has played is evident in the construction process of languages and identity.

Language standardisation has received positive attention in Hyltenstam and Stroud's research (1991) into the Sámi languages and their use in Sweden. The new, uniform terminology that modern society needs can be created once the standard language is in us in a modern context. This type of language modernisation has an impact on language revitalisation. The aforementioned researchers also stressed that a new, standardised Sámi literary language might reinforce the identity of all Sámi. A standard language is also crucial for use by the government, in the press, in research conducted in one's own language, and particularly for children to learn to write their own language at school. (Todal 2002: 137, 139.)

On the other hand, the significance of literary languages should not be exaggerated. Those languages that do not have a literary language of their own do not "slowly crumble into dialects" as Hobsbawm (1994: 64) states. These "non-literary-language" languages are also not less developed than languages with their own literary language. Sámi and all other languages too, have been, as a result of, and are, independent languages regardless of when a literary language was created for them. Languages that do not have a literary language are simply without a literary language. Their speakers live in a diglossia where the written and spoken forms of their language are two different languages. It would also be preferable for modern literary languages to be able to allow variation and to support diversity.

Even around the time the Sámi literary language was created, many of the older generation felt that the standardisation was problematic and inquired as to why their tradition-rich language, 'a heritage language', was not suitable for use in schools. Furthermore, it can be noted that the literary language of North Sámi, which is the form most often taught in schools, has started to homogenise the spoken language, thus impoverishing the way the language is used. In addition, it must also be noted that only a few people in the Sámi and other communities are active users of the literary language. (Todal 2002: 137–138.)

To conclude this section, literary languages do, however, have a symbolic value. Language generates the idea of a unified modern community. Speakers realise that they form a community that reaches beyond the boundaries of their local community. A literary language joins people by creating solidarity and a single mythic past, whose political significance is just as important as its cultural significance. (Hobsbawm 1994: 65–73.) The ability to read and write as well as negotiate with the state are key factors in the survival of an ethnic group in the modern world (Eriksen 2001 [1995]: 288).

### 5.2.3. A breakthrough in literary and artistic activities and the media

In the 1970s, a breakthrough in literary and artistic activities and in the media occurred that launched the Sámi cultural renaissance, thanks to a new type of Sámi movement led by the Sámi born leaders.

The renaissance had begun even before the new unified literary language; for example, a committee to promote Sámi literature had already been established. The first steps to establish the committee were taken at the 'ČSV' seminar held in 1972 in Sirma, Norway, by Sámi activists from various associations. (Čállagat 1 1973: 2.) The committee published a literary anthology called *Čállagat* in 1973. *Čállagat* was considered to be the stepping stone for many current Sámi authors. The first Sámi theater group, *Dálvadis*, was founded in Jokkmokk, Sweden and the first art center was opened in Máze, Norway (Seurujärvi-Kari 2005h: 412). Sámi artists formed ties across the borders of the Nordic countries: *Sámi Girječálliid Searvi*, a Sámi authors' association, and *Sámi Dáiddačehppiid Searvi*, a Sámi artists' association were founded in 1979; and *Sámi Teahtersearvi*, a Sámi theater association was founded in 1980. The goal of these organisations was to champion their own professional causes, to achieve professional equality at the Nordic level and to enhance the Sámi identity. (Seurujärvi-Kari 2005a: 23.)

The printed word, literature, art and theater all play a role in the construction of an ethnic community as they can be used to rapidly disseminate information amongst the people. The era of the press actually writing about Sámi issues commenced in 1958, when the newspaper *Ságat* started to be published in Norwegian. The magazine *Sápmelaš*, which was distributed free to every Sámi household until 1990, had already been launched before that in Finland. In reaction to *Ságat*, a weekly newspaper named *Sámi Áigi*, backed by Sámi organisations and proposed by the Sámi Conferences, was launched in Karasjok, Norway in 1979. *Sámi Áigi* was written in North Sámi and was meant for the entire Nordic market. The weekly immediately started to act as a channel for the Alta Movement and validated the organisations' ideology amongst the Sámi. Where there is a national publication that is read by an entire community, new publications will develop. The publications validated the Sámi's national feeling and dealt with the group as a cohesive unit, thus promoting the learning of the standard language. People learned to read the written language and were able to practice it daily. At the same time, the community's members also reasserted the difference between inside and outside and defined what was going on in the world. Later, two rival newspapers, *Áššu* and *Min Áigi*, which took up where the defunct *Sámi Áigi* left off, merged into a biweekly, pan-Scandinavian newspaper *Ávvir*. (Seurujärvi-Kari 2005d: 282–286.)

Other media, particularly radio and TV have had a major impact on linguistic development and ethnic unity. Sámi Radio is the oldest and most established Sámi mass medium. Begun as a joint Nordic cooperative project, it has become an ever more significant means of communication for the Sámi. *Sápmi*, the concept of Sámi unity has been manifest in the operations of Sámi Radio ever since the 1960s. A joint Nordic news programme in the North Sámi language was broadcast from Tromsø in Norway in 1964, and a current affairs programme from Kiruna in Sweden from 1973 to 1986. Since 1986 broadcasts have been shared between the different countries. In Finland, the reception range of Sámi Radio is limited to the Sámi area, although over a third of Sámi people live outside it. In Norway and Sweden most of the transmissions can be heard throughout these countries. The programmes of Norwegian and Swedish Sámi Radio are broadcast in North, South and Lule Sámi, while in Finland there are almost daily transmissions in Inari and Skolt Sámi in addition to programmes in North Sámi. Nowadays, *Oddasat*, the Sámi TV news programme is broadcast nationwide across Scandinavia in North Sámi with subtitles in the majority language of Norway, Sweden and Finland. Sámi news and other programmes can also be read and listened to on the internet. (Seurujärvi-Kari 2005e: 291–292.)

### 5.3. The Alta Movement: making a language legitimate and visible

The Sámi revitalisation movement was not just about culture as such, that is culture in its narrower sense. The concept of culture has many definitions. It is usually defined as comprising those abilities, notions and forms of behaviour persons have acquired as members of society (Eriksen 2001 [1995]: 3). Most of all, culture is a process, and it is changing and blending. Culture is also seen as a way to perceive and shape the world, which is how evaluation of culture as high or low can be prevented. Cultural difference is also very much emphasised in this changing world. Thus common culture is regarded as a concrete example of a group's characteristics to both the group itself and outsiders. In this sense culture and ethnicity can mean almost the same thing. In the broader sense, culture is not only about non-material but also material aspects, such as nature, natural resources and livelihoods, "Sámi have their own culture and social life, which are connected to their own history, traditions, language, livelihoods and future visions... for Sámi land and water form the basis of culture" (Pohjoismainen saamelaissopimus. Suomalais-norjalais-ruotsalais-saamelaisen asiantuntijatyöryhmän 27. lokakuuta 2005 luovuttama luonnos. Oslo. 2005: 9).

In the Sámi movement it was, and still is, also question about rights, the right to determine one's own path and direction for the future by using the past, the right to territory and traditional livelihoods, the right to educate children in one's own mother tongue on their own culture's terms, and the right to participate in decision-making on a large scale. As a result, the minority language and culture ended up at loggerheads with the dominant language and culture, and this was a partial cause for the Alta Controversy in 1979–1981. The project to dam the Alta-Kautokeino River was a controversy in Norwegian society that also attracted worldwide attention. The Norwegian state-owned energy company NVE had already put forward a proposal in 1968 for harnessing the water resources of the Finnmark. At the time of the Alta-Kautokeino dispute, the Sámi movement was led by a group of trained Sámi professionals who were able to work with the media and the public. The Sámi leaders made strong demands to get the state to recognise Sámi peoples' special rights, such as the rights of their way of living and language and culture as an indigenous people. The movement that fought against the damming of the Alta-Kautokeino Rivers had Sámi organisations working side-by-side with international environmental activists. This boosted the morale of the Sámi and reinforced their collective identity and sense of community.

The relationship between the majority and the minority is always a question of power, as the majority is in a governing position, they own the economic, social and culture capital that the minority does not have. Conflicts arise when the majority wants to take over and control resources, ecological, economic or intellectual, that are important to the minority, as occurred with the Alta Controversy. Indigenous peoples have traditionally lived in their own territories, depended on natural resources, practiced their own cultures, and spoken their own languages. Various colonisation and assimilation processes have resulted in the change or disappearance of many of their traditional ways of life.

The Alta Controversy was a turning point in Sámi politics in Norway, and it has also had significant, positive consequences for Sámi politics everywhere. The Alta Controversy resulted in a committee report being published in Norway in 1984 about the legal status of the Sámi (NOU 1984:18), and a committee report on cultural and educational issues, *Samisk kultur og udanning*, the following year (NOU 1985: 14). The latter proposed a law be enacted on the Sámi language. This draft language act corresponded to various international conventions and treaties that demanded stronger protection for minority languages, (e.g., *Covenant on Civil and Political Rights of 1966* (Article 27), and *Indigenous and Tribal Peoples Convention C169*, which Norway was one of the first countries in the world to ratify June 20th, 1990. Finland and Sweden have yet to ratify the convention. Due to Norway's new Sámi politics, in 1989 King Olav V apologised at the opening of the Norwegian Sámi Parliament to the Sámi for their suffering at the hands of the state during Norwegianisation. Similar apologies have since appeared in various places around the world, the last time in 2007 when the Australian prime minister apologised to the country's Aborigines for the oppression and mistreatment they suffered. From 1910 to 1970 at least 100,000 Aboriginal children in Australia were wrenched from their families and homes and placed with white families in order to assimilate them in accordance with racist policies. The children who have experienced this racism and violence are referred to as the 'stolen generation'. (Sturcke 2008.)

Norway has become a pioneer for Sámi issues, with Sweden and Finland following its lead. However, Finnish policies towards traditional minorities and the Sámi people have been more favorable than Sweden's policies, at least until 2000 and in particular, concerning language policies, as you can also read in the following paragraphs. In Norway, for example, financial resources allocated for the promotion of Sámi language have always been much bigger than in Finland and Sweden and, more importantly, even special language centres to reinforce languages and language identity have been established. In 2003 34,5 million krones were allocated by the Norwegian state to municipalities for the promotion of bilingualism and language projects, and in the following year financial support was 42 million krones (roughly over 5 million euros; Sámedikki 2003 bušeahtta). In comparison, for example, with Finland, where the whole 2003 budget of the Sámi Parliament was 1 120 000 euros and state support for the implementation of the language law 83 638 euros. (Saamelaiskäräjien toimintakertomus 2003: 13–14.) The financial support for Finnish Sámi languages and culture is not much better today, the whole 2010 budget of the Finnish Sámi Parliament is about 2 million euros of which 433,000 for its language section (Saamelaiskäräjien talousarvio 2010).

Sámi language acts came into force in Norway and Finland in 1992. In Finland, the language act was later amended and the new Sámi language act (1086/2003) entered into force at the beginning of 2004 at the same time the new language acts for Finnish and Swedish were enacted. Sweden has lagged behind Norway and Finland, as it was only in 2000 that Sámi became an official national minority and regional language there (Seurujärvi-Kari 2005c: 177–180). In 2010 the new act on minorities and minority languages entered into force in Sweden (Lag (2009: 724) om nationella minoriteter och minoritetsspråk.) According to this new language act, for example the language administrative area was expanded from four northern municipalities to 17 municipalities including even such city areas as Strömsund, Umeå, Åre and Östersund. This now affords Sámi the same status as the dominant languages within these areas, and ensures that Sámi can be used in official domain.

The recognition of minority and indigenous languages (in Norway and Finland, Sámi is classified as an indigenous language) in legislation has had a positive effect on language use. In society, Sámi has also become a more legitimate and visible language compared to its previous status as a problem that should be kept hidden and secret. The language acts have raised the self-esteem of speakers and provided them with the legitimacy to act in the political arena. (Huss & Lindgren 2005: 253–255, 268, 276–277, Seurujärvi-Kari 2005c: 177–180, 2005f: 345–346, SOU 2006:19, 135.)

It should be mentioned that only after the language acts had been enacted were Norway and Finland ready to ratify *the European Charter for Regional or Minority Languages of the Council of Europe*. The charter, which entered into force in 1998 is the only international instrument that specifically pertains to the status of national regional and minority languages. It was 2000 before Sweden ratified the charter, i.e., years after Norway and Finland. The same year, Sweden finally approved the Sámi languages spoken in Sweden as official minority languages. (European Charter for Regional or Minority Languages of the Council of Europe, Seurujärvi-Kari 2008.)

## 6. Challenges for the Sámi language community and policies in the new millennium

Article 4 of *the Declaration from the Second Sami Parliamentarian Conference*, held in Rovaniemi, Finland on October 28th, 2008 states the following:

> *The right to maintain, use and develop one's own language is a fundamental human right. The Sámi have the right to use their own language and to be understood in their own language. The Sámi should themselves take care of their own languages through the Sámi Parliaments. The countries should fulfill their national and international obligations towards the Sámi languages.*

Since 1974, the Sámi Language Board has been responsible for transnational language cooperation among the Sámi and for monitoring the use and status of the Sámi languages. In 1992, Russian representatives of Kildin, Akkala and Ter Sámi joined the board. The Sámi Parliamentary Council, a joint body consisting of the various Sámi Parliaments, currently appoints the 12 members of the Language Board (2000). Each individual Sámi Parliament also has its own body that deals with language issues.

The Sámi Parliaments have a great deal of responsibility for ensuring that the Sámi language is transmitted to future generations and that the Sámi-language school system works. For this reason, the coordinating body of the Sámi Parliaments has started to boost and reorganise language cooperation with the objective of establishing a joint language center for maintaining and conducting research on the Sámi languages.

However, the most important question is still to be asked: Has the Sámi movement really succeeded in restoring a language?

Even though the social and legal prerequisities for reinforcing the Sámi language and education in Sámi and about Sámi have improved in recent decades, the revitalisation process is still underway and language shift to the dominant languages is still occurring. Based on the assessment of the results of recent research and reports (eg. Hirvonen

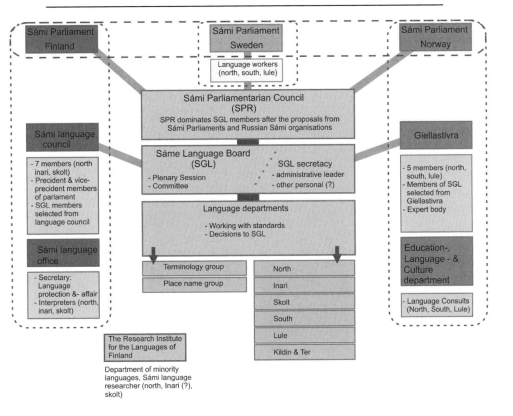

Figure 2. Transnational Sámi language co-operation and organisations as of 2008.

2003, Lindgren 2000, Näkkäläjärvi 2007), assimilation is continuing, particularly at the edges of the Sámi territory, due to school policies and the linguistic choices made by officials

The authorities are not either providing the Sámi-language with the proper services that have been set out in the language acts. Sámi is not being used enough in official contexts (Näkkäläjärvi 2007). I give here just some examples of these deficiencies. In Finland the implementation of the language act seems to work arbitrarily in practice mostly due to the lack of a sufficient number of officials able to speak the Sámi language. That's why the use of the language in relations with the administration and authorities still varies in practice. As regards Skolt and Inari Sámi, there is also a lack of translators and interpreters, although the demand for translation has grown significantly since the Sámi language act came into force in 2004. There is no North Sámi periodical published in Finland to be distributed to all Sámi-speaking households, as it used to be some ten years ago.

An actual language policy is still missing from society and even from the Sámi schools – even though they have partially succeeded in boosting Sámi language teaching and revitalising Sámi – on how the Sámi languages can be supported and reinforced (Aikio-Puoskari 2007: 82–83, Hirvonen 2008: 35–37). Several schools have failed to create language policy programs for the Sámi languages. In addition, they do not have clear target programs pertaining to the bilingualism of their staff. A major challenge to society and the Sámi community is that the majority of children and young people living outside the Sámi territory do not receive any education in Sámi or about Sámi. One of the problems of education is that Sámi language and culture classes are isolated from the natural use of Sámi language to school rooms and separate Sámi lessons (Todal 2002: 216). Sámi languages, traditions and livelihoods should be properly included in the curriculum.

Thus the linguistic rights of the Sámi are not implemented in practice. The underlying reason for this is that the deeply entrenched practices of society are difficult to change. For the Sámi community, the external way of thinking is so firmly entrenched that they do not notice the majority wielding power over them (Hirvonen 2003: 149-150). The Sámi have internalised the basic values and worldview of the majority. (Kuokkanen 2007a: 11–12, 2007b: 149–150.) This kind of internalisation has been a long process, and it has influenced even people's minds. Sámi people are often put to shame when using their language in official contexts, because they also know the dominant language. That's why they have not had courage, e.g., to use their language.

For this reason, steps to get people to decolonialise their ways of thinking and make them think and act better from the viewpoint of the Sámi culture must be taken. This would mean that people also start to use their traditional knowledge, experiences and practices that have accumulated over generations. Traditional knowledge refers to a system of knowledge which is constituted in response to way of life, nature and cosmology. It is not based on the experiences of an individual, but rather on a "collective cognitive experience" shared and communicated by the members of the community through language and oral traditions (Kuokkanen 2007: XVIII). Language is a valuable library of traditional knowledge, and that's why the use of the Sámi languages should also be as natural as the use of other languages in all life's domains. This is the only way that a real change, e.g., a Sámi school based on the viewpoint, content and basic values of the Sámi, can be achieved. This would then fulfill the obligations set out in the language acts and curricula: multiculturalism and bilingualism. New models should be created to improve knowledge of Sámi and the opportunity to study Sámi language and culture for both the Sámi themselves and the authorities dealing with Sámi issues (Samisk handbok).

As soon as possible, a national revitalisation program for the Sámi languages must be created by the state in cooperation with Sámi. The program must focus on preschool education in Sámi; education in and about Sámi at all educational levels, up to and including university; and the extent to which Sámi is used privately and publically. In Finland concrete and resolute actions have lately been claimed for to be taken to revitalise Sámi throughout the country since 70 % of Sámi children already live outside of the Sámi homeland area. (e.g. Länsman 2008: 3, 29–35, sámediggi: aloite 1.3.2010.)

As stated in the draft version of the Sámi Convention of 2005 (Pohjoismainen saamelaissopimus. Suomalais-norjalais-ruotsalais-saamelaisen asiantuntijatyöryhmän 27. lokakuuta 2005 luovuttama luonnos. Oslo. 2005, Articles 6, 7 and 27) presented to the ministries responsible for Sámi Affairs, it is the duty of the states to ensure that the Sámi have access to the environment that allows them to maintain and develop their language, culture and life in society. The states are also responsible for creating favourable conditions for Sámi research, recruiting more Sámi researchers and promoting transnational research cooperation throughout the country.

Since the establishment of the Nordic Sámi Institute, Sámi research has directed its criticism towards the approaches, methods and results of research on the Sámi and their culture carried out by non-Sámi (Keskitalo 1974/1994). Its superficial approach and its way of operating have been criticised for turning the Sámi and their culture into something they are not. At the same time, this criticism can be seen as testament to the scientific activeness of the Sámi themselves. Current discourses in Sámi Research are incorporated into a broader global discourse on indigenous research where the different theoretical and methodical problems of indigenous research become topical. It might seem slightly paradoxical that indigenous peoples are developing their own "ethnomethodology", considering that they have adopted the basic strategies of the dominant culture in constructing their identity and "people". This paradox, however, holds within it hope, in the sense that powerful research using the past and traditions to construct the future is needed for rebuilding the language. At the same time, cultures, as well as, people are constantly interacting with each other and thus blending and changing.

## 7. Conclusion

By exercising persistent identity politics the Sámi movement succeeded in forming the Sámi community both at the national level and across borders. The original goal of the Sámi movement was to raise the level of education by means of an educational system that had its foundations in the Sámi language and culture; an "ideological clarification" campaign was waged for the adoption of the writing system of the Sámi language, the teaching of the Sámi language in schools, teacher training colleges and universities. Further education grew strongly, and publication, radio and TV broadcasting and cultural activism in the Sámi language increased. The Alta Controversy (1979–1981) was an event of great significance in raising the Sámi conscience when the Sámi activists organised themselves to oppose the plans of damming the Alta-Kautokeino river. By the end of the 1980s, organisational activities had noticeably succeeded in creating conditions for a redefinition of the Sámi identity within the Sámi community and for a new political unity. Today, the unity of the Sámi people is based on a common ethnic identity and a common language maintained and developed by an indigenous Sámi administration and this administration's cultural politics. The movement used language as a driving force in the construction and strengthening of Sámi identity, which in turn made it possible for the Sámi to function as "an imagined political community". In all, the Sámi's right for autonomy is stronger than before, which has resulted in a new legislative foundation in the Nordic Countries. Today, the Sámi people are recognised as an indigenous people with a right to cultural self-government realised by the Sámi Parliaments in Finland, Norway and Sweden.

Ethnicity is constructed through the symbolic, such as linguistic and informational indicators, instead of external cultural characteristics. Language is a significant ethnic symbol, and language and ethnic identity are reciprocally related: language use influences the formation of group identity, and group identity influences patterns of language attitudes and usage.

Language is an important indicator of identity and a constructor of a sense of togetherness for the Sámi. However, there are also other symbols and signs of Sáminess that are linked to identity formation and preservation: family, 'a sense of place' pertaining to a common living area or place of origin, Sápmi, and memories of traditions. Although these vary to the extent that they are real or fictitious, they are nevertheless essential. Sámi identities are situational and relative. They are constantly shifting and blending. It appears, however, that the Sámi have preserved their connection with their own language and culture. This connection is also maintained by participating in the activities and events of Sámi associations and organisations, which in turn create the feeling of a connection in the Sámi movement and amongst the Sámi.

Norway is a pioneer in Sámi issues, showing the way to maintain and develop the Sámi languages and cultures. In addition, it has boldly provided other countries with a model to follow by implementing a new type of politics that is more favorable towards the Sámi.

In summary, it can be said that in the Sámi's efforts towards a more extensive right to self-determination, it is language that provides the Sámi with a voice that fortifies the Sámi community and enables them to identify with their national identity.

# Literature

Act on the Sámi Parliament (974/1995). – <http://www.finlex.fi/en/laki/ kaannokset/1995/en19950974.pdf> 15.2.2009.

Aikio, Samuli 1987: Yksi mieli, yksi kieli. – *Virittäjä* 91: 457–490.

Aikio-Puoskari, Ulla 2007: Saamelaisopetus osana suomalaista peruskoulua – kielenvaihdoksen vai revitalisaation edistäjä? – *Sámit, sánit, sátnehámit. Riepmočála Pekka Sammallahtii miessemánu 21.beaivve 2007.* Helsinki: Suomalais-Ugrilaisen Seuran Toimituksia = Mémoires de la Société Finno-Ougrienne 253. Helsinki: Suomalais-Ugrilainen Seura. 73–84.

Anderson, Benedict 1991 [1983]: *Imagined Communities: Reflections on the Origin and Spread of Nationalism.* London – New York: Verso.

Barth, Fredrik. 1969. Introduction. – Fredrik Barth (ed.), *Ethnic Groups and Boundaries: The Social organization of Culture Difference.* Oslo – Bergen – Tromsø: Universitetsforlaget. 9–38.

Bergsland, Knut 1952: Hvordan den samiske rettskrivningen ble til. – *Sámi aellin – Sameliv* 1951–52. 28–50.

Collinder, Björn 1957: Lapskans betydelse för samerna och samekulturen. – *Sámiid dilit. Föredrag den nordiska samekonferensen Jokkmokk 1953.* Oslo: Svensk, norska och finsk utgåva. 184–198.

*Constitution of Finland* (1999). (731/1999, amendments up to 802/2007 included.) – <http://www.finlex.fi/en/laki/kaannokset/1999/en19990731.pdf> 15.2.2009.

*Covenant on Civil and Political Rights of 1966.* – <http://www.hrcr.org/docs/ Civil& Political/intlcivpol.html> 15.2.2009.

*Čállagat* 1 1973. Láv´degåd´di åvdidan dittii sámegiel girjálášvuođa. Kárášjohka: Nårga Kulturráđđi.

Declaration from the Second Sami Parliamentarian Conference 2008. – <http://www.samediggi.fi> 15.2.2009.

Eidheim, Harald 1985: Indigenous peoples and the state: the Sámi case in Norway. – Jens Brøsted, Jens Dahl, Andrew Gray, Hans Christian Gulløv, Georg Hanriksen, Jørgen Brøchner Jørgensen and Inge Kleivan (eds), *Native power.* Bergen: Universitetsforlaget. 155–171.

Eriksen, Thomas Hylland 2001 [1995]: *Small Places, Large Issues. An introduction to Social and Cultural Anthropology.* 2nd Edition. London – Sterling, Virginia: Pluto Press.

—— 2002 [1993]: *Ethnicity and Nationalism. Anthropological Perspectives.* 2nd Edition. London: Pluto Press.

European Charter for Regional or Minority Languages of the Council of Europe. – <http://conventions.coe.int/treaty/Commun/QueVoulezVous. asp?NT=148&CM=1&CL=ENG> 15.2.2009.

Fishman, Joshua 1991: *Reversing Language Shift. Theoretical and Empirical Foundations of Assistance to Threatened Languages.* Multilingual Matters 76. Clevedon – Philadelphia – Adelaide: Multilingual Matters.

Hall, Stuart 2003: Kulttuuri, paikka, identiteetti. – Mikko Lehtonen ja Olli Löytty (eds), *Erilaisuus.* Tampere: Vastapaino. 85–128.

Henriksen, John Bernard, Scheinin, Martin & Åhrén, Mattias 2005: Saamelaisten itsemääräämisoikeus. Liite 3. Pohjoismaisen saamelaissopimuksen taustamateriaalia. – *Pohjoismainen saamelaissopimus. Suomalais-norjalais-ruotsalais-saamelaisen asiantuntijatyöryhmän 27. lokakuuta 2005 luovuttama luonnos.* Oslo. 263–315.

Hirvonen, Vuokko 2003: *Mo sámáidahttit skuvlla? Reforpma 97 evalueren.* Kárásjohka: Čálliid Lágádus.

—— 2008: 'Out on the fells, I feel like a Sámi': Is There Linguistic and Cultural Equality in the Sámi School? – Nancy H. Hornberger (ed.), *Can Schools Save Indigenous Languages.* Policy and Practice on Four Continents. Houndsmills, Basingstoke, Hampshire RG21 6S and New York: Palgrave Macmillan. 15–41.

Hobsbawm, E. & Ranger, T. (eds) 1984 [1983]: *The Invention of Tradition.* Cambridge: Cambridge University Press.

Hobsbawm, Eric 1994: *Nationalismi.* Tampere: Vastapaino.

Huss, Leena 1999: *Reversing language shift in the Far North. Linguistic Language Revitalization in Northern Scandinavia and Finland.* Acta Universitatis Upsaliensis. Studia Uralica Upsaliensia 31. Uppsala: Uppsala universitet.

Huss, Leena & Lindgren, Anna-Riitta 2005: Monikielinen Skandinavia. – Marjut Johansson and Pirkko Pyykkö (eds), *Monikielinen Eurooppa. Kielipolitiikkaa ja käytäntöä.* Helsinki: Gaudeamus. 246–280.

Hyltenstam, Kenneth & Stroud, Christian 1991: *Språkbyte och språkbevarande.* Lund: Studentlitteratur.

*Indigenous and Tribal Peoples Convention C169* (1989). – <http://www.ilo.org/ilolex/cgi-lex/convde.pl?C169> 25.9.2010.

Itkonen, Erkki 1951: Suomen kirjakielen kehitysvaiheet. – *Virittäjä* 55: 169–183.

Johansson, Marjut & Pyykkö, Pirkko 2005: Johdanto: monikielisyys ja kielipolitiikka. – Marjut Johansson and Pirkko Pyykkö (eds), *Monikielinen Eurooppa. Kielipolitiikkaa ja käytäntöä.* Helsinki: Gaudeamus, 9–26.

Keskitalo, Alf Isak 1974/1994: *Research as an interethnic relation*. Acta Borealia nr 13. Rovaniemi: Arctic Centre, University of Lapland.

Korhonen, Mikko 1981: *Johdatus lapin kielen historiaan*. Helsinki: Suomalaisen Kirjallisuuden Seuran Toimituksia 370. Helsinki: Suomalaisen Kirjallisuuden Seura.

Kulonen, Ulla-Maija & Irja Seurujärvi-Kari & Risto Pulkkinen (eds) 2005: *The Saami – a cultural encyclopaedia*. Helsinki: Suomalaisen Kirjallisuuden Seura.

Kuokkanen, Rauna 2007a: *Reshaping the university. Responsibility, Indigenous Epistemes, and the Logic of the Gift*. Vancouver – Toronto: UBC Press.

—— 2007b: Saamelaiset ja kolonialismin vaikutukset nykypäivänä. – Joel Kuortti & Mikko Lehtonen & Olli Löytty (eds), *Kolonialismin jäljet. Keskustat, periferia ja Suomi*. Helsinki: Gaudeamus, 142–155.

Lag (2009:724) om nationella minoriteter och minoritetsspråk. – <http://www.notisum.se/rnp/sls/lag/20090724.htm> 30.03.2010.

Liebkind, Karmela 1999: Social Psychology. – Joshua A, Fishman (ed.), *Handbook of Language and Ethnic Identity*. New York – Oxford: Oxford University Press. 140–151.

Lindgren, Anna-Riitta 2000: *Helsingin saamelaiset ja oma kieli*. Helsinki: Suomalaisen Kirjallisuuden Seura.

Linnankivi, Jaakko 1993: *Saamen kielen opetuksen kehittämisestä 1973–93*. Opetushallitus. (Unpublished.)

Länsman, Anne 2008: *Saamen kieli pääkaupunkiseudulla*. Vähemmistövaltuutetun julkaisusarja 5. Helsinki: Vähemmistövaltuutettu.

Magga, Ole Henrik 1985: Davvisámi čállinvuohki: čállinvuohkebargu 1973 rájes. – *Giella: dutkan, dikšun ja oahpaheapmi*. Diedut 2. Sámi Instituhtta. 42–67.

May, Stephen 2001: *Language and Minority Rights. Ethnicity, Nationalism and the Politics of Language*. Harlow, England: Pearson Education Limited.

Minutes. 10th session of the Sámi Council March 8–9, 1966 in Enontekiö; Asia 3/1966 Saamelaisopettajien kokouksessa Masissa elokuussa 12–14.

Nettle, Daniel & Romaine, Suzanne 2000: *Vanishing Voices. The Extinction of the World's Languages*. New York: Oxford University Press.

NOU 1980: 59. Sámegiella vuoddoskuvllas. Oslo–Bergen–Tromsø: Universitetsforlaget.

NOU 1984: 18. Om samenes rettsstilling. Oslo–Bergen–Tromsø: Universitetsforlaget.

NOU 1985: 14. Samisk kultur og utdanning. Oslo–Bergen–Stavanger–Tromsø: Universitetsforlaget.

NSR-dieđáhusat. NSR's meldingsblad. 1974. Nr. 1.

Näkkäläjärvi, Klemetti 2007: *Selvitys saamen kielilain toteutumisesta 2004–2006*. Inari: Saamelaiskäräjät.

*Pohjoismainen saamelaissopimus. Suomalais-norjalais-ruotsalais-saamelaisen asiantuntijatyöryhmän 27. lokakuuta 2005 luovuttama luonnos.* Oslo.

*Press release of the Supreme Administrative Court of Finland.* September 22nd, 1999.

Rantala, Leif & Sergina, Aleftina 2009: *Áhkkila sápmelaččat. Oanehis muitalus sámejoavkku birra, man maŋimuš sámegielalaš olmmoš jámii 29.12.2003.* Roavvenjárga: Kasvatustieteiden tiedekunta.

Romaine, Suzanne 2006: Planning for the Survival of Linguistic diversity. – *Language Policy,* 5: 441–473.

Ruong, Israel 1969: *Samerna.* Stockholm: Aldus/Bonnier.

Saamelaiskäräjien talousarvio 2010. Saamelaiskäräjät. Inari.

Saamelaiskäräjien toimintakertomus 2003. Saamelaiskäräjät. Inari.

Sámediggi: aloite 1.3.2010. – <http://www.samediggi.fi> 1.3.2010.

Sámedikki 2003 bušeahtta. Sámediggi. Kárášjohka.

*Sámiid kulturpolitii'ka. Samernas kulturpolitik. Saamelaisten kulttuuripoliittinen ohjelma* 1974: Helsset: Davviriikkaid sámiráđđi.

Sámi Language Act 1086/2003. <http://www.finlex.fi> 15.2.2009.

*Sámepolitihkkálaš prográmma.* 1989. 2. prenttus. Ohcejohka: Sámiráđđi.

*Samisk handbok.* – <http://www.samediggi.se> 15.2.2009.

Scheinin, Martin 2006: *Ihmisen ja kansan oikeudet – kohti Pohjoismaista saamelaissopimusta.* Lakimies 1/2006: 27–41.

Seurujärvi-Kari, Irja 2000: Esipuhe. – Irja Seurujärvi-Kari (ed.), *Beaivvi mánát. Saamelaisten juuret ja nykyaika.* Tietolipas 164. Helsinki: Suomalaisen Kirjallisuuden Seura. 9–15.

——— 2005a: Artists' organizations. – Ulla-Maija Kulonen, Irja Seurujärvi-Kari and Risto Pulkkinen (eds), *The Saami – a cultural encyclopaedia.* 23.

——— 2005b: Assimilation. – Ulla-Maija Kulonen, Irja Seurujärvi-Kari and Risto Pulkkinen (eds), *The Saami – a cultural encyclopaedia,* 24–25.

——— 2005c: Language legislation. – Ulla-Maija Kulonen, Irja Seurujärvi-Kari & Risto Pulkkinen (eds), *The Saami – a cultural encyclopaedia.* Helsinki: Suomalaisen Kirjallisuuden Seura. 176–180.

—— 2005d: Press. – Ulla-Maija Kulonen, Irja Seurujärvi-Kari & Risto Pulkkinen (eds), *The Saami – a cultural encyclopaedia*. Helsinki: Suomalaisen Kirjallisuuden Seura. 282–286.

—— 2005e: Radio. – Ulla-Maija Kulonen, Irja Seurujärvi-Kari and Risto Pulkkinen (eds), *The Saami – a cultural encyclopaedia*. Helsinki: Suomalaisen Kirjallisuuden Seura. 291–292.

—— 2005f: Saamen kieli ja saamelaisten kielelliset oikeudet 2000-luvulla. – Marjut Johansson and Pirkko Pyykkö (eds), *Monikielinen Eurooppa. Kielipolitiikkaa ja käytäntöä*. Helsinki: Gaudeamus. 338–357.

—— 2005g: Saami movement. – Ulla-Maija Kulonen, Irja Seurujärvi-Kari & Risto Pulkkinen (eds), *The Saami – a cultural encyclopaedia*. Helsinki: Suomalaisen Kirjallisuuden Seura. 347–350.

—— 2005h: Theatre. – Ulla-Maija Kulonen, Irja Seurujärvi-Kari & Risto Pulkkinen (eds), *The Saami – a cultural encyclopaedia*. Helsinki: Suomalaisen Kirjallisuuden Seura, 412–413.

—— 2008: Eurohpa ráđi guovllugielaide dahje vehádatgielaide guoski vuođđugirji ja dan mearkkašupmi sámegillii. – *Sámi dieđálaš áigečála*. 1, 2008. Sámi Allaskuvla, Guovdageaidnu, Romssa universitehtta sámi dutkamiid guovddáš. Romsa. 51–70.

Skutnabb-Kangas, Tove 1999: Education of Minorities. – Joshua A, Fishman (ed.), *Handbook of Language and Ethnic Identity*. New York – Oxford: Oxford University Press. 42–59.

Skutnabb-Kangas, Tove & Phillipson, Robert 1989: *Wanted! Linguistic Human Rights*. ROLIG-papir 44. Roskilde: Roskilde Universitetscenter.

Smith, Anthony D. (1994) 2002: The Politics of Culture: Ethnicity and nationalism. – Tim Ingold (ed.): *Companion Encyclopedia of Anthropology*. London – New York: Routledge. 706–733.

Solbakk, Aage (ed.) 2006: *Bures daddjon – Sápmelaš dajai ja maid earát leat cealkán*. Karasjok: Čálliid Lágádus.

SOU 2006 = *Att återta mitt språk. Åtgärder för att stärka det samiska språket*. Statens offentliga utredningar 2006: 19. Stockholm: Fritzes.

Sturcke, James 2008: Australia says sorry for racist past. – <http://blogs.guardian.co.uk/news/2008/02/it_has_been_a_long.html> June 1st. 15.2.2009.

Svakko, Anna-Stina 1991: *Virvelvind=VV*. Jokkmokk: Sámi Girjjit.

Todal, Jon 2002: *"-jos fal gáhttet gollegielat": vitalisering av samisk språk i Noreg på 1990–talet*. Avhandling (dr. art.). Universitet i Tromsø.

Wright, Sue 2004: *Language Policy and Language Planning. From Nationalism to Globalisation*. New York: Palgrave Macmillan.

# "Válddiimet gielamet ruovttoluotta"
## – sápmelaš identitehta ráhkadeapmi sámelihkadusas ja sámegiela rolla 1960-logus jahkái 2008

*Irja Seurujärvi-Kari*

Gieđahalan dán artihkkalas sámegiela rolla sámelihkadusa kollektiiva identitehta ráhkadanprošeavttas áiggis 1960–2008. Fokuseren sámelihkadusa identitehtapolitihka, giela, revitalisášuvnna ja etnihkalašvuođa gaskasaš oktavuhtii sámeservoša dásis.

Modearna etnopolitihkas gielas lea boahtán kultuvrra guovddáš symbola. Sámiid revitalisašuvdnlihkadusa ulbmilin bođii ovdasajis iežas giela ruovttoluotta váldin, ovddideapmi ja ođđasit guorahallan. Dán revitalisášuvnna ideologalaš vuđđui, 'ideological clarification' (Joshua Fishmana tearbma 1991), mii huksejuvvui 1960–1970-logus, vuođđuduvvá maŋit ealáskahttindoaibma. Servodatdási revitalisášuvdna oidno das, ahte giella standardiserejuvvui, máhcahuvvui skuvlii, geavahuvvogođii medias ja dáidagis ja suodjaluvvui lágain (sámi giellalágat fápmui Norggas ja Suomas 1992 ja Ruotas 2000).

Giella lea dehalaš identitehta-indikáhtor ja sámiid oktavuođadovddu huksejeaddji, muhto identitehtaid šaddamii ja seailluheapmái laktásit earáge sápmelašvuođa symbolat ja mearkkat, sohka, dovdu oktasaš ruovttuguovllus dahje oahpes báikkiin, the sense of place, muittut árbevieruin ja álgoboahtimušas, duogážis. Dát aspeavttat leat eanet dahje uhcit duođalaččat dahje fiktiivvalaččat, muhto goittotge leat mearkkašahtti. Daid oktavuohta dollojuvvo ealasin oassálastimiin sámeservviid doaimmaide ja dáhpáhusaide, ja dan bokte ráhkaduvvo oktavuođa dovdu sámelihkadussii ja sámiid gaskavuhtii.

Sámiid gielalaš vuoigatvuođat eai goit otne ollašuva geavadis. Sivvan lea dat, ahte servodahkii čiekŋalassii cieggan vuogádagaid lea váttis nuppástuhttit. Virgeoapmahaččat eai fála giellalágain dárkkuhuvvon sámegielat bálvalusaid ja sámegiella ii geavahuvvo doarvái virggálaš oktavuođain. Stuorra hástalussan stuorraservodahkii ja sámeservošii lea dat, ahte sámeguovllu olggobealdi ássi mánáin ja nuorain stuorámus oassi báhcá sámegiela oahpahusa olggobeallái. Sámeidentitehtat maiddái rivdet ja seahkanit geažosáigge. Loahpas, sámiid rahčamis viidásut iešráđđenvuoigatvuođa guvlui, giella lea dat dahkki, mii addá sámiide jiena. Sámeáššiin Norga lea dat álgojalgejeaddji, mii lea čájehan luotta sámiid giela ja kultuvrra seailluheapmin ja ovddideapmin ja maiddái čájehan roahkkadit eará riikkaide málle ollašuhttimiin ođđalágan sámiide miehtemielalaš politihka ovttasbarggus ieš sámiiguin ja sámedikkiin.

ELISABETH SCHELLER

# The Sámi Language Situation in Russia

## Abstract

The article presents an overview of the Sámi language situation in Russia. In Russia there are or used to be found four Kola Sámi languages (Kildin Sámi, Ter Sámi, Skolt Sámi and Akkala Sámi), plus a newcomer, North Sámi, which has been used by some Kola Sámi community members since the 1990s. Today, all four Kola Sámi languages are seriously threatened by a language shift from Sámi to Russian. However, a revitalisation process in respect to Kildin Sámi is currently occurring. The present article starts with a general introduction to the Sámi, who are one of the indigenous minority peoples in the Russian Federation. After that, sources of data will be presented and categories of language competence, categories of language users, their numbers and their visibility inside and outside the language community will be discussed. The figures for Sámi language users in Russia are presented in a table below. A description of the actual Sámi language situation(s) in Russia, describing each language variation separately, follows. Finally, conclusions are drawn about the language situation with regard to the potential for language revitalisation, which is the main focus of the article.

*Ethnic and Linguistic Context of Identity: Finno-Ugric Minorities.* 79–96.
Uralica Helsingiensia 5. Helsinki 2011.

# 1. Introduction

The Sámi are an indigenous ethnic minority group living in Norway, Sweden, Finland and on the Kola Peninsula in north-western Russia. The Sámi languages belong to the Finno-Ugric language family and can be divided into two groups: the Eastern Sámi language group and the Western Sámi language group. Kildin, Skolt, Inari, Ter, and Akkala Sámi belong to the Eastern Sámi language group (Map 1). North, Lule, Pite, Ume and South Sámi represent the Western Sámi language group. Today, less than 20,000 of the 70,000–100,000 Sámi speak a Sámi language (cf. Aikio 2003: 34–35). According to criteria for judging whether a language is endangered recommended by both J. A. Fishman (1991: 381–415) and UNESCO (2003), all Sámi languages are seriously endangered.

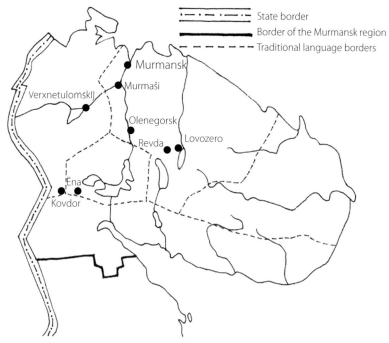

Map 1. The Sámi in Russia: Traditional language borders. (Map according to Misjura 2003 [2007]; traditional language borders according to Sammallahti 1998: 5.)

## 2. The Sámi in Russia

The Russian Federation has a population of slightly over 145 million people. It is a multi-national state with more than 200 different ethnic groups, of which half are indigenous. Although the Russian ethnic group is the largest, approximately 30 million Russian citizens are not ethnic Russians (cf. VPN 2002). Most of the ethnic groups in Russia have been heavily influenced by Russian culture, and Russian is used as the official language of communication across the whole country.

There are about 2000 Sámi in Russia who mainly live in the Murmansk region of the Kola Peninsula (Map 1) – a region that has always been quite important for Russia, both industrially, economically and strategically. After a heavy influx of migrant workers, which was at its strongest in the 1960s and 1970s, more than 100 several ethnic groups now live in the Kola Peninsula. The Sámi, who are the indigenous people of this region, have been displaced and assimilated over the last centuries, and they are today one of the smallest ethnic groups in the region (cf. VPN 2002). As a result of the forced displacements by the Soviet authorities of several Sámi groups from across the whole Kola Peninsula during the 1960s and 1970s, most Kola Sámi language users today live as a minority group in the centralised multi-ethnic municipality of Lovozero (Kildin Sámi *Lujavv'r*).

The Kola Sámi languages have been strongly influenced by Russian. After the 1917 Russian revolution, there was a short period when the Soviet state implemented certain practical measures to develop and protect the Sámi languages and the Sámi culture. This was followed by almost 20 years of repression and russification, which had a negative influence on the Kola Sámi languages and increased the language shift process from Sámi to Russian. The freedom after the Soviet period opened up new opportunities for the political, cultural and language development of the Sámi. However, there were new economic and social difficulties to contend with. According to the law, the Sámi have several rights to language sovereignty and the use and development of their languages (Krjažkov 1994: 129–140). Yet, their ability to exercise their rights depends on the economic situation in Russia and on the attitudes of the authorities and the majority Russian population towards the Sámi.

## 3. The Sámi language situation in Russia today

According to the last official census, carried out in 2002, 787 of a total of 1991 Sámi living in Russian territory speak Sámi (cf. VPN 2002). Even though this census is one of the most extensive national censuses ever undertaken, it still gives a rather incomplete picture of the Sámi language situation in Russia. The figures are based on voluntary information and self-identification. The statistics do not give any information about spoken varieties and dialects or about the language competence, frequency or context of language usage of those informants who consider themselves Sámi speakers. (cf. VPN 2002).

To get a more precise picture of the Sámi language situation in Russia, the author of this article conducted a survey using a sociolinguistic questionnaire over the period March 2007 to August 2008 as part of the *Kola Sámi Documentation Project* (KSDP 2009). The aim of the survey was to reach as many members of the Sámi community in Russia as possible, and to get more extensive quantitative and qualitative information on the Sámi language situation in Russia, both at the individual level and at the level of the community.

As a result of the survey, 1105 completed questionnaires were collected from several places in the Kola Peninsula and other places in Russia. In other words more than half the Sámi population in Russia answered the questionnaire. The results of the survey will be presented and analysed in my doctoral thesis, which will present a more extensive description of the Sámi language situation in Russia and suggest a model for a revitalisation of Kildin Sámi, the Kola Sámi language with the best prospects.

According to the author's own observations during four years of fieldwork, and from the first results of the questionnaire survey, qualitative interviews and the 2002 Russian census, it is likely that approximately 800 people in Russia have some knowledge of Sámi. "Knowledge of Sámi" in this case means *any* kind of language knowledge, ranging from fluency to a rudimentary understanding.

## Potential language users

Among the 800 individuals who have knowledge of Sámi, probably at least 200 are "potential language users", which means people who have good passive language skills. They understand all or most of the language and can often speak it, but for several reasons they do not speak the language actively or do not speak it at all. These people usually grew up with Sámi as their first language and spoke it actively in their childhood but then stopped speaking it during childhood or when they started at school. Most of the potential Sámi language users in Russia are middle-aged, which means people between 30 and 50 years. This age group was subjected to greater discrimination, assimilation and stigmatisation than the older and the younger generation. Today, very few from this age group use Sámi on a daily basis and those who are parents do not transfer the Sámi language to their children.

It is likely that most of these potential language users would start speaking Sámi fluently (again) if they were in a language environment where Sámi had a high status and was actively used as an everyday language.

## Active speakers

Probably less than 100 of the 800 people with a knowledge of Sámi are active speakers. "Active speakers" means people who speak Sámi fluently as their first or second language. Unlike potential language users, active speakers use Sámi naturally in their everyday life at *all levels* of communication, that is, they use Sámi as an everyday language inside and outside their homes, independently of the conversation topic.

This group also includes people who do not necessarily use the language on a daily basis at home, but who regularly use it actively in high level contexts as a professional language, as do, for example, interpreters.

Most of the active speakers belong to the older generation, that is, the over 50s. However, there are also some active speakers who are

83

middle-aged. Normally, active speakers grew up with Sámi as their first language and many did not speak Russian at all after they started to attend school.

## Symbolic language use

A language can be analysed not only in respect to its active and passive use, but also in respect to its symbolic use. In this case, "symbolic language users" are, for example, people who use Sámi to emphasise their ethnicity or signify their membership of a group, but who do not otherwise use it as a language of communication. A potential language user, who uses the language passively, can be, but is not necessarily, a symbolic language user. In the Kola Sámi language community, Sámi is often used symbolically in a public context, for example, when opening meetings and exhibitions. It also seems to be common to use Sámi as a "show language" for the Sámi culture. Here it is used in connection with folklore performances and traditional festivals or when tourists and guests come for a visit. The symbolic use of Sámi seems to be common irrespective of individual language knowledge. Potential language users and community members who only have a restricted knowledge of Sámi constitute the majority of symbolic language users. However, symbolic use of Sámi also occurs among active speakers. Symbolic language use seems to be expressed most strongly among people who are engaged in Sámi public life, for example, among politicians, cultural workers, Sámi language teachers and, to a certain extent, even among language activists.

## Visibility of language users

Most Sámi language users in Russia are not visible. Those who are visible tend to be language activists and so-called language specialists: language teachers, language users with a higher education, older active speakers who are engaged in language maintenance. The most visible group is people who are engaged in public life and people who have a high social status, for example, politicians and people in leading positions. The majority of these people only use Sámi passively and symbolically. Nevertheless, as official representatives of the Sámi language outside the Sámi community, they are the most visible language users. Active Sámi speakers are not usually involved in societal, political or cultural life, which makes them invisible, especially for outsiders who do not have a deeper insight into the language community. The "invisible group" also includes the majority of potential language users, especially the younger generation, that is, people who are younger than 30 years of age. The younger generation is the so-called "lost generation". Their parents did not transfer the Sámi language to them; however, many of them heard it from the older generation when they were growing up. It is unusual for the younger generation to speak Sámi fluently; many do not speak it at all. However, there is a group of young people who have a good passive knowledge of Kildin Sámi. Their interest in learning and using the language has grown during recent years. However, their language competence is not usually acknowledged by the rest of the community, and especially, not by the *language specialists*.

Another important group among invisible Sámi language users comprises people with a low social status, for example, mentally ill, alcoholics and social outsiders. However, these people are also part of the language community, and many of them are active speakers of Sámi. Unfortunately, they are usually ignored both by the majority of the language community and by researchers.

In addition, people with competence in Sámi but who are not ethnic Sámi are not normally visible in the Kola Sámi language community. This group includes, for example, non-Sámi members in Sámi families, people who are not Sámi but work in an environment in which the Sámi language is used and members of other ethnic groups who learned Sámi out of personal interest in the Sámi language and culture.

Having discussed language use and visibility, I now present the figures for Sámi language users in Russia in Table 1. I will then describe the situation for each Sámi language in Russia separately.

| Sámi language | Knowledge of Sámi (any)[1] | Potential Language Users | Active Speakers |
|---|---|---|---|
| Kildin Sámi | < 700 | > 200 | < 100 |
| North Sámi[2] | > 100 | ? | > 1 |
| Ter Sámi | < 20 | < 10 | 1–2 |
| Skolt Sámi[3] | < 20 | < 10 | – |
| Akkala Sámi | 2 (?) | 1 (?) | – |

Table 1. Sámi Language knowledge among Sámi in Russia.

## Kildin Sámi

Kildin Sámi is the most widely spoken Sámi language in Russia today. Of the approximately 700 people with a knowledge of Kildin Sámi, there are probably more than 200 potential language users and about 100 active speakers. Four dialects of Kildin Sámi are still used: *Lujavv'r* (Lovozero dialect) is the most spoken dialect, followed by *Kīllt* (Kildin dialect), *Koarrdegk* (Voron'e dialect) and *Ārsjogk* (Varzina dialect). Today, most users of the four Kildin Sámi dialects live in the municipality of Lovozero.

Kildin Sámi is most commonly used within the family and between close acquaintances. According to accounts from the older generation and retired Sámi reindeer herders, Kildin Sámi is no longer used as a working language in reindeer herding because most of the active Kildin Sámi speaking reindeer herders have retired and the younger herders, who constitute the majority of reindeer herders, do not have sufficient knowledge and interest to use Sámi as their professional language. The languages used in reindeer herding today are probably Russian and Komi.[4] Even if Kildin Sámi may not be heard as a working language among reindeer herders anymore, this does not mean that there are no active Kildin Sámi speakers working and using the language in the reindeer herding work teams today. Kildin Sámi

---

1. This category includes the other categories "potential language users" and "active speakers".
2. These figures concern those people with knowledge of North Sámi permanently living in Russia.
3. These figures concern the Skolt Sámi community in Russia.
4. This information is not completely reliable. For my doctoral work I plan to investigate language use among reindeer herders more precisely.

has a written language standard based on the Cyrillic alphabet. There is literary form of Kildin Sámi, but the literature mainly consists of prose and poems for children. There are some poems and prose translations from Russian into Kildin Sámi, but there is no literature for adults originally written in Kildin Sámi.

Today, compulsory teaching of Kildin Sámi only takes place in one vocational school, Pu-26, in Lovozero. Until 2004, there was compulsory teaching of Kildin Sámi and Komi for pupils from grade 1 to grade 4 at Lovozero's boarding school. When, in 2004, the boarding school lost its status as a national school for Sámi and Komi children, the compulsory lessons in Kildin and Komi were replaced with one hour of optional teaching a week. Optional Kildin Sámi language courses for adults and children are held in Lovozero, Murmansk, Revda, Olenegorsk and Ёna. However, these courses are mainly for beginners, have no permanent funding and do not take place regularly.

The existing teaching material for Kildin Sámi was mainly developed for school children. There is a serious lack of modern teaching materials for adults and advanced students. There is also a lack of modern and effective teaching methods within Kildin Sámi language teaching.

In addition to the language teaching mentioned above, there is one Kildin Sámi nursery group in Lovozero functioning once a week. However, the main language of communication in this group is Russian.

The *Kola Sámi Radio,* established by an Interreg-Sápmi project that was financed by 19 funders in five countries (Norway, Sweden, Finland, Denmark and Russia), is an independent Kola Sámi radio station and has to finance itself, for example, by selling TV-news to the Nordic Sámi TV. (Cf. Somby, 2005: 20, Barentsobserver, 2009.) This radio station has the responsibility of broadcasting transmissions in Kildin Sámi, but there have been no regular transmissions in Kildin Sámi during the last two years and most of the broadcasts have been in Russian. For financial reasons the Kola Sámi Radio was in danger of closing at the end of 2009 (Barentsobserver 2009). During the last three years, the movement for the revitalisation of Kildin Sámi has become more active in Lovozero. Active speakers, potential language users, adults and children who are learning Kildin Sámi, have started to meet regularly for language evenings, where they practise the active use of Kildin Sámi. During this time, Kildin Sámi summer language camps have also been organised for adults and children (cf. SKS 2007, SKS 2008). As a result, new teaching materials for adults and advanced students have been developed. In March 2009, the first issue of *Kīl Kjājjn* came out in Lovozero. *Kīl Kjājjn* is an unofficial newspaper written in Kildin Sámi which encourages people with knowledge of Kildin Sámi to use the language actively by writing articles in the newspaper (cf. KK 2009). In order to further promote this revitalisation work Kildin Sámi language activists plan to establish a language centre in Lovozero (cf. PZCHD 2009).

## North Sámi

Surprisingly, today the second most spoken Sámi language in the Kola Peninsula is not an original Kola Sámi language, it is in fact North Sámi, a western Sámi language, originally spoken in the north of Norway, Sweden and Finland. North Sámi came to the Kola Peninsula in the 1990s after the fall of the Soviet Union, when it became possible to establish regular cultural and political cooperation between the Nordic countries and Russian Sámi. Courses in North Sámi, which are financed by the Nordic Sámi community and the Nordic countries, are regularly held in the municipality of Lovozero and in Murmansk. Russian Sámi are offered scholarships to go to the Nordic countries to learn North Sámi or even to complete a higher education in the language.

It seems likely that there are at least two active North Sámi speakers of Kola Sámi origin living in Russia today. However, they do not necessarily use North Sámi in their private lives or in the home. As, for example, interpreters or employees of the Barents Secretariat or Kola Sámi Radio, they would use North Sámi actively and on a daily basis as a working language. It also seems probable that there are more than 100 people with some knowledge of North Sámi in the Kola Peninsula today. Some of them may have gained a knowledge of North Sámi through participating in language courses held in Russia, others during intensive language courses, and others have studied it in Norway or Finland. This group also includes people who are potential users of North Sámi. Typically, these people have spent some time in the Nordic countries, where they learnt and used North Sámi, but stopped using the language after their return to Russia.

North Sámi has the highest status among the Sámi languages. It receives most state support, has come furthest in the language revitalisation process and is used as a lingua franca among Sámi people from all four countries. However, the popularity of North Sámi among the Russian Sámi is not only motivated by reasons of status and communication, personal economic interests also play a part. Studying North Sámi leads to lucrative scholarships and the chance to travel to a Western European country. As a result of their studies, many Sámi students from Russia emigrate to a Nordic country for economic reasons. This is natural and understandable and it has benefited the revitalisation of North Sámi. Nevertheless, despite the Nordic Sámi community's good intentions in supporting cultural, social and political cooperation by giving Kola Sámi community members the opportunity to learn North Sámi, it inevitably creates problems for the maintenance of the Kola Sámi languages. The social and economic problems of many Kola Sámi and the lack of comparable financial and ideological support for the maintenance and revitalisation of the Kola Sámi languages has caused a power imbalance between North Sámi and the Kola Sámi languages which strongly influences the individual language choices of the Kola Sámi.

## Ter Sámi

Of the 20 people with a knowledge of Ter Sámi there are probably only two active language users today. Both are over 70 years old and live in Lovozero and Revda. Less than ten people have sufficient knowledge of Ter Sámi to count as potential language users, and they are over 60 years old. In addition they live far away from each other, spread out across the Kola Peninsula and around the city of St Petersburg.

Currently, there are no teachers of Ter Sámi and, hence, no teaching takes place. However, there is a Ter Sámi grammar and a published collection of poems, written in Ter Sámi on the basis of the Kildin Sámi alphabet. There are also audio recordings of Ter Sámi, which were collected by the Russian Academy of Science in the 1960s and 1970s.

## Skolt Sámi

At best, half of the 20 or so people in Russia today with a knowledge of Skolt Sámi are potential language users. It seems there is not a single active speaker left in the Skolt Sámi community in Russia today. There is both teaching material and literature in Skolt Sámi. It is written in the Latin alphabet and is used by the Skolt Sámi community in Finland. In Verxnetulomskij and Murmaši, optional courses in Skolt Sámi are sometimes offered to adults. However, these courses are not held regularly and have no permanent funding.

## Akkala Sámi

Akkala Sámi is the most endangered Kola Sámi language. In 1992, about seven or eight elderly Akkala Sámi speakers were counted (c.f. Sergejeva, 1993: 178). But by 2003 the last speaker of Akkala Sámi passed away (c.f. Rantala, 2009: 67). That means that no active speakers of Akkala Sámi are left. However, there are at least two people, both aged 70, with some knowledge of Akkala Sámi. One of them learned Akkala Sámi as a first language as a child. The other is a potential Skolt Sámi user, who understands Akkala Sámi and can translate older Akkala Sámi audio recordings into Russian. Skolt Sámi and Akkala Sámi are quite close and Skolt and Akkala Sámi speakers with a good command of their languages can understand each other (c.f. Pekka Sammallahti: p.c. 19.11.2009).

There is an Akkala Sámi grammar and there are audio recordings of Akkala Sámi, which were collected by the Russian Academy of Science in the 1960s and 1970s.

Today, a group of around 80 Akkala Sámi live in a closely knit community in Ёna, in the municipality of Kovdor, near the boarder with Finland, which is a closed military zone. However, it seems that nobody in the Kovdor region speaks Akkala Sámi today, although the Akkala Sámi language situation has not yet been properly investigated. The information we have comes from Kildin Sámi language specialists and politicians, who do not themselves have any competence in Akkala Sámi. According to middle-aged Akkala Sámi from Ёna, nobody of this generation has learned Akkala Sámi from their parents, but many have heard the language in their childhood. There are probably people both among the generation of middle-aged Akkala Sámi and the older generation who are potential speakers of Akkala Sámi.

There is a group of Akkala Sámi in Ëna who are learning Kildin Sámi as an "intermediate language", in the hope of switching more easily to Akkala Sámi after they have acquired a good knowledge of Kildin Sámi. On this group's initiative, optional teaching of Kildin Sámi for adults, adolescents and children has been regularly organised since 2004. The courses are financed by external funding because the municipality of Kovdor does not have the resources to support the courses. However, according to Akkala Sámi informants, the municipality of Kovdor and the local authorities in Ëna have a fairly positive attitude towards the revitalisation of Sámi culture and language, and they support the Sámi community as much they can. In addition to Kildin Sámi language courses, once a week the Akkala Sámi community in Ëna also runs a language and folklore circle for children at Ëna's culture centre.

The language situation of the Ter, Skolt and Akkala Sámi has not been investigated as extensively as Kildin Sámi. In my doctoral thesis I will investigate the situation of these Kola Sámi language groups more thoroughly.

## 4. Conclusion

All four Kola Sámi languages are seriously endangered by the ongoing language shift from Sámi to Russian. Akkala Sámi is almost extinct and the situation for Ter Sámi and Skolt Sámi is not much better. North Sámi, the Sámi language with the highest status, is gaining more and more language users even in the Kola Peninsula. The Kola Sámi language with the best chance of revitalisation and survival is Kildin Sámi. Language revitalisation in terms of a reintroduction of Kildin Sámi as the everyday language on all levels of communication is plausible due to the large invisible group of active speakers and potential language users. Nevertheless, successful language revitalisation requires teachers with modern and effective language teaching methods, new teaching materials and language courses for adults and advanced students. More opportunities to practise active language use are also a prerequisite. A better communication between the generations and more cooperation between Sámi language activists and officials is needed. It is also important to give the Kola Sámi languages a higher status, by, for example, promoting situations where Kola Sámi language competence is expressly required. Another way of giving the language a higher status could be for Nordic Sámi communities to direct more attention and interest towards the Kola Sámi languages. This could be achieved through joint Kola Sámi language courses for Sámi community members from Russia and the Nordic countries, and including the Kola Sámi languages in the highly effective Nordic Sámi language development programs.

## References

Aikio, Ante 2003: The geographical and sociolinguistic situation. – Jukka Pennanen & Klemetti Näkkäläjärvi (eds), *Siiddastallan: from Lapp Communities to Modern Sámi Life*. Inari. 34–40.
Barentsobserver 2009: Kola Sami Radio might be closed. – <http://www.barentsobserver.com/kola-sami-radio-might-be-closed.4548612-16149.html> 22.01.2009.
Fishman, Joshua A. 1991: *Reversing language shift: theoretical and empirical foundations of assistence to threatened languages*. Clevedon: Multilingual Matters.
KK 2009 = Антонова, А. А. & Виноградова, Г. А. & Данилова, С. С. & Медведева, М. Г. & Шаршина, Н. С. (ред.) 2009: *Кӣл кӣййн*. Нюххчманн 2009 ы. № 1 (1) Ловозеро: Самиздат.
Krjažkov 1994 = Кряжков, В. А. (сост.) 1994: *Статус малочисленных народов России: Правовые акты и документы*. Москва: Юридическая литература.
KSDP 2009 = *Kola Sámi Documentation Project*. – <http://www2.hu-berlin.de/ksdp> 11.08.2009.
Misjura 2003 [2007] = Мисюра, М. Г. (ред.) 2003 [2007]: *Схема Северо-западного федерального округа*. Санкт Петербург: Роскартография.

PZCHD 2009 = Данилова, С. & Шаршина Н. 2009: Проект завершился. Что дальше? – *Ловозерская правда*. № 11 (8450) 20.03.2009. 2.

Rantala, Leif & Aleftina Sergina, 2009: *Áhkkila sápmelaččat. Oanehis muitalus sámejoavkku birra, man maŋimuš sámegielalaš olmmoš jámii 29.12.2003*. Roavvenjárga.

Sammallahti, Pekka 1998: *The Sámi languages. An introduction*. Kárášjohka: Davvi Girji.

Sergejeva, Jelena, 1993: The situation of the Sámi people in Kola. – E. Gayim & K. Myntti 1995: *Indigenous and tribal peoples rights*. Juridica Lapponica 11, Rovaniemi. 176–188.

SKS 2007 = Scheller, Elisabeth & Riessler, Michael 2008: *Sām' Kīll Sījjt – Språkläger i kildinsamiska Lujavv'r, 13.08.–26.08.2007. Rapport*.

SKS 2008 = Scheller, Elisabeth 2008: *Sām' Kīll Syjjt – Språkläger i kildinsamiska Lujavv'r, 03.07.–17.07.2008. Rapport*.

Somby, Liv Inger 2005: *Prosjekt Kola Saami Radio i Russland. Rapport 01.06.02–31.10.05*. Guovdageaidnu/Kautokeino.
– <http://www.saamicouncil.net/files/20060123163858.pdf>

UNESCO Intangible Cultural Heritage Unit's Ad Hoc Expert Group on Endangered Languages, March 10, 2003: *Language Vitality and Endangerment*. Paris.

VPN 2002 = *Всероссийская перепись населения 2002 года*.
– <http://www.perepis2002.ru> 11.08.2009.

# Рӯшш-ёммьне сӣмь кӣл туй

*Elisabeth Scheller*

Кыррьй вӭзхалл Рӯшш-ёммьне сӣмь кӣл туй я пыянт, кӣххт пэря вуаннче пайнэ кӣл. Тӣрьм Куэлнэгк нёарк соӣме пугк нёлльй кӣл лӯв вэсьт кӣдтмэдтӭ я кӣлоаннӭй выйтнэв сӣмь кӣлэсьт рӯшш кӣлле. Кӣлт, таррьй я нюхьт-явьр кӣл вэсьтэ вял ӣннъюввэв. Ахькэль (Ӣкьявьр) кӣлл, вуайй цӣлльке, кӣдэ, ноа лӯв вял ӣллмэ, кӣсьт кӯдтъенҍ тэнн кӣл рӯяс тӣд. Таввялсамь кӣлл, ку пӯдӭ Рӯшш-ёммьне 1990 ыгень, коаппч ӣна я ӣна сӣн оаннҍет, кӣххт Скандинавиясьт, ныдтҍ э Куэлнэгк нёаркэсьт. Кӣнн гоарренҍ ель вэльшэхьт тэнн ӭл, ноа кӣлт соӣме кӣл пайнэмушш пай эвтэс манн.

Тӣррьм, кӯсстай, альт 800 ӣллмэнҍ Рӯшш-ёммьнесьт лев тӣд сӣмь кӣл баяс. Сӣнэнҍ, вуайй пыйнӭ, 200 ӣллмэдтӭ вуайй коаххче «потенциальнэ кӣл оаннҍегуэйм». Сӣнэнҍ лӯв кӣл шӣг рӯяс тӣд: сыйй оӣнтшэв пугк лубэ ӣннэ, ӣннэ сыйе мӣххьтэв сӣррнэ сӣмь кӣлле, ноа югке рӭзэ гуэйке сыйй ев сӣрн кӣйнханна, вӣймленне лубэ вӣфьсе ев сӣрн. Рӯшш-ёммьнесьт тӣрьм вӣнӣ 100 вӣймлэсь сӣмь кӣл оаннҍедтӭ ӣллев. Сӣмас вӣймлесь сӣррнъедтӭ, вуайй цӣлльке, лев ӣллмэ, кугк пуэраст я вӣллтъенне сӣррнэв йжесь кӣлле кӣххт авьтма кӣлле, ныдтҍ э нымьп кӣлле, я кугк оаннэв сӣмь кӣл югке пӣйв я югке саесьт.

Сӣмь кӣлл тоӣййв ӣннъювв вӭзхэллэм (символичсскэ) кӣлэнҍ, вӣлльтэ, вӯзьхемь гуэйке, манҍтӭ олма ли – сӣмь вай мудта. Ныдтҍшэ вӭзхэллэм кӣл ӣнньювв ӭххтса сӣмь ялэсьт, лубэ, го «шоу кӣлл» вӭзхалл йжесь ӣллмэ культура. Вӭзхэллэм кӣл оаннэв ев лышшэ ӣллмэ, вӣнас тӣдтӭй кӣл, ноа э ӣллмэ, пуэраст тӣдтӭй кӣл. Ёнамп вӭзхэллэм кӣл оаннэв ӣллмэ, кугк вӣймельт кӯскнэв ӭххтса сӣмь ялла. Янаш сӣмь кӣл оаннӭй ев кӯсстэ. Чӯтӓ кӯсстъев сӣмь кӣлл вӣйймлесь, кугк вӣймельт кӯскнэв ӭххтса сӣмь ялла, ӣллмэ кӣсьт ли ӭлл сайй ялэсьт я ял выгкэй, го политик я шурьмуз (лидеры). Ноа янаш сӣмь кӣл вӣймлесь оаннӭй ев кӯсстэ. Тэнн "эйй кӯсстъей" ӣллмэ туххка ныдтҍшэ мӭнънэв янаш потенциальнэ кӣл оаннӭй, нӯрр пуллдэг, ōллмэ эйй соāменҍ выййтма я ōллмэ вӯлльгесь я̄л сэенҍ, вāлльтэ, кэ̄бп вōйвишна ōллмэ, вуаййпей роавас чоāзенҍ я мудта рэ̄зэгуэйм вуаййпей ōллмэ.

Го кӣл пайнэмушш лōгэнч вāсьт яллхэ кӣлт кӣл, гу югке-пяййвса кӣл, ку вāллтъенне ōннъюваххч югке сэенҍ, танна кӣлт кӣл вāймлесь я потенциальнэ оаннэ̄й эйй кӯсстъей туххк лыххк шӯрр потенциал. Эвтэс, кунт гуэйке вāсьт кӣл пайнэ, бэдҍсуввэв ōххпэй, тӣдтэ̄й ōдт я тāррмъя кӣл ōххпэм тӯетҍ, ōдт ōххпэм кырьетҍ я кӣл ōххпэм оанҍхесь кэскэтҍ лыгксаххьтэмь гуэйке эвтэс ōххпмуж. Лашшенҍ кӣл ōххпэм оанҍхэсь кэскэтҍ бэдт лыххкэ ēна вуаннчмужэтҍ кӣл вāймля оаннэ̄мь гуэйке сāмас сāррнэм пāль югкепийве вуанчнэм вāрэсьт сāмас сāррнэм вырькэтҍ. Āннъюввв э сāмь ōллмэ эхтнэг сыськасьт кэскэсьт югке пуллдэгэ ēна э̄ххтса кӣл тӯетҍ выгкэ я ныдтҍшэ выгкэ э̄ххтса тӯетҍ кэскэсьт сāмь кӣлл вāймлегуэйм, пāйхьк я̄л выг-кэ̄й чӯрьвэгуэйм. Ныдтҍшэ шӯрр тӯйй ли аннҍтэ Куэлнэгкнӗарк соāме кӣлэтҍ ēннгэдтэ̄ аля я̄лл сай, вāлльтэ, лыххкэ вēххькенҍ мугка тӯетҍ, кугк āннэв кӣлт соāме кӣлэтҍ оаннмуж. Кӣл сай пайнэмь гуэйкэ вял э мугка вуэйймушш лӣннчле вуаяхч, вāлльтэ, Скандинавскэ сāмь ōллмэ вāлтченҍ шуря пя̄дцэльвуд я тыввь-вудт Куэлнэгкнӗарк соāме кӣлэ альн. Тэ̄йт тӯетҍ вуаяхч йилькье пэ̄йель э̄ххтса оанҍхэсь кӣлт кӣл ōххпэм кэскэ Скандинавскэ соāме я Куэлнэгкнӗарк соаме гуэйке. Вял кӯсстай мугка лыххк, вāлльтэ, Куэлнэгкнӗарк соāме кӣлэтҍ э̄ххтэ Скандинавскэ шӣг программатҍ пайнэмь гуэйке сāмь кӣлэтҍ.

Сāмь кӣлле пыйень Сāндрэ Антонова
я Элизабет Шеллер

## Соагнэххьк

вӣймлесь кӣл оаннӭй – активный носитель языка
вуаннчмушш, вуэйӣмушш – возможность
вӭзхэллэм кӣлл – символический язык
эвтэс ōххпмушш – продвинутый этап обучения
кӣл ōххпэм оанҍхесь кэск – языковые курсы
кӣл пайнэмушш – ревитализация языка
кӣл вӣӣӣмль – языковой активист
оанҍхесь кырьй – резюме
пыйнэ – предполагать, решать
тӣррьмъя – современный
тыввьвудт – интерес
чуэррьв – чиновник, начальник, руководитель, вождь, председатель
ōлл ӣлл сай – высокий статус
ōххтса ӣллмушш – общественная жизнь

VILMOS TÁNCZOS

# The Moldavian Csángós
# – Questions of Demography and
# Linguistic Assimilation

## Abstract

The article deals with the ongoing ethnic and linguistic assimilation processes of the Moldavian *Csángós*, that is a population of Hungarian origin living in the Romanian province of Moldavia. The Csángós speak extremely archaic dialects of the Hungarian language; their folk culture is extremely archaic too, preserving several medieval elements.

The Csángós, who settled in Moldavia during the Middle Ages (the 13th and 14th centuries), have been strongly Romanianised linguistically during the last few centuries. Of the Roman Catholic Csángó population in Moldavia (232,045, according to the 2002 Romanian census), only about a quarter speak Hungarian dialects (the estimated number is approximately 62,000). In some villages linguistic assimilation into Romanian is complete, or almost complete, while in others the middle and older generations still speak their original language.

The assimilation process, which has led to a language shift, is presented in a historical perspective based on existing data from the 17th century until the present day. The characteristics of the collective identity of the Csángós are also discussed. Their linguistic assimilation is partly a consequence of this specific identity.

*Ethnic and Linguistic Context of Identity: Finno-Ugric Minorities.* 97–119.
Uralica Helsingiensia 5. Helsinki 2011.

# 1. The Etymology of the 'Csángó' Name, the Csángó Dialects

People of Hungarian origin living in the Romanian province of Moldavia are called *Csángós*, officially as well as unofficially (Map 1).

Map 1. The Csángós live in the eastern part of Romania.

The word Csángó derives from the verb *csang/csáng* (which means wander, stroll, ramble, rove etc., cf. EWU 1993) and thus the name of this ethnic group clearly refers to the migratory, colonising character of the Csángós. (Benkő 1990: 6; Gunda 1988: 12–13; Szabó T. 1981: 520.)

According to the 2002 Romanian census, the size of the Roman Catholic Csángó population in Moldavia is 232,045. All the Csángós living in Moldavia speak the official language of the state, which is Romanian, to a certain extent. However, the number of speakers of the Csángó dialects (which are archaic dialects of the Hungarian language) is much less: about 62,000 Csángós use the Csángó dialects in their everyday life, especially in the home. Both as a result of spontaneous and natural assimilation processes and also of systematic forced assimilation, today the majority of the Csángós do not know the language of their ancestors and consider themselves Romanian. In some Csángó villages linguistic assimilation with the Romanian speaking majority is complete, or almost complete. However, there are also villages where the middle and older generations still speak the archaic Csángó dialects.

## 2. Origin and Settlement

It is generally accepted that the original Csángós settled in Moldavia during the Middle Ages, in the course of the 13th and particularly the 14th centuries as part of a systematic Hungarian imperial policy. Their task was to control and defend the eastern frontier of Hungary. This systematic settlement of Moldavia, which was intended to safeguard the border region, could not have been carried out before the very end of the 13th century, after the 1241–1242 Mongol Invasion, and later in the early 14th century. Historians believe that the original settlers came from the west rather than the east. (Arens & Bein 2003; Auner 1908; Baker 1997; Benda 1989; Benkő 1990; Lükő 1936; Mikecs 1941, 1943; Năstase 1934, 1935; Rosetti 1905.)

References to Moldavian Hungarians appear in historical sources from the 13th century onwards. So far, however, there is no scientifically convincing explanation of their origins. One rather romantic view, according to which the Csángós are the successors of the Cumans (Jerney 1851; Munkácsi 1902; Veress 1934), has long been refuted, while a small minority believe that the Moldavian Csángós descend from a group of Hungarians who did not take part in the Hungarian Conquest of the Carpatian Basin at the end of the 9th century (Domokos 1931; Gunda 1987; Rubinyi 1901; Viviano & Tomaszewski 2005). These romantic statements, however, are also very difficult to prove.

The territory inhabited by the medieval Moldavian Hungarian settlers was considerably larger than that which their descendants occupy today (Map 2). There are only two language enclaves where the descendants of the medieval Moldavian Hungarians have survived: "the northern Csángós" north of the town of Roman and "the southern Csángós" in some villages south of the town of Bacu.

The central geographical location of these villages and their favourable economic conditions suggest that they were among the first settlements to be established in this province. The dialects and

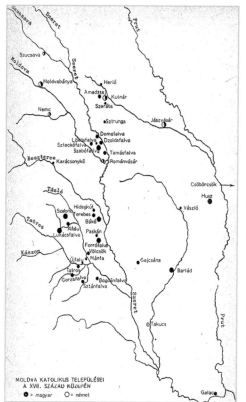

Map 2.   Catholic settlements in Moldavia at the middle of the 17th century: the Northern and the Southern block. (Source: Benda 1989. 26.)

folk culture of both northern and southern Csángós are extremely archaic preserving several medieval elements (see for example, Domokos 1931, Wichmann 1936, Bosnyák 1980, Kiss 2003, 2004). (Picture 1.)

The number of Hungarians in Moldavia was reduced significantly in the 16th and 17th centuries by wars, epidemics and, importantly, by linguistic and religious assimilation with the Romanians. Their numbers only began to rise again in the 18th century, as the result of an increasing influx of Szeklers (another Hungarian ethnic group living in the

Picture 1. Hungarian folklore motif on a medieval glazed tile (King Saint László pursues the Cumanian warrior; Moldvabánya/Baia, 15th century).

100

eastern part of historical Hungary, which was assigned the military role of safeguarding its eastern borders from the Middle Ages to the 18th century). In particular, many Szeklers moved to Moldavia after the Siculeni/Madéfalva Massacre of the Szeklers by the Habsburgs in 1764 (also called the 'Siculicidium'). Most of the existing "Szeklerised" Csángó villages date back to this time. The 18th century Szeklers settled exclusively around the southern Csángó villages (around the town Bacău). Some of the villages became mixed, although the Szeklers did also found several new settlements of their own. (Benda 1989: 30–35; Mikecs 1941: 242–255.) The northern Csángó villages clearly preserved their Medieval culture and language (see the Csángó dictionary by Wichmann 1936; Pictures 2 & 3).

Pictures 2 & 3. Yrjö Wichmann and his dictionary of the North Csángó dialects.

## 3. Inner Division: Two Groups

As we have seen, the Moldavian Csángós do not constitute a homogeneous group, either historically or linguistically/ethnographically. Some researchers speak about *Moldavian Hungarians* and *Moldavian Szeklers* (Lükő 1936; Mikecs 1941), while others use the terms *Csángó Hungarians* and *Szekler Hungarians* to distinguish between the two groups (Benkő 1990). Today, both groups use the term Csángó to describe someone who belongs to neither side, someone who is no longer either Romanian or Hungarian, while at the same time it has come to have the pejorative connotations of imperfection and degeneracy.

The huge increase in Moldavia's Roman Catholic population over the last two centuries cannot be considered exclusively the result of the immigration of Roman Catholic Szeklers. The number of Catholics living in Moldavia more than doubled between 1930 and 1992 owing to the high birth-rate within the Csángó population. Even today we see that Csángó families usually have many children.

## 4. Linguistic Assimilation Processes

Prior to the battle against the Osman Turks in Mohács, in 1526, Moldavian Csángós, an ethnic group vital to imperial policy, had enjoyed the security provided by a powerful, centralised Hungarian Kingdom. After the Battle of Mohács, the Hungarian empire was divided into three parts. Since that time, the ethnic group of Moldavian Csángós has been *isolated both culturally and religiously*. The Catholic episcopacies were no more, and Moldavia became a missionary region in which, during the 17th–19th centuries, the missionary organisation De Propaganda Fidei sent Italian, Polish and Bosnian priests from Rome, who did not speak the mother tongue of the population. The missionary reports sent to Rome by these priests in the 18th and 19th centuries already speak of the linguistic, and often religious, assimilation of Moldavian Catholics with the Romanians. Later accounts by Hungarian travellers in Moldavia confirm that the process of assimilation had resulted in an increasing loss of the population's mother tongue. (See: Auner 1908: 48; Benda 1989: 30–35; Domokos 1931 [1987]: 116–119, 1938: 295–308; Mikecs 1941: 242–255.)

From the 19th century onwards we can rely on exact, detailed data from *official censuses* (Lahovari & Brătianu & Tocilescu 1898–1902; Manuilă 1938; Szabados 1989: 89–102; Official census returns 1992 and 2002). The data referring to the mother tongue of the census taken in 1859 are especially valuable. According to official Romanian censuses in the 20th century, the Catholics in Moldavia, in respect to both their mother tongue and their nationality, became Romanians; the number of Hungarian Catholics became completely insignificant. The official Romanian opinion – "scientific," "religious" and political – of the Hungarian Csángós from Moldavia even today maintains that this ethnic group *practically does not exist*. The 2002 census records only 2,015 Hungarian Catolics in the Moldavian counties. This figure is, quite obviously, only a fraction of the real number of Hungarian-speaking Catholics in Moldavia. (Table 1 & Figures 1 & 2.)

| Year | A) Evolution of the number of Catholics | B) The evolution of the number of Catholics who declares themselves Hungarian in censuses | C) Evolution of the speakers of Hungarian (of the Csángó dialects), estimated numbers |
|---|---|---|---|
| The beginning of the XVIth century | 25–30,000 (of which Hungarian approx. 20–25,000) | – | – |
| 1591 | 15,000 | – | – |
| 1646 | 5,577 | – | – |
| 1744 | 5,500 | – | – |
| 1807 | 21,307 | – | – |
| 1844 | 43,244 | – | – |
| 1859 | 52,811 | 37,825 | – |
| 1899 | 88,803 | 24,276 | approx. 30,000 |
| 1930 | 109,953 | 23,894 | approx. 45,000 |
| 1992 | 240,038 | 1,826 | approx. 62,000 |
| 2002 | 232,045 | 2,015 | – |

Table 1. The evolution of the absolute number of the Moldavian Catholics (A), of those declaring Hungarian identity in cencuses (B), speakers of Hungarian (C) between 1500–2002. (Sources: Auner 1908: 48; Benda 1989: 30–35; Domokos 1931 [1987]: 116–119, 1938: 295–308; Lahovari & Brătianu & Tocilescu 1898–1902; Manuilă 1938; Mikecs 1941: 242–255; Szabados 1989: 89–102; Tánczos 1998, 2002; Official census returns 1992 and 2002.)

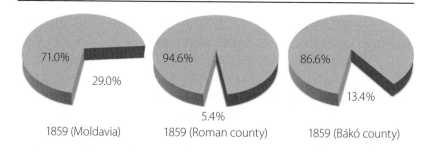

Figure 1. The percentage of declared Hungarians within the number of Catholics according to the first official Romanian census (1859) in Moldavia, respectively in the Bákó/Bacău and Roman counties.

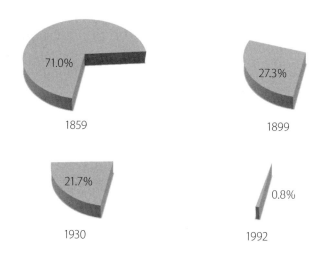

Figure 2. The evolution of the percentage of Hungarians within the Catholic population according to official censuses.

104

Old nationalist pseudo-scientific theories (Pal 1942, Râmneanţu 1944, Mărtinaş 1985, Bucur 1997, Ciobotaru 1998–2005, Stan–Weber 1998 – most of them having been republished nowadays) still persist in the Romanian cultural and political discourse regarding the questions of the Csángós, and provide an ideological foundation for the forceful assimilation of the ethnic Csángós. Naturally there have also been and there still are Romanian researchers, human rights activists who discuss these questions objectively and with scientific foundation, rejecting the above pseudo-scientific theories, but the number of these is rather small (e.g. Rosetti 1905, Năstase 1934–1935, Andreescu 2001, Andreescu–Enache 2002, Diaconescu 2005).

Still, we can ask the question: If a language is spoken by tens of thousands of people, why doesn't this fact appear in official censuses? *How many of the Moldavian Csángós can speak their ancestors' language?*

I have been conducting research – primarily of an ethnographical nature – in Moldavia among the Catholic Csángós since 1980. In addition to this, I studied Csángó identity in 110 Moldavian towns and villages between 1994–1996. In 83 of these, I have found a Hungarian-speaking population. I have published my findings in several studies. (Tánczos 1998, 1999, 2002, 2006, etc.) At present I am working on new research repeating the same surveys today. (Tánczos 2009.)

I have found that the number of Hungarian Csángós – in contrast to the official data – is still relatively large. From the number of originally Hungarian speaking Catholic Csángó in Moldavia (232,000) today an *estimated 62,000 still speak Hungarian*, that is, only a quarter of the whole Moldavian Catholic Csángó population. In some villages linguistic assimilation was complete, or almost complete, whereas in others only the middle and older generations still speak a Hungarian dialect. (See Map 3.)

It is a pity that the loss of language in the Csángó villages in the north and the south, that is to say in exactly those groups of medieval origin, has advanced so far. Today their dialect is only spoken by 17,000 people and they are scattered among several villages. (See Figure 3.)

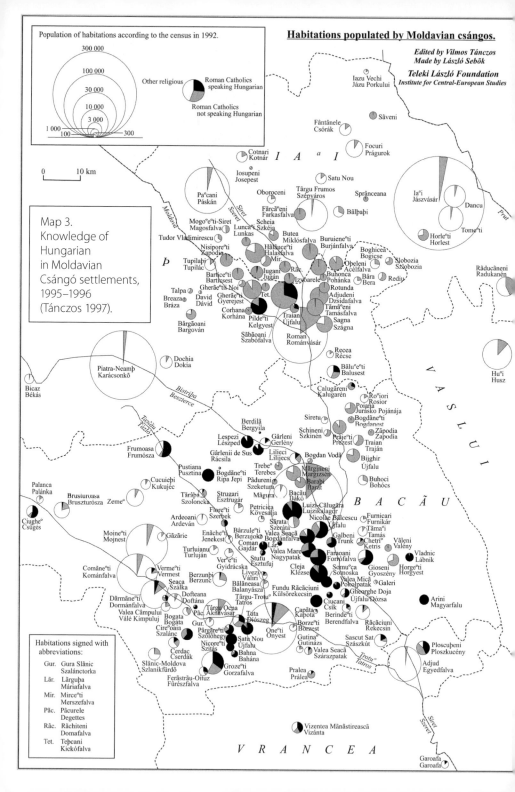

Population of habitations according to the census in 1992.

300 000
100 000
30 000
10 000
3 000
1 000
100          300

Other religious    Roman Catholics
                   speaking Hungarian
Roman Catholics
not speaking Hungarian

0      10 km

Map 3.
Knowledge of
Hungarian
in Moldavian
Csángó settlements,
1995–1996
(Tánczos 1997).

**Habitations populated by Moldavian csángos.**

*Edited by Vilmos Tánczos*
*Made by László Sebők*

*Teleki László Foundation*
*Institute for Central-European Studies*

Habitations signed with
abbreviations:

Gur.   Gura Slănic
       Szalánctorka
Lăr.   Lărguța
       Máriafalva
Mir.   Mirceşti
       Merszefalva
Păc.   Păcurele
       Degettes
Răc.   Răchiteni
       Domafalva
Tet.   Tețcani
       Kickófalva

Iazu Vechi
Jázu Porkului

Săveni

Fântânele
Csórák

Focuri
Prágurok

Cotnari
Kotnár      I  A    a    I

Iosupeni
Josepest                    Satu Nou

Paşcani    Oboroceni        Târgu Frumos    Sprânceana
Páskán                      Szépváros
                                            Bălţaţi              Iaşi            Dancu
Mogoşeşti-Siret   Scheia                                         Jászvásár
Magosfalva        Lunca şi Szkéja
Tudor Vladimirescu  Lunkas                                       Horleşti    Tomeşti
                  Farcăşeni                                      Horlest
                  Farkasfalva
                                                                              Răducăneni
Nisiporeşti   Butea                                                           Radukanén
Zápóda        Miklósfalva
                Hălăuceşti    Buruieneşti
Tupilaţi        Halasfalva    Burjánfalva
Tupilác         Mir                           Boghiceá
          Barticeşti        Iugani    Răc.    Bogise
          Bartosest         Iugán           Opeleni  Slobozia
Gherăeşti-Noi              Izvoarele        Acélfalva  Szlobozia
Talpa    Gherăeşti                          Buhonca  Bâra   Rediu
Breaza   David  Gyerejest                   Pohánka  Bera
Bráza    Dávid         Tet.                  Rotunda
         Corhana                             Adjudeni
         Korhána   Pildeşti                  Dzsidafalva
                   Kelgyest    Traian        Tămăşeni
Bârgăoani                     Újfalu         Tamásfalva
Bargován          Săbăoani                   Sagna
                  Szabófalva    Roman        Szágna
                               Románvásár
                                             Recea
                                             Récse
         Dochia
Piatra-Neamţ  Dokia                    Băluşeşti
Karácsonkő                             Balusest                        Huşi
                                                                       Husz
Bicaz                                  Calugăreni
Békás          Bistriţa                Kalugarén            V
                                                Roşiori        A
                                                Rosior     Poiana  S
                                                           Jurasko Pojánája  L
                                       Siretu          Bogdăneşti          U
Berdilă                               Schineni  Prăjeşti  Bogdanest   Zăpodia
Bergyila                              Szkinén  Prezest  Traian  Zapodia        I
Lespezi          Gârleni                              Traján
Lészped          Gerlény       Lilieci  Bogdan Vodă  Bijghir
          Gârlenii de Sus      Liliecs              Újfalu
          Rácsila    Trebeş   Mărgineni
Frumoasa          Bogdăneşti  Terebes  Marizsén     Buhoci
Frumósza          Ripa Jepi  Pădureni  Barabi      Bohócs
Pustiana                     Szeketura  Barat
Pusztina      Tărâţa  Strugari  Bacău
Cucuieţi      Szoloncka  Esztrugár  Dákó  B  A  C  Ă  U
Kukujéc              Flore  Petricica  Luizi-Călugăra
Palanca  Brusturoasa  Zerne  Szerbek  Kövesalja  Luizikalagár
Palánka  Bruszturósza        Sărata    Nicolae Bălcescu  Furnicari
                     Ardeoani          Szeráta  Újfalu  Furnikár
Ciugheş              Ardeván  Enăcheşti  Bărzuleşti  Valea Seacă  Galbeni  Tămăşi
Csügés                       Jenekest  Berzujok  Bogdánfalva  Trunk  Tamás  Văleni
          Moineşti                     Coman  Lárga  Chetri  Valény
          Mojnest    Găzărie  Turluianu  Gajdár  Valea Mare  Faraoani  Vladnic
                              Turluján  Vereşti  Stufu  Nagypatak  Forrófalva  Lábnik
Comăneşti                              Gyidrácska  Esztufuj  Cleja  Someşca  Gioseni  Horgeşti
Kománfalva  Vermeşti                   Livezi  Klézse  Somoska  Gyoszény  Horgyest
            Vermest  Berzunţi  Bălăneasa          Valea Mică  Galeri
Dărmăneşti  Seaca  Berzunc  Balanyásza  Fundu Răcăciuni  Pokolpatak  Gheorghe Doja
Dormánfalva  Szálka  Dofteana  Târgu-Trotuş  Külsőrekecsin  Újfalu-Dózsa  Arini
            Valea Câmpului  Doftána  Tatros             Ciucani  Berindeşti  Magyarfalu
            Válé Kimpuluj  Bogata  Păc.  Aknavásár  Csík  Berendfalva  Răcăciuni
                          Bogáta         Tóta                Rekecsin
            Cireşoaia  Gur.  Pârgăreşti  Dioszeg  Capăta  Sascut Sat
            Szalánc           Szőlőhegy          Kápota  Onyest  Borzeşti  Szászkút
                  Cerdac  Nicoreşti  Satu Nou  Oneşti          Borzest  Ploscuţeni
                  Cserdák  Szitás  Újfalu          Gutina          Ploszkucény
            Slănic-Moldova  Bahna                  Gutinázs  Valea Seacă  Adjud
            Szlanikfürdő  Bahána                    Szárazpatak  Egyedfalva
                          Groześti  Pralen
            Ferăstrău-Oituz  Gorzafalva  Prálea
            Fűrészfalva                                          Garoafa
                                                                 Garoafa
                          Vizantea Mănăstirească
                          Vizánta

V  R  A  N  C  E  A

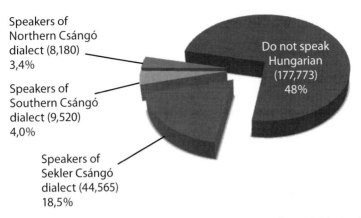

Speakers of
Northern Csángó
dialect (8,180)
3,4%

Speakers of
Southern Csángó
dialect (9,520)
4,0%

Speakers of
Sekler Csángó
dialect (44,565)
18,5%

Do not speak
Hungarian
(177,773)
48%

Figure 3. The number of the people speaking/not speaking Moldavian Hungarian Csángó dialects within the whole Csángó population (source: Tánczos 1997).

My research has shown that there is a *language shift* taking place: owing to linguistic changes the exclusive use of the Csángó (Hungarian) dialects has switched to the exclusive use of Romanian. (See a summary of linguistic research done by others in: Tánczos 2004. And see, in this respect, also: Bodó 2004; Sándor 2005; Tánczos 1998, 1999, 2006, 2009.) My studies referring to the linguistic competence of different generations show a strong deterioration in the state of the Csángó dialects in all villages. Although there are considerable differences in the stages of the evolution towards a total language shift in the villages, the knowledge of the younger generations has dramatically worsened compared to that of the older generations in every settlement. (See Figures 4, 5 and 6.)

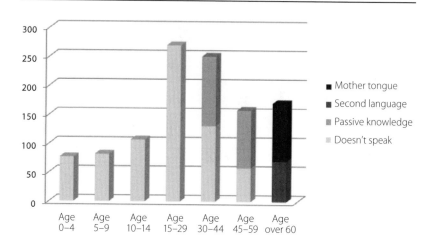

Figure 4. Hungarian language knowledge of generations in Vizánta/Vizantea village (within the community of Catholic Csángós), 2008. NB: Children are divided into three groups with intervals of 5 years according to age, and other generations into four groups, i.e. three with intervals of 15 years and 60 years and over.

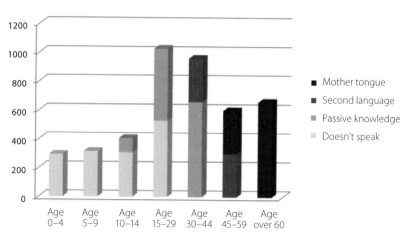

Figure 5. Hungarian language knowledge of generations in Gorzafalva/Grozeşti village (within the community of Catholic Csángós), 2008. NB: Children are divided into three groups with intervals of 5 years according to age, and other generations into four groups, i.e. three with intervals of 15 years and 60 years and over.

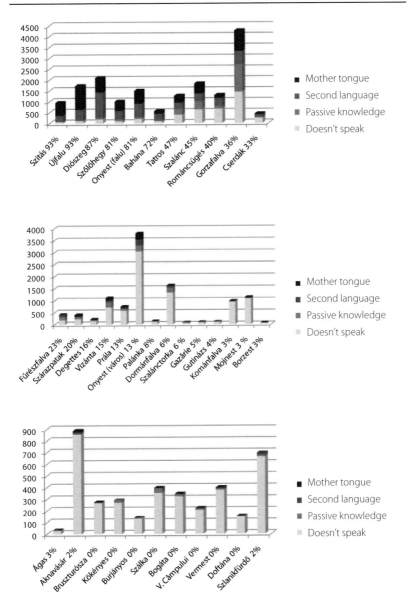

Figure 6. The stages of the language shift in the Csángó villages near the Tatros/
Trotuş river (2008).

109

## 5. Causes of the assimilation: the special Csángó identity and the lack of intelligentsia and institutions

The official figure for speakers of the Csángó dialects is arrived at partly by the manipulative, distortional methods used in the carrying out of the 1992 and 2002 censuses and by the unique concept of identity of the Csángós. The census commissioners were ordered to cover up the presence of ethnic Hungarians and Hungarian speakers, the Church conducted a powerful propaganda campaign among the Csángós, those who declared themselves Hungarian were threatened with forced repatriation to Hungary, and both the censuses were carried out in an atmosphere of nationalism fired by the mass media.

Nevertheless, assimilation (language shift, language loss) can be seen not only in the figures of the official censuses but also in reality. The causes can be found: 1) in the special relationship between language and culture, in the characteristics of *the Csángó identity*, that 2) is explained by *the lack of intellectuals and institutions* in the Csángó community.

Moldavian Csángós living beyond the Carpathian Mountains played no part in the great historical movements of the first half of the 19th century which created the modern Hungarian nation and society (language reforms, political and cultural movements of the "Reform Age", the 1848 War of Independence). The Moldavian Csángós were therefore the only group of Hungarian speakers who did not become part of the Hungarian nation. Consequently, the most important factors for unification are absent. (On this specific modern Csángó identity see: Bodó 2004; Pozsony 2002, 2006; Tánczos 2009.) The most important characteristics of this identity are enlisted below.

1.     Beyond its practical role as a means of communication, the Moldavian Csángós do *not attribute any symbolic or cohesive value* to their own dialects. (Their relation to language use is free of ideology, thus they regard the phenomenon of language loss as an inevitable part of modernisation rather than as a tragedy.) The Csángós are well aware of the fact that their archaic dialects are not identical to the Hungarian literary language or the Hungarian dialect spoken in Hungary, so they consider that the prestige of the archaic local dialects are inferior.

In the Hungarian dialects of the Csángós there are several loan words from the Romanian language, mostly for newer concepts, and therefore almost all Csángós are convinced that their language is neither Hungarian nor Romanian, but a sort of a "mongrel" language, a "mixture" of questionable value. Consequently, for the Csángós, the archaic dialects are not a symbol of their national identity. These dialects do not have a written form, therefore they have no value in modern life, for example, in the school, in administration or in the press.

Not only the official authorities, but the Csángós themselves, *stigmatise their language*. Because the value of the local dialects in social communication is decreasing, passing on the Hungarian Csángó dialects to newer generations is more and more difficult.

2. Today the majority of Csángós are already bilingual, that is *they also know a "real" language* – the Romanian literary language. Therefore they easily declare themselves to be Romanian in official censuses.

3. They are unaware of the national values contained within *folklore and folk culture*, and of the fact that traditional culture can be a powerful means for strengthening national unity.

4. They have virtually no contact with *Hungarian "high culture"*, the values of which remain out of their reach due to the absence of a proper institutional network and low levels of literacy in Hungarian.

5. Since their migration, the history and historical awareness of the Csángós has been distinct from that of the Hungarians in the Carpathian Basin. The consciousness of common origins is fading away even among Szeklerised Csángós.

The Csángós confused identity is also caused by the fact that the Csángós have never had their own intellectuals. In Europe it has always been the intellectuals who have played the most important role in relating people to the nation's constituent features. In Moldavia, however, no ecclesiastical or secular intelligentsia emerged.

In the modern age (that is beginning from the end of the 19th century) the identity of Csángó intellectuals was formed by the Romanian national state, thus their own intellectuals were the ones who facilitated their assimilation.

The state has always taken care to send priests, teachers and officials brought up in the spirit of Romanian nationalism to Moldavia, to act as channels of the official ideology (e.g. of the view that Csángós are Magyarised Romanians, *Roman* Catholics are, in fact, *Romanian* Catholics, Csángó "pidgin-talk" is something to be ashamed of, etc.).

This meant that the Catholic Church, which had for centuries been the most important factor in the separation of Moldavian ethnic Hungarians from Romanians and in the survival of the Hungarian language, became, from the end of the 19th century, a vehicle of Romanianisation. (See: Barszczewska forthcoming; Pozsony 2006: 72–119; Sándor 1999: 317–331, 2005: 163–186.)

After the establishment of a network of modern state-owned schools, the language of education in Moldavia became exclusively the state language. The speaking of the local Hungarian dialects was forbidden in schools, and numerous accounts reveal that teachers punished students who used Hungarian, urging parents to speak Romanian, even at home.


## 6. Human Rights, European Council Recommendation

In Romania it is considered officially that the culture, ethnicity and identity of the Csángós have never existed. In other words: among the Csángós there have never been any processes of assimilation, nor, in the present, are there any problems because the Csángós are supposed to be Romanians, the traditions or cultural values of the Csángós are only endangered by the processes of modernisation.

Nevertheless, some important facts on the forceful assimilation of the Csángós have reached the Western European media. In July 1999, the European Council and the Federal Union of European Nationalities (FUEN) sent a joint delegation to Moldavia in order to write a report on the situation of the Moldavian Csángós. The then Finnish minister of education, Ms. Tytti Isohookana, was a member of this delegation, and wanted to get direct information in the Csángó area. So we have to thank her personally for the fact that, in 2001, the European Council accepted recommendation No. 1521. This document made it compulsory for Romania to protect the culture, traditions and language of the Moldavian Csángós. One of the most important statements in this document is a declaration according to which the Csángós speak ancient, archaic dialects of the Hungarian language. At the same time it officially accepted the Hungarian written form of the name of the ethnic group (that is, Csángó), which had been formerly mentioned in official documents as "Csangó." The real value of the document is mostly that it provided a general legal framework for the protection of legal rights; it provided a basis for future negotiations that could no longer be ignored.

There have been no spectacular changes since the recommendation of the European Council and since Romania joined the European Union. The religious ceremonies of the Catholic Church are almost exclusively performed in Romanian; the priests only speak with members of their congregation in Romanian. Little progress has been made in the field of Hungarian language education. Beginning in only one or two villages, but now already in 22 – with sustained human effort – the Hungarian language has been introduced as the mother tongue at school, but only for 2 to 3 hours a week. However, only about 10% of the children still speaking Hungarian dialects take part in such Hungarian language education.

The Romanian state does not officially recognise the existence of the Moldavian Hungarian ethnic group and, since it regards the Csángós as Romanians, it does not grant them the most basic minority rights, thus forcing the complete linguistic assimilation of this ethnic group with the Romanians. Local initiatives are occasionally taken to form or maintain Hungarian identity, but these are suppressed with the connivance or the silent consent of the local authorities. In fact, the majority of the Catholic population has been entirely Romanianised linguistically.

# References

Andreescu, Gabriel 2001: Investigaţia din Moldova. In: *Ruleta. Români şi maghiari, 1990–2000. Jurnal tematic.* Iaşi: Polirom. 236–243.

Andreescu, Gabriel & Enache, Smaranda 2002: Raport asupra situaţiei ceangăilor din Moldova. Problema ceangăilor maghiari. Altera VIII. 17–18. 90–104.

Arens, Meinolf & Bein, Daniel 2003: Katolische Ungarn in der Moldau. Eine Minderheit im historischen Kontext einer ethnisch und konfessionell gemischten Region. *Saeculum* 54: 2. 213–269.

Auner, Károly 1908: *A romániai magyar telepek történeti vázlata.* Temesvár: Szent László Társulat.

Baker, Robin 1997: The Moldavian Csángos. – *The Slavonic and the East European Rewiew* 75: 4. 659–680.

Barszczewska, Agnieszka [forthcoming]: Language and Religion as Community-Building Factors in the Moldavian Csángó Society in the Second Half of the 19th Century. *Ungarn-Jahrbuch* 29. München.

Benda, Kálmán (ed.) 1989: *Moldvai csángó-magyar okmánytár1467-1706 = Documenta Hungarorum in Moldavia, 1467-1706.* I–II. *Szerkesztette, a bevezető tanulmányt és a jegyzeteket írta Benda Kálmán.* A Magyar Tudományos Akadémia Történettudományi Intézete. Budapest: Magyarságkutató Intézet.

Benkő, Loránd 1990: *A csángók eredete és települése a nyelvtudomány szemszögéből.* A Magyar Nyelvtudományi Társaság Kiadványai 188. Budapest: Magyar Nyelvtudományi Társaság.

Bodó, Csanád 2004: Nyelvi szocializáció és nyelvi érintkezés a moldvai magyar-román kétnyelvű beszélőközösségekben. – Jenő Kiss (ed.): *Nyelv és nyelvhasználat a moldvai csángók körében.* A Magyar Nyelvtudományi Társaság Kiadványai 221. Budapest: Magyar Nyelvtudományi Társaság. 37–66.

Bosnyák Sándor 1980: A moldvai magyarok hitvilága. Budapest: MTA Néprajzi Kutató Csoport. Folklór Archívum 12. 11–145.

Bucur, Ioan Micu 1997 Încercări violente de maghiarizare a „ceangăilor" români. 1944–1997. Bucureşti: Bravo Press.

Ciobotaru, Ion H. 1998–2005: Catolicii din Moldova. Universul culturii populare. I–III. Iaşi: Editura Presa Bună.

Diaconescu, Marius 2005: A moldvai katolikusok identitáskrízise a politika és a historiográfiai mítoszok között. – István Kinda & Ferenc Pozsony (eds): Adaptáció és modernizáció a moldvai csángó falvakban. Kolozsvár: Kriza János Néprajzi Társaság. 9–20.

Domokos, Pál Péter 1931: *A moldvai magyarság.* Csíksomlyó. (Also 5th enlarged edition (1987), Budapest: Magvető Kiadó.)
—— 1938: A moldvai magyarság történeti számadatai. *Hitel* 3: 295–308. (Republished unchanged in: *Honismeret* 1986. 14: 3. 16–22.)

EWU 1993 = *Etymologisches Wörterbuch des Ungarischen* I. Hrsg. Loránd Benkő. Institut für Sprachwissenschaft der Ungarischen Akademie der Wissenschaften. Budapest: Akadémiai Kiadó.

Gunda, Béla 1987: Ursprung der Moldau-Ungarn. – Benda Kálmán & Thomas von Bogyay & Horst Glassl & Zsolt K. Lengyel (eds), *Forschungen über Siebenbürgen und seine Nachbarn. Festschrift für Attila T. Szabó und Zsigmond Jakó.* Band I. München: Trofenik Verlag. 267–285.

—— 1988: A moldvai magyarok eredete. *Magyar Nyelv* 84/1, 12–24.

Jerney, János 1851: *Keleti utazása a "Magyarok" őshelyeinek kinyomozása végett. 1844 és 1845.* Vol. I–II. Pest.

Kiss, Jenő 2003: A moldvai magyar nyelvjárásokról. – Jenő Kiss (ed.), *Magyar dialektológia.* Budapest: Osiris Kiadó. 195–199.

—— (ed.) 2004: *Nyelv és nyelvhasználat a moldvai csángók körében.* A Magyar Nyelvtudományi Társaság Kiadványai 221. Budapest: Magyar Nyelvtudományi Társaság.

Lahovari, George Ioan & Brătianu, C. I. & Tocilescu, Grigore G. (eds) 1898–1902: *Marele Dicţionar Geografic al României.* Vol. I–V. Bucureşti: Societatea Geografică Romînă.

Lükő, Gábor 1936: *A moldvai csángók. I. A csángók kapcsolatai az erdélyi magyarsággal.* Budapest.

Manuilă, Sabin (ed.) 1938: *Recensământul general al populaţiei României din 29 Decemvrie 1930.* Vol. II. Neam, limbă maternă, religie. Bucureşti: Institutul Central de Statistică.

*Marele Dicţionar Geografic* I–II. Bucureşti, 1898–1902.

Mărtinaş, Dumitru 1998: Originea ceangăilor din Moldova. Bacău: Editura Symbol. (First ed. 1985, Bucureşti, Editura Ştiinţifică şi Enciclopedică.)

Mikecs, László 1989 [1941]: *Csángók.* [Budapest:] Bolyai Akadémia.

—— 1943: Kárpáton túli magyarság. – József Deér & László Gáldi (eds), *Magyarok és románok* I. Budapest: Magyar Történettudományi Intézet. 441–507.

Munkácsi, Bernát 1902: A moldvai csángók eredete. – *Ethnographia* 13: 433–440.

Năstase, Gh. I. 1934, 1935: Ungurii din Moldova la 1646 după „Codex Bandinus". – *Arhivele Basarabiei* 6: 397–414, 7: 74–88.

Pal, Iosif Petru M. 1942: *Origenea catolicilor din Moldova şi Franciscanii, păstorii lor de veacuri.* Săbăoani–Roman. Bacău: Tipografia Serafica.

Pozsony, Ferenc 2002: The Historical Consciousness of the Moldavian Csángós. – *Hungarian Heritage.* Vol. 3. Budapest: European Folklore Institute. 28–41.

—— 2006: Religious life in the Moldovan Hungarian Communities. – *The Hungarian Csángó of Moldova.* Buffalo–Toronto: Corvinus Publishing. 72–119.

Râmneanţu, Petru 1944: Die Abstammung der Tschangos. Sibiu: Centru de Studii şi Cercetări Privitoare la Transilvania.

Rosetti, Radu 1905: *Despre unguri şi episcopiile catolice din Moldova.* Bucureşti: Extras din Analele Academiei Române. Seria II. Tom. XXVII. Instit. de Arte Grafice „Carol Göbl".

Rubinyi, Mózes 1901: A moldvai csángók múltja és jelene. – *Ethnographia* 12: 3. 115–124, 4. 166–175.

Sándor, Klára 1999: Contempt for Linguistic Human Rights in the Service of the Catholic Church: The Case of the Csángós. – Miklós Kontra & Robert Phillipson & Tove Skutnabb-Kangas & Tibor Várady (eds), *Language: A Right and a Resource Approaching Linguistic Human Rights.* Budapest: CEU Press. 317–331.

—— 2005: The csángós of Romania. – Anna Fenyvesi (ed.), *Hungarian Language Contact Outside Hungary.* Studies in Hungarian as a minority language. Amsterdam/Philadelphia: John Benjamins Publishing Company. 163–186.

Stan, Valentin & Weber, Renate [1998]: *The Moldavian Csango.* [Budapest]: International Foundation for Promoting Studies and Knowledge of Minority Rights.

Szabados, Mihály 1989: A moldvai magyarok a romániai népszámlálások tükrében. [Moldavian Hungarians in the Romanian Censuses.] – *Magyarságkutatás. A Magyarságkutató Intézet Évkönyve.* Felelős szerkesztő: Kiss Gy. Csaba. Budapest: Magyarságkutató Intézet, 89–102.

Szabó T., Attila 1981: A moldvai csángó nyelvjárás kutatása. [Research on the Moldavian Csángó Dialect.] – *Nyelv és irodalom* V. Bukarest: Kriterion Könyvkiadó. 482–527, 599–609.

Tánczos Vilmos 1998: *Hungarians in Moldavia.* Teleki László Foundation. Institute for Central European Studies. Occasional Papers 8. [Budapest:] Teleki László Foundation. – <http://www.kia.hu/konyvtar/erdely/moldvang.pdf>.

—— 1999: Über die Bevölkerungszahl der Moldauer Tschangos. – *Aufgetan ist das Tor des Ostens. Volkskundliche Essays und Aufsätze.* Csíkszereda: Pro-Print. 228–275. – <http://www.kia.hu/konyvtar/erdely/moldvnem.pdf>.

—— 2002: About the Demography of the Moldavian Csángós. – László Diószegi (ed.), *Hungarian Csángós in Moldavia. Essays on the Past and Present of the Hungarian Csángós in Moldavia.* Budapest: Teleki László Foundation – Pro Minoritate Foundation. 117–147.

—— 2004: A moldvai csángók nyelvészeti kutatása. 1945–2004. – Jenő Kiss (ed.), *Nyelv és nyelvhasználat a moldvai csángók körében.* A Magyar Nyelvtudományi Társaság Kiadványai 221. Budapest: Magyar Nyelvtudományi Társaság. 208–285.

—— 2006: A moldvai csángók asszimilációja történeti perspektívában. – László Diószegi (ed.), *A moldvai csángók. Veszélyeztetett örökség – veszélyeztetett kisebbségek.* Budapest: Teleki László Alapítvány. 26–46.

—— 2009: A Tatros menti székelyes csángók magyar nyelvismerete 2008-ban. – Diószegi László (ed.), *Moldvai csángók és a változó világ.* Budapest–Szombathely: Teleki László Alapítvány – Nyugat-magyarországi Egyetem Savaria Egyetemi Központ, 177–222.

Veress, Endre 1934: A moldvai csángók származása és neve. – *Erdélyi Múzeum* 39: 29–64.

Viviano, Frank & Tomaszewski, Tomasz 2005: In the shadow of Attila. Romania's Csángós cling to fading customs and beliefs–folkways of the nomadic Asians they claim as ancestors. *National Geographic* June 2005: 67–83.

Wichmann, Yrjö 1936: *Wörterbuch des Ungarischen Moldauer Nordcsángó und des Hétfaluern Csángódialektes.* Herausgegeben von Bálint Csűry und Artturi Kannisto. Lexica Societatis Fenno-Ugricae IV. Helsinki: Suomalais-Ugrilainen Seura.

# Ceangăii din Moldova – Probleme demografice și de asimilare lingvistică

*Vilmos Tánczos*

Termenul „ceangău"/„csángó" în sensul său mai larg este folosit pentru denumirea populației româno-catolice din Moldova. Numărul catolicilor, adică a ceangăilor din Moldova după datele recensământului din 2002 este 232.045, deci aproape un sfert de milion de suflete.

În literatura referitoare la ceangăi găsim suficiente date privind românizarea continuă a acestei populații de origine medievală maghiară multiseculară. Din secolele XVI–XVIII rapoartele, conscrierile bisericești, relatările diplomatice, descrierile de călătorie reprezintă surse importante. Începând cu secolul al XIX-lea ne putem baza și pe datele exacte și detaliate ale recensămintelor oficiale. Datele referitoare la limba maternă a recensământului din 1859 sunt deosebit de valoroase. Rezultatele acestor măsurători evidențiază din cei 52.881 de catolici din Moldova existența a 37.825 (71,6%) de locuitori cu limba maternă maghiară, ceea ce înseamnă că celelalte 15.058 de suflete (28,4%) aveau deja limba maternă română. Măsurătorile oficiale românești din secolul XX referitoare la maghiarii din Moldova pot fi considerate ca autentice doar în privința apartenenței confesionale, ele fiind cu totul inadecvate pentru formarea unei imagini cât de cât reale despre cunoștințele de limbă maghiară, despre identitatea etnic-națională, adică despre gradul de asimilare ale catolicilor moldoveni. Potrivit recensămintelor oficiale românești din secolul XX catolicii din Moldova, atât din punct de vedere al limbii materne cât și al naționalității, au devenit integral români, numărul ceangăilor maghiari a devenit total nesemnificativă (în 1992 total 1826 de suflete, din care în medul rural doar 525 de suflete). Opinia oficială – „științifică," „religioasă" și politică – românească despre ceangăii maghiari din Moldova susține și astăzi teoria „variantei zero:" această etnie nu există.

Autorul studiului a efectuat cercetări de teren privind conștiința identitară și situația lingvistică a ceangăilor și pe baza acestor cercetări constată că astăzi numărul ceangăilor vorbitori și de limba maghiară din Moldova poate fi estimat la cca 62 de mii de suflete, aceştia constituie doar un sfert al catolicilor din Moldova. Statul român şi biserica catolică nu recunoaşte în mod oficial existenţa etniei maghiare în Moldova, şi li se refuză şi cele mai elementare drepturi minoritare, forţând astfel asimilarea totală, lingvistică şi identitară, a acestora la populaţia românească.

MAGDOLNA KOVÁCS

# Ethnic and linguistic identities of Hungarians and their descendants in Finland

## *Abstract*

The aim of this article is to investigate how strongly ethnicity and language are tied to the identity of Hungarians and their descendants in Finland. Hungarians in Finland are a small minority of people numbering approximately 2,000. The data were collected with the aid of an internet questionnaire, which was filled in by 107 first and 30 second generation respondents.

In the analysis, both quantitative and qualitative methods are used: quantitative analysis of the answers given by first and second generation Hungarians was compared to micro-level analyses of open-ended comments. The role of the Hungarian immigration history, self-organisation of the group and Finnish language policy in supporting the maintenance of the Hungarian identity is also discussed.

Recent research considers identity to be a dynamic, multilayered and negotiable phenomenon that emerges in linguistic interaction. In harmony with this, the article reveals that some respondents, after choosing their identities in the questionnaire, re-negotiated these identities in their open comments.

*Ethnic and Linguistic Context of Identity: Finno-Ugric Minorities.* 121–159.
Uralica Helsingiensia 5. Helsinki 2011.

# 1. Introduction

Ethnic identity has been related to categories such as (myth of) a common ancestry or origin, descent, culture, history, nationality, common religion, race, tribe, caste etc. However, the validity of these categories as markers of identity has been criticised. (Chandra 2006.)

Many sociolinguists underline the link between language and ethnicity. However, this link is not always obvious and its strength can vary from one group to another. (Fishman 1997, Joseph 2004, Bartha 2006.) Smolicz (1981) and Smolicz and Secombe (1985) call the elements that play a central role in a culture's integrity 'core values'. According to Smolicz and Secombe (2003: 4–5), in many ethnic groups language is the strongest core value and losing it results in the existence of the group as a distinct entity becoming threatened. Smolicz and Secombe (2003: 4–5) also draw attention to the fact that in some ethnic groups other values (religion, family structure etc.) can have higher significance than language.

Recent studies on identity have emphasised that identity in the modern world is less stable and less fixed than it was in earlier times (or this is thought to be so). Identity is not seen anymore as an unchangeable end product but a dynamic characteristic which can be re-constructed, re-negotiated from one situation to another; it is not necessarily exclusionary (the "we" and "they" opposition) but can be hybrid and multilayered. People usually have more than one identity (Bucholtz and Hall 2005, Omoniyi 2006, Omoniyi and White 2006a, b, Brettell and Nibbs 2009). According to Bucholtz and Hall's (2005) approach, "identity as a relational and sociocultural phenomenon that emerges and circulates in local discourse contexts of interaction rather than as a stable structure located primarily in the individual psyche or in fixed social categories."

Stability in "place" (or external environment, that is, physical, social, cultural) has been seen as a maintenance factor of (fixed) identity, with mobility as a factor playing a role in identity change. However, according to Easthope (2009), this simplification obscures the dynamic nature of (negotiable) identities.

This paper aims to combine the more traditional identity research methods used to search for a group identity with recent ones in order to give a more comprehensive and detailed picture of the identities of Hungarians and their descendants.

## 2. Demography and living places

Before the 1980s there is only some sporadic statistical data on Hungarians in Finland. According to Straszer (2009: 12), there were only 67 people born in Hungary living in Finland in 1960, and 81 Hungarian citizens in 1980.[1] Statistics on Hungarians in Finland can be accessed in the electronic database of the Finnish statistics office (Statistics Finland 2010) from 1990.

According to official statistics (Table 1), in 2009 there were 1,442 people who were born in Hungary and 1,198 Hungarian citizens living in Finland. The number of the people who spoke Hungarian as their mother tongue was 1,799 in 2009. (This is comparable to the number of the indigenous people in Finland whose mother tongue is Sámi, with 1,789 native speakers in 2009.) For comparison, Table 1 shows the statistics also for 1990 and 2000, since the number of Hungarians in Finland is growing continuously.

|  | 1990 | | | 2000 | | | 2009 | | |
|---|---|---|---|---|---|---|---|---|---|
|  | W | M | A | W | M | A | W | M | A |
| Country of birth: Hungary | 244 | 278 | 522 | 389 | 484 | 873 | 660 | 782 | 1,442 |
| Mother tongue: Hungarian | 261 | 312 | 573 | 488 | 601 | 1,089 | 839 | 960 | 1,799 |
| Citizenship: Hungarian | 148 | 160 | 308 | 290 | 364 | 654 | 546 | 652 | 1,198 |

Table 1.   Hungarians in Finland in the statistics: country of birth, mother tongue and citizenship (Statistics Finland 2010). W = Women, M = Men, A = Altogether.

---

1.   However, the number of the Hungary-born people was surely higher in 1981, if we compare it to the tendency in the later statistics (see Table 1). Finland did not allow dual citizenship before 2003 (KANSALAISUUSLAKI 2003) and many Hungarians in Finland changed their citizenships from Hungarian to Finnish because of the convenience provided by a Finnish passport when travelling in other countries (personal discussions with immigrants).

However, the categories in Table 1 do not provide the exact number of Hungarians and their progeny in Finland. First, the category "Citizenship: Hungarian" tells the least about the number of Hungarians because it does not include the many people who changed their Hungarian citizenship to Finnish or whose citizenship was originally not Hungarian (but, for example, Romanian). Second, the category "Country of birth: Hungary" does not include Hungarians who moved to Finland from countries other than Hungary. Third, the category "Mother tongue: Hungarian" includes neither those second or third generation people who have Hungarian ancestors but cannot speak Hungarian nor those who do speak Hungarian but their mother tongue is Finnish (or rarely Swedish) in the official statistics, as Statistics of Finland does not recognise bilingualism.

Table 2 provides statistics on the country of the birth of people who spoke Hungarian as their mother tongue in Finland in 2007. Most Hungarian speaking people in Finland (71.0%) were born in Hungary but 12.1% are from Romania (which has the largest Hungarian speaking minority in the world). Less than 2% were born in other countries neighbouring Hungary (the former Czechoslovakia and the former Yugoslavia). According to the statistics, 193 (13.3%) people, who were born in Finland, had Hungarian as their mother tongue in 2007. Taking into account the shortcomings of mother tongue statistics, this number is slightly underestimated.

| Country of birth | Mother tongue Hungarian | Total % |
|---|---|---|
| Hungary | 1,034 | 71.0 |
| Finland | 193 | 13.3 |
| Romania | 176 | 12.1 |
| Former Czechoslovakia | 16 | 1.1 |
| Former Yugoslavia | 12 | 0.8 |
| Other | 26 | 1.8 |
| Total | 1,457 | 100 |

Table 2. Country of birth of the people in Finland in 2007 with Hungarian as mother tongue (Statistics Finland).[2]

2. Cross tabulation for Table 2 and 3 was kindly provided by Markus Rapo, Statistics Finland (via e-mail 18.2.2009).

Cross tabulation of the mother tongue and country of birth (Table 3) reveals that 92.2% of the Hungary-born population in Finland also spoke Hungarian as their mother tongue in 2007. Among the Hungary-born people there are also Finnish (4.5%) and Swedish (0.6%) speakers together with individuals that speak another language as their mother tongue. Finnish and Swedish speakers could refer to Hungarians (born to Hungarian parents or to mixed marriages) who moved to Finland in their childhood but probably also for some people born to Finnish parents in Hungary who later moved to Finland.

| Mother tongue | Born in Hungary | % |
|---|---|---|
| Hungarian | 1,034 | 92.2 |
| Finnish | 52 | 4.6 |
| Swedish | 7 | 0.6 |
| Other | 28 | 2.5 |
| Total | 1,121 | 100 |

Table 3. The mother tongue of Hungary-born individuals living in Finland in 2007 (Statistics Finland).

Taking into consideration the above statistics in Table 3 and that there are also third generation individuals of Hungarian origin, Hungarians and their progeny in Finland might be somewhat more numerous than individuals with Hungarian mother tongue, thus, altogether around 2,000.

According to Statistics Finland, about two-thirds of the 347 marriages that involved Hungarians were mixed marriages (135 involved a Finnish man and Hungarian woman, and 100 a Finnish woman and Hungarian man) in 2007.[3]

According to Statistics Finland (2010), people with Hungarian as mother tongue could be found in all of the 20 Finnish counties in 2009. However, 45.5 % of them were concentrated in *Uusimaa*, where the capital city, Helsinki, and its neighbouring cities (Espoo and Vantaa) are located. In addition, the following counties have more than 100 people each with Hungarian as mother tongue: *Pirkanmaa*

---

3. Data kindly provided by Markus Rapo, Statistics Finland (via e-mail 18.2.2009).

(172 persons; the main city is Tampere), *Pohjois-Pohjanmaa* (North Ostrobothnia, 135; Oulu), *Etelä-Pohjanmaa* (South Ostrobothnia, 130; Seinäjoki), *Varsinais-Suomi* (119; Turku) and *Pohjanmaa* (Ostrobothnia, 103; Vaasa). (See Map 1.) In other counties of Finland the number of people with Hungarian mother tongue is between 4 and 47.

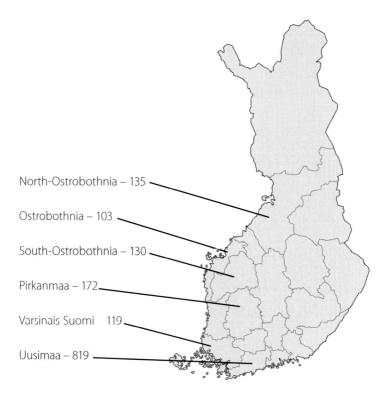

North-Ostrobothnia – 135

Ostrobothnia – 103

South-Ostrobothnia – 130

Pirkanmaa – 172

Varsinais Suomi  119

Uusimaa – 819

Map 1. Seven Finnish counties where the number of the Hungarians is over 100. (Statistics Finland 2010.)

People whose mother tongue is Hungarian are relatively young (Table 4): the largest group is between 30–39 years old (34.0%); only 7.1% are over 60 years old. This is a consequence of recent immigration to Finland.

| Age | Hungarian as mother tongue | |
| --- | --- | --- |
| | Number | % |
| 0–9 | 213 | 11.8 |
| 10–19 | 125 | 6.9 |
| 20–29 | 285 | 15.8 |
| 30–39 | 612 | 34.0 |
| 40–49 | 248 | 13.8 |
| 50–59 | 188 | 10.5 |
| 60–69 | 96 | 5.3 |
| 70– | 32 | 1.8 |
| Total | 1,799 | 100 |

Table 4.   The age of the Hungarian speaking population
in Finland in 2009. (Statistics Finland 2010.)

In sum, the total number of Hungarians and their progeny in Finland
is around 2,000. Most Hungarians born in Hungary also speak the
language. Around two-thirds of the second generation were born in
mixed marriages which, according to earlier minority research (e.g.,
Pauwels 1985, de Bot and Clyne 1994), is not a supporting factor for
language maintenance.

## 3.   Hungarian immigration history in Finland
   – a supporting factor with relation
   to identity?

Hungarian immigration to Finland does not follow the "classic" Hungarian emigration waves. Namely, the first and the largest Hungarian
immigration wave targeting North America dates back to the turn
of the 19th and 20th centuries. At that time people of mostly agrar-
ian and working class backgrounds left their home country for economic reasons. After that time, the main emigration waves were as
follows: before and after World War II (first liberal democrats and
Jewish people, who continued the emigration also after WWII, then
educated professionals, aristocrats; politically right wing individuals
etc.), around the year 1948 when Hungary became a communist country, during and after the 1956 revolution (many young people, factory

127

workers but also university students and intelligentsia) – mainly due to political reasons. From the end of the 1960s and especially from the 1980s economic reasons started to play a greater role in emigration. Hungarians emigrated from the countries neighbouring Hungary[4] as well (e.g., after the Treaty of Trianon in 1920 and after WWII; guest workers from Yugoslavia especially to Germany; during the Ceausescu regime from Romania; after the collapse of communism from many countries in the Carpathian Basin and during the Yugoslav war in the 1990s). Today around 1–2 million Hungarians live outside the Carpathian Basin (A. Kovács 1999: 49, Fenyvesi 2005a: 2–3, Fenyvesi 2005b: 265–272, HTMH 2006).

In comparison, the Nordic countries, except for Sweden, where people of Hungarian origin live in larger numbers (14–35,000 people), were not destinations of Hungarian mass immigration. About 2,000 Hungarians and their progeny live in Finland (for a detailed demography see above), 2,000–4,000 in Denmark, around 3,000 in Norway and some 50 individuals in Iceland. For a comparison with other parts of Europe: there are, for example, around 120–160 thousand Hungarians in Germany and 35–42 thousand Hungarians in Switzerland. (HTMH 2006; KUMSWITZ 2005, KUMDAN 2007; for statistics in Sweden see Straszer's article in this volume.)

Before the 1970s, only sporadic immigration trickled from Hungary to Finland. However, Finnish-Hungarian cultural relations started to develop already in the 19th century via personal contacts and visits due to a growing interest in the shared Finnish and Hungarian linguistic prehistory. The first Hungarian immigrants who we know about arrived in Finland as a consequence of these contacts.[5]

The linguist Heikki Paasonen (1865–1919) stayed on a scholarship in Hungary in 1893 – and already in 1894 he married a Hun-

---

4. Around 2.7–3 million in the countries neighbouring Hungary as autochthonous minorities, as a consequence of the Hungarian border changes under the Treaty of Trianon after World War I (1920).
5. It is beyond the scope of the article to discuss all sporadic migration in detail. My aim is to illustrate the main tendencies of the immigration by mainly singling out persons who became well known in Finnish society. The other reason to present these details is that this is the first time they have been collected together in the same article as part of the history of the Hungarian immigration to Finland.

garian, Mária Palásthi Paskay (1864–1951), but first the couple lived in Hungary for a few year. Of their four children, Aladár Paasonen (1898–1974; born in Hungary) became a well-known colonel in Finland: during the what is called the 'Continuation war' against the Soviet Union he was the head of intelligence (1942–44) of Marshal Mannerheim (1867–1951). He also married a Hungarian, Flóra Barta in 1938 (Korhonen et al. 1983: 63–78, Brantberg 1999, KESKUS-ARKISTO 2004). Another Finno-Ugrist linguist, Yrjö Wichmann (1868–1932) married Julie (Júlia) Herrmann (1881–1974), daughter of the well-known Hungarian ethnographer Antal Herrmann (1851–1926) in 1905. Before moving to Finland in 1908, Julie took part in her husband's fieldwork studying the Mari and Csángó people and later published a book on Mari ethnography (Wichmann 1913, Korhonen et al. 1983: 79–94, KESKUSARKISTO 2004).

Official cultural contacts and Lutheran Church cooperation between Hungary and Finland started in the 1920s. Lutheran Church student and young priest exchanges started in 1927 and continued regularly until the end of World War II. (Koren & Voipio 1988: 30–51.) Some of the church exchange students later returned to Finland for the rest of their lives – after marrying a Finn. For example, Lajos Garam senior (1910–1994), who studied for one year in Finland in 1932–33, married the pianist Sole Kallioniemi (1909–1995) in 1936. The family lived first in Hungary but moved to Finland in 1943. Besides his work as a lecturer of church history in Helsinki's Munkkiniemi co-educational school (1946–1966), Lajos Garam also taught Hungarian at the University of Helsinki (Koren & Voipio 1988: 74–77, GAR-AML, KLASSINEN SK).[6] The priest Rudolf Molnár (1915–2003; Th.D), who stayed in Finland in 1941–1944 on a scholarship, also married a Finn. He moved to Hungary with his Finnish wife, Elmi (née Helkiö) but returned to Finland in 1957. Rudolf Molnár became

---

6. Several members of the Garam family, became well known musicians in Finland, for example, the second generation violinist Lajos Garam (1939–) and cellist Károly Garam (1941–) as well as the third generation pianist Virva Garam (1980–). Third generation Sami Garam is a famous chef in Finland and Helsinki slang writer and translator (GARAML, GARAMS, KLASSINEN GK, KLASSINEN GL, KLASSINEN GV, KLASSINEN SK; part of the information by email from Lajos Garam junior, 9.3.2010).

a priest in Masku (1966–78). He also taught Hungarian at the University of Turku (Koren & Voipio 1988: 110–111, CRUX 2003, MASKU-LAINEN 2009, PAPPISLUETTELO). Some Finnish scholarship students, who visited Hungary, also returned to Finland with a Hungarian partner (Koren & Voipio 1988: 156). Later also church music players got scholarships to Finland and some settled down in Finland. For example, Ákos Papp (1920–2006), who was a scholarship student in 1958–59 in Finland and immigrated to the USA, later returned to Finland and worked as a choirmaster, organist and music reviewer in Jyväskylä (Koren & Voipio 1988: 114, Vainio 2005).

The first cultural congress was held in 1921, and the first bilateral agreement – including lecturer and other academic exchange and scholarships – signed in 1937 (Numminen 1985: 10 –11). Gyula Weöres (born 1899) was the first Hungarian lecturer from Hungary at the University of Helsinki in 1925–41. He returned to Hungary but his offspring moved back to Finland. Lately, some other Hungarian teachers stayed and married in Finland as well. According to Numminen (1985: 17), mixed marriages became a tradition in the Finnish–Hungarian cultural relationship.

Turning back to the 1930s, Nándor Mikola (1911–2006) moved to Finland in 1935 as young painter and became a well-known water colour painter in the new country (MIKOLAMUSEO). István Rácz (1908–1998) spent four years in Finland during World War II (1939–43), then moved back to Hungary, but finally settled down in Finland in 1956. He became a renowned photographer and also translated the Finnish national epos, Kalevala, into Hungarian (Kalevala 1976, Borbándi 1992).[7]

Hungarian immigration to Finland was sporadic until the 1960s. The anti-communist revolution in 1956 did not raise the number of Hungarians in Finland. While Denmark, Norway, and especially Sweden took high numbers of Hungarian refugees, Finland did not officially encourage Hungarians to immigrate to Finland. Only about twenty Hungarian students arrived in Finland; almost all of them left the country in fear of being extradited to the Soviet Union or Hungary (Halmesvirta & Nyyssönen 2006: 8, 168).

---

7.    Imre Szente (1922–), another Kalevala (1987, 2001) translator, lived also temporarily in Finland between 1968–1980. (Borbándi 1992.)

In the late 1960s and 1970s, more and more Hungarian musicians and music teachers moved to Finland (HTMH 2006, Kovács M. 2009, Straszer 2009). Hungarian musicians and music teachers played a great role in developing the Finnish music schools. Among them the Szilvay-brothers, Géza Szilvay (1943) and Csaba Szilvay (1941) have been very influential persons in the Finnish music life since 1971. They developed a Kodály-based, new music teaching method, called "colourstrings", in which children are taught to play strings from notes marked with different colours. Many Finnish musicians, nowadays internationally known, were once their students. For his work, Géza Szilvay got the honorary title of professor from the Finnish president in 2009 (KLASSINEN SzG, KLASSINEN SzCs). His daughter Réka Szilvay (1972–) is also a well-known violinist and violin professor in Finland (SZILVAYR).

First, second and third generation people with Hungarian backgrounds are represented in other arts as well. Hungary-born sculptor and jewellery designer Zoltán Popovits (1940–) left Hungary at the age of four with his parents at the end of World War II and arrived in Finland in 1965, living until then in Austria, Germany, Australia and the USA (Kerkékgyártó 1999, SKT). The children's writer Harri István Mäki (1968–) represents the second generation, while the comic artist Kati Kovács (1963–), who has now lived longer in Italy, the third generation (TAMMI; COMMICS).

Since the late 1960s, the Hungarian immigration to Finland has continued. Mainly highly educated people (teachers, researchers, medical doctors, IT workers, etc.) moved to the country (HTMH 2006, Kovács M. 2009a). Several of them took positions in Finnish higher education.

From the end of the 1980s, Hungarian immigrants arrived in Finland also from the countries neighbouring Hungary (HTMH 2006) for political and economic reasons. After Hungary joined the EU in 2004, manual workers, especially welders, have also looked for better lives in Finland, mainly in the Ostrobothnian counties (Silander 2006, Hallikainen 2007).

In sum, Hungarian immigration to Finland differs from the main lines of typical Hungarian emigration. Before the late 1960s it was rather sporadic: personal contacts, love, church and cultural contacts played a role here. The immigration from the late 1960s and 1970s and also later was mainly caused by economic reasons but also personal contacts played a role in it. During this time musicians, music teachers and other high educated people moved to Finland. The appreciation of the immigrants by Finnish society and the mainly non-refugee based immigration history as well as Finnish-Hungarian linguistic affinity (which is understood by many people and politicians to be due to a genetic relationship between Hungarians and Finns) might have positive effects on the maintenance of Hungarian identity, at least for the first generation.

## 4. Self organised groups and other institutions that support the maintenance of language, culture and identity

The *Association of Hungarians in Finland* (in Hungarian: *Finnországi Magyarok Egyesülete*, FME) is a registered association which was established in 1993. The association organises some Hungarian events together with the Hungarian Centre of Culture and Science (see below), for example Santa Claus evenings for children (which is traditionally celebrated on the 6th of December in Hungary), Hungarian puppet shows, Winter carnivals, Goulash parties and also some cultural events. It is a member of the *Federation of National Organisations of Hungarians in Western Europe* (in Hungarian: *Nyugat-Európai Országos Magyar Szervezetek Szövetsége*). Hungarian societies in Tampere and Turku also maintain contact with the national association, but they are not registered officially (Kovács M. 2009, Straszer 2009: 17, NyEOMSz 2009, FME 2010).

The *Hungarian Christian Community in Finland* (in Hungarian: *Finnországi Magyar Keresztény Közösség*; functioning in Helsinki) is an ecumenical, registered association that organises church services in Hungarian, holds a Bible circle once a week and a church service once a month. Occasionally also Roman Catholic Masses are organised by the community because Finland is a Lutheran country and most Hungarians are Roman Catholic. (FMK 2010.) The *Hungarian*

*Parish in Finland* (in Hungarian: *Finnországi Magyar Gyülekezet*; since 1997) also has a website but it is not active, there have been no programmes or home page changes between 2008 and 2010 (FMGY 2010, Kovács M. 2009a, Straszer 2009: 17).

The *Bóbita* play school group meets in Espoo every second Saturday (from 1998; BÓBITA 2009). Another play school group started in Tampere in 2005 (Straszer 2009: 17). In addition to self organised groups and associations, Hungarians in Finland can also use the services of the *Hungarian Centre of Culture and Science in Helsinki* (*Magyar Kulturális és Tudományos Központ* in Hungarian; since 1980) which is maintained by the Hungarian Ministry of Education and Culture (from 2010: Ministry of National Resources). The Centre organises exhibitions, concerts, film series, lectures of Hungarian relevance, and it also has a collection of Hungarian books, journals and newspapers (HUNCULT 2010). The *Finnish-Hungarian Society* (*Suomi-Unkari Seura* in Finnish) was originally established for and by Finnish people who were interested in Hungary and Hungarians, but some members of the Hungarian community also attend their events. It has over 50 member societies all around Finland, organising Hungarian cultural events, language teaching and Hungarian cultural weeks at schools (SUS 2009).

University level Hungarian language and culture teaching is offered at three universities in Finland (in Helsinki: BA, MA and PhD level; in Jyväskylä MA and PhD level; in Turku: BA level) and a few second generation Hungarians can also be found among the students (Kovács M. 2009b).[8] The three university libraries have a considerable number of Hungarian books, journals and newspapers (for example, around 8000 books in Helsinki). In addition, a Centre for Hungarian Literature with about 4,000 Hungarian books, journals and newspapers has operated from Pori town library since 1986 (PORI).

In sum, there are organisations and many events for the relatively small Hungarian community. However, most of them are concentrated in the capital and in other big cities.

---

8. There has also been part-time teaching at the University of Oulu and occasionally also at the University of Tampere.

## 5. Finnish language policy – a supportive device for Hungarian descendants?

Finland is usually regarded as a country with very positive minority language policy. In 1995, Phillipson and Skutnabb-Kangas (1995) saw Finland as one of the countries which has the high level maintenance-oriented language policy for the Swedish speaking language group, a medium-level support for Sámi language but they did not mention any other language groups in Finland.

Finland is officially a bilingual country. The *Constitution of Finland* recognises Finnish and Swedish as national languages. According to the Constitution, "The Sami, as an indigenous people, as well as the Roma and other groups, have the right to maintain and develop their own languages and culture" (CONSTITUTION 2009: Section 17). "Other groups" are not specified. The *Language Act* (2003) mostly describes the rights to use the national languages, refers to the separate Sámi Language Act (Saamen kielilaki 2003)[9] and also briefly deals with the Romani and sign languages. The right to use "other languages" is not specified in the Language Act (2003), but there is a passing reference in it to other statutes of different authorities (§ 9). The *Equality Act* (2004, § 6) prohibits discrimination on the basis of "ethnic or national origin, citizenship, language".[10]

When it comes to supporting the linguistic identity and this consequently, also supports language maintenance of a minority group, a ban on discrimination is not enough support. The language in which education is conducted with attendant mother tongue teaching is extremely important for succeeding in this aim. Although Finland provides opportunities for immigrants to learn Finnish at all levels of education (IMMIGREDU), mother tongue support exists at a much weaker level for other languages. The *Decree 1777/2009 of the Finnish Ministry of Education and Culture* (OPM 2009, §3) defines the sup-

---

9. For the Sámi situation see Seurujärvi-Kari's article in this volume.
10. In Finnish: "Ketään ei saa syrjiä iän, etnisen tai kansallisen alkuperän, kansalaisuuden, kielen, uskonnon, vakaumuksen, mielipiteen, terveydentilan, vammaisuuden, sukupuolisen suuntautumisen tai muun henkilöön liittyvän syyn perusteella." (Yhdenvertaisuuslaki 2004, § 6.)

port of the mother tongue teaching for students with foreign language backgrounds. For the year of 2010, the 4/2010 bulletin of the Finnish National Board of Education (passage 2) defines the circumstances of this support: support can be given for mother tongue (/ home language) teaching for 2 hours per week for groups with at least 4 students (OPH 2010).[11] In practice, this type of mother tongue teaching has been supported in the same way before the decree from the 1990s. However, realisation of the instruction depends on the activity and interests of the municipalities (and of parents, of course).

Hungarian mother tongue (/ home language) teaching at 2 hours per week was organised for a total of 39 students in autumn 2006 in four places: Espoo (15), Helsinki (12), Tampere (6) and Turku (6).[12] This is around 27% of the students of primary and high school age 7–19[13] that had Hungarian as their mother tongue (Statistics Finland 2010). For the school year 2009–2010, the number of the Hungarian learning students (aged 7–15) increased to 54. Of that number, 24 were in Espoo (4 groups), 8 in Vantaa (after a few years' break), 7 in Helsinki, 7 in Tampere (breaking in autumn 2009 but starting again in spring 2010), 4 in Turku and 4 in Jyväskylä.[14] According to answers from authorities in these cities, the longest tradition of Hungarian teaching has been in Espoo: it started with voluntary teaching in the 1970s, continued with official support for remedial instructions in Hungarian in 1982–83 and from 1988 with mother tongue teaching

11.  In Finnish: "Vieraskielisten oppilaiden oman äidinkielen tai hänen kotonaan puhuman muun kielen opetukseen [...] myönnetään valtionavustusta enintään kahdesta tunnista viikossa jokaista neljän oppilaan laskennallista ryhmää kohti." (OPH 2010, kohta 2.)
12.  Finnish National Board of Education. (Email-answer: 9.3.2010).
13.  In 2006, there were 168 people with Hungarian as mother aged 5–19. If we deduct from that number the children aged 5–6 (about 40% deduction from the 66 pupils aged 5–9), the number of the school age students (between 7–19) estimates to be 142. However, as highlighted above: students whose home language is (also) Hungarian but their mother tongue is Finnish(/Swedish) in the statistics are not included in this estimation because of the difficulties to get statistics on them.
14.  The latest information above is collected via email or phone, addressed to employees in charge of organising the mother tongue teaching for immigrants in different municipalities. Answers from the authorities via email: 9.3.2010 (Helsinki and Tampere), 10.3.2010 and 15.3.2010 (Espoo), Jyväskylä 15.3.2010 (Jyväskylä) 16.3.2010 (Turku). Answer via phone: 9.3.2010 (Vantaa).

(2 hours per week). The latest city teaching Hungarian is Jyväskylä (from 2007). According to Straszer (2009: 18), in Helsinki, Hungarian mother tongue teaching started in 1990, in Vantaa (later stopping) and in Kauniainen (no teaching in recent years) in 2000, in Turku in 2003 and in Tampere in 2006.

In sum, Finnish language policy supports Swedish and Sámi teaching, but there is much less instruction for other, immigrant communities. However, for example, among Hungarians, even the existing possibilities are not made full use of as less than a third of the students entitled to it used the opportunity to receive 2 hours of Hungarian teaching per week.

## 6. Data

The data contains the responses of 137 people of Hungarian origin to a sociolinguistic survey on language use and identity: 107 first generation and 30 second generation informants. (An informant is considered to be second generation if (s)he was born in Finland and at least one of her/his parents are Hungarians, or (s)he moved to Finland in her/his childhood with his/her Hungarian parent(s).

The sociolinguistic survey was conducted between August and November 2008. Most of the respondents were reached by email via the Association of Hungarians in Finland and filled in the questionnaire on the Internet. Others were reached via a Hungarian intermediate or via personal contacts. It was not an easy task to contact second generation informants, that is why there are fewer of these than first generation respondents.

The language of the survey was optionally Hungarian or Finnish but filled in mainly in Hungarian (123/137); only 4 first generation respondents (3.7%) and 10 second-generation respondents (33.3%) used Finnish to answer the questionnaire.

In the questionnaire, there were 39 questions. In the present study, I deal with the answers to questions 3, 4 and 7 as background information, 12, 16, 21, 23, 24, 25 and 26.

Most informants were born in Hungary (71.5%), about one-sixth (16.8%) in Romania, 9.5% in Finland and 2 persons elsewhere. If we compare this to Table 2, which shows the country of birth of those Hungarians whose mother tongue is Hungarian, we can see that people born in Romania are slightly overrepresented and people born in Finland are underrepresented in the data.

| Country of birth | Number | % |
|---|---|---|
| Hungary | 98 | 71.5 |
| Finland | 13 | 9.5 |
| Romania | 23 | 16.8 |
| Other | 2 | 1.5 |
| Not known | 1 | 0.7 |
| Total | 137 | 100 |

Table 5.   The country of birth of the respondents.

The majority of the respondents (65; 47.4%) live in Helsinki or its surroundings, 33 (24.%) in Tampere and 12 (8.8%) in Turku or their surroundings, and 27 elsewhere (19.7%). The main cities and its surroundings (altogether 80.3%) are more represented as places of residence among the respondents than they are represented as places of residence of the people of Hungarian origin in the 2009 Finnish statistics (compare to Map 1 and its description).

The respondents' educational levels follow the typical trend described above in the Hungarian immigration history: 92 (67.2%) of the 137 respondents have university degrees (and work usually as musicians or music teachers, other teachers or in the technological fields and information technology). Of those 30 (21.9%) who have senior high school diplomas several are studying at universities. Only five (3.6%) have vocational school diplomas. Of the nine (6.6%) respondents with junior high school diplomas, several are in secondary level schools. (One respondent's educational level is not known.) According to Statistics Finland (2010), there were 960 men and 839 women whose mother tongue was Hungarian in Finland in 2009. In the data, women (80 persons) are more represented than men (54 persons); three respondents did not report their gender.[15]

---

15.   Counted from the answers to questions 3 and 4.

Of the second generation informants, 13 were from Hungarian-Hungarian marriages, 16 from Hungarian-Finnish marriages, and only one informant is from a Hungarian and other nationality (mixed) marriage.

In sum, the country of birth, place of residence and educational level of respondents in the data follows the tendencies shown in Finnish statistics on Hungarians and Hungarian origin people in Finland; although the proportion of women to men is higher in the data than in the official statistics.

The data is also possibly positively biased because people who did not speak Hungarian to their children at all or those representatives of the second generation who are not interested in Hungarian values are not represented among the respondents.[16]

## 7. Positioning oneself

The aim of this section of the paper to discuss whether Hungarians and their descendants in Finland identify themselves as being more Hungarian or Finnish or if they have dual identities.

According to Hatoss (2003), Australian Hungarians, for example, identify themselves as more Hungarian than Australian – in spite of the big distance to the home country. Not only the majority (72.4%) of those who migrated as adults to Australia identify themselves more Hungarian than Australian but also a great part (65.1%) of those who migrated with their parents as children (Hatoss 2003: 73).[17]

In the present survey, question 24 asked the respondents how they positioned themselves, i.e., as Hungarians or Finns. The response options provided included the possibilities of the dual identity and one different from Hungarian or Finnish (Table 6). Open comments were also welcome. These comments shed light on the motivations that led to the choice of a certain category in the questionnaire.

---

16. Personal discussions with some people who did not wish to complete the questionnaire.
17. The data is most possibly biased because, according to Hatoss (2003: 73), many informants were active members of the Australian Hungarian community.

| Feeling her-/himself | Gen. I. | % | Gen. II. | % |
|---|---|---|---|---|
| Hungarian exclusively | 47 | 43.9 | 2 | 6.7 |
| Hungarian in Finland | 31 | 29.0 | 8 | 26.7 |
| Hungarian and a bit Finnish | 11 | 10.3 | 0 | 0 |
| Hungarian and Finnish equally | 0 | 0 | 3 | 10.0 |
| Finnish and a bit Hungarian | 1 | 0.9 | 8 | 26.7 |
| Finnish exclusively | 1 | 0.9 | 8 | 26.7 |
| Other | 11 | 10.3 | 1 | 3.3 |
| Not known | 5 | 4.7 | 0 | 0 |
| Total | 107 | 100 | 30 | 100 |

Table 6. The ethnic identity of Hungarians and people of Hungarian origin in Finland.

According to the findings, the ethnic identity of the first generation is clearly Hungarian-dominant (Table 6). A total of 78 out of 107 felt that they were only 'Hungarian' or 'Hungarian in Finland' and 11 'Hungarian and a bit Finnish'. These 89 persons make up 83.2% of the first generation. Only two persons felt that they were Finnish or 'Finnish and a bit Hungarian'. Of the 11 people who felt other than the given categories above, several wanted to emphasise their minority background as 'Transylvanian Hungarians' (*erdélyi magyar*) or 'Hungarians from outside Hungarian borders' (*határon túli magyar*). Thus, they have a double minority identity. One felt that she was a 'citizen of the world' (*világpolgár*), and one expressed the feeling of being 'alien' (*idegen*) both in the old and the new country (Example 1):

(1) *Itt örökre idegen maradok otthon meg már idegen lettem.*[18]
'Here I will always be an alien and at home [= in the home country] I am already alien'. <G1>

18. The quotations are cited in the form as they were written by the respondents in their answers or comments, no orthographic or other correction are done unless misspelling or word mistake do not disturb understanding (see, e.g., example 2). Most examples are in Hungarian. A few examples are in Finnish and, in these examples, the language is marked after the example. The translations were done by the current author.

In comparison, second generation persons have more of a Finnish than a Hungarian identity (Table 6): 16 (53.4%) of the 30 persons feel that they are 'exclusively' Finnish or 'Finnish and a bit Hungarian'. One crystallises this in the following way (Example 2):

(2)  *Mivel hogy kicsi körömtöl [= koromtól] itt lakom, és itt nöttem fel, persze finnek tartom magam, de nagyon is büszke vagyok a szarmazásomról.*

'Because I have lived here [= in Finland] since I was a small child, of course, I feel that I am a Finn but I am still very proud of my [Hungarian] descent.' <G2>

The above cited opinion can be understood as negotiating identities after choosing one of the available choices in the questionnaire: besides the chosen, exclusively Finnish identity, the respondent would like to draw attention to also 'proudly' belonging to the Hungarian side. Three respondents had chosen an equally dual Hungarian and Finnish identity in the questionnaire, but one of them, similarly to example 2, negotiates this in his comments as shown in example 3. The young informant, who was born in Hungary and moved with his Hungarian parents to Finland and lived there for over 10 years, negotiates another, a bit more Hungarian than Finnish, identity for himself in his comments:

(3)  *Ez egy olyan kérdés, amire még mindig nem tudok válaszolni. Ha kettôt választhatok, az egyik 'finnországi magyarnak', a másik 'magyarnak és finnek egyformán'.*

'This is the type of question which I cannot answer yet. If I were allowed to choose two, one would be 'Hungarian in Finland' and the other 'Hungarian and Finnish equally''. <G2>

From the second generation, 8 persons feel that they are 'Hungarian in Finland' and 2 'Hungarians exclusively'. Cross tabulation reveals that all but one had been born in Hungary. Additionally, both their parents are Hungarians, with one exception. In comparison, of those 16 persons who chose Finnish identity exclusively or 'Finnish and a bit Hungarian', only three respondents had parents who were both Hungarians, the other 13 were born to mixed marriages. Being born in Hungary to Hungarian parents seems to induce a more Hungarian than Finnish identity, while being born in Finland to a mixed marriage a more Finnish identity.

The answers to question 25 reveal the importance of being Hungarian in the respondents' lives (Table 7). In both groups, for the majority of the people, being Hungarian has a great role in their lives: second generation respondents consider being Hungarian to have even more importance in their lives (for 83.3% very big or big role) than the first generation (for 73.8%, a very big or a big role).

| Degree of importance | Gen. I. | % | Gen. II. | % |
|---|---|---|---|---|
| Very big | 35 | 32.7 | 6 | 20.0 |
| Big | 44 | 41.1 | 19 | 63.3 |
| Small | 19 | 17.8 | 5 | 16.7 |
| Not importance | 6 | 5.6 | 0 | 0 |
| Not known | 3 | 2.8 | 0 | 0 |
| Total | 107 | 100 | 30 | 100 |

Table 7.  The importance of being Hungarian in the respondents' lives.

At first glance, the results seem surprising, but they are not: for those first generation Hungarians who were born and raised in Hungary, being Hungarian was "naturally" present in everyday life without any additional emphasis – and for some Hungarians, it is the same in Finland (examples 4–6):

(4)  *Büszke vagyok rá, de ezen kivül a hétköznapi életemet, az, hogy magyar vagyok nem befolyásolja.*
'I am proud of it but the fact that I am Hungarian does not influence my everyday life.' <G1>

(5)  *Így természetes.*
'It is natural like this.' <G1>

(6)  *Egyszerüen magyar vagyok, erre büszke is vagyok, mi értelme lenne ezen változtatni??*
'I am just simply Hungarian, I am also proud of it, is there any sense in changing that??' <G1>

141

In contrast, second generation representatives realise already in their childhood that they live in two worlds: inside the family (with 'Hungarianness'), which can be different from those outside the family. For them being Hungarian is present via their Hungarian parent(s), the language and various customs, or for some it is present all the time, sometimes invisibly and negatively (examples 7–9):

(7) *mert magyarok a szüleim és sokszor beszélek magyarul.*
'because my parents are Hungarian and I often speak Hungarian.' <G2>

(8) *puhun päivittäin, käymme ainakin kerran vuodessa Unkarissa, vaikka olen suomalaistunut paljon, edelleen paljon unkarilaisia tapoja ym.* <in Finnish>
'I speak [Hungarian] every day, we visit Hungary at least once a year, although in many aspects I have become more like a Finn, I still have many Hungarian customs, etc.' <G2>

(9) *mert még akkor is szerepe van, amikor nekem nem tetszik. láthatatlan erőként hat.*
'because it has a role even in those moments when I do not like it, it acts as an invisible force.' <G2>

Those first generation speakers in whose life being Hungarian has an important or very important role describe that it is important because of the Hungarian language, culture (example 10), ethnicity (example 11), and because the maintenance of language and culture is an everyday issue with the children and needs an additional effort (example 12):

(10) *Anyanyelv és kultúra nagyon sokat számít.*
'Because one's mother tongue and culture has a very big importance.' <G1>

(11) *Nemzetiségem, hazám Mo.*
'My nationality [is Hungarian], my fatherland is Hu[ngary].' <G1>

(12) *Mert a magyarság és megőrzésének kérdése nap mint nap fel-
merül a gyerekekkel, hogy magyarul beszélek-e, hogy a gyere-
kek magyarul válaszolnak-e, örülnek-e magyarságuknak vagy
szenvednek töle stb.*

'Because the issue of being Hungarian and the maintenance
of it is present every day with children: do I speak to them in
Hungarian, do they answer in Hungarian, does being Hungarian
make them happy or does it cause suffering to them, etc.' <G1>

Those first generation members who feel that being Hungarian does
not play an important role either feel that it is a 'natural condition' (see
examples 4–6 above) or they are somehow dissatisfied with it, especially with Hungarian politics (example 13) or dissatisfied with the
unsuccessful maintenance efforts in the new country (example 14).
One argues about the time factor: the long period in the new country
diminishes the importance of being Hungarian (example 15):

(13) *Mert nem igazan vagyok buszke arra hogy magyar vagyok.
Csak ahhoz ertunk hogy hogyan kell tonkretenni egy orszagot
(lasd mai magyar politika).*

'Because I am not very proud of being Hungarian. We are
expert in ruining our country (see today's Hungarian politics).'
<G1>

(14) *Mar nem orzom a kulturat, hisz a kutyat nem erdekelte ez a
tevekenysegem.*

'I do not maintain the Hungarian culture anymore because
nobody cared about my activities connected to it.' <G1>

(15) *Többet éltem itt, mint otthon.*

'I have lived here longer than in [the] home [country].' <G1>

Only two first generation respondents contrast the Hungarian ("we")
and the Finnish ("they") culture, in arguing about the importance of
maintaining a Hungarian identity, as it is put into words in example
16:

143

(16) *Elsosorban a kultura, a szokasok, a hagyomanyok, az oriasi viselkedesbeni es ertekrendi kulonbseg miatt.*
'First of all because of the culture, the customs, traditions, and the enormous differences in behaviour and values.' <G1>

In sum, the quantitative analysis reveals that the ethnic identity of first generation is dominantly Hungarian, but there is more dispersion in second generation (cf. Hatoss for Australian Hungarians). Slightly over half of this generation feel dominantly Finnish and 10% feel equally Finnish and Hungarian. However, one-third reported they had more Hungarian than Finnish identity. In this last group there were Hungary-born persons both of whose parents are Hungarian.

## 8. Language – the most essential marker of identity

The threat of modern globalisation to keeping the Hungarian language alive is an issue which has been brought up before in Hungarian communities. Language has been a central issue for Hungarians for centuries. From the Middle Ages to 1844 Latin was the official language for most Hungarians, who were surrounded by Indo-European languages and far from people speaking other Finno-Ugric languages. They also lived in fear that Hungarian would melt linguistically into Slavic languages or German. As a consequence of the Treaty of Trianon in 1920, around a third of the Hungarian speaking population became Hungarian minorities in neighbouring countries. This fact raised the importance of language among Hungarians even more.

According to Czibere (2007: 33–34), the Hungarian language is still a very important issue for Hungarians both living in Hungary and outside the Hungarian borders. In Czibere's (2007: 36) survey, 83% of students studying the Hungarian language and literature as major subjects at a Slovakian university regard language 'as the most essential component' of identity. In a Hungarian university, 75% of those students, whose university subjects were the Hungarian language and literature, agreed with this opinion, as did 63% of students at the University of Technology. According to Hatoss (2003:74), Australian

Hungarians are also language-centred: 50% of them agree and 43% strongly agree with the statement that "the Hungarian language helps keep my Hungarian identity".

In the present survey, question 26 aimed to find out what position language has among other Hungarian valued carriers of Hungarianness among the respondents. A list of these was provided: drinks, food, Gypsy music, handicraft, history, language, literature and national costumes, and the respondents were also asked to add others. The most important notions for first generation are literature, language and history. Most of the 107 respondents consider literature (101/107) and language (100/107) as very important or important, and 92/107 consider history to be as well. (Other notions were important or very important for 24–55/107 persons.) Language and history are also very important or important for most second generation respondents (language for 29/30 and history for 25/30). However, the third most important valued notion for them was not literature but food (21/30). Other carriers were important or very important for 6–18 persons.). Few respondents came up with suggestions of their own. However, there were suggestions of how to maintain the core notions of Hungarianness: the importance of the Internet was emphasised in many comments. According to the respondents, Hungarian books, music, films, more Hungarian television channels should be available free for them via the Internet. Some also underlined that some of these carriers of Hungarianness, for example books and recipes, should be available also in Finnish – for Finnish people and probably for the second generation.

The answers to question 26 confirm the findings that the Hungarian language is considered by both generation respondents to be a core value. This is in line with Czibere's (2007) survey on the importance of language.

Question 23 asked for the mother tongue of the respondents. Hungarian was the mother tongue for first generation respondents, with four exceptions (Table 8). The exceptions involve individuals who were young adults when they moved to Finland, individuals that have had long stays in Finland as well as individuals who had had multiple migrations between Hungary and Finland. Cross tabulation with birth place has revealed that only one respondent who was born in Finland claimed that his mother tongue was Hungarian, and only one who was born in Hungary claimed her mother tongue to be Finnish.

| Mother tongue | Generation I | % | Generation II | % |
|---|---|---|---|---|
| Hungarian | 103 | 96.3 | 9 | 30.0 |
| Finnish | 1 | 0.9 | 8 | 26.7 |
| Hungarian and Finnish | 2 | 1.9 | 13 | 43.3 |
| Not known | 1 | 0.9 | 0 | 0 |
| Total | 107 | 100 | 30 | 100 |

Table 8. The claimed mother tongues of the respondents.

Cross tabulation of mother tongue and parents' nationality in the second generation (Table 9) reveals that respondents whose parents were both Hungarians are likely to consider their mother tongue to be Hungarian or Hungarian and Finnish. Mixed marriages are likely to produce individuals with Finnish mother tongue or Hungarian-Finnish mother tongues.

| Parents' nationality | Mother tongue of the second generation's respondents | | | |
|---|---|---|---|---|
| | Hungarian | Finnish | Hungarian and Finnish | Total |
| Hungarian-Hungarian parents | 7 | 1 | 5 | 13 |
| Hungarian-Finnish parents | 1 | 7 | 8 | 16 |
| Hungarian-other nationality parents | 1 | 0 | 0 | 1 |
| Total | 9 | 8 | 13 | 30 |

Table 9. Cross tabulation of mother tongue and parents' nationality in the second generation.

Question 21 investigated how important it is to teach Hungarian to the next generation within the family. Most respondents both in the first (100/107) and second generations (28/30) thought that it is very important – and no respondent thought it was not important at all.

A closer analysis of the comments of the respondents shows that passing the Hungarian language to the next generation is important for different reasons for the first and the second generation. First generation individuals think that identity and language go hand-in-hand; language is the main instrument to maintain the culture, to find the roots and to be in connection with relatives and friends in Hungary (Examples 17–19). These arguments are only marginally presented in the second generation comments (Example 20).

(17) *Hogy tudja, hogy ő magyar.*
'So that [the child] knows that (s)he is Hungarian.' <G1>

(18) *Hogy továbbvigye a nyelvet, s vele talán valamiféle magyar kulturát is, identitást.*
'So that [the child] would keep with the language also some Hungarian culture and identity.' <G1>

(19) *Főként a gyermek identitása miatt. Legyen büszke a magyarsá-gára, értse meg és beszélje szülöje nyelvét, tudjon kapcsolatot teremteni a rokonsággal, más magyarokkal.*
'Mostly because of a children's identity. So that they would be proud of their Hungarian identity, could understand their parents' language, could be in contact with relatives and other Hungarians.' <G1>

(20) *Segít az identitást megtalálni és megérteni a hátteret.*
'It helps to find one's identity and understand one's background.' <G2>

For some first generation respondents language is so important that they want to express the problem which people can face in writing Hungarian using a keyboard: it is not always possible to get a Hungarian keyboard or the right Hungarian diacritic marks (example 21):

(21) *Specialis ekezetek nelkul fogok mindent irni - sajnos a laptop, amirol irok nem tud magyar ekezeteket.*[19]
'I'll write everything without special diacritics – unfortunately the laptop which I am writing on now does not produce Hungarian diacritics.'

In contrast, second generation respondents underline the usefulness of language knowledge in general (Example 22). This aspect is also raised by some first generation respondents (Example 23). However, two second generation individuals who chose the option that passing Hungarian to the next generation is not important, underline the low "market" value of Hungarian in Finland (Example 24).

(22) *Kaksikielisyys on rikkaus.* <in Finnish>
'Bilingualism is an enrichment.' <G2>

(23) *A ket nyelv tudas kincs es a gyerek könnyen megtanulja.*
'Knowing two languages is a treasure and children learn them easily.' <G1>

(24) *Englanti, saksa ja ranska hyödyllisempiä mm. työelämässä.* <in Finnish>
'English, German and French are more useful, for example, in working life.' <G2>

In sum, language maintenance seems to be the key to the maintenance of Hungarian identity and to cultural maintenance for the first generation. In their comments, second generation did usually not connected Hungarian language maintenance to identity issues but to general language knowledge, which is an enrichment for everyone.

---

19. Diacritic marks mark length of a vowel and differentiate between front and back vowels. The sentence in example 21 with diacritic marks would be as follows: *Speciális ékezetek nélkül fogok mindent írni – sajnos a laptop, amiről írok, nem tud magyar ékezeteket.*

## 9. Facing the values and desires with the action

As has already been discussed, Hungarian self organisations and some other organisations and institutions provide Hungarian events, language learning, play school for children etc., which can support Hungarian identity.

The respondents were asked to specify how often they take part in Hungarian events in Finland (Question 16). The statistics are provided in Table 10. There is a significant difference between the first and second generations: 37.4% of the first generation respondents attend at least 3–5 Hungarian events monthly. Over half of the second generation (53.3%) did not attend Hungarian events at all, while 30.0% of them attended events less than once a year.

| Frequency of visits | Generation I | | Generation II | |
|---|---|---|---|---|
| | | % | | % |
| Monthly | 15 | 14.0 | 0 | 0 |
| 3–5 times a year | 25 | 23.4 | 0 | 0 |
| 1–2 times a year | 30 | 28.0 | 4 | 13.3 |
| Less than once a year | 8 | 7.5 | 9 | 30.0 |
| Usually do not visit | 17 | 15.9 | 16 | 53.3 |
| Not known | 12 | 11.2 | 1 | 3.3 |
| Total | 107 | 100 | 30 | 100 |

Table 10. Visiting Hungarian events in Finland.

Those first generation representatives who rarely attend Hungarian events in Finland or do not attend them at all gave excuses for their absence such as a lack of time, unsuitable dates (the events are often organised during the working week), and the long distances between their homes and events held in the capital. For some an unofficial circle of Hungarian friends in Finland is enough. Representatives of the second generation felt that the events are not in the focus of their interests and are often boring; they cannot meet young people of their age group at these events. One, for example, suggested that discos for young Hungarian-Finnish bilinguals should be organised. The results above reveal that Hungarian events in Finland are not identity supporting factors for second generation individuals and are only partly so for the first generation.

Hungarian language knowledge is considered by both first- and second-generation respondents to be very important. Finnish language policy makes it possible to organise Hungarian language teaching for school and high school age students, as described above.

In the studied group, only three representatives of the second generation took part in officially organised Hungarian teaching in Finland, and eleven did not study Hungarian at all (answers to Question 12). Thus, this is not a language supporting factor in this group. According to real time sociolinguistic research (e.g., Janulf 1998 in Sweden), a few hours of mother tongue instructions per week while at school are hardly enough to successfully maintain the minority mother tongue of an adult. Almost half (14/30) of the questionnaire's respondents, however, studied Hungarian at home for 2–9 years. Many parents seem to be conscious of the importance of Hungarian language teaching (and some other subjects, too) to the next generation – and act actively to realise it. This might be in connection with the fact that most Hungarians in Finland are highly educated and some of them are teachers by profession.

As described above, people in the studied group draw attention to the importance of the Internet in supporting minority identity and language maintenance, which seemed to be a significant marker of identity. The Internet makes Hungarian culture available to those outside Hungary and gives them the opportunity to have Hungarian contacts in their homes even if they live alone.

The use of the Hungarian language on the Internet, is also looked into as part of Question 26. Table 11 shows the results of the answers.

| Frequency of use | Generation I | | Generation II | |
|---|---|---|---|---|
| | | % | | % |
| Daily | 59 | 55.1 | 7 | 23.3 |
| Couple of times/week | 22 | 20.6 | 7 | 23.3 |
| Couple of times/month | 6 | 5.6 | 4 | 13.3 |
| Couple of times/year | 4 | 3.7 | 6 | 20.0 |
| Usually none | 3 | 2.8 | 3 | 10.0 |
| Not known | 13 | 12.1 | 3 | 10.0 |
| Total | 107 | 100 | 30 | 100 |

Table 11. The use of the Hungarian language on the Internet.

A considerably large proportion of the first generation (75.7%) use Hungarian on the Internet daily or a couple of times per week. In the second generation this activity is less common but still 46.6 % use it actively. For them the Internet could be a supporting device for language maintenance.

## 10. Summary

The identity of Hungarians and their descendants in Finland has been studied with the help of a survey involving 107 first and 30 second-generation respondents.

The identity of the first generation is strongly Hungarian-dominant. Most consider themselves only "Hungarian" or a "Hungarian in Finland". Some respondents wished to express their doubled minority identity and, thus, make a difference between a "Hungarian from Hungary" and their own "Transylvanian-Hungarian" or "Hungarian from a neighbouring Hungary" identity. There is a greater dispersion in second-generation identity. Respondents with parents who are both Hungarians have a Hungarian-dominant identity. In contrast, those who have a Hungarian and a Finnish parent, feel more Finnish than Hungarian. Because the questionnaire gave the possibility to choose only one option, some second-generation informants negotiated another identity, different from the one they had chosen, for themselves in their comments. This is in line with recent research, which points out that a person's identity is not stable and unchangeable but dynamic. "Hungariannes" is important for both the first and second generations. A Hungarian identity is "natural" for some first generation respondents; others point out in their comments that it is important for them because of the maintenance of the Hungarian language, culture and customs. For the second generation, it is important because of their parents and the language, but sometimes because it can be a chore as well.

Language is strongly tied to identity in the first generation mind and it is a core value for members of this generation. Second generation respondents consider the importance of passing on the Hungarian language to the next generations but in their comments they describe this as a general benefit (just like other language proficiency).

Supporting factors for the maintenance of a Hungarian identity have been looked for in the immigration history, self-organisation of the group in Finland, and Finnish language policy. However, these do not seem to support second-generation identity in the studied group, whereas using Hungarian language on the Internet might also support minority values and identity in the second generation.

## Bibliography

Bartha, Csilla 2006: Nyelv, identitás és kisebbségek. A nemzeti identitás fogalmának értelmezései egy országos kutatás tükrében. – Ágnes Tóth & János Vékás (eds), *Egység a különbözőségben. Az Európai Unió és a nemzeti kisebbségek*. Budapest: Friedrich Ebert Stiftung. 57–84.

BÓBITA 2010: = <http://www.bobita.fi>; <http://bobita.nyito.com> 1.2.2010.

Borbándi, Gyula 1992: Nyugati Magyar Irodalmi Lexikon és Bibliográfia. Budapest: Hitel. – <http://mek.niif.hu/04000/04038/html> 1.3.2009.

Borbély, Anna 2001: *Nyelvcsere. Szociolingvisztikai kutatások a magyarországi románok közösségében*. Budapest: MTA Nyelvtudományi Intézetének Élőnyelvi Osztálya.

Brantberg, Robert 1999: *Sotaupseerit*. [Tampere:] Revontuli (Jyväskylä: Gummerus). – <http://kotisivu.suomi.net/brantberg/Sotaupseerit%20-%20Aladar%20Paasonen.htm> 15.1.2010.

Brettell, Caroline B. & Nibbs, Faith 2009: Lived Hybridity: Second-Generation Identity Constructions through College Festival. – *Identities* 16. 678–699.

Bucholtz, Mary & Hall, Kira 2005: Identity and interaction: a sociocultural linguistic approach. – *Discourse Studies* 7. 585–614.

Chandra, Kanchan 2006: What is ethnic identity and does it matter? – *Annual Review of Political Science* 9, 397–424. doi: 10.1146/annurev.polisci.9.062404.170715. 02.22.10.

COMICS = Kati Kovács. <http://finnishcomics.info/authors/kati-kovacs> 15.1.2010.

CONSTITUTION 2009 = Constitution of Finland. 11 June 1999 (731/1999, amendments up to 802/2007 included). Unofficial translation. Ministry of Justice, Finland. – <http://www.finlex.fi/fi/laki/kaannokset/1999/en19990731.pdf>. [The Constitution in Finnish: Suomen perustuslaki 11.6.1999/731. – <http://www.finlex.fi/fi/laki/ajantasa/1999/19990731>.] 1.2.2010.

CRUX 2003 = He saavat levätä. Crux 2003/5, p. 14. – <http://www.pappisliitto.fi/liitteet/akiliitot-00010338-1.pdf> 15.1.2010.

Czibere, Márta 2007: How important a factor is language in the formation of identity? – Rogier Blokland & Cornelius Hasselblatt (eds), *Language and Identity in the Finno-Ungric World*. Proceedings of the Fourth International Symposium on Finno-Ugric Languages at the University of Groningen, May 17–19, 2006. Maastricht: Shaker Publishing BV. 32–43.

de Bot, Kees & Clyne, Michael 1994: A 16-year Longitudinal Study of Language Attrition in Dutch Immigrants in Australia. – *Journal of Multilingual and Multicultural Development* 15/1. 17–28.

Easthope, Hazel 2009. Fixed Identities in a Mobile World? The Relationship Between Mobility, Place, and Identity. – *Identities: Global Studies in Culture and Power* 16. 61–82.

Equality Act 2004 = Yhdenvertaisuuslaki 21/2004. – <http://www.finlex.fi/fi/laki/ajantasa/2004/20040021> 10.1.2010.

Fishman, Joshua 1997. Language and Ethnicity. The View from Within. Florian Coulmas (ed.), *The Handbook of Sociolinguistics*. Blackwell Handbooks in Linguistics 4. Oxford: Blackwell Publishers.

FME 2010. = <http://www.magyarutca.org/fme> 18.1.2010.

FMGY 2010. = <http://magyarutca.org/fmgy> 3.11.2008 and 10.1.2010.

FMK 2010. = <http://www.magyar-kozosseg.com> 1.2.2010.

GARAML = <http://www.lajosgaram.net/index.php?option=com_content&view=article&id=19&Itemid=27> 15.2.2010.

GARAMS = <http://fi.wikipedia.org/wiki/Sami_Garam> 5.2.2010.

Hallikainen, Raija 2007. Hitsareille tarjolla töitä Taivalkoskella. *Tekniikka & Talous*. 27.9. 2007. – <http://www.tekniikkatalous.fi/metalli/article33806.ece> 16.12.2009.

Hatoss, Anikó 2003: Identity Formation, Cross-Cultural Attitudes and Language. Maintenance in the Hungarian Diaspora of Queensland. – <eprints.usq.edu.au/1158/1/Hatoss_Deakin_paper.pdf> 11.12.2009.

HTMH 2006. = 2006-os jelentés a Kárpát-medencén kívül élő magyarság helyzetéről. Határon Túli Magyarok Hivatala. – <http://www.hhrf.org/htmh/?menuid=060209&news026_id=1765> 10.8.2008.8.

HUNCULT 2010 = Helsinki Magyar Tudományos és Kulturális Központ. – <http://www.magyarintezet.hu/index2.jsp?HomeID=6>; <http://www.unkarinkulttuuri.com> 2010. 1. 15.

IMMIGREDU = Immigrant education in Finland. Finnish National Board of Education. – <http://www.oph.fi/english/publications/2006/immigrant_education_in_finland> 12.1.2010.

Janulf, Pirjo 1998: *Kommer finskan i Sverige att fortleva? En studie av språkkunskaper och språkanvändning hos andragenerationens sverigefinnar i Botkyrka och hos finlandssvenskar i Åbo.* Acta Universitatis Stockholmensis. Studia Fennica Stockholmiensia 7. Stockholm: Almqvist & Wiksell International.

Joseph, John E. 2004: *Language and Identity: National, Ethnic, Religious.* Basingstoke: Palgrave Macmillan.

*Kalevala* 1976. Fordította Rácz István. [Helsinki]: [I. Rácz].

*Kalevala* 1987. Fordította Szente Imre. München: Nemzedékek – Nemzetőr.

*Kalevala* 2001. Fordította Szente Imre. Minoritates Mundi, Literatura. Szombathely: Berzsenyi Dániel Főiskola.

KANSALAISUUSLAKI 2003 = Kansalaisuuslaki 16.5.2003/359. – <http://www.finlex.fi/fi/laki/ajantasa/2003/20030359> 10.1.2010.

Kerékgyártó, István 1999: Odüsszeusz az ezredfordulón. – *Napút* 1999/7. <http://www.napkut.hu/naput_1999/1999_07/065.htm> 12.12.2009

KESKUSARKISTO 2004 = Helsingin yliopiston keskusarkisto. – <http://www.helsinki.fi/keskusarkisto/virkamiehet_2/P-O.pdf> 5.2.2010.

KLASSINEN GK = Károly Garam. – <http://klassinen.fi/profiili/9944> 5.2.2010.

KLASSINEN GL = Lajos Garam. – <http://klassinen.fi/profiili/9945> 5.2.2010.

KLASSINEN SK = Sole Kallioniemi. – <http://klassinen.fi/profiili/9293> 5.2.2010.

KLASSINEN SzCs = Csaba Szilvay. – <http://klassinen.fi/profiili/13398> 5.2.2010.

KLASSINEN SzG = Géza Szilvay. – <http://klassinen.fi/profiili/13399> 5.2.2010.

KLASSINEN GV = Virva Garam. – <http://klassinen.fi/profiili/13979> 5.2.2010.

Koren, Emil – Voipio, Martti 1988: *Sukukansojen uskonyhteys: Unkarin ja Suomen kirkkojen suhteet.* [Lapua:] Herättäjä-yhdistys.

Korhonen, Mikko & Suhonen, Seppo & Virtaranta, Pertti 1983: *Sata vuotta suomen sukua tutkimassa: 100-vuotias Suomalais-Ungrilainen Seura.* Espoo: Weilin+Göös.

Kovács, Andor (1999): *A világ magyarsága: Történeti áttekintés és címtár. Európa I.* [Hungarians in the world: A historical overview and address list. Europe, Vol.1.] Budapest: Magyarok Világszövetsége.

Kovács, Magdolna 2005. Nyelvpolitika elméletben és gyakorlatban: kétnyelvűség a finnországi egyetemeken. In: Kontra Miklós szerk. 2005. *Sült galamb? Magyar egyetemi tannyelvpolitika.* Konferencia a tannyelvválasztásról Debrecenben, 2004. október 28–31-én. Somorja–Dunaszerdahely: Fórum Kisebbségkutató Intézet – Lilium Aurum Könyvkiadó. 41–54.

——— 2009a: A finnországi magyarok egy csoportjának identitása és nyelvi attitűdjei. – Borbély Anna & Vančoné Kremmer Ildikó & Hattyár Helga (ed.), *Nyelvideológiák, attitűdök és sztereotípiák. 15. Élőnyelvi Konferencia Párkány (Szlovákia), 2008. szeptember 4–6.* MTA Nyelvtudományi Intézet – Gramma Nyelvi Iroda – Konstantin Filozófus Egyetem Közép-európai Tanulmányok Kar. Budapest – Dunaszerdahely – Nyitra: Tinta könyvkiadó. 359–366.

——— 2009b: Unkarin opiskelu Suomen yliopistoissa. *Suomi-Unkari* 2009/3, 13. KUMDAN 2007 = <http://www.mfa.gov.hu/kum/hu/bal/Kulpolitikank/Ketoldalu_kapcs/Europa/dania> 1.2.2010.

KUMSWITZ 2005 = <http://www.mfa.gov.hu/kum/hu/bal/Kulpolitikank/Ketoldalu_kapcs/Europa/svajc> 1.2.2010.

Language Act 2003 = Language Act 423/2003. Unofficial translation. Ministry of Justice, Finland. <http://www.finlex.fi/fi/laki/kaannokset/2003/en20030423.pdf>.

MASKULAINEN 2009 = Kirkkotiellä Maskussa. *Maskulainen. Maskun kunnan ja seurakunnan tiedotuslehti.* No 14. 20.8.2009. <http://www.masku.fi/wp-content/uploads/maskulainen_14_09_n.pdf>.

MIKOLAMUSEO = <http://www.mikolamuseo.com/press/bioSuomi.pdf>.

155

NETTIMATRIKKELI = Suomen nuorisokirjailijoiden nettimartikkeli. <http://www.nuorisokirjailijat.fi/main.php?s=k&k=80> 5.2.2010.

Numminen, Jaakko 1985: Introduction. The Development of Cultural Relations between Hungary and Finland. – *Friends and relatives. Finnish-Hungarian Cultural relations.* Budapest: Corvina. 9–18.

OPH 2010 = Opetushallitus. Tiedote 4/2010. Valtionavustus vieraskielisten sekä saamen- ja romanikielisten oppilaiden ja opiskelijoiden esi- ja perusopetuksen sekä lukiokoulutuksen järjestämiseen vuonna 2010. – <http://www.oph.fi/instancedata/prime_product_julkaisu/oph/embeds/119884_Tiedote_4_2010.pdf> 15.2.2010.

Omoniyi, Tope 2006: Hierarchy of Identities. – Omoniyi, Tope & White, Goodwith (eds), *Sociolinguistics of Identities.* Advances in Sociolinguistics. London: Continuum. 11–33.

Omoniyi, Tope & White, Goodwith 2006a: Introduction. – Omoniyi, Tope & White, Goodwith (eds), *Sociolinguistics of Identities.* Advances in Sociolinguistics. London: Continuum. 1–8.

—— (eds) 2006b: *Sociolinguistics of Identities.* Advances in Sociolinguistics. London: Continuum.

OPM 2009 = Opetusministeriön asetus vieraskielisten sekä saamenkielisten ja romanikielisten oppilaiden täydentävään opetukseen perusopetuksessa ja lukiokoulutuksessa myönnettävän valtionavustuksen perusteista. 1777/2009. – <http://www.finlex.fi/fi/laki/alkup/2009/20091777> 5.2.2010.

PAPPISLUETTELO = Pappisluettelo – Masku. Kirkkoherrat. – <http://hiski.genealogia.fi/seurakunnat/srk?CMD=PRIESTS&ID=322&TYPE=HTML&LANG=FI> 19.2.2009.

Pauwels, Anne 1985: The role of mixed marriages in language shift in the Dutch communities. – Clyne, Michael (ed.), *Australia, Meeting Place of Languages.* Pacific Linguistics Series C – No. 92. Canberra: Department of Linguistics, Research School of Pacific Studies, The Australian National University. 39–55.

Phillipson, Robert & Skutnabb-Kangas, Tove 1995: Linguistic Rights and Wrongs. *Applied Linguistics* 16/4: 483–504.

PORI = The Center of Hungarian Literature, Porin kaupunginkirjast – Satakunnan maakuntakirjasto. <http://www.pori.fi/kirjasto/unkari-english.html> 18.12.2009.

SÁMI LANGUAGE ACT 2003 = Saamen kielilaki 1086/2003. – <http://www.finlex.fi/fi/laki/smur/2003/20031086> 17.11.2009.

Silander, Maria 2006: Ole valmis – taantuma tulee. Talouselämä, 3.10.2006. <http://www.talouselama.fi/uutiset/article156429.ece> 16.12.2009.

SKT = Suomen kuvataiteilijat. Verkkomatrikkeli. <http://www.kuvataiteilijamatrikkeli.fi/cv.asp?id=1121>.

Smolicz, J. 1981: Core Values and Cultural Identity. – *Ethnic and Racial Studies* 4: 75–90.

Smolicz, J. & M. J. Secombe 1985: Community Languages, Core Values and Cultural Maintenance: The Australian Experience with Special Reference to Greek, Latvian and Polish Groups. – Michael Clyne (ed.), Australia, Meeting Place of Languages, Canberra, ANU / Pacific Linguistics. 11–38.

Smolicz, Jerzy J. & Secombe, Margaret J. 2003: Assimilation or pluralism? Changing policies for minority languages education in Australia. – *Language Policy* 2: 3–25.

Statistics Finland 2010 = Tilastokeskus.
– <http://pxweb2.stat.fi/database/StatFin/vrm/vaerak/vaerak_fi.asp>; <http://pxweb2.stat.fi/Dialog/Saveshow.asp> 15.4.2010.

SUS 2009 = Suomi-Unkari Seura. – <http://www.suomiunkari.fi> 12.12.2009.

Straszer, Boglárka 2009: Unkarilaiset Suomessa. – *Siirtolaisuus–Migration* 36/1: 12–21.

SZILVAYR = Réka Szilvay. – <http://www.rekaszilvay.com> 10.2.2010.

TAMMI = Harri István Mäki.
– <http://www.tammi.fi/kirjailijat/kirjailija/101> 10.2.2010.

Vainio, M. 2005: Ákos Papp: kuoronjohtaja, urkuri ja musiikkikriitikko. – *Keskisuomalainen* 2.10.2005.

Wichmann, Julie 1913: *Beiträge zur Ethnography der Tscheremissischen.* Travaux ethnographiques – Kansantieteellisiä julkaisuja 5. Helsinki: Société Finno-Ougrienne.

# A finnországi magyarok etnikai és nyelvi identitásának néhány összetevője

*Magdolna Kovács*

Tanulmányom elején bemutattam a mintegy 2000 főt kitevő finnországi magyarok bevándorlástörténetét, amely a bevándorlás nagysága, ideje és a bevándorlók összetétele alapján eltér a tipikus magyar kivándorlástörténettől.

A finnországi magyarok első és második generációja egy csoportjának nyelvi és etnikai identitását egy internetes felmérés alapján vizsgáltam. Az adatbázis 107 első és 30 második generációs magyar származású adatközlő 39 kérdésre adott válaszát tartalmazza; ebből jelen tanulmányomban csak néhány kérdést emeltem ki.

A felmérés alapján a megkérdezett csoportban az első generáció etnikai és nyelvi identitása erősen magyardomináns. Többségük csak magyarnak vagy finnországi magyarnak tartja magát, illetve magyar kisebbségi származását hangsúlyozza (erdélyi magyar, határon túli magyar). A második generáció azon tagjai, akik vegyes házasságban születtek, inkább finnek érzik magukat. A kérdéseknél ugyan csak egy választ lehetett bejelölni, a kérésekhez fűzött megjegyzéseikben azonban többen is árnyalják, sőt újraértelmezik identitásukat. Ez az eredmény összhangban van azokkal a kutatásokkal, amelyek az identitás dinamikus voltát hangsúlyozzák.

Az etnikai és nyelvi identitás az első generáció tagjai esetében szorosan összekapcsolódik: szerintük a magyar nyelv megőrzése Finnországban a magyarság, a magyar kultúra és a szokások megőrzésének alapja is egyben. A nyelv megőrzése mellett a magyar irodalmat és történelmet tartják a legfontosabb magyar értékeknek, s megőrzésük fontos számukra. A második generáció tagjai is fontosnak tartják a magyar nyelv megőrzését, de inkább csak egy általános nyelvtudás hasznosságának a szempontjából. Ez nem feltétlenül segíti elő a nyelv megőrzését hosszabb távon. Ők a nyelv mellett a történelmet és a magyar ételeket tartják a legfontosabb magyar értékeknek, valamint kiemelik az internet szerepét a magyar nyelv és kultúra megőrzésében.

Tanulmányomban a finn nyelvpolitika és a finnországi magyarság önszerveződésének fórumait, illetve egyéb hivatalos fórumakat is vizsgáltam a magyarság megőrzésének szempontjából. Ezek csak részben bizonyultak a nyelv és kultúra megőrzése fórumainak, egyrészt azért, mert az adott lehetőségek nem mindenki számára elérhetők (pl. a lakóhely miatt), másrészt azok sem használják ki őket, akik számára helyileg elérhetők lennének, harmadrészt pedig ezek a fórumok gyakran nem elégítik ki a második generáció igényeit.

BOGLÁRKA STRASZER

# Language and Identity among Hungarians in Sweden

## Abstract

The article provides an overview of some factors of language maintenance and shift among Hungarians in Sweden, above all at the
group level. First, the historical background of their immigration,
demography, settlement patterns, activity in Hungarian associations
and mother tongue instruction are described. Second, the article presents the linguistic situation of second generation Hungarians at the
individual level where the main focus is on language transmission
within the family, their self-assessed language proficiency in Swedish and Hungarian, the domains of minority language use and attitudes towards their Hungarian roots, culture, language and traditions.
Finally the future prospects for language maintenance or language
shift are discussed. The entire article is based on my own data, which
I collected for a comparative socio-linguistic study on the role of
minority language and identity among second generation adult Hungarians in Finland and Sweden.

*Ethnic and Linguistic Context of Identity: Finno-Ugric Minorities.* 161–195.
Uralica Helsingiensia 5. Helsinki 2011.

# 1. Hungarians in Sweden

## 1.1. The historical background

There are around 25,000–35,000 Hungarians or people with Hungarian roots in Sweden. Hungarians have a long history of contact with and immigration extends to Sweden. According to Svanberg & Tydén (1992: 104), Hungarians have been found on Swedish soil since the time of King Gustav Vasa and, for example, during the Hungarian revolution and struggle for independence between 1848 and 1849. In the 19th century, there were, however, only some twenty Hungarians recorded in Sweden, while at the end of the First World War their number was roughly one hundred (Szabó 1988: 463–464). Hungarians became visible in Swedish society after the First World War when Hungarian communists, exiled Social Democrats, high-level officials and a hundred evacuated children were accepted together with other refugees by Sweden (Svanberg & Tydén 1992: 255–256). During the interwar years, many academics, authors, artists, musicians and politicians came to the country (Szabó 1988: 464). The first organised immigration was that of a group of Hungarian Jews who, as a result of the 1945 Bernadotte Offensive, were rescued from German labour and concentration camps. However, some of them died shortly thereafter or continued their emigration in third countries. (Szabó 1988: 464, Svanberg & Tydén 1992: 397.) The Hungarian political system changed from democracy to communism in 1947–1948, after which even more Hungarians arrived to Sweden. This time it was an organised influx of foreign labour from the northern and northeastern parts of Hungary, including approximately 400 Hungarian agricultural labourers and 100 forestry workers, and their immediate family members. These Hungarians came to Sweden on a two year contract, but after the communists took power in Hungary in 1948, most families refused to return. They were either granted political asylum or they emigrated again to third countries. (Szabó 1988: 464; Svanberg & Tydén 1992: 328.)

The most extensive immigration of Hungarians to Sweden occurred during and after the Hungarian Uprising in the autumn of 1956 and the winter of 1957. Sweden was one of the first countries to receive Hungarians, a decision made the day after the Soviet invasion.

From 1956 to 1958, Sweden received approximately 8,000 Hungarians, which was, at the time, the largest number of immigrants from a single country to come to Sweden since the Second World War (Svensson 1992: 13, 142). Sweden also received Hungarian refugees who were suffering from tuberculosis (TB) and their family members; in total they numbered almost one thousand persons (Szabó 1988: 464). Thanks to Hungarian immigration, Sweden received a valuable contribution to its labour force, since those arriving mainly consisted of young people with a high level of education. Roughly 60% of these Hungarian immigrants were under 25, many were students, and the men outnumbered the women. There were also a great number of metal workers, engineers, technicians, textile workers, agricultural labourers, construction workers, office workers and doctors. Motor mechanics, chauffeurs, masons, relief workers, labourers, assistant nurses, nurses, waitresses and teachers were also well represented. (Svensson 1992: 153–154.)

Hungarians continued to immigrate to Sweden at a steady rate, though on a lesser scale than during the big refugee wave, until the end of the 1980s (See SCB 1987: 75). On average, approximately 300 persons arrived annually during those years, and, according to Statistics Sweden, it is estimated that in all 15,000 Hungarians emigrated to Sweden, a figure which includes those refugees who came during the 1980s to escape political persecution. The latter contained a high concentration of Hungarians who came from outside the present borders of Hungary, mostly from Romania, Slovakia and the former Yugoslavia. Immigration from Hungary to Sweden during the second half of the 1990s amounted to approximately 165 persons annually, rising to 200 individuals during the early 2000s (SCB 2006: 310).

Hungarian immigration in the 2000s consists of individuals and families often looking for temporary work. When the European Union extended membership to Hungary and other former Eastern European states in the spring of 2004, the Swedish government feared a wave of "social tourism", but this so-called Eastern European migration never occurred (see Zsiga 2007: 47–52). In 2008, a shortage of labour led many Swedish municipalities to recruit labour from Hungary, for example, Småland needed workers in the iron and metalworking industries and Södermanland needed medical doctors (see SP 2008; FOLKET 2008).

163

## 1.2. Demographic development and geographical area

Immigrants in Sweden are registered according to their citizenship and country of birth, which means that Hungarian speakers from the vicinity of Hungary, who ethnically and linguistically identify themselves as Hungarians, are excluded from the statistics. Also excluded are those Hungarians who have changed their citizenship and the majority of second and third generation Hungarians. Hence it is impossible to determine the number of Hungarians in Sweden, it is only possible to make an estimation with the help of the data available. Mátyás Szabó, a Swedish Hungarian who has investigated change of citizenship among Hungarians, estimates that in 1995 there were roughly 27,000 Hungarians in the country, the majority of whom were already naturalised (see Szabó 1997: 199). However, according to other sources (for example Szöllősi 1999: 68), the number of Swedish Hungarians can run up to 30,000, and in some Hungarian documents (for example HTMH 2006) as many as 35,000 (cf. MV 1996: 14–15; Kovács 1999: 49; Borbándi 1996: 118). Table 1 shows the number of Swedish Hungarians according to data from Statistics Sweden.

Table 1 shows the demographic development of emigration to Sweden among Hungarian citizens and persons born in Hungary. From 1900–2000 demographic development is shown in 10–30 year periods, whereas between 2000–2007 it is shown for each year.

| Year | Hungarian citizens | Born in Hungary | Year | Hungarian citizens | Born in Hungary |
|------|--------------------|-----------------|------|--------------------|-----------------|
| 1900 | 47    | 50     | 2000 | 2,988 | 14,127 |
| 1930 | 64    | 108    | 2001 | 2,727 | 14,027 |
| 1950 | 1,800 | 2,030  | 2002 | 2,463 | 13,935 |
| 1960 | 8,404 | 8,544  | 2003 | 2,303 | 13,794 |
| 1970 | 4,493 | 10,650 | 2004 | 2,309 | 13,672 |
| 1980 | 2,695 | 12,929 | 2005 | 2,349 | 13,600 |
| 1990 | 3,155 | 15,045 | 2006 | 2,560 | 13,711 |
| 2000 | 2,988 | 14,127 | 2007 | 3,104 | 14,057 |

Table 1.   Hungarian citizens and those born in Hungary living in Sweden between 1900 and 2007. (Source: SCB 1987, 1990, 1994b, 2004, 2006, 2007a, 2008a, 2008b.)

Between 2000 and 2007 an average of 160 persons were naturalised annually (see SCB 2008a: 72).

The distribution of age and gender among Hungarians living in Sweden is shown in Table 2. From this we can see that of those born in Hungary, most are relatively old with the largest age group comprising those between 50 and 64. Among those who are Hungarian citizens most are in the age group 40–49. In the group of those born in Hungary, small children between the ages of 0 and 3 form the smallest group, while in the group of Hungarian citizens, young people between the ages of 18 and 19 form the smallest group. The number of school age children in the group born in Hungary is slightly more than 200 and among the Hungarian citizens roughly 300. The male to female ratio among persons born in Hungary is almost one to one, though there are slightly more women than men. Among the Hungarian citizens women are also slightly more numerous.

| Year 2006 | Born in Hungary | | | Hungarian citizens | | |
|---|---|---|---|---|---|---|
| Age | Both sexes | Men | Women | Both sexes | Men | Women |
| 0–6 | 85 | 55 | 30 | 134 | 76 | 58 |
| 7–17 | 304 | 154 | 150 | 253 | 150 | 103 |
| 18–29 | 1,058 | 512 | 546 | 515 | 230 | 285 |
| 30–39 | 1,580 | 709 | 871 | 697 | 325 | 372 |
| 40–49 | 1,327 | 513 | 814 | 415 | 172 | 243 |
| 50–64 | 4,950 | 2,424 | 2,526 | 382 | 148 | 234 |
| 65– | 4,407 | 2,431 | 1,976 | 164 | 50 | 114 |
| Total | 13,711 | 6,798 | 6,913 | 2,560 | 1,151 | 1,409 |

Table 2. Hungarian citizens and those born in Hungary living in Sweden in 2006 according to age and sex. (Source: SCB 2007a: 42–43, 64–65.)

When trying to show the number of second generation Hungarians in Sweden, there are difficulties not only because of the aforementioned shortcomings in gathering the statistics concerning Hungarians from the neighbouring countries and changes of citizenship, but also because of the way Statistics Sweden defines persons with a foreign background. In the statistics guidelines, persons with a foreign background are defined as persons born abroad or persons born in Sweden with two parents who were born abroad (SCB 2002). However, since 1947, children who were born abroad were not recorded as such, if the mother was, at that time, registered as a national of Sweden (SCB 2007a: 410). One additional problem concerning the statistics of the second generation is that if a person has dual Hungarian-Swedish citizenship, Swedish citizenship is the one given priority, which leads to that person being omitted from the statistics as a Hungarian citizen (SCB 2007a: 412). According to earlier statistics, for example 1986, the number of first and second generation Hungarians totalled 17,844 persons of whom 4,200 represented the second generation. (SCB 1987.) According to other statistics, in that same year there were 3,604 children between 0 and 17 years of age who were the children of Hungarian-born married or unmarried cohabiting couples. 2,579 of these children were born in Sweden and were Swedish citizens. Furthermore, in that same year there were 2,332 children between the ages 0 and 17 who were born to married couples of whom one of the parents had been born in Hungary (SCB 1987). The situation today concerning the number of second generation Hungarians, and distribution according to age and sex is shown in Table 3.

| Year 2006 | | Born in Sweden with two parents born in Hungary | |
| Age | Total | Men | Women |
| --- | --- | --- | --- |
| 0–6 | 369 | 194 | 175 |
| 7–17 | 973 | 524 | 449 |
| 18–29 | 1,264 | 689 | 575 |
| 30–39 | 1,200 | 645 | 555 |
| 40–49 | 1,701 | 872 | 829 |
| 50–64 | 403 | 190 | 213 |
| 65– | 8 | 4 | 4 |
| Total | 5,918 | 3,118 | 2,800 |

Table 3. Persons born in Sweden with parents born in Hungary, by age and sex, for the year 2006. (Source: SCB 2007a: 54–55.)

Regarding the distribution of Hungarians in Sweden, more than half of those born in Hungary live in Götaland. Slightly less than half live in Svealand, and a very small number live in Norrland. Table 4 (below) shows persons born in Hungary according to their regional distribution in Sweden in exact figures for the year 2006 in descending order according to how many reside in the various counties. The table shows that the largest number live in the counties of Stockholm, Skåne and Västra Götaland (see also Straszer 2006a, 2006b).

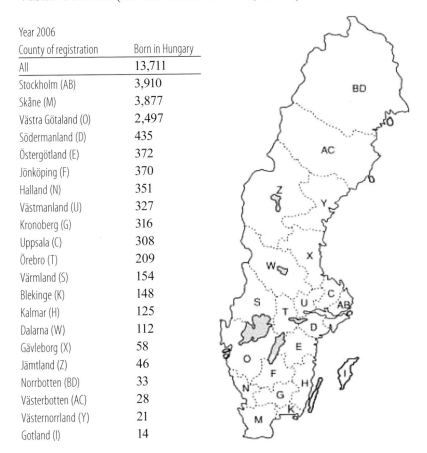

| Year 2006 | |
| --- | --- |
| County of registration | Born in Hungary |
| All | 13,711 |
| Stockholm (AB) | 3,910 |
| Skåne (M) | 3,877 |
| Västra Götaland (O) | 2,497 |
| Södermanland (D) | 435 |
| Östergötland (E) | 372 |
| Jönköping (F) | 370 |
| Halland (N) | 351 |
| Västmanland (U) | 327 |
| Kronoberg (G) | 316 |
| Uppsala (C) | 308 |
| Örebro (T) | 209 |
| Värmland (S) | 154 |
| Blekinge (K) | 148 |
| Kalmar (H) | 125 |
| Dalarna (W) | 112 |
| Gävleborg (X) | 58 |
| Jämtland (Z) | 46 |
| Norrbotten (BD) | 33 |
| Västerbotten (AC) | 28 |
| Västernorrland (Y) | 21 |
| Gotland (I) | 14 |

Table 4. Regional distribution for the year 2006 of persons born in Hungary in descending order according their numbers in each county. (Source: SCB 2007a: 88–89.)

167

During 2006, the level of education among persons born in Hungary between the ages of 25 and 26 was relatively high, as half had an upper secondary school education and more than a third had a post-upper secondary school education (SCB 2008c).

The Swedish Hungarian priest Pál Molnár-Veress estimates that roughly 60% of Swedish Hungarians are Catholic, while the majority of those remaining (40%) are Protestant. More than half of the Protestants are reformed with the remaining half being predominately Lutheran and Unitarian, and a smaller number belonging to the Baptist Church or other Free Churches. There are also Hungarian Jews in Sweden who consider themselves followers of various different faiths. In addition there are Swedish Hungarians who do not practise any religion and therefore do not belong to any of the Hungarian religious communities.[1]

It can be concluded that Hungarians in Sweden form a very heterogeneous group, not only in terms of their reasons for and time of immigration, but also in their area of residence and in terms of their culture. Even their religious convictions and educational backgrounds differ.

## 1.3. Organisations

The first Hungarian associations were founded in connection with the organised immigration of Hungarians in 1957 (Svensson 1992: 176, 226). In the 1960s there were already roughly 60 active Hungarian associations throughout Sweden, including religious congregations, sports clubs, song and dance groups (Szabó 1988: 466). The most active associations were located around big cities, that is, in Stockholm, Gothenburg and Malmö, and in industrial centres such as Västerås, Södertälje and Olofström. A national committee was established in 1974, which was the precursor of Svédországi Magyarok Szövetsége (SMOSZ; [The Swedish Federation of Hungarians][2]), which was founded in 1976 and is still active today. This national federation is for civil associations of Swedish Hungarians and is politi-

---

1. The information is based on a recorded interview with the Hungarian priest Pál Molnár-Veress 26 April 2007.
2. In Swedish *Ungerska Riksförbundet.*

cally independent. Its objectives are to facilitate Hungarians in their integration into Swedish society, preserve the Hungarian language, culture and customs, maintain good relations between Hungary and Sweden and support and encourage the activities of local associations (SMOSZ 2008). The Swedish Federation of Hungarians has grown steadily and today it has 39 local associations and more than 5000 paying members (see SMOSZ 2008). These 39 local associations are active in 18 towns all over Sweden. There are local associations in Skåne (Helsingborg, Kristianstad, Malmö), Halland (Halmstad), Jönköping (Jönköping), Kronoberg (Ljungby, Markaryd, Växjö), Östergötland (Norrköping), Södermanland (Eskilstuna), Örebro (Örebro/Kumla), Stockholm (Södertälje, Stockholm), Uppsala (Uppsala) and Västmanland (Västerås).[3] The bilingual local association in Uppsala is the northernmost, with approximately 50 members.[4] Above all, these local associations carry out cultural activities, such as celebrating Hungarian national and memorial days.

In addition to the local societies, there are special cultural associations in Gothenburg, Lund, Solna and Stockholm. Since 2005, *Ungerska Kulturföreningen Kőrösi Csoma Sándor* [The Hungarian Cultural Society Kőrösi Csoma Sándor] has annually arranged the Hungarian Culture and Art Festival in Gothenburg. In addition to this, there are other cultural interest groups with active members throughout the country, such as *Transsylvanska Bokvänner* [Transylvanian Book Club], *Vänskapsföreningen Ághegy-Liget* [Friendship Society Ághegy-Liget], *Ungerska Konstens Vänner* [Friends of Hungarian Art] and *Sällskapet för ungersk litteratur* [Society for Hungarian Literature]. Most Hungarian organisations are, however, in the Stockholm metropolitan area, and many of them were founded by local interest groups. There is a trade association, a society for Hungarian medical students, for architects, for senior citizens, for scouts and for native teachers of Hungarian. Furthermore, there is a nationwide association for young people. Besides the aforementioned associations, there are also aid organizations, which send aid back home, to acquaintances and relatives and other Hungarians in their native countries who face

---

3. See map above.
4. The information is based on personal correspondence with the chairwoman of the association Ingela Pronchev. 5 August 2008.

economic difficulty or have been the victims of various disasters, such as floods. There is even one aid association established to provide for orphans. *SMOSZ* [The Swedish Federation of Hungarians] also plays an active role in *Nyugat-Európai Országos Magyar Szervezetek Szövetsége* [The Western European Association of Country Organisations of Hungarians]. (HTMH 2006; SMOSZ 2008. See also Straszer 2006b.)

The *SMOSZ* has two headquarters, the first of these is in Bromma, Stockholm. This has been used since 1971 as a meeting place for various associations. The Federation has owned it since 1996. The building is called *Magyar Ház* [The Hungarian House]. The other "Hungarian house" is called *Dél-svédországi Magyar Otthon* [South-Swedish Hungarian Home] and has belonged to the Federation since 2005. It is located in Kristianstad. The buildings are intended for events, meetings and seminars and as general meeting places. In addition, there is a Hungarian church community hall in Tångagärde, in the municipality of Ulricehamn, which also serves as an important meeting place for Swedish Hungarians. Many scout camps, language and translation camps, meetings and festivities have taken place here over the course of several decades. (See among others HTMH 2006; SMOSZ 2008.) These Hungarian organisations arrange altoghether approximately 1200–1300 events each year, for which they receive support via *SMOSZ* from the Swedish State (HTMH 2006).

The Church also plays an important role for many Swedish Hungarians. After the largest wave of immigration in the autumn of 1956, a Hungarian speaking priest was appointed and regular services in Hungarian began. In addition to these regular church services, the Church provided support and the opportunity to engage in social interaction with other Hungarians. According to Szabó (1988: 468), throughout the Church's history it has had a social function, and he claims that there are many instances of overlap between the roles of church groups and those of the civil associations.

Taking part in church services and in Christian holy days provided an opportunity for many Hungarians to meet other Hungarians and to belong to a community characterised by a common language.[5] The latest addition to the Hungarian organisations and associations

---

5.    The information is based on a recorded interview with the Hungarian priest Pál Molnár-Veress 26 April 2007.

is a Hungarian choir, which was founded in Stockholm in 2007. One of the choir's most important tasks is to foster Hungarian culture and language through music. The choir collaborates with several other Hungarian organisations in Sweden. (Pap 2008.)

Last but not least, there is the Swedish Hungarian institute, the *Északi Magyar Archívum*[6] [The Hungarian Archive]. The Archive was founded in 1973 and is maintained privately in Stockholm. The material in the Archive, which mostly deals with Hungarian immigrants in 53 countries, consists of around 20,000 books and 3,000 periodicals and papers. Furthermore, the Archive contains tens of thousands of articles, documents from Hungarian associations and different interest groups, official historical documents, various publications, posters, postcards, business cards, stamps, photos and audiovisual material.[7]

Concerning the activities of Swedish Hungarians in the associations, it has been noted that some Hungarians distinguish between those Hungarians who have come from Hungary and those who are from neighbouring countries. Szabó (1988: 466) is not alone in observing that Hungarians from Romania have distinct ideas regarding their cultural identity. This has been attributed to the fact that this group is the most active in the associations. For many Swedish Hungarians, activity in the associations constitutes a natural part of their lives. This is especially true of the first generation and newcomers, while second and third generation Hungarians participate less.[8]

## 1.4. Mother tongue instruction

In connection with the organised emigration of Hungarians to Sweden, a Hungarian secondary grammar school was founded in Gothenburg in 1957 for Hungarian refugees who had been forced to interrupt their studies due to the Uprising in the autumn of 1956 and who wished to continue their studies at Swedish colleges and enter the workforce. The school closed after the 1960/1961 school year. Between 1957–61

---

6. Which in Swedish is called *Ungerska Arkivet*.
7. This information is based on personal correspondence with the founder of the archive Antal Szöllősi 20 October 2008. See also Szöllősi (2008) and Borbándi (1996: 125).
8. The claim was also emphasised by the Hungarian priest Pál Molnár-Veress in the interview on 26th April 2007.

roughly 100 pupils studied there, of whom 34 completed their studies successfully.[9]

From the 1960s every child with an immigrant background who uses a language other than Swedish at home, got the opportunity to receive teaching in the mother tongue. This means in most cases one lesson weekly, when children can practise the language and speak about the culture and habits in their or their parents' country of origin. So-called mother tongue instruction is important for the strengthening of identity, maintenance of the language and culture and for the development of attitudes towards the child's roots. (Hyltenstam & Tuomela 1996: 29–30.) From the beginning of the 1970s, Swedish Hungarian children[10] received lessons in Hungarian in Stockholm, Gothenburg and Borås (György-Ullholm 2004: 286; Tóth 2007; cf. SCB 1984b: 120). Later, education in Hungarian was extended and during the 1970s and 1980s Hungarian became a middle-ranking language in terms of the frequency with it was taught in schools (Beijer 2008: 305). Most of the teachers in Hungarian were well educated, and several were trained as teachers in Sweden. Teacher training was available in Stockholm and Malmö, and in 1982 the College for Teachers in Malmö sent a group of over 30 teachers from 23 municipalities to Hungary for a few days of in-service training. (Beijer 2008: 305.) Today, teaching in Hungarian takes place in over 100 municipalities,[11] although frequently by teachers lacking pedagogical training. There is no special education offered to mother-tongue teachers in Sweden today (Ikonen & Straszer 2006: 28), forcing each language group to arrange further education on their own. (See also Straszer 2008).

The number of primary school pupils (grades 1–9) eligible for training in the Hungarian language as a mother tongue during the 1980s and the early 1990s was approximately 2000. The number reached its peak during the 1990/1991 school year. The participation

9.   The information is partly based on documents concerning the Hungarian upper secondary school which I have studied in *The Regional Archives in Gothenburg* and partly on Svensson (1992: 155–163).
10.   Only children who use Hungarian in their everyday life at home are entitled to receive teaching in Hungarian as a mother tongue (see SV 2002: 22).
11.   This information is based on personal correspondence with Ulla Ekander Liew 25 February 2005, who is responsible for school statistics in the *Statistics Sweden.*

rate during the 1980s was between 51% and 58%. It reached a peak of 61% during the 1989/1990 school year, but in the 1990s it sank to below 40%. Today the number of pupils entitled to language training is roughly half what it was in the 1980s (SCB 1979, SCB 1984a, SCB 1992, SCB 1994a and 1994b). The participation rate has also sunk drastically. For example, in autumn 2003 there were, according to Statistics Sweden, 1192 pupils in Swedish primary schools eligible to receive training in Hungarian as a mother tongue, but only 32.8%, that is, 391 of them participated in the teaching. The eligible pupils attended 593 different schools, 527 of which were state schools and 66 of which were private. The schools were distributed throughout 112 municipalities across Sweden.[12] The situation is much the same today. The number of pupils eligible for mother-tongue instruction at secondary school level (grades 10–12) is much lower and the participation rate is less than 20% (see SCB 1979: 23, 32).

Apart from the instruction provided by the educational system, teaching in Hungarian is also provided by the private sector. In some regions Hungarian speaking children have the possibility of obtaining instruction in Hungarian under the direction of Swedish Hungarian associations through weekend classes, music and game clubs, and summer and scout camps (see for example Boross 2006; Stuber 2006). In 1997 an association to support the maintenance of the Hungarian language and culture in Sweden was founded. The association's[13] objective is to organise language camps for children and arrange lectures and training for parents and teachers in the mother tongue. (See Alapszabály 2007.) The association arranges teaching in Hungarian with the help of volunteers in nine cities: Eskilstuna, Gothenburg, Halmstad, Jönköping, Kristianstad, Ljungby, Lund, Norrköping and Stockholm.[14] Summer camps are arranged in two locations and children and young people from all over Sweden participate. It is esti-

---

12.   The information is based on personal correspondence with Ulla Ekander Liew 25 February 2005, who is responsible for school statistics in the Statistics Sweden.
13.   The name of the association is *Őrszavak / Custos Anyanyelvápolók Egyesülete.*
14.   This information comes from personal correspondence with Ildikó Tóth 4 April 2008.

mated that roughly 100–130 children and adolescents participate each year [15] (see also Straszer 2008).

Hungarian can also be studied at university level, but today only at Uppsala University. Furthermore, Hungarian can be studied in some of the country's adult education centres.

## 2. Language and identity among second generation Hungarians

Concerning second generation Hungarians, their knowledge of Hungarian and their linguistic and ethnic identity, there is very little information to be found. For this reason I carried out a study between 2004 and 2009. My research consisted of a comparative socio-linguistic study in which I concentrated on the role of language and identity among second generation [16] Hungarian adults in two Nordic countries. For my study I collected research material with the help of a questionnaire which was completed by 38 informants from Finland and 50 from Sweden. Moreover, I conducted in-depth interviews with a few of the informants.

In my study I was interested in the linguistic situation of the second generation and the kind of relationship they had with their own Hungarian roots and the Hungarian language and culture. I first studied the informants' background: how their parents transmitted the Hungarian language and motivated them to use it in their everyday life, what kind of relationship they had in their childhood with Hungary and Hungarian speaking relatives and if they had had the possibility to attend classes in their mother tongue at school. I also studied the current situation in their everyday life as adults and their own estimation of their competence in Hungarian and Swedish, how

---

15. This information comes from personal correspondence with Ildikó Tóth 4 April 2008. Cf. György-Ullholm (2004: 287, 292).
16. In my investigation, the informants fulfilled the following criteria: they were (1) adults permanently resident in Sweden or Finland, i.e. they had reached the age of 18, who (2) were born in Sweden or Finland or had moved to Sweden or Finland before attending school. Furthermore (3) at least one of the parents should have had Hungarian as their mother tongue and should have been born and raised in Hungary and moved as an adult directly to or via another country to Sweden or Finland.

often they used the minority language, and the importance Hungarian culture and traditions had in their personal lives. Furthermore, I studied their attitudes towards what it means to be "Hungarian" and whether they aimed to maintain their "Hungarian heritage" and pass it on to the next generation. I compared the linguistic situation, sense of identity and attitudes of second generation Hungarians in Finland and Sweden and tried to pin-point both macro and micro level factors which influence the linguistic situation and the future prospects for language maintenance or language shift (Straszer 2010a and forthcoming 2).[17] In this article the focus is on Hungarians in Sweden and the results below concern only the Swedish material.

Among my 50 Swedish Hungarian informants, there were 27 women and 23 men. More than half were under the age of 35 (10 were between 18 and 25 and 17 between 26 and 35), while 14 informants were between the ages of 36 and 45 and nine informants were older than 45. More than half (28) were well educated. Only four informants were born in Hungary, the rest were born in Sweden. 33 informants had lived their entire life in Sweden, while 7 informants had at some time in their lives also lived or spent a shorter period of time in Hungary. Most of the informants (43) had only Swedish citizenship, the remainder dual or triple citizenship. Almost all informants (45) lived near a Hungarian association.

Of the 50 informants, more than half (29) came from families where both parents were Hungarian speaking. However, four informants had a Hungarian speaking mother and a Swedish speaking father and three had a Hungarian speaking mother and a father whose mother tongue was a neither Swedish nor Hungarian (English, Spanish and Polish). 14 of the informants had a Swedish speaking mother and a Hungarian speaking father. The majority of Hungarian fathers (31 of 43) had come to Sweden from Hungary as refugees in 1956–57 and only three had moved for family reasons. Half the Hungarian mothers (18 of 36) had come to Sweden from Hungary as refugees, 12 for family reasons and two came to work. The majority of parents were well educated. However, there were also some who had only completed elementary school. The mothers had a slightly lower level of education

---

17. See also other publications about this study: Straszer (2006a, 2006b, 2009, 2010b) and Straszer (forthcoming 1).

than the fathers. Among the parents there were, for example, doctors, teachers, engineers, agronomists and economists, some parents had already retired. A large percentage, above all the fathers, were active members of Hungarian associations.

## 2.1. Language transmission during the informants' childhoods

There was no clear pattern between the various informants' childhood exposure to the mother tongue: at home their parents did not exclusively use their mother tongue when speaking with each other or with the children. Several different patterns of communication between the informants and their parents emerged. Roughly quarter of the informants' mothers used Hungarian exclusively when talking to the informants and the same proportion used Hungarian predominantly, while they only used Swedish to a limited extent. One-third of the fathers exclusively used Hungarian and almost half exclusively used the majority language. Furthermore, it occurred rather often that the Hungarian speaking parent, especially the mother, code-switched and also to some extent used Swedish when communicating in the family. It is also interesting that in some families the parents used a different language with other siblings than with the informant. One-third of the informants only used Hungarian at home as a child while one-third only used Swedish or a third language. Among the remaining third, the extent to which both Hungarian and Swedish were used at home varied.

During the informants' childhoods, the Hungarian language and culture was often present thanks to the fact that the families maintained contact with their Hungarian relatives and acquaintances by travelling to Hungary regularly. Eight informants visited Hungary several times a year, while roughly one-third (17) visited once a year and 13 on average every other year. A quarter (12) visited Hungary seldom or never. It was most common to visit Hungary during the summer vacation, but many families also travelled there during the Christmas holidays. One informant mentioned that her family always travelled to Hungary in the spring, around Easter. In some families the trips were repeated annually until the children grew up.

The opportunity to receive teaching in Hungarian is appreciated by many Hungarians in Sweden. 75% of informants had, on some occasion, participated in a class in Hungarian. Twenty informants had attended classes during their childhood and seven had received their first instruction in Hungarian as adults. Eleven informants had participated in teaching both as children and as adults. Most commonly informants had received teaching in the mother tongue at primary school (24), nursery school (13) or upper secondary school (14). Of the informants 13 had studied Hungarian at university level, while some informants (11) had received teaching in other ways, for instance, at summer camps, adult education institutions or through private lessons. (Cf. Straszer 2010b: 200–201.)

## 2.2. Language proficiency

The informants compared their language proficiency in Hungarian to proficiency in Swedish in the following way: 10% said that their knowledge of Hungarian is as good as Swedish, while the majority said that their knowledge of Hungarian is not quite as good as Swedish (40%) or much worse (38%). Six informants had no knowledge of Hungarian at all. It is interesting that no one of the informants claimed that their knowledge of Hungarian is either slightly better or a lot better than Swedish. The following table shows the informants' assessment of their proficiency in Hungarian and Swedish. Language proficiency is here divided into the abilities of listening comprehension, speaking, reading and writing.

|  | Listening comprehension | | Speaking | | Reading | | Writing | |
|---|---|---|---|---|---|---|---|---|
|  | Hung. | Swe. | Hung. | Swe. | Hung. | Swe. | Hung. | Swe. |
| Very good | 21 | 50 | 11 | 50 | 6 | 48 | 6 | 48 |
| Good | 15 | 0 | 14 | 0 | 11 | 2 | 9 | 2 |
| Not good & not poorly | 6 | 0 | 11 | 0 | 8 | 0 | 10 | 0 |
| Poorly | 3 | 0 | 8 | 0 | 13 | 0 | 7 | 0 |
| Very poorly | 5 | 0 | 6 | 0 | 12 | 0 | 19 | 0 |
| Total | 50 | 50 | 50 | 50 | 50 | 50 | 51* | 50 |

Table 5.  Informants' estimation of their proficiency in Hungarian and Swedish. (*One informant chose two answers.)

Table 5 clearly shows that the informants' own estimation of proficiency in the minority language is considerably lower than for Swedish. This difference is particularly evident in secondary language skills, that is, in reading and writing. Proficiency in the majority language seems to be high in all areas among second generation Hungarians. (Cf. Straszer 2010b: 202.) The informants described their knowledge of Hungarian with the following statements:

*"Since I have only ever attended Swedish school, I am more proficient in this language* [Swedish], *but my feelings come out in Hungarian.* [...] *"New Hungarian words and sayings can create difficulty, and technical terms."*
(male, 64 years old, both parents Hungarian)

*"I have never needed to write* [in Hungarian], *only attended one term of mother tongue instruction. Since* [Swedish] *is used every day, it's easier to be better at Swedish."*
(female, 23 years old, both parents Hungarian)

*"I can participate in a conversation in a Hungarian kitchen, but when they broadcast on television from Parliament, I don't even try to understand. On the other hand, I don't daily follow the Swedish Parliament either."*
(male, 40 years old, both parents Hungarian)

*"*[I understand] *some* [Hungarian] *words, greetings, sayings, numbers... I can read it and I know how the words should be pronounced, but I don't understand it."*
(female, 42 years old, Swedish mother and Hungarian father)


## 2.3. Domains of Hungarian in Sweden

First of all, it is interesting to investigate how Hungarian is available to second generation Hungarians today, inside and outside the home. Almost all the informants had Hungarian speaking relatives and half also had acquaintances and friends who spoke Hungarian as their mother tongue. Most informants (35 of 50) had Hungarian books and music (32). However, much less than half (16 of 50) had videos or DVDs in Hungarian at home. Only four regularly subscribed to a Hungarian language newspaper or magazine and four subscribed to one or more Hungarian TV channels at home. It was more common to have an internet connection, which enabled them to read Hungarian websites and listen to Hungarian programmes.

How often and in which domains, to coin Joshua Fishman's expression (see Fishman 1964, 1965, 1972), do people with a Hungarian background use the Hungarian language in their everyday life today? There was only one informant who read books in Hungarian a few times a week and another who read them a few times a month. In contrast, most informants (33 of 50) never read books in Hungarian. The situation is almost the same with Hungarian newspapers. It was, however, slightly more common to read websites on the internet in Hungarian. Three informants did this every day and two several times a week. Five informants read these websites at least once a month, and less than half (21 of 50) never read them at all. To listen to Hungarian music or radio channels was more popular than reading Hungarian. Seven informants listened to Hungarian music or radio channels at least once a week, eight at least once a month, and 18 not at all. Half sometimes watched Hungarian TV programmes and videos or DVDs: eleven informants at least once a month, five a few times a year. Writing cards was not so common, but writing short text messages on the mobile was quite popular. The situation was quite similar concerning the writing of letters and e-mails. There were 22 informants who never wrote in Hungarian, five who wrote short messages and letters or e-mails at least a few times a week, five who did this at least once a month and 14 a few times a year. Among this group of second generation Hungarians the language was most commonly used on the fixed-line telephone or mobile. Eleven informants did this every day, and seven a few times a week; 13 informants never spoke Hungarian on the telephone or mobile. (Cf. Straszer 2010b: 202–203.)

Most of the informants (39 of 50) used Hungarian with their relatives, above all with their parents and relatives living in Hungary. Additionally, 12 informants often used Hungarian with friends and four used it in their spare time activities. However, it is clear that in everyday life, at home and in other private spheres, Hungarian is not a frequently used language. Because the informants were adults, most of them no longer lived with their parents. However, a few still did, and a few lived with other adults in student accommodation. Those informants were not yet married and did not have children of their own. (Because the circumstances of a person's private life can differ so much I shall here name every adult living with an informant as "flat mates" in the plural form, independent of their relationship.) Among my informants, only three used Hungarian exclusively at home with their flat mates and one used both Hungarian and Swedish. The remainder only used the majority language. There was only one informant who spoke Hungarian exclusively and three who tried to use both Hungarian and Swedish at home when they spoke with their children. Those who did not have children also answered the question about communication with children. It was, however, a hypothetical question about what they planned to do if they had children. It is interesting that the answers to the hypothetical question were much more positive than the reality among those who already had children. Two informants said that they would speak Hungarian exclusively and 14 informants stated that they planned to use some Hungarian when raising their future children. Some informants had pets and three said they only used Hungarian with them. Furthermore, approximately one third (18 of 50) used Hungarian slightly more often than Swedish when thinking or speaking to themselves.

A few informants also had other contacts with the Hungarian culture and language. Four informants actively participated in the activity of Hungarian associations and eight were occasional participants and almost half the informants (20 of 50) regularly met other persons with a Hungarian background at least once a month. Almost everybody had relatives in Hungary and half also had friends there. As a result, 16 informants travelled to Hungary at least once a year and 11 every other year. Of the informants 27 always spent a minimum of a few weeks there when they travelled to Hungary. Obviously, the informants did not travel to Hungary as much as during their childhood, nor did they stay there for long periods. Furthermore, 19 informants regularly followed, at least once a month, what was going on in Hungary and 35 paid attention to other Hungarians in

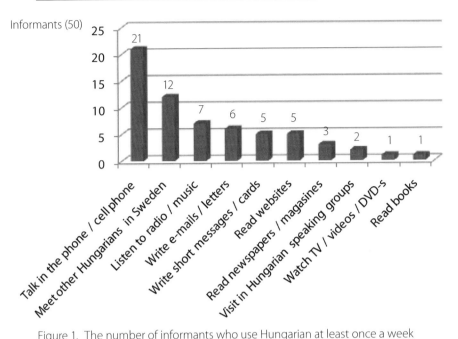

Figure 1. The number of informants who use Hungarian at least once a week according to various domains.

Sweden. Figure 1 summarises those domains in which the informants use Hungarian at least once a week today. The chart shows that Hungarian is most often used when informants speak on the phone.

The use of Hungarian in everyday activities was common for only 32 % of the informants (16 of 50). Thirteen informants estimated that they used it at least once a week, five at least once a month and the remainder even less. Altogether, six informants never used Hungarian. In summary, it can be stated that in the everyday lives of these second generation Hungarians, the majority language, Swedish, is more frequently used than Hungarian. Hungarian is a language reserved, above all, for relatives and it is a symbol of heritage. Many informants lacked proficiency in Hungarian, and therefore did not use it much. As a rule, it was easier for many of the informants to speak Hungarian to themselves or to their pets than to use it with native Hungarian speakers, possibly because they did not need to be afraid of critical comments concerning their communication skills.

## 2.4. Identity

Many of the questions in my study concerned the relationship of the informants to the Hungarian culture and language, multilingualism, and their Hungarian background. Ten informants considered Hungarian their sole mother tongue while 11 considered both Hungarian and Swedish their mother tongues. More than half (29 of 50) considered Swedish their sole mother tongue. However, the informants did not always consider the mother tongue the most natural language to use, for in answer to this question 43 chose Swedish. One informant could not answer this question, while six said that both Hungarian and Swedish felt natural to use. Interestingly enough, nobody thought Hungarian was the most natural language to use. It is also worth restating that eleven informants said Hungarian was their most natural language choice earlier in their lives, so the role of the languages and the informants' relation to them had changed. (Cf. Straszer 2010b: 203–206.)

Regardless of their real knowledge of Hungarian most informants (42) thought it was important for a person with a Hungarian background to know Hungarian and they commented on this as follows:

*"When you have Hungarian family members, it is much more interesting and informative when you can converse 'for real' in Hungarian."*
(female, 24 years old, Swedish mother and Hungarian father)

*"It is important for cultural identity."*
(male, 49 years old, both parents Hungarian)

"[It's important to know Hungarian,] *but the feeling deep inside is even more important."*
(female, 35 years old, both parents Hungarian)

In spite of this, almost half of the informants (22) thought that Hungarian should not be spoken in the presence of others (who do not understand Hungarian), in order to be polite.

Some of the open questions in the questionnaire related to ethnic identity and dealt with, among other things, what the informants considered the most important components of Hungarian identity. Ten informants said they considered themselves "Hungarians in Sweden", 20 considered themselves Hungarians in Sweden on occasion and the remaining 20 never identified themselves in this way. When in Hungary, only eight informants felt they could identify themselves as Hungarians, and half felt they could not. For the other informants, the feeling of "belonging" was dependent on the situation. Furthermore, every informant felt that Sweden was their home, while less than half, 20 informants, also felt at home in Hungary. When somebody abroad asked the informants who they were and where they were from, 20 informants only answered that they were Swedish or that they were from Sweden. Nine informants occasionally added that they were also Hungarian. Another 15 informants always said that they were both Swedish and Hungarian, while only four said that they were Hungarians or from Hungary or that they had a Hungarian background. (Cf. Straszer 2010b: 206–210.)

Some of the informants' comments concerning identity:

1.   Feeling of belonging in Sweden:

*"I am divided, but when it comes down to it I am pretty Swedish."* (male, 23 years old, both parents Hungarian)

*"No* [I don't think of myself as Hungarian] *because I feel I have a Swedish mindset. When I was younger I was more open."* (female, 34 years old, Swedish mother and Hungarian father)

"[No I don't think of myself as Hungarian]. *I feel a connection with others who share a similar background, like my friends who also have parents from other countries."* (female, 42 years old, Swedish mother and Hungarian father)

2. Feeling of belonging in Hungary:

"[I feel Hungarian when I am in Hungary] *or at least I want to.*" (male, 25 years old, Swedish mother and Hungarian father)

"[I feel Hungarian when I am in Hungary] *even though others usually consider me Swedish.*"
(male, 64 years old, both parents Hungarian)

*"It depends on the situation, but usually I don't* [feel Hungarian in Hungary]. *Everyone looks upon me as being Swedish, but I am OK with that."*
(female, 35 years old, both parents Hungarian)

3. I feel "at home" in Sweden:

*"I know how the system works here."*
(male, 40 years old, both parents Hungarian)

"[I feel at home here]. *Always. This is where I grew up."*
(male, 64 years old, both parents Hungarian)

*"Here I understand how folk think and why they do the things they do better than in Hungary. I have learned the social and cultural codes here."*
(female, 34 years old, Swedish mother and Hungarian father)

4. I feel "at home" in Hungary:

*"When I'm with friends and family I feel at home. But if we're talking about dealing with governmental agencies, I don't have any sense of what is considered "correct". Do people still bribe doctors in order to get help earlier?"*
(male, 40 years old, both parents Hungarian)

*"With people and places* [I feel at home], *but not in a meeting with public officials, etc."*
(male, 25 years old, Swedish mother and Hungarian father)

*"There are a lot of things that are familiar, and I know how things work, but I don't feel at home in the same way that I feel at home in Sweden."*
(female, 34 years old, Swedish mother and Hungarian father)

The informants were also asked to describe those persons whom they considered Hungarian. Among the criteria used, the one most commonly stated was "the feeling", that is, Hungarians are "those who feel so in their heart". Just as important was to have a connection with Hungary, mostly in the sense of being born or growing up there. Their roots were, according to the informants, the most important criterion; the language itself was not so important. Among the other criteria mentioned were: the Hungarian way of life, having an interest in the language and culture, having typically Hungarian features, having a Hungarian upbringing, eating Hungarian food, having a Hungarian name, having Hungarian citizenship and feeling an affinity with Hungarian music.

The informants felt that the most "characteristic" part of Hungarian identity was the language, though by that they meant not only a person's knowledge of Hungarian but also a particular accent and a special way of speaking Swedish. The second most important "Hungarian characteristic" was Hungarian food culture, including knowledge of making Hungarian dishes and the habit of eating Hungarian meals. Hungarian culture and literature, history and politics also played a part in Hungarian identity according to the informants. They also mentioned things such as the habit of visiting Hungary, having Hungarian relatives and roots, listening to Hungarian music and having character traits and a value system which the informants thought typical of Hungarians. Figure 2 shows what the informants believed best distinguishes Hungarian identity. (Cf. Straszer 2010b: 211–212.)

Informants (50)

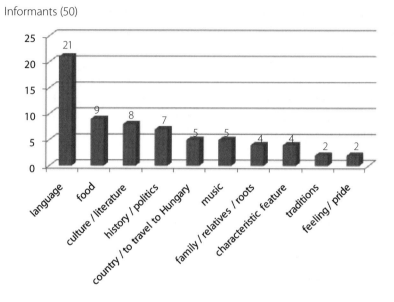

Figure 2. Informants' estimation of the most characteristic features of Hungarian identity.


## 3. Informants' view of future prospects

Language maintenance is closely connected with the identity of speakers and their inclination to transmit the language to their children. Therefore, the informants were asked which language or which languages they would like their children (or their future children, if any) to learn. To this question, 21 informants answered that they would like their children to learn Hungarian and Swedish and possibly a third language. Twelve chose just the majority language, while eight chose the majority language and one or more other languages (but not Hungarian). Five chose other languages, above all English, and four were undecided.

Less than half the informants (21) thought it is important that their own children are interested in learning Hungarian, while ten did not think it is important at all. Learning Hungarian considered as even less important, since only 14 informants answered affirmatively on the question concerning participation in teaching. The answers showed that the informants believed that language was not as important for future generations as having an interest in Hungary and their own Hungarian background. Altogether, 37 informants agreed that it was important to have an interest in Hungary and their Hungarian background, five did not think that it was important and eight could not answer the question.

## 4. Results and discussion

If you ask Swedish Hungarians how the future looks and especially about maintaining the language and culture, their answers suggest that culture is more important than language. In his book *Language Policy Evaluation and the European Charter for Regional or Minority Languages* (see Grin 2003: 43–44) François Grin presents three conditions necessary for the use of a language: *capacity* (C), *opportunity* (O) and *desire or willingness* (D). Capacity (C) means a person must know the language and if they do not know it, they should have the opportunity to learn it. Capacity is a necessary requirement of language use. Opportunity (O) to use the language is also a prerequisite. In the case of some minority languages, linguistic vitality is limited to language use within the private sphere. In consequence, a governmental language policy and the support it gives can be significant for users of a minority language. The third prerequisite for minority language use is connected to the behaviour of the individual. The minority language is used only if speakers have a desire or willingness (D) to use it. Grin points out that in most cases minority speakers are bilingual or multilingual, and consequently can choose whether to use the minority or the majority language. Through their language choice, speakers can themselves favour the minority language. These three components are necessary for the use of minority languages and despite the fact that each component in and of itself represents an important part in the attempt to use and maintain the minority language, individually they are unable to secure the survival of the language; all three components must be present. Capacity (C) without opportunity and the desire to use the language is not sufficient, nor are opportunity (O) and desire (D) sufficient without capacity. Table 6 summarises the results of my investigation.

| 3 dim. COD | 2 dimensions CO | OD | CD | 1 dimension C | O | D | None | Total number of informants in Sweden |
|---|---|---|---|---|---|---|---|---|
| 9 | 1 | 11 | 2 | 1 | 3 | 20 | 3 | 50 |

Table 6. Grin's three dimensions and their distribution among the informants. (C = Capacity, O = Opportunity, D = Desire.)

The table shows that all three dimensions only occurred in a fifth of the informants (9 out of 50). According to Grin's theory, these informants have the prerequisites to maintain the language. In contrast, more than half had none or only one of these dimensions, which clearly means that they did not have sufficient prerequisites for language maintenance. The table also shows the number of informants with two dimensions, the most common being the "OD" group. This means they used Hungarian and had a positive attitude towards it, but did not possess sufficient knowledge of the language. Two informants belonged to the "CD" group, which means they had a good knowledge of the language and also a positive attitude, but less opportunity to use Hungarian. Furthermore, one informant belonged to the "CO" group, which indicates that the informant had both the knowledge and the opportunity to use Hungarian, but lacked the desire. Of those informants with only one dimension, most commonly they had the desire to use Hungarian, but they lacked the knowledge and the opportunity to use the language (see column "D" in the table). Three informants used the language despite lacking sufficient knowledge of it and having only a limited interest (see column "O" in the table). Only one informant was in the position of knowing the language well, but lacked the desire to use it (see column "C" in the table). The results show that the Hungarian language in Sweden is a threatened immigrant language, since only a quarter of the informants knew the language sufficiently well and only one fifth possessed the prerequisites for language use, that is, the knowledge, opportunity and desire to maintain it.

As shown at the beginning of the article, Hungarians are a rather large immigrant population in Sweden. The results of my investigation point to a Swedish Hungarian group with major differences: a first generation which has preserved the language and culture because of their internal value, and a second generation that is almost completely assimilated into the Swedish culture, considerably less active in Hungarian associations and activities, and with much less interest in culture and language preservation. The second generation does not know the Hungarian language to the same extent as their parents, consequently they do not have sufficient knowledge and self-confidence to be able to pass on the language to future generations. For the second generation, "Hungarianness" means different things than for the first generation. Above all else, "Hungarianness" means having a Hungarian background and roots, although to some it is a way of life. There is variation in the strength of the connection to the Hungarian language of second generation Hungarians. Some, for example, use it with relatives and acquaintances, some listen to music in Hungarian, some read websites in Hungarian while for others the connection to Hungarian culture may be limited to cooking Hungarian food or travelling to Hungary. For most second generation Hungarians, "Hungarianness" only means a feeling of being different or a knowledge of their Hungarian background. For many of them, their Hungarian heritage lives on through their parents, who usually live close by, and through other relatives and acquaintances, many still residing in Hungary. Yet they themselves do not show a great interest in maintaining their Hungarian heritage and do not take responsibility for the preservation of the language and culture for future generations. This, in most cases, is due to a lack of knowledge of Hungarian.

## Acknowledgment

I would like to express my gratitude to Björn Lundqvist and Sharelle Sånglöf for their great help with translation and editing.

# References

Alapszabály 2007 = *Az Őrszavak / Custos Anyanyelvápolók Egyesületének Alapszabálya*. Elfogadta és jóváhagyta a 2007. augusztus 11-i közgyűlés. Custos Anyanyelvápolók Egyesülete. Stockholm.

Beijer, Mai 2008: *Mest språk. Språk- och kulturkunskap i ett alltmer gränsöverskridande samhälle.* Stockholm: Myndigheten för skolutveckling.

Borbándi, Gyula 1996: *Emigráció és Magyarország. Nyugati magyarok a változások éveiben 1985–1995.* Basel-Budapest: Európai Protestáns Magyar Szabadegyetem.

Boross, Katalin 2006: „Az iskolák fölöttéb szükséges voltáról". Tömör helyzetfeltárás. – *Magyar Liget* 7. évfolyam 26. szám (2006/1). 20.

Fishman, Joshua 1964: Language Maintenance and Language Shift as a Field of Inquiry. – *Linguistics* 9. 32–70.

—— 1965: Who speaks what language to whom and when? – *Linguistics* 2. 67–88.

—— 1972: Domains and the Relationship between Micro- and Macrolinguistics. – Gumperz, John & Dell Hymes (eds), *Directions in Sociolinguistics. The ethnography of Communication.* New York: Holt, Rinehart and Winston.

FOLKET 2008 = Ungrare kan råda bot på läkarbristen i Flen. – *Folket* 01.08.2008.

Grin, François 2003: *Language Policy Evaluation and the European Charter for Regional or Minority Languages.* Hampshire and New York: Palgrave Macmillian.

György-Ullholm, Kamilla 2004: Language planning between pluralism and assimilationism. Reflections on Hungarian mother tongue instruction in Sweden. – *Estudios de Sociolingüística* 5(2). 277–298.

HTMH 2006 = 2005-ös jelentés a Kárpát-medencén kívül élő magyarság helyzetéről. Határon Túli Magyarok Hivatala. – <http://www.hhrf.org/htmh/printable_version.php> 13.1.2006.

Hyltenstam, Kenneth & Tuomela, Veli, 1996: Hemspråksundervisningen. – Kenneth Hyltenstam (ed.) *Tvåspråkighet med förhinder? Invandrar- och minoritetsundervisning i Sverige.* Lund: Studentlitteratur. 9–109.

Ikonen, Kristiina & Straszer, Boglárka 2006: *Maahanmuuttajaoppilaiden äidinkielen opetuksen asemasta ja opettajan koulutuksesta – opetuksen käynnistämisestä tähän päivään. Selvitys 2005.* Opetushallituksen julkaisemattoman selvityksen käsikirjoitus.

Kovács, Andor 1999: *A világ magyarsága.* Európa I. Budapest: MVSZ.

MV 1996 = *Magyarok Világszövetsége a nemzet szolgálatában.* World Federation of Hungarians. Második javított kiadás. Budapest: MVSZ Hivatala.

Pap, Veronika 2008: Énekszóval a svédországi magyarságért. – *Híradó* XXVI (110). 30.

SCB 1979 = *Grundskolan och gymnasieskolan 1978/79. Elever med annat hemspråk än svenska hösten 1978.* Statistiska meddelanden. Stockholm: Statistiska centralbyrån.

SCB 1984a = *Statistisk årsbok för Sverige 1985.* Årgång 71. Sveriges officiella statistik. Stockholm: Statistiska centralbyrån.

SCB 1984b = *Tema invandrare. Levnadsförhållanden.* Rapport 38. Sveriges officiella statistik. Stockholm, Örebro: Statistiska centralbyrån.

SCB 1987 = *Folkmängd 31 dec 1986 enligt indelningen 1 jan 1987.* Del 3. Fördelning efter kön, ålder, civilstånd och medborgarskap i kommuner mm. Sveriges officiella statistik. Stockholm: Statistiska centralbyrån.

SCB 1990 = *Folkmängd 31 dec 1989 enligt indelningen 1 jan 1990.* Del 3. Fördelning efter kön, ålder, civilstånd och medborgarskap i kommuner mm. Sveriges officiella statistik. Stockholm: Statistiska centralbyrån.

SCB 1991 = *Tema invandrare. Levnadsförhållanden.* Rapport 69. Sveriges officiella statistik. Stockholm: Statistiska centralbyrån.

SCB 1992 = *Utbildningsstatistisk årsbok 1992. Sveriges officiella statistik.* Stockholm: SCB, Publikationstjänsten.

SCB 1994a = *Statistisk årsbok för Sverige 1995.* Årgång 81. Sveriges officiella statistik. Stockholm: Statistiska centralbyrån.

SCB 1994b = *Befolkningsstatistik del 3, 1993.* Statistik över folkmängden fördelad efter kön, ålder, civilstånd och medborgarskap i hela riket, län och kommuner. Stockholm: Statistiska centralbyrån.

SCB 2002 = *Meddelanden i samordningsfrågor för Sveriges officiella statistik. Raports on Statistical Co-ordination for the Official Statistics of Sweden. 2002: 3. Personer med utländsk bakgrund. Riktlinjer för redovisning i statistiken. Statistics on persons with foreign background. Guidelines and recommendations.* Örebro: Statistiska Centralbyrån.

SCB 2004 = *Befolkningsstatistik del 3, 2003.* Statistik över folkmängden fördelad efter kön, ålder, civilstånd, födelseland och medborgarskap i hela riket, län och kommuner. Stockholm: Statistiska centralbyrån.

SCB 2006 = *Tabeller över Sveriges befolkning 2005.* BE01 Befolkningsstatistik. Sveriges officiella statistik. Örebro: Statistiska centralbyrån.

SCB 2007a = *Tabeller över Sveriges befolkning 2006.* BE01 Befolkningsstatistik. Sveriges officiella statistik. Örebro: Statistiska Centralbyrå.

SCB 2007b = *Utbildningsstatistisk årsbok 2008.* Tabeller. Utbildning och forskning. Sveriges officiella statistik. Stockholm: Statistiska centralbyrån.

SCB 2008a = *Tabeller över Sveriges befolkning 2007.* BE01 Befolkningsstatistik. Sveriges officiella statistik. Örebro: Statistiska Centralbyrå.

SCB 2008b = Statistiska Centralbyråns databas: <http//www.ssd.scb.se/databaser> 14.8.2008.

SCB 2008c = *Befolkningens utbildning. Utbildningsnivå efter födelseland och kön 2006, 25-64 år.* – <http://www.scb.se/templates> 1.4.2008.

SMOSZ 2008 = Ungerska Riksförbundets hemsida, Svédországi Magyarok Országos Szövetsége. – <http://www.smosz.org/sindex.htm> 20.2.2008.

SP 2008 = Ungrare bidrar till levande samhälle. – *Smålandsposten 31.7.2008.*

Straszer, Boglárka 2006a: Femtio år i Sverige. – *Invandrare och minoriteter* 5: 9–12.

—— 2006b: Ungrare – en osynlig men aktiv invandrargrupp i Norden. – Gunilla Ransbo (ed.), *Humanister forskar. Humanistdagen vid Uppsala universitet 2006.* Uppsala: Uppsala universitet. 211–217.

—— 2008: Unkarilaistaustaiset lapset äidinkielen opetuksessa Uppsalassa – havaintoja vanhempien odotuksista ja opettajan kokemuksista. Abstract in Swedish. Ungerskspråkiga barn i modersmålsundervisningen i Uppsala ur föräldrar- och lärarperspektiv. – Ulla Börestam, Satu Gröndahl & Boglárka Straszer: *Revitalisera mera! En artikelsamling om den språkliga mångfalden i Norden tillägnad Leena Huss.* Uppsala Multiethnic Papers 50. Centrum för multietnisk forskning. Uppsala: Uppsala universitet. 179–196.

—— 2009: Unkarilaiset Suomessa. – *Siirtolaisuus/Migration* 1/2009: 12–21.

—— (2010a): *Ungrare, ungerska och ungersk kultur i Sverige och Finland. En översikt.* ["Hungarians, Hungarian and Hungarian culture in Sweden and Finland. A survey."] Digitala skrifter från Hugo Valentin-centrum 1. Uppsala: Uppsala universitet. <http://urn.kb.se/resolve?urn=urn:nbn:se:uu:diva-133236>

—— (2010b): "Unkarilaisuus tekee minusta persoonallisen". Pohdintoja toisen polven suomenunkarilaisten kieli-identiteetistä. – Martikainen, Tuomas & Lotta Haikkola (eds) *Maahanmuutto ja sukupolvet.* Tietolipas 233. Nuorisotutkimusverkoston julkaisuja 106. Helsinki: Suomalaisen Kirjallisuuden Seura & Nuorisotutkimusseura. 193–216.

—— (forthcoming 1): Embracing Hungarian: top-down emancipation of an immigrant language in Finland. – Leena Huss & Nolan J. Shaun (eds), The Many Faces of Language Emancipation. Special issue of *International Journal of the Sociology of Language*. No. 209.

—— (forthcoming 2): *"Ungerska för rötternas skull"*. *Språkval och identitet bland andragenerationens ungrare i Sverige och Finland*. Dissertation for the degree of Doctor of Philosophy in Finno-Ugric languages. Doctoral Thesis. Acta Universitatis Upsaliensis. Studia Uralica Upsaliensia. Uppsala: Uppsala universitet.

Stuber, György 2006: Anyanyelv, kultúra és kapcsolatok az új Európában. – *Híradó* XXV(99), 11.

SV 2002 = Flera språk – fler möjligheter. Utveckling av modersmålsstöd och modersmålsundervisningen 2002. Rapport till regeringen 15 maj 2002. Dnr 01-01: 2751. Skolverket.

Svanberg, Ingvar & Tydén, Mattias 1992: *Tusen år av invandring. En svensk kulturhistoria*. Stockholm: Gidlunds Bokförlag.

Svensson, Anders 1992: *Ungrare i folkhemmet, Svensk flyktingpolitik i kalla krigets skugga*. Cesic Studies in International Conflict 7. Lund University Press. Lund: Studentlitteratur.

Szabó, Mátyás 1988: Ungrare. – Ingvar Svanberg & Harald Runblom (eds), *Det mångkulturella Sverige. En handbok om etniska grupper och minoriteter*. Centrum för multietnisk forskning vid Uppsala universitet. Stockholm: Gidlunds Bokförlag. 463–471.

—— 1997: *Vägen mot medborgarskap. Studier i medborgarskapsbyte och integration*. Malmö: Bokförlaget Arena.

Szöllősi, Antal 1999: *Svédországi magyarság 1956-ig*. Stockholm: Ungerska Arkivet.

—— 2008: 35 éves az Északi Magyar Archívum. – *Híradó* XXVI (110), 14–15.

Tóth, Krisztián 2007: A magyar nagykövetség hírei. – *Híradó* XXVI (110): 14.

Zsiga, Erik 2007: *Hejdå Östeuropa!* Stockholm: Timbro.

# Nyelv és identitás a svédországi magyarok körében

*Boglárka Straszer*

E tanulmány a Svédországban élő magyarok történetébe, demográfiai és geográfiai felosztottságába és nyelvhasználati lehetőségeibe, valamint a második generációt képviselő 50 informáns nyelvválasztásába és azonosságtudatába nyújtott betekintést. A vizsgálati eredmények szerint a gyermekkori nyelvhasználat a családban, valamint bizonyos mértékben a kapcsolat a magyar nyelvvel és kultúrával magyarországi utazások és magyar anyanyelvi oktatásban való részvétel formájában a legtöbb esetben egyenesen arányos a későbbi magyar nyelvi kompetenciával és ezzel részint szerepet játszik a nyelvválasztásban és az identitástudat kialakulásában is.

A vizsgálatban részt vevő, Svédországban élő második generációs magyar informánsok harmadrésze csak a magyar nyelvet használta a szüleivel és testvéreivel való kommunikációban gyermekkorában, míg mások a magyart is és a svédet is vagy csak a svédet és egy harmadik nyelvet használtak a családi kommunikációban. Az informánsok fele évi rendszerességgel utazott Magyarországra, amíg egy negyed résznek nagyon ritkán vagy sohasem volt lehetősége ellátogatni Magyarországon élő rokonaikhoz és ismerőseikhez. Az informánsok jelentős része részesült élete valamely stádiumában magyar nyelvoktatásban, leggyakrabban még általános iskolás korában.

A magyar nyelvi kompetenciájukat az informánsok jóval gyengébben ítélték meg, mint a svéd nyelvi kompetenciájukat, főképpen az olvasás/szövegértés és az írás területén. A magyar nyelv használatát viszont nem kizárólag csak a kompetencia, hanem az informánsok jelenlegi családi helyzete, érdeklődése és lehetőségei határozzák meg a vizsgált anyagban. A magyar nyelvet az informánsok egyharmada használja naponta. A nyelvet leggyakrabban családtagokkal való telefonbeszélgetések és találkozások alkalmával használják, míg más doménekben a magyar nyelv használata igencsak behatárolt. Saját gyermekével csak egyetlen egy informáns használja a magyar nyelvet, ennek ellenére az informánsoknak közel fele szeretné, ha gyermeke megtanulna magyarul. Az informánsok a nyelvnél jóval fontosabbnak tartják a magyar kultúra, valamint a magyar gyökerek és Magyarország ismeretét. Magyar azonosságtudatukat részint a nyelv, részint pedig a kultúra ismerete és gyermekkori emlékek határozzák meg. A nyelvi kompetenciától függetlenül az informánsoknak közel fele anyanyelvének tartja a magyart és az informánsoknak több mint a fele magyarnak vagy magyarnak is és svédnek is tartja magát. Ennek ellenére csak néhányan azonosulnak a magyarsággal magyarországi tartózkodásuk idején, mégis az informánsoknak közel fele otthonának érzi Magyarországot is.

A nyelvmegőrzési lehetőségekről Grin elméleti modelljét alkalmazva az a következtetés vonható le a vizsgált anyagból, hogy Svédországban veszélyeztetett helyzetben van a magyar nyelv, hiszen csak az informánsok ötödénél van jelen a nyelvmegőrzés mindhárom feltétele.

A tanulmányban szereplő adatok finn-svéd összehasonlító nyelvszociológiai kutatásom eredményeire alapulnak, amelyben a magyar nyelv használatát és szerepét vizsgáltam meg Finn- és Svédországban élő magyar származású felnőttek körében.

RAIMO RAAG

# I'm Estonian – What Is Your Excuse? – Ethnic and Linguistic Aspects of the Identity of Estonians in Sweden

## Abstract

The key topic of my article is the question of selection of informants and generalisation about the identity and linguistic development of ethnic minorities such as Estonians in Sweden. A sketch of the historical background of the Estonian diaspora in Sweden illuminates the grounds for a division of the population into three groups: the mainstream group, outsiders and the fringe group. The designation "diaspora Estonian" or "Estonian abroad" usually refers to the mainstream group and scholarly work done on diaspora Estonian history, identities, and language focuses on precisely this group. Thus, we know little about the fringe group and, especially, of the outsiders.

The linguistic build-up of Swedish Estonian includes pre-war Estonian lexemes and Swedish influence which occurs in the lexicon as well as in the grammar of Swedish Estonian usage. The use of such characteristics combined with an ambition to avoid using alleged or real Soviet Estonian words and expressions became linguistic markers of group affiliation.

Today, the Estonian language in Sweden is considered to be a migrant language, notwithstanding the fact that it fulfills the requirements of an official minority language as formulated in the European Charter for Regional or Minority Languages, Strasbourg, 5.XI. 1992, and the Framework Convention for the protection of National Minorities, Strasbourg, 1.II 1995, ratified by Sweden in 2000. In January, 2009, a petition for the recognition of Estonian as a minority language in Sweden was submitted to the Swedish Minister of Integration.

*Ethnic and Linguistic Context of Identity: Finno-Ugric Minorities.* 197–216.
Uralica Helsingiensia 5. Helsinki 2011.

# 1. Introduction

In the early 1980s, young expatriate Estonians could been seen on the streets of Stockholm wearing T-shirts displaying the words "I'm Estonian – what is your excuse?" I am quoting verbatim as the words were in English. The choice of language was not surprising as English had already become part of everyday life in Sweden by then. In fact, I suspect the fad of wearing T-shirts with these words actually came from Estonians living in North America, as did perhaps the T-shirts themselves. Many elderly Estonians in Sweden found the message either objectionable or, at the very least, odd. This was because Estonians were being made to look deviant by the mere fact of their nationality. However, as far as I know, the older generation tolerated the T-shirts and let the young people have their way.

This event took place some thirty five years after the end of the Second World War, and the young people wearing the T-shirts were without doubt born outside Estonia. If approached and asked, they would have described themselves either as simply 'Estonians', 'Estonians in Sweden', or 'Swedish Estonians'. However, the question of identity has not always been so clear for Estonians in Sweden. Soon after the arrival in Sweden of more than 22,000 Estonians and nearly 6,000 Estonian Swedes (Berge 1992: 33), an event which mainly took place during two rather turbulent months in the autumn of 1944, the refugee group experienced a split. The split was a result of the choice that all refugees and migrants have to make soon after arrival in their new country of residence: whether to adopt the new language and culture, or attempt to preserve the language and culture of the homeland.

John Widdup Berry and Uichol Kim identify four courses of 'acculturative' action undertaken by emigrants in their new environment. If a person preserves his or her old culture but at the same time engages with the new society, this is termed *integration*; if the old culture is preserved but the new one rejected, this is termed *separation*; if the old culture is abandoned and the new one embraced, this is termed *assimilation*; and if both the old and the new cultures are rejected, this is termed *marginalisation* (Berry & Kim 1988; Berry 1990: 243–246; Raag 2004: 179). However, before we concern ourselves with ques-

tions of the language and identity of Estonians in Sweden, we should
consider matters in their wider context by examining the background
information on the Estonian diaspora in general (section 2) and on
Estonians in Sweden in particular (section 3).

## 2. The rise of Estonian communities in the West

The phrase "Estonians abroad" is commonly associated with Estonian
refugees who fled to the West during the Second World War, and their
descendants. This is, however, not the whole truth. As a matter of fact,
on the eve of the Second World War some 176,000 Estonians already
lived outside Estonia. They mainly lived in the Soviet Union, where
they numbered 143,500. In contrast, only 32,500 Estonians lived in
other countries abroad, notably in the USA, Canada, Australia, and
Brazil, and also in the neighbouring countries of Latvia and Finland.
Nonetheless, the arrival of some 70,000 Estonian war refugees represented a significant addition to the relatively small number of Estonians scattered throughout the West. It was this group of Estonians who
managed to attract a great deal of attention to their diverse political,
cultural and social activities, and consequently, they became connected with the phrase "Estonians abroad", while the more numerous
expatriate Estonians behind the Iron Curtain – in central and northwest Russia, West Siberia, on Russia's Pacific coast, in the Crimea and
Georgia – received little or no attention.

Excluding the political arrests, executions, and mass deportations
carried out by the Soviets and the Nazis between 1940–1944, the wartime exodus from Estonia took place mainly between mid-August and
early October 1944.[1] Most refugees left for Finland, Sweden or Germany. Virtually all the Estonians who fled to Finland then proceeded
on to Sweden, in order to avoid being handed over to the Soviet Union.
This fear grew even greater when Finland and the Soviet Union signed

---

1. For details on population losses in Estonia during the war, see the Reports of the
Estonian International Commission for the Investigation of Crimes Against Humanity (Hiio, Maripuu & Paavle 2006) and Rahi-Tamm (2007).

the Moscow Armistice on September 19, 1944. When the war drew to a close, some 40,000 Estonians had arrived in Germany (Kool 1999: 8–11) and more than 22,000 in Sweden (Berge 1992: 33).[2]

The refugees were placed in camps where they generally refused, on political grounds, to return to Soviet-occupied Estonia. While the camps in Sweden were closed down by the summer 1945, by which time their occupants had either been absorbed into Swedish society or re-emigrated, the majority of Estonians in Germany had to survive in camps for displaced civilians for several years (Tegeler 2007). The last camps were not closed down until 1951. Under the International Refugee Organization resettlement project, which ran between 1947 and 1951, 27,096 of the Estonians in Germany were sent to more than 25 different countries (in Western Europe, the Americas, Africa, Asia, and Oceania) across the world (Madise 1966; Raag 1999: 64–73). Others migrated on their own initiative. Only those who were unable to emigrate because of old-age or ill health, and those who had already found a job and a place to live remained in Germany.

By the end of the 1950s, after the resettlements, the largest Estonian communities in the West were to be found in the United States, Canada, Sweden, and Australia (see table 1). Approximately three quarters of all Estonians in the West lived in one of these four states.

---

2. For a comprehensive study on the exodus to Sweden, see Andræ (2004, in Swedish; 2005, in Estonian). See also the contributions to the conference "[The] Great Exodus in 1944. The Flight of Estonians to the West and its Influences" in Kumer-Haukanõmm et alii (2006) and recent surveys by Kumer-Haukanõmm (2009) and Raag (2009b).

| Country | 1945 | ca 1960 | 1997–2008 |
|---|---|---|---|
| Germany | 40,000 | 3,000 | 4,469 (1997) |
| Sweden | 22,500 | 16,000 | 26,438 (1997) |
| United States | 9,000 | 19,938 (1960) | 26,760 (1990) |
| Canada | 2,200 | 18,550 (1961) | 10,848 (2008) |
| Finland | 2,000 | n.d. | 22,357 (2008) |
| Brazil | 1,800 | 2,000 | 120 |
| Australia | 1,100 | 6,549 (1954) | 6,884 (1988) |
| Denmark | 700 | n.d. | 50 |
| United Kingdom | 300 | 4,000 | 2,730 (1992) |
| Russia | 130,498 (1939) | 78,566 (1959) | 28,113 (2002) |
| Latvia | 7,014 (1935) | 4,610 (1959) | 2,537 (2005) |
| Georgia | n.d. | 2,148 (1959) | 1,800 |
| Other countries | 26,100 | 14,600 | 26,900 |

Table 1.  The number of expatriate Estonians in 1945, circa 1960, and 1997–2008,
by country of residence. Note: Round figures are approximations. The figures for
1945 include both pre-war residents of Estonian extraction and war refugees; n.d.
= no data available. Sources: Aun (1985), *Eesti entsüklopeedia* (2003), *Eesti kroonika*
(1957), Estonian Central Council in Canada (2009), Haas & Siska (1988), Madise
(1966), Mela (2007), Ministry of Science and Education (2009), Pennar, Parming &
Rebane (1975), Raag (1999), Statistics Finland (2009).

By the 1950s, the refugees had established themselves in their new
environment and many had even managed to achieve a degree of
material comfort equal to, or even higher than that available to them
in pre-war Estonia. In this respect, the Estonians in Sweden were at an
advantage to their compatriots in (what was then) West Germany and
other countries, as they had reached their new country of residence as
early as 1944 and 1945, whereas most Estonians who left Germany or
Sweden for other Western European countries, or who left the conti-
nent altogether, only arrived in their new countries between 1947 and
1954.

Estonians' adaptation to and absorption into their new societies
occured simultaneous to the creation of a large number of "Mini-Esto-

nias", which were established where a sufficient number of Estonians had settled, in other words, practically throughout the world. This was due to the fact that many refugees, even if they did not form an actual majority, had a strong wish to retain their Estonian identity and language. This is an attitude typical of political refugees. In contrast, economic migrants tend to view the retention of the old language and culture as less significant.

In order to preserve their language and culture, Estonian expatriate communities were created virtually on arrival in the new country. As a consequence, exile societies very soon included associations for various occupational groups, clubs for socializing and hobby activities, athletic clubs, political parties and elected or self-appointed representations, churches, students' associations, Scout and Guide troops, publishing houses, newspapers and journals, and last but not least, ethnic schools – especially Sunday schools, which became very numerous in Estonian exile communities.[3]

The sphere of activity for the bulk of these associations was limited to a particular city. Alongside these, there arose societies and clubs of a broader scope, covering either whole provinces, larger regions, or the whole country. Some even became international, spanning the continents of Europe, North and South America, Australia, and Africa. Therefore, Estonian expatriate associations can be distinguished according to whether they are local, regional, national or international (Raag 2004: 182). Eventually the central organisations in Canada, Sweden, Australia, the United Kingdom, West Germany and the United States, supported by smaller Estonian communities in Belgium, France and South Africa, agreed to work together, adopting the name the Estonian World Council (*Ülemaailmne Eesti Kesknõukogu*), and setting up their headquarters in the United States. The official date for this event was October 1, 1955, when representatives from the central organisations met in New York (<http://english.uekn.org/>).

---

3. A list of Estonian organisations, including congregations, schools and outdoor areas abroad, can be found at the home page of the Ministry of Science and Education of Estonia, <http://www.eesti.ee/rahvuskaaslased/index.php?lang=en>.

## 3. Estonians in Sweden: a thumbnail sketch

At the time of the events described in the previous paragraph, the number of Estonian expatriate organisations in Sweden was remarkably high, numbering several hundred. According to a list of past and present Estonian organisations in Sweden, more than 700 different organisations had been active at some time or other prior to Estonian re-independence in 1991 (Äro *s.a.*).[4] In the 1960s and 1970s, the Estonian exile community in Sweden openly admitted that it was internally divided and overorganised, joking that: "Wherever there are two Estonians, there are at least three Estonian central organisations".

After Estonia regained its independence, many organisations, especially those with overt political aims, closed down, since the goal – reestablishment of Estonian independence – had been reached. During this period some organisations also merged and new ones were established.

Today, there are about 100 active Estonian organizations. They are mainly to be found in the large central Swedish cities of Stockholm and Gothenburg, the industrial towns of Uppsala, Gävle, Eskilstuna, Örebro, Norrköping, the districts of Värmland and Gotland, the southern Swedish cities of Lund and Malmö and the northern Swedish city of Luleå. Estonians maintain a weekly newspaper, *Eesti Päevaleht* (The Estonian Daily), which currently has a circulation of slightly more than 2,000, and the political and cultural periodical *Rahvuslik Kontakt* (National Contact) which is published quarterly.

As for instruction in Estonian, in Stockholm there are two Estonian nursery schools and a primary school for children between the ages of seven and sixteen, and in Gothenburg a Swedish-Estonian bilingual nursery school. In addition, Estonian is taught twice a week in primary and secondary schools (gymnasiums) in about ten municipalities, mainly in Central Sweden. Furthermore, Estonian language courses are organised by Swedish adult educational associations. Finally, Estonian is taught as a major subject at Uppsala University.

---

4.   For a comprehensive report on Estonian societal life in Sweden after the Second World War, still unsurpassed as to coverage and accuracy, see Kangro (1976a; in Estonian) and Kangro (1976b; in Swedish).

Swedish legislation distinguishes between national minorities and minority languages on the one hand, and immigrant groups and immigrant languages on the other. Estonians in Sweden have twice applied for recognition as a historical minority, appealing to the fact that Estonians have been living in Sweden since at least the 18th century, when thousands of Estonian peasants fled serfdom by crossing the Baltic Sea in small boats and set up home on Swedish soil (for details, see Raag 1999: 33–34 and Raag 2010) and that parts of Estonia were a part of Sweden for more than 150 years. The last appeal was filed with the Minister for Integration and Gender Equality in early 2009 (Raag 2009a), but it was swiftly rejected. Consequently, Estonians in Sweden are still considered immigrants by the authorities.

In Sweden, the Estonian way of life is currently upheld by some four to five thousand Estonians.[5] This core is made up of former war refugees, and their children and grandchildren, immigrants who predominantly came to Sweden from Soviet Estonia in the 1970s and 1980s, and Estonians who have recently moved from re-independent Estonia to Sweden. The language of Estonian social life in Sweden is Estonian, the command of which, albeit not flawless on the part of all participants, actually serves as an implicit 'ticket of admission' to Estonian social events.

A crucial factor in the development of the Estonian exile community in Sweden was that the refugee group arriving during the Second World War included individuals from all the social classes of pre-war Estonian society. In addition to the small farm-holders and coastal dwellers, who made up the majority of refugees, there were many ordinary townspeople and also a sufficient number of educated

---

5. It must be mentioned that immigration from Estonia to Sweden began again on a larger scale after the collapse of the Soviet Union and after Estonia had regained its independence in 1991. The net immigration of ethnic Estonians to Sweden during the last two decades amounts to approximately 3,100 persons. At the end of 2007, a total of 9,800 Estonian-born persons (3,938 males and 5,862 females) lived in Sweden. In addition there were 5,192 Swedish-born persons (2,630 males and 2,562 females), who had two Estonian-born parents. These numbers, however, fail to give a true picture of the size of the Estonian group in Sweden, because Swedish statistics record population by country of birth and citizenship, not by language or ethnic affiliation.

people, including artists and politicians, who were able to lead the exile community.

It is sometimes claimed that the exodus of Estonians during the Second World War mainly consisted of intellectuals. This is not really the case, at least regarding Estonians in Sweden. In 1953, slightly over half the Estonians living in Sweden had completed compulsory elementary school education, nearly 14 percent secondary school, almost 24 percent high school and less than ten percent university education (Reinans 2008: 1329, table 4). It is, however, a fact that the Estonian refugee group in Sweden differs, in terms of education, from the Swedish population in that, the proportion of Swedes with a university degree is considerably lower, as Reinans (1999: 13–16; 2004: 1328) reports.

It is beyond the scope of this article to look for reasons for the fact that Estonians are more highly educated. However, two such reasons may be that pre-war Estonia placed a strong emphasis on education, which resulted in an excess of university graduates. In Sweden, the situation was different. In pre-war Sweden, university education was still not easily accessible to middle and working class Swedes. As a consequence, the level of education of the population at large was inevitably lower than in Estonia. Secondly, Swedish family traditions largely determine whether children proceed to higher education or not. The attitude of working class Swedes towards education tends to be negative whereas Estonian attitudes to education are much more favourable. Consequently, in Sweden, Estonians from all levels of society are keen on their children going into higher education. This explains why Swedish Estonians generally have a higher level of education not only than Swedes, but also than those Estonians who remained in Estonia, as Reinans (1999: 16) reports.

## 4. The core, periphery, and the fringe

Far from all refugees participated in the activities organised by the exile community of their new country of residence. In 1955, Andrus Saareste, a former professor of Estonian at the University of Tartu, who went on, as a refugee to work at Uppsala University, claimed that

10,000 of his compatriots in Sweden were failing to fulfil their moral duty as political refugees by their non-participation in the activities organised by the Estonian community (Saareste 1955). They had, instead, abandoned Estonian culture and embraced the new culture in Sweden; to use the terminology of Berry and Kim (1988; quoted from Berry 1990) they had become assimilated. This is the split within the refugee group I referred to above.

Even if we take the number of 'lost souls' mentioned by Saareste with a pinch of salt, the fact remains that Estonian identity abroad was, and is, maintained principally by people who – to use the term proposed by Berry and Kim (1988; quoted from Berry 1990) – have become integrated, who are loyal citizens of their new country but who have entered its cultural sphere without rejecting their Estonian roots. Those 'hermetically sealed' or marginalised Estonians have also helped to maintain Estonianness, but they have been far fewer in number. However, when taken together, marginalised Estonians and those who have integrated form the core of the Estonian exile community (Raag 2004: 192).

Around this core we find the periphery. This consists of people who, for one reason or another, do not take part in Estonian social or cultural life abroad. The reasons vary a great deal, from the purely personal, e.g. starting a family, looking after children, maintaining a career, or from a world view incompatible with that of the core Estonians, to reasons determined by geography, e.g. from living away from Estonian centres of activity in Sweden (Raag 2004: 192). Such people may take pride in their national background and its traditions, but they seldom maintain any traditions. Usually they are rather poor at Estonian or do not speak the language at all. However, they might still consider themselves Estonians or Swedish Estonians, even if they were born in Sweden. Consequently, one could say they have an Estonian identity under certain circumstances, or that theirs is a 'symbolic ethnicity', which is a term used by Herbert Gans (1978). This implies the possibility of movement or 'migration' from the core to the periphery, or *vice versa*; both groups appear to be open-ended.

It is important not to confuse those on the periphery with the very many people who form the passive audience for Estonian culture and ethnic activities abroad. Even if they are just the audience, just consumers of Estonian culture, they belong to the core and their role in supporting Estonian culture abroad cannot be overestimated.[6]

Where the periphery stops, we find the outsiders. To this group belong people of Estonian extraction who, quite like the people on the periphery, never take part in Estonian social or cultural life abroad. They neither speak Estonian, nor maintain contact with relatives in Estonia. They are the 'lost souls' of the Estonian community in Sweden, the assimilated, in the terminology of Berry and Kim (1988; from Berry 1990).

Thus the split in the Estonian community in Sweden developed into a permanent division into the core (or mainstream) group, the periphery and the outsiders. This division reflects people's different attitude towards their Estonian 'heritage' and to their new home country, and its culture and language.

## 5. Language use among Estonians in Sweden

We now proceed to a linguistic account of Swedish Estonian. The first problem we face is deciding what 'Swedish Estonian' actually is. Should only the language used by the core group be recorded and analysed, or should the usage of outsiders also be included in the analysis? Needless to say, the designation 'diaspora Estonian' or 'Estonians abroad' (*väliseestlased* in Estonian) usually refers to the language of the mainstream group. Scholarly work on diaspora Estonian history, identities and language focuses on just this group. Thus we know very little about the periphery and even less about the outsiders.

The usual procedure in classical dialectology was to select informants who were not only elderly, but who were also uneducated and untravelled, and who could produce examples of 'genuine' dialect. It was a long time before dialectologists realised that 'genuine' dialect did not necessarily mean 'typical' (Chambers & Trudgill 1980: 56). Who would be the most 'typical' Swedish Estonian informant? A young person, an educated person, a well-travelled person?

---

6. Recent accounts of cultural activities of Estonians abroad, including Sweden, have been published by Valmas (2003; publishing), Hirvesoo (1996; music), Järv (2009; theatricals), and Lääne (2000; athletics).

Obviously, standard sociolinguistic procedure should be applied: informants should be selected at random in such a way that the whole spectrum of linguistic usage is reflected in the recordings and subsequent analysis. This method gives us a picture of Swedish Estonian that is characterised by great variation. This variation is manifested in informants' differing proficiency in Estonian, the extent to which they use Swedicisms, dialectisms and archaisms in lexicon, grammar and pronunciation, and their capacity or willingness to adhere to the rules of the current standard variety of Estonian. (See, e.g. Raag 1982, 1983, 1985, Lindström 1998, Laagus et alii 2004.) It is the task of the scholar to record the facts of this diversity. However, even if it is difficult to generalise about the linguistic usage of Estonians in Sweden, there is a sufficient number of informants with shared lexical, grammatical and phonological or phonetic characteristics to justify recognising Swedish Estonian as a regional variety of Estonian in its own.

Estonians who fled to Sweden during the Second World War had an understandable need to dissociate themselves from Soviet-occupied Estonia while still wanting to emphasize their Estonianness in their new country, both within the expatriate community and externally, vis-à-vis Swedish society. The linguistic means of achieving these ends was to preserve the Estonian language in as "pure" and "uncorrupted" form as possible. In practise this meant preserving pre-war lexemes, and, above all, avoiding the neologisms of the Soviet era. This explains the refusal of many Swedish Estonians to adopt the Standard Estonian word *korrus* 'storey, floor' and to stick to its traditional synonym *kord*, or *majakord*. The Standard Estonian word was considered a Sovietism, and therefore objectionable. In actual fact, however, the idea that *korrus* is a Sovietism is not entirely correct as *korrus* was introduced into Estonian by the building trade just before the Second World War. Nonetheless, *korrus* only began to replace *kord/majakord* in common usage only after its inclusion in an Estonian dictionary printed in 1946, after which it was adopted by the print media.

Disapproval of Soviet neologisms was particularly strong if they had ideological overtones, or if they were thought to be of Russian origin. For example, the word *natsionalism* was used in the pre-Soviet sense of 'nationalism; patriotism', as was its pre-war synonym *rahvuslus*. In contrast, the new Soviet meaning was 'bourgeous (i.e. anti-Soviet) nationalism'. In the West it was also completely out of the question, to refer to the so-called "forest-brother" (*metsavend*), the Estonian anti-Soviet guerrilla, as *bandiit*, literally 'bandit', which was a designation that originated from Soviet Russian criminal law. (It was not until 1961 that Soviet Estonia had its own criminal code.)

Disapproval could also be directed towards seemingly "pure" Estonian neologisms. Such was the case with *tuusik* 'a voucher for a rest home'; a word introduced in the early post-war years as an Estonian equivalent for the Russian *путёвка*. Another example is *raal*, introduced in 1967, which means 'computer'. This word was objectionable to Estonians abroad on account of its alleged Russian origin; *raal* was claimed to originate from the (Russian) name of the first Soviet computers, *Урал*, literally 'the Ural Mountains'.

A further way of maintaining the "purity" of the beloved mother-tongue (to speak with Fishman's term), was to introduce Western substitutes for odious Sovietisms. For example, *terpsulg*, 'a ball-point pen', was introduced to compete with, and perhaps replace, both the Soviet Estonian neologism *pastapliiats* and Swedish Estonian *küülspetspenna*, which was a Swedish lexical import. However attractive this word was, it failed, however, to become established either in Swedish Estonian or to spread to (Soviet) Estonia.

Even the use of Swedicisms like *end klaarima* 'to manage, get on, make out' (Standard Estonian: *hakkama saama, toime tulema*) might be interpreted as a means of signifying affiliation with the Estonian community in Sweden, regardless of the fact that Estonians in Sweden thought Swedicisms should be avoided – for the sake of the purity of the language. In order to introduce Estonian equivalents for "words that are urgently needed", around the end of the 1950s, a language committee was established in the Estonian Learned Society in Sweden under the guidance of Valter Tauli, an Estonian linguist living in Uppsala. The committee's task was to introduce Estonian words for a number of Swedish and English loanwords. However, most of the words introduced by this language committee failed to enter into common usage in either Swedish Estonian or Estonian in Estonia (Raag 1982: 114–116, 121–122, 126), and indeed the very existence of these words is totally unknown, even to Estonian linguists, in Estonia today.

Today, after Standard Estonian has, for the third time in a century, again been forced to adapt to a completely new social order, it seems much easier for Swedish Estonians to adopt Standard Estonian neologisms. It must, however, be mentioned that Swedish Estonians sometimes distance themselves from Standard Estonian words or expressions by adding the phrase *nagu nüüd üteldakse* 'as the saying now goes' after the word or expression in question. This could be an indication that the Standard Estonian word or expression has not been fully accepted. At the same time, there are signs of a certain polarisation within the Estonian community in Sweden as not all Swedish Estonians have adopted Standard Estonian.

In conclusion, the use of pre-war lexemes and Swedicisms combined with the avoidance of Soviet Estonian neologisms are the linguistic markers of group affiliation for Estonians in Sweden. It could even be claimed that fifty years of separate development has given rise to a new geographical variety of Estonian, a variety that, in addition to certain internal innovations and pre-war pecularities, has been coloured by Swedish, the majority language of the host country.

I will refrain from presenting a list of lexical, grammatical and phonological or phonetic characteristics of Swedish Estonian here, and simply refer to two forthcoming publications in which descriptions of Swedish Estonian are to be found. The first is a collection of articles covering ten varieties of Estonian spoken outside Estonia, including Swedish Estonian (Praakli & Viikberg 2010). This collection will be published in Estonia. The second publication will be exclusively devoted to the phonetic, grammatical, lexical, and pragmatic aspects of Swedish Estonian and is being compiled at the Department of Modern Languages in Uppsala (Keevallik et alii forthcoming).

In summary, the text on the T-shirts that young expatriate Estonians wore in Stockholm in the early 1980s, "I'm Estonian – what is your excuse?", were certainly not meant as a challenge to elderly Estonians, nor did they imply that Estonians per se were in some way deviant. The word had a plain message: they were an overt demonstration of ethnic affiliation and ethnic pride. As the American experimental physicist and Nobel Prize winner Leon Lederman claimed in 1984: "If a basic idea is too complicated to fit on a T-shirt, it's probably wrong."

# References

Andræ, Carl Göran 2004: *Sverige och den stora flykten från Estland 1943–1944*. Acta Academiae Regiae Gustavi Adolphi, LXXXIII. Uppsala: Kungliga Gustav Adolfs Akademien för svensk folkkultur.

—— 2005: *Rootsi ja suur põgenemine Eestist 1943–1944*. Tallinn: Olion.

Äro, Johannes (*s.a.*): *Eesti organisatsioonide register*. Manuscript.

Aun, Karl 1985: *The Political Refugees. A History of the Estonians in Canada*. Toronto: McClelland and Stewart.

Berge, Anders 1992: *Flyktingpolitik i stormakts skugga. Sverige och de sovjetryska flyktingarna under andra världskriget*. Uppsala Multiethnic Papers 26. Uppsala: Centrum för multietnisk forskning.

Berry, John W. 1990: Psychology of Acculturation: Understanding Individuals Moving Between Cultures. – Richard Brislin (ed.), *Applied Cross-Cultural Psychology*. Cross-Cultural Research and Methodology Series 14. Newbury Park, Calif., London, New Delhi: Sage Publications. 232–253.

Berry, John W. & Uichol, Kim 1988: Acculturation and mental health: toward applications. – P. R. Dasen, J. W. Berry & N. Sartorius (eds), *Health and Cross-Cultural Psychology*. Cross-Cultural Research and Methodology Series 10. Newsbury Park, Calif.: Sage. 207–236.

Chambers, J. K. & Trudgill, Peter 1980: *Dialectology*. Cambridge: Cambridge University Press.

*Eesti entsüklopeedia 12. Eesti A–Ü*. Tallinn: Eesti Entsüklopeediakirjastus. 696–697.

*Eesti kroonika 1957*. Esimene aastakäik. Stockholm: Kirjastus EMP.

Estonian Central Council in Canada (*Eestlaste Kesknõukogu Kanadas*), *Estonians living in Canada*. – <http://www.ekn.ca/edemog.phk> 29.12.2009.

Estonian World Council (*Ülemaailmne Eesti Kesknõukogu*) – <http://english.uekn.org> 15.3.2009.

Gans, Herbert 1978: *Symbolic Ethnicity: The Future of Ethnic Groups and Culture in America*. New York: The Free Press.

Haas, Õie & Siska, Voldemar (eds) 1988: *Eestlased Austraalias*. Adelaide: Austraalia Eesti Seltside Liit.

Hiio, Toomas & Maripuu, Meelis & Paavle, Indrek (eds) 2006: *Estonia 1940–1945. Reports of the Estonian International Commission for the Investigation of Crimes Against Humanity*. Tallinn: Estonian National Commission for the Investigation of Crimes Against Humanity.

Hirvesoo, Avo 1996: *Kõik ilmalaanen laiali: lugu Eesti pagulasmuusikutest*. Tallinn: Kupar.

211

Järv, Ants 2009: *Väliseesti teater: väliseestlaste seltsi- ja teatritegevuse põhijooni.* Tartu: Vanemuise Seltsi Kirjastus.

Kangro, Bernard 1976a: *Eesti Rootsis. Ülevaade sõnas ja pildis.* Lund: Eesti Kirjanike Kooperatiiv.

—— 1976b: *Estland i Sverige. Översikt i ord och bild.* Lund: Eesti Kirjanike Kooperatiiv.

Keevallik, Leelo & Krull, Diana & Raag, Raimo & Raag, Virve (forthcoming): *The Estonian Language in Sweden.* Uppsala.

Kool, Ferdinand 1999: *DP Kroonika. Eesti pagulased Saksamaal 1944–1951.* Lakewood, New Jersey: Eesti Arhiiv Ühendriikides.

Kumer-Haukanõmm, Kaja 2009: Eestlaste põgenemine Saksamaale. – Terje Hallik & Kristi Kukk & Janet Laidla (toim.), *Eestlaste põgenemine Läände Teise maailmasõja ajal. Artiklid ja elulood.* Tartu: Korp! Filiae Patriae. 13–53.

Kumer-Haukanõmm, Kaja & Tiit Rosenberg & Tiit Tammaru (eds) 2006: *Suur põgenemine 1944. Eestlaste lahkumine läände ning selle mõjud.* 22. oktoobril 2004 Tartus toimunud rahvusvahelise teaduskonverentsi artiklite kogumik. Tartu: Tartu Ülikooli Kirjastus.

Laagus, Aino & Klaas, Birute & Allik, Mari 2004: *Lõuna-Rootsi eestlased ja nende keel. Valimik intervjuusid.* Tartu Ülikooli eesti keele (võõrkeelena) õppetooli toimetised 4. Tartu: Tartu Ülikool.

Lindström, Liina (ed.) 1998: *Väliseestlaste keelest.* Tartu Ülikooli eesti keele õppetooli toimetised 9. Tartu: Tartu Ülikool.

Lääne, Tiit 2000: *Välis-Eesti spordielu 1940–1991: Austraalias ja Uus-Meremaal, Saksamaal, Rootsis, Kanadas, USAs ja teistes riikides.* Tallinn: Maalehe Raamat.

Madise, Juhan 1966: Emigratsioon Saksamaalt. – *Eesti saatusaastad 1945–1960,* IV. Stockholm: Kirjastus EMP. 179–189.

Mela, Marjo 2007: *Läti eestlased. Ajalugu, keel ja kultuur.* Tallinn: Eesti Keele Sihtasutus.

Ministry of Science and Education of Estonia (*Teadus- ja haridusministeerium*) – <http://www.eesti.ee/rahvuskaaslased/index.php?lang=en> 29.12.2009.

Pennar, Jaan & Parming, Tõnu & Rebane, P. Peter 1975: *The Estonians in America 1627–1975. A Chronology & Fact Book.* Ethnic Chronology Series 17. Dobbs Ferry, New York: Oceana Publications, Inc.

Praakli, Kristiina & Jüri Viikberg (eds) 2010: *Eestlased ja eesti keel välismaal.* Tallinn: Eesti Keele Sihtasutus.

Raag, Raimo 1982: *Lexical Characteristics in Swedish Estonian*. Acta Universitatis Upsaliensis. Studia Uralica et Altaica Upsaliensia 13. Uppsala: Uppsala University.

—— 1983: *Estniskan i Sverige*. FUSKIS/FIDUS 6. Uppsala: Uppsala universitet, Finsk-ugriska institutionen.

—— 1985: The Direct Object in Swedish Estonian. – *Eesti Teadusliku Seltsi Rootsis aastaraamat/Annales Societatis Litterarum Estonicae in Svecia* IX: 201–211.

—— 1999: *Eestlane väljaspool Eestit. Ajalooline ülevaade*. Tartu: Tartu Ülikooli Kirjastus.

—— 2004: The National Identity and Culture of Estonians Living in the West 1944–1991. – Jean-Jacques Subrenat (ed.), *Estonia. Identity and Independence. On the Boundary of Two Worlds. Identity, Freedom, and Moral Imagination in the Baltics* 2. Amsterdam, New York, NY: Rodopi. 179–197.

—— 2009a: Kiri minister Nyamko Sabunile vähemuskeele staatuse andmise kohta eesti keelele. – *Eesti Päevaleht* (Stockholm), nr 4 (6606), 4. veebruaril 2009: 6. [Also published on the Internet by the Language Committee of the Estonian National Congress in Sweden (Rootsi Eestlaste Liidu keeletoimkond) – <http://keeleveeb.blogspot.com/2009/01/eestlased-taotlesid-vhemusrahvuse.html>]

—— 2009b: Eestlaste põgenemine Rootsi Teise maailmasõja ajal. – Terje Hallik & Kristi Kukk & Janet Laidla (eds), *Eestlaste põgenemine Läände Teise maailmasõja ajal. Artiklid ja elulood*. Tartu: Korp! Filiae Patriae. 55–64.

—— 2010: Eestlased ja eesti keel Rootsis. – Kristiina Praakli & Jüri Viikberg (eds), *Eestlased ja eesti keel välismaal*. Tallinn: Eesti Keele Sihtasutus. 385–432.

Rahi-Tamm, Aigi 2007: Deportations in Estonia, 1941–1951. – Kristi Kukk & Toivo Raun (eds), *Soviet Deportations in Estonia: Impact and Legacy. Articles and Life Histories*. Tartu: Tartu University Press. 9–52.

Reinans, Alur 1999: *Rootsieestlaste teine põlvkond*. Rahvastiku-uuringud. Seeria B; nr 41. Tallinn: Eesti Kõrgkoolidevaheline Demouuringute Keskus.

Reinans, Alur 2008: Rootsi eestlased 1953. aastal. – *Akadeemia* 20: 1028–1047, 1327–1360.

Saareste, Andrus 1955: Kadunud kümmetuhat ja ka teised. – *Eesti Üliõpilaste Seltsi Album* XII. Stockholm: Eesti Üliõpilaste vanematekogu kirjastus. 31–41.

Statistics Finland 2009. – <http://pxweb2.stat.fi/Dialog/Saveshow.asp> 29.12.2009.

Tegeler, Tillmann 2007: Esten, Letten und Litauer in Nachkriegsdeutschland. Von rechtlosen Flüchtlingen zu heimatlosen Ausländern. – Christian Pletzing & Marianne Pletzing (eds), *Displaced Persons. Flüchtlinge aus den baltischen Staaten in Deutschland.* Colloquia Baltica 12. München: Martin Meidenbauer Verlagsbuchhandlung. 13–27.

Valmas, Anne 2003: *Eestlaste kirjastustegevus välismaal 1944–2000,* I–II. Tallinn: Tallinna Pedagoogikaülikool. [Includes a summary in English: Publishing activities of the Estonians outside Estonia during 1944–2000.]

# Olen eestlane – millega sina end vabandad?
# – Rootsi eestlaste identiteedi etnilisi ja keelelisi aspekte

*Raimo Raag*

Artikkel käsitleb rahvusliku identiteedi väljendust Rootsi eestlaste eesti keeles. Taustaks kirjeldatakse lühidalt eesti kogukondade teket Läänes ja iseloomustatakse üldjoontes praegust Rootsi eestlaskonda. Organiseeritud eesti rahvuslikust tegevusest osavõtu ja eesti identiteedi olemasolu põhjal jagatakse Eesti päritoluga inimesed Rootsis tuumikuks, perifeeriaks ja kõrvalseisjateks. Nimetus „Rootsi eestlased", „eestlased Rootsis" ja „Rootsi eestlaskond" käibib üldiselt just tuumiku kohta, sest tuumik kannab organiseeritud eesti elu Rootsis. Tuumikusse kuulub praegu hinnanguliselt 4000–5000 eestlast. Perifeeriasse kuuluvad need, kes peavad end eestlasteks või tunnevad Eesti vastu sümpaatiat, kuid kes ühel või teisel põhjusel ei osale organiseeritud rahvuslikus tegevuses. Kõrvalseisjate näol on tegemist inimestega, kes ei pea end eestlasteks. Teadustöö Rootsi eestlaste kohta, olgu see identiteedi-, sotsioloogia- või keelealane uurimus, käsitleb üldjuhul tuumikusse kuuluvaid eestlasi. Perifeeriat ja eriti kõrvalseisjaid uuritakse vähe, kui üldse. Sellest tõuseb üldistuste kandepinna küsimus.

Rootsi eesti keelele aluseks on enne Teist maailmasõda Eestis kõneldud eesti keel. Sellest johtuvalt esineb ennesõjaaegseid keelendeid isegi Rootsis sündinud ja võrsunud põlvkondade esindajate eesti keeles. Rootsi eestlaste keelt on veel mõjutanud asukohariigi põhikeel, see on rootsi keel. Rootsipärasusi võib kohata nii sõnavaras kui grammatikas. Tänapäeva eesti standardkeele seisukohast vananenud keelendite ja rootsipärastuste kasutamine ning sellele lisanduv püüe vältida uuemaid vene laensõnu, eriti nõukogulikke sõnu ja väljendeid, on muutunud Rootsi eestlaste rühmakuuluvuse märgisteks, seda nii tuumikusse kui perifeeriasse kuuluvate eestlaste puhul.

Praegu peetakse Rootsis eesti keelt immigrantkeeleks, kuigi eesti keel vastab nendele vähemuskeele kriteeriumidele, mis on sõnastatud Euroopa regionaal- või vähemuskeelte hartas (koostatud Strasbourg'is 5. novembril 1992) ja Vähemusrahvuste kaitse raam-

215

konventsioonis (koostatud Strasbourg'is 1. veebruaril 1995), ning mis Rootsi ratifitseeris aastal 2000. Kriteeriumidele vastavusele toetudes ning neid põhjendades saatis Rootsi Eestlaste Esindus jaanuaris 2009 Rootsi integratsiooniministrile esildise, milles taotleti eesti keelele ametliku vähemuskeele seisundit Rootsis. Esildis lükati poliitilise tahte puudumise tõttu tagasi.

KRISTIINA PRAAKLI

# The New Estonian Community in Finland

## Abstract

The Estonian diaspora is the result of three waves of emigration, of which two are complete and one is still in progress. A detailed survey on the formation of the Estonian diaspora is presented by Tiit Tammaru (Tammaru et alia, 2010, to be published). The eastern diaspora, or the Estonian communities in Russia, emerged as a result of mass emigration beginning in the middle of the 19th century and lasting until the start of World War I. The second mass emigration, which was caused by World War II, took place in a westward direction. As a result of it, the Estonian diaspora emerged or grew in the West. The third (ongoing) wave of emigration is mainly directed to the west (see detailed survey by Tammaru et alia, 2010).[1]

In this article, the Estonian community in Finland, which is of late origin, is explored. The article presents a short survey on the formation of Estonian-language communities and discusses language and identity issues. Proceeding from the age structure of the new communities, the article focuses on the observation of the linguistic behaviour and language use of first generation Estonians in Finland.[2]

---

1. In 2000–2007, the main destination of emigration was Finland, where over 17,000 people moved during eight years. Fewer people moved to Germany (over 1,200), the USA, Sweden and Great Britain (less than 1,000 to each country).
2. In the present article, "first generation" means persons having changed the country of residence in adulthood. The language informants mentioned in the article, 25 Estonians speaking Estonian as their mother tongue and living in Tampere or in the surrounding areas, are first generation immigrants who had been living in Finland for an average of ten years at the time the data was gathered (2002–2005). All language informants were born in Estonia and emigrated to Finland in their adulthood (i.e. older than 18).

*Ethnic and Linguistic Context of Identity: Finno-Ugric Minorities.* 217–246.
Uralica Helsingiensia 5. Helsinki 2011.

## 1. The formation of the Estonian population in Finland

As neighbouring countries there has always been a strong migration link between Finland and Estonia. Seemingly, as early as at the beginning of the 18th century, Estonians emigrated to Finland, mainly to the area around Kirkkonummi (Kulu 1992: 123), there are even sporadic data about still earlier emigration (see Raag 1999: 13–14, 29–31). The exodus of Estonian peasants to Finland in the 16–18th century has been most thoroughly explored. Various sources are also available about emigration at the beginning of the 20th century. One of the most important sources is a survey by August Nigol (1918) *Eesti asundused ja asupaigad Wenemaal* (*Estonian colonies and residences in Russia*). Although the Estonian population in Finland has been the subject of several studies from a variety of perspectives (e.g. the emigration of peasants to Finland, "Finnish boys", Finnish-Estonian cultural relations, the Estonian language minority viewed from social perspectives), there is still no consistent research about the diaspora. The period 1945–1990 has not been studied either, mainly because of the delicacy of this political issue. A few memoires shed light on the period (for example, Talve 1999, Nivanka 2002). Memoires should be critically treated, but at the same time, they are of utmost relevance from the point of view of describing the period and they can partly fill the gap in the missing scientific literature.

The first large-scale Estonian emigration to Finland took place in the first decade of the 20th century when many Estonian social and cultural figures (e.g. Friedebert Tuglas, Eduard Vilde, Nikolai Triik, Konrad Mägi and others) chose to live in Finland because of the oppressive political atmosphere at home. It is at the beginning of the 20th century that the emergence of the Estonian population in Finland took place. When Estonian independence was declared in 1918, there was a considerable Estonian community living in Finland, according to various sources, around 2,000 people, mostly in Helsinki (Nigol 1918: 9, 78; Välis-Eesti Almanak (Foreign Estonian Almanac) I 1929: 25; Kulu 1992: 123; Raag 1999: 51). Estonians also lived in the

Kabböle seaside village (Pernaja rural municipality, Itä-Uudenmaa).[3] In addition to the Tallinn-Helsinki direction, Estonians also chose to emigrate from Narva to Viipuri at various times (in more detail Pullat 1992: 79).

## 2. The Demographic Development of Estonians in Finland

In the early 1930s there were still approximately 1,500 Estonians residing in Finland. The majority of the Estonian population were women. They were mostly domestic servants and shop assistants and the men artisans and factory workers. There were also 20 farmers, approximately 30 businessmen and merchants, 2–3 manufacturers, and some students (Välis-Eesti almanak (Foreign Estonian Almanac) 1933: 35). Between 1928–1944, the size of the Estonian population was approximately 1,300. The data from Finnish Annual Statistics (STV) 1948 reveal that the number of Estonian citizens has steadily decreased since the 1930s (see Table 1). They returned to Estonia, emigrated to other parts of Europe, or applied for Finnish citizenship (for more detailed data on Estonians who acquired Finnish citizenship between 1928–1944 see STV 1946: 80).

| Year | 1930 | 1931 | 1933 | 1935 | 1937 | 1938 | 1941 | 1942 | 1944 |
|---|---|---|---|---|---|---|---|---|---|
| Number | 1,320 | 1,154 | 821 | 681 | 607 | 556 | 425 | 350 | 277 |

Table 1. Estonian citizens in Finland from 1930–1944 (STV 1948: 6). There are no statistical data for the years 1939 and 1940.

---

3.    It is known from the history of Kabböle that the village was founded at the beginning of the 20th century (in 1906 according to data from Raimo Raag) when nine Kuusalu families emigrated to the coast between Porvoo and Loviisa in Pernaja parish (see Raag 1999). Today, the Estonian language has vanished from the village (see also Mäkeläinen 2006). According to August Nigol's data (1918: 78–79), the number of Estonians in the village amounted to 80.

An annual average of 34 Estonians received Finnish citizenship between 1928 and 1940. The number of Estonians who acquired Finnish citizenship quadrupled (115 successful applications) in 1941 (STV 1944–1945: 50, 80). This growth is probably related to the difficult wartime situation in Estonia, which caused many Estonians staying in Finland to consider it more prudent to apply for Finnish citizenship. In 1945, the number of Estonian citizens living in Finland was 207 (STV 1948: 6). The next data on the size of the Estonian population in Finland can be found in STV 1990.

According to Aigi Rahi-Tamm (2004: 16), during the German occupation of Estonia (1941–1944) some 6,000 people fled to Finland. On 19th September 1944, Finland and the Soviet Union signed a truce, which forced Estonians living in Finland to leave the country because remaining there meant potential deportation to the Soviet Union (Jürjo 1996: 7; Rahi-Tamm 2004: 8). After the truce was finalised – and even before that – many Estonians living in Finland moved from Finland to Sweden, either legally or illegally (for more detail see Uustalu & Moora 1993; Roiko-Jokela 1997; Relvik 2003; Leskinen & Juutilainen 2005). Local Estonian societies were closed down before the end of World War II or immediately after the war at the latest (Raag 1999: 110–111; Nivanka 2002: 179, 187–188) and Estonian cultural public activities were suspended. The political situation also suspended emigration from Estonia to Finland.

It is difficult to find information and precise data about those Estonians who remained in Finland after World War II. The last numerical wartime data are available for 1945 (207 persons with Estonian citizenship), in the statistical data for 1947, Estonians are no longer mentioned. The next data are available in the statistics for 1990. In 1956–1987 the records mention Estonians, Latvians and Lithuanians among those Soviet Union citizens who had acquired Finnish citizenship, but do not present any precise figures (STV 1989: 102).

Although Finland is considered a relatively homogeneous country – foreigners comprise only 2.9% of the total population (<http://www.suomi.fi>) – due to large-scale immigration starting at the beginning of the '90s, Finland has in fact changed from a homogeneous society into a multilingual and multicultural society. From the end of World War II until the 1980s, the number of residents without

Finnish citizenship remained rather steady. The immigrant population started to grow in the '80s and soared a decade later. This can be attributed to a rapid growth in the number of economic immigrants and asylum seekers (caused by the Somalian Civil War, the disintegration of Jugoslavia and the Gulf wars) and the start of intensive immigration during the collapse of the Soviet Union. Notwithstanding the rapid increase in the number of immigrants, the number of foreigners is still among the smallest in Europe.[4]

The new Estonian communities in Finland are the result of the intensive waves of emigration which followed the collapse of the Soviet Union in 1991. Emigration from Estonia to Finland began in the mid-1980s: in 1990 there were 1,394 native Estonian speakers living in Finland, in 1995 the number rose to 8,710, and by the end of year 2004 to 13,978 (Statistics Finland 2005: 116–117). According to the data published by the Statistical Office of Estonia (Statistikaamet 1995: 77; 1999: 57), this process reached its peak in 1995 when 1,067 Estonians emigrated from Estonia to Finland. The data also show that since that time, an annual average of 500 people have emigrated from Estonia to Finland.

Emigration to Finland increased after Estonia joined the European Union in 2004. Different sources confirm that in the following years the number of Estonian citizens more or less permanently residing in Finland dramatically increased. According to the latest data, Estonians in Finland now number 29,000 (31.12.2009, <http://www. suomi.fi>). Nevertheless, these numbers should be treated with caution as when gathering data the Statistical Office of Estonia proceeds from the country of birth, not mother tongue. This group is therefore likely to include quite a few people whose mother tongue is Russian or Ukrainian, etc., as well as Ingrian Finns whose first language is either Russian, Estonian or Ingrian Finnish.

Migration is never an independent phenomenon, it is influenced by the political, economic and social developments which take place

---

4. In Germany, the immigrant population forms approximately 7% (<http://www. destatis.de>), in Belgium 9% (Jamin 2003: 3) of the total population. As of at 2009, 155,660 foreign citizens lived in Finland, Russians (28,214) are at first place, Estonians (25,416), Swedes (8,568) and Somals (5,549) are next (data as of 31.12.2009, <http:// www.suomi.fi/suomifi/suomi/tietopaketit/perustietoa_suomesta/vaesto/index.html>).

in society (Kulu 2000: 7; see also Eamets, Philips 2004). Push and pull factors can be differentiated according to whether the incentive for migration is in the home or destination country. Push factors can be a high rate of unemployment or a low level of income in the home country, pull factors are available jobs and better remuneration in the potential target country (referred to Kulu 2000: 7; see also Eamets, Philips 2004: 13). The large increase in the size of the Estonian population in Finland can be attributed to different factors. Among the more general reasons for Estonian citizens to emigrate to Finland are ethnic remigration of Ingrian Finns with Estonian citizenship, marriage to a Finnish citizen, family reunification (Pohjanpää et al. 2003: 55–56, Liebkind et al. 2004: 22), and also studying abroad. After Estonia joined the European Union (1 May 2004), economic migration increased rapidly. A new migration trend is that where people oscillate between the two countries: the workplace is in Finland but the home is still in Estonia.

The Estonian-speaking population in Finland is supported by immigration consistency, the very large size of the local Estonian population and the concentration of Estonians in big cities. Since 2005, more than half of the Estonians in Finland have resided in the capital city region and surrounding counties: in Uusimaa, 8,101, Varsinais-Suomi, 1,336 and Pirkanmaa, 847 (Statistics Finland 2005: 116–117). At the same time, the average age of people in the new Estonian communities in Finland is substantially lower than in older Estonian communities in the east and west (for more detail see Tammaru et al. 2010).

Local Estonian societies play an important role in Estonian cultural life in Finland. In October 1997 the Tampere Estonian Club was established (TEK, <http://www.eestiklubi.fi>). In addition to club activities, TEK published an Estonian language newsletter "Eesti Leht (Estonian Newspaper)" four times a year (from 1997–2003; in 2003–2004 it was named "Binokkel (Binoculars)". The main activity of the Club involves organising Estonian cultural events and children-oriented activities, celebrating national holidays and arranging Estonian language classes. Estonian societies in Finland also operate in Kotka (Estonian Society in Kotka), Turku (Estonians of Turku Region), Iisalmi (Iisalmi Estonian Society), Oulu (Oulu Estonian Club), Lappeenranta (Lappeenranta Estonian Society) and in Helsinki (East-Helsinki

Estonian Club "Koit" and Helsinki Children's Club). These societies' activities mainly take place mainly at the local level, typical activities being the organising of an Estonian Christmas party, celebrating the anniversary of the Republic of Estonia, children's clubs and summer camps (Finnish-Estonian Union 2006). In November 2002, the Estonian Union in Finland (SEL) was established in Tampere by the representatives of Estonian associations from the different regions.

There are many societies and institutions in Finland dealing with Estonian culture and teaching the Estonian language. The most renowned among Finnish Estophiles is the Tuglas Society (Tuglas-Seura), which was established in 1982 in Helsinki. Nine years later (1991), the Union of Estonian Societies in Finland (SVYL) was founded, which is a national organisation whose main objective is to develop Estonian-Finnish relations in various fields. There are about 40 Estonian societies and the members are mainly Finnish speaking. The main objective of these small societies is to introduce the Estonian culture to the Finnish population through different activities. At the national level, the Estonian Embassy in Finland and the Estonian Institute in Finland play the most important role in the introduction of Estonian culture and language.

## 3. The Importance of Language and Culture

For citizens of Estonia, particularly for persons speaking Estonian as their mother tongue, emigration to Finland is less painful in terms of language, culture and psychology, than for citizens of other Member States of the European Union or third countries. Finland is geographically close, and the similar culture and language favours contacts with Finns. The relationship between the languages and closeness of the cultures, the size of the Estonian speaking population, the geographical closeness to Finland and close contacts with Estonia, and also the activities regulated by legislation to support the educational and cultural activities of Estonian language minorities in Finland, can be considered important factors. Quoting a language informant, *"it is easy to be and remain an Estonian in Finland. Everybody knows who we are and where we come from, why we are here and what we do here"*. However, the closeness of the cultures and the relationship of the languages can also cause problems, which can favour becoming a Finn: *The Finns' positive attitude, the relationship between languages and the similarity between the cultures can support being Estonian, but they can be a problem at the same time. Our culture and languages are so close that becoming a Finn is very easy. Changing your first name is enough.*

Changing the country of residence influences and shapes a person's identity and their linguistic behaviour. A new aspect of self-determination is belonging to a minority group, which eventually raises the question of a person's belonging, the determination of their ethnic and cultural identity and relations with the majority group. Ethnic identity is not static, it is a constantly developing process which flexibly responds to changes in the social context (Valk & Karu-Kletter 2005: 1979–1981). A change of identity, like other cultural and psychological processes which take place during long-term contact between two cultures, is termed aculturisation (see Berry 1992; Liebkind et al. 2004). Of all the new groups, the linguistic behaviour, identity issues and the language use of the representatives of the Tampere Estonian group have been most thoroughly studied using interviews and participatory observation (Praakli 2009). Based on these interviews, it can be said that all forms of aculturisation can be found among Tampere Estonians: 1) integrated Estonians: they relate to both cultures and a dual cultural identity has been established; 2) assimilated Estonians: they relate to the majority group or Finns; 3) marginalised Estonians: they lack relations with either group (i.e. Finns and Estonians), and 4) separated Estonians: they identify themselves solely with their group of origin.

Instead of firm self-determination, many language informants determine themselves as carriers of dual identity: they are conscious of and appreciate belonging to two cultural spaces, both of which are considered equally relevant. Dual identity provides richer opportunities, enabling the person to participate in the activities of the other cultural group (common hobbies, spare time, celebrating family events) and to belong to Finnish networks. One language informant's comment describes their self-determination most expressively: *"Although for an Estonian it is important to spend Midsummer Eve and the long summer holidays in Estonia, it is equally important to celebrate St Philip's Day, to watch Ice Hockey, "Strictly Come Dancing", and to sympa-*

*thise with Finns in the Eurovision Song Contest."* Naturally, there are other viewpoints where the necessity of being Finnish is placed in the forefront: *"I would not stress being Estonian too much. Living in Finland we also have to be Finnish, if only because of our children."*

It can be concluded from the interviews that being Estonian means the common ethnic origin and mother tongue. The most relevant of the components of being Estonian is the language: the Estonian language as the common mother tongue and people who speak Estonian as their mother tongue. In the interviews the following components of being Estonian were also considered important:

— common roots and common historical and cultural experience (participation in the events of regaining independence: Baltic Chain, Night Song Festivals);
— use of the Estonian language as the home language (or one of the home languages);
— sticking to Estonian customs and traditions, and celebrating holidays (Midsummer Night, Christmas, St. Martin's Fair);
— frequent visits to places in Estonia such as Tallinn, Saaremaa and Pärnu.

The language of the Estonians plays two roles in identity: on the one hand, it is a means of communication with members of the group, on the other it is a criterion for differentiating one's own people from others. Thus, Estonian language skills are one of the main attributes for delineating the group.

## Language Choice of Estonian Communities in Finland

When living in another language environment, being Estonian also means using Estonian as the home language (or one of the home languages).[5] While in case of marriage within the same national group (both are Estonians), the language informant and spouse's main communication language was Estonian (excluding switches to Finnish

---

5.  The Estonian language as an important feature of being Estonian is also revealed in the results of questionnaires answered by Estonians in Sweden (for more detail see Valk & Karu-Kletter 2006).

during the conversation for some reason), in Estonian–Finnish mixed families there are different language choices in which the Finnish language plays a dominant role.[6] Based on informants' comments, four main motives for language change can be observed: 1) the spouse's negative attitude to the Estonian language, 2) children's negative attitude to the Estonian language, 3) children's difficulties in acquiring the language, and 4) the language informant's personal reasons.

Whether or not the Estonian language was used as the home language was substantially influenced by the timing of the informants' arrival in Finland and the political situation in Estonia at that time. Language informants who arrived in Finland during the Soviet period or immediately after Estonia regained independence tend to prefer Finnish. Those persons who arrived in Finland in the mid-1990s, however, are in contrast, language retainers. The time of arrival in Finland is in turn related to the language informants' common historical experience and Estonian identity. Language informants who have personally experienced Estonia regaining independence and have taken part in the political events preceding it (Baltic Chain, Singing Revolution) are also more language-concious about using their mother tongue. Still, there are no grounds for assuming that the decision to use Finnish reflects a negative attitude toward Estonia or anything related to the Estonian language. As many studies confirm, changing language does not automatically mean a loss of identity or loyality to the group (Jürgenson 2002: 200). Changing language is mostly related to personal reasons which need not be connected with the person's attitude to the particular language or group. Many language informants had deliberately chosen Finnish as the main family language, but at the same time participated actively in the Tampere Estonian Club's activities and promoted the Estonian language, cultural and educational events.

Karmela Liebkind et al. (2004) have studied the language choices of Finnish new minority groups in different fields of language use and in the transfer of the language to the next generation. The results of her study reveal a connection between Finnish language skills and language choice which defines the heterogeneity of language

6. The informants for the current study were 25 Estonians residing in and around Tampere. The linguistic material in the study consisted of recordings of oral speech. This material was collected using the interview method.

choices: the better respondents can speak Finnish, the exclusive used the mother tongue in family communication with children. Approximately half of the Russian and two thirds of the Estonian women living in Finland use primarly or exclusively Finnish for communicating with their children, which can in turn be explained by the multiplicity of exogamic marriages. Liebkind also assesses the role of the level of education in language choices. It appears that language informants who have a higher education (excluding Ingrian Finnish) use their own language (Estonian or Russian) more, independently of how well they can speak Finnish.

The Estonian population in Finland is an extremely heterogeneous group in terms of their linguistic behaviour, and this fact is also referred to in the results of a study by Minna Suni and Merja Tarnanen (2005: 10–11).

The communication networks of the Estonian population in Finland have been explored in four surveys (Pohjanpää et al. 2003; Liebkind et al. 2004; Tarnanen & Suni 2005; Reuter & Jaakkola 2005). The main emphasis of all these surveys is on the analysis of the immigrants' integration society. Immigrants' social relations, as one component of immigration, are also studied. According to a study by Karmela Liebkind et al., half the Estonians participating in the study described their friends as consisting mostly or entirely of Finns. One fifth of Estonians, however, had groups of friends who are all or mostly Estonians. Compared to Russian-speaking and Ingrian Finnish groups, Estonians' integration into Finnish networks is more robust even when the respondents' age, gender, duration of residence in Finland, size of the region, marital status, socio-economic position, Finnish language skills and the impact of the spouse's ethnic background are considered.

Kirsti Pohjanpää (2003) obtained similar results. According to her study, approximately 70% of the people in her in Estonian respondents' networks were native Finns. According to a study by Tarnanen and Suni (2005: 21), the Russian-speaking population in Finland (which does not concern the indigenous Russian minority in Finland, but only concerns the new Russian population) and the Estonians have the closest relations with Finns: almost everybody has Finnish friends and many of their spouses were born in Finland. Only in rare cases (3–6%) did an Estonian not belong to Finnish networks (Tarnanen &

Suni 2005: 14). According Liebkind (2004: 184), half of the Estonians had groups of friends who were mostly or entirely made up of Finns, every fifth had friends who were mostly or exclusively Estonian.

The conclusion can be drawn that the new Estonian language groups in Finland are heterogeneous in terms of their linguistic and sociodemographic structure and that they do not form a uniform ethnic and linguistic minority group. They are united by the same mother tongue and country of birth (in case of first generation), but are differentiated by socioeconomic factors such as their time of arrival in Finland, reasons for emigration, objectives and profession, linguistic attitudes and attitudes to the majority and minority groups.

## 4. A Finnish Variety of the Estonian language

The Estonian language spoken in Finland can be called a Finnish variety of the Estonian language. The Finnish variety of the Estonian language is a special regional variety spoken in one geographical space. This can also be called a contact based language variety (or *immigrant language variety,* a term used by, for example, Extra, Verhoeven 1998: 9; Backus 2004: 711; also *diaspora variety,* term by Johanson 1993: 197–198*)* which arises from the immigration of small groups or single persons to another country and their joining the local population (Riionheimo 2007: 29; see also Thomason 2001: 10–12, 18–19). The immigrant language variety is not a standardised language, it is a local spoken variety influenced by the country of residence, generally an oral language variety characterised by asymmetry (i.e. unequal relations between languages), dynamics, change over time and variable use in communication between generations. Contact-induced language varieties are never uniform (see Pajusalu 1998; Viikberg 2001; Hennoste 2003a).

Many development scenarios have been presented in contact linguistics for linguistic processes taking place in immigration stuations. Relying on data from different studies, two likely linguistic developments proceeding from contact with the other group: divergence from old native codes and convergence towards new foreign codes. Most changes in immigrant varieties can be attributed to these factors or to combinations of the two (for more detail see Johanson 2006: 7).

In immigrant contact situations, relations between the two groups or languages are never equal. They are characterised by asymmetric or unequal sociolinguistic relations proceeding from the unequal social status of the languages, functions, possibility of use and the speakers' language skills (for more detail see Halmari 1997: 69; see also Thomason 2001: 8–11; Myers-Scotton 2002: 41). In a contact situation this is manifested in the dominant linguistic impact of one language. It means that changes from language A into language B appear more frequently than changes from language B into language A, generally from a sociolinguistically stronger language towards a sociolinguistically weaker language (= the speaker's mother tongue). There is no language level immune to linguistic impact. The most receptable to foreign impact in contact situations is the lexical level (which is also the mildest form of contact impact), but contact manifestations are never confined to the lexical level, they also reach the morphological and syntactic levels (Thomason 2001: 10–13; Backus 2004: 711–712; see also Sankoff 2001).

The Estonian communities' contact situation type can be termed the maintenance of the language. It means that speakers use Estonian as their main language communicating with their compatriots. At this point, the peculiarity of the contact situation under study must be taken into account: the language informants of the present study are adults, they have acquired the Finnish language in adulthood, the time of the contact situation is relatively short (language informants had lived in a Finnish language environment for ten years on average), the speakers are mostly able to keep both languages apart and the borders between the languages are generally clearly differentiable for them. At the same time, the contact situation is not the same for all members of the group, and the same can be said of the characteristics of language retention by Estonian groups in Finland. Any language choice and the speaker's linguistic behaviour are always related to different sociolinguistic factors, including the speaker's views and language attitudes, which do not exclude the changing of the main language even among first generation speakers.

In the Tampere example, the bilingual language use of first generation speakers is characterised by major switchovers to Finnish within a sentence. In the language material under study, copying[7] reaches all language levels, but it is typically more dominant for first generation speakers at the lexical level. Here, typical copies are single words which are generally (but not always) phonologically and/or morpho-syntactically integrated. The most frequent types of words are substantives (64%), discourse particles (18%) and verbs (8%), the rest (pronouns, conjunctions) are of marginal frequency.

Here the Estonian-Finnish language data correspond to the results presented in various bilingual studies according to which first generation representatives mainly transfer single word units into their mother tongue. Observing the number of copied substantives in different spoken texts, we see that they always form over 50% of the total number of copied words (see e.g. Poplack 1980: 602–603; Appel, Muysken 1987: 170–172; Halmari 1997: 53–58; Backus 1998: 267; see also Muysken 2000; Kovács 2001: 129–130; Backus 2006: 263–267 and many others).

The language data under study reveal that not all Finnish units are of equal importance for the speaker. The speakers copy primarily those Finnish units which are more attractive to them for some reason or which are more prominent because of their having certain properties. Such properties could be the meanings of the units, particularly their semantic specifity, and also the simplicity of their structure, transparency and linguistic economy. From the language data it appears that it is attractive for speakers to copy the vocabulary of social and culturally specific fields, which mark their relation and contact points with the new cultural space. The dominant occurrence of substantives and discourse particles can be explained in many ways: they are simple, transparent by structure, have specific meaning (substantives in particular) and are frequently used in Finnish. There are only about ten Finnish verbs in the data, which is of very little used compared to the frequency of substantives. The low frequency of simple verbs can be attributed to their lack of semantic utility. Unlike substantives, verbs do not express the speaker's connection with the

---

7. The analysis of bilingual language use is based on the Code-Copying Model of Lars Johanson (1993).

surrounding language space, which could raise their attractiveness and influence the frequency of their use in the language informants' speech.

Various names (e.g. names of institutions and companies) also fall into semantically specific units. The copies of names mostly lack a precise equivalent in the Estonian language, therefore their global copying is logical. Names are not semantically transparent, copying them assumes familiarity with their context:

(1)  INF8:  *Kela helistas mulle eile, ei tea mingi jama on jälle vist.*
'*Kela* called me yesterday, I don't know, seems like there's something wrong again.' (*Kela = Kansaneläkelaitos,* Social Insurance Institution of Finland)

In the conscious use of Finnish elements, the changed or changing dominant relations of model and base codes can be observed. Proceeding from that, the use of Finnish elements is in many cases a forced choice for the speaker: the speaker has to make choices in favour of Finnish units because there are no Estonian equivalents to these Finnish words in their linguistic repertoire, or Finnish units may be more suitable, precise, specific for some reason, or have other features which are important for the speaker. Although the reason for using the two languages alongside each other may be the context of the conversation and the marking the speaker's linguistic environment, an linguistic economy can not be ruled out either. Thus, the Finnish substantive *gradu* might be shorter and easier to pronounce for the speaker than the Estonian equivalent *magistritöö*:

(2)  INF13:  *Nüüd ma olen nii tihedalt teinud oma lõputööd, seda (.) gradut noh et ma ei ole lugend, aga siin üldiselt ma ennem lugesin absoluutselt iga päev. Kõik need kolm lehte, Õhtuleht, Päevaleht ja Postimees.*
'Right now I'm so busy with my thesis, this (.)*MA thesis,* you know, that I haven't been reading at all, but I used to read every day here. All three papers, *Õhtuleht, Päevaleht* and *Postimees.*'

231

KRISTIINA PRAAKLI

Let us now examine example 3. The reason for copying the substantive *maahanmuuttaja* (*immigrant* in Estonian and English) is probably the topic of conversation: when talking about social problems, Finnish is more dominant for the speaker, but it cannot be assumed that there is no mother tongue equivalent for word *maahanmuuttaja* in the speaker's linguistic repertoire:

(3)  KP:      *Kuidas sa ise sellesse sõnasse suhtud?*
     INF3:    *Joo, kõik kardavad hirmsasti ja häbenevad*
              *praegusel ajal **sitä** või **maahanmuuttaja.***
     KP:      'What do you think of this word?'
     INF3:    'You know, nowadays everybody is really afraid
              and ashamed of it or *immigrant.*'

Semantically speaking, the Finnish element need not be absolutely identical with the mother tongue equivalent. It is possible that the substantives *maahanmuuttaja* and *immigrant* do not carry the same meaning for the speaker and when speaking about new immigrants the use of term *maahanmuuttaja* is more precise according to the speaker's assessment. It is a prerequisite that the conversation partner possesses the same code as the language informant, and that the choice of code does not hinder further communication. The use of the Finnish noun can also be explained by the speakers' belonging to a common sociocultural linguistic group. The speakers wish to express themselves in a way which is characteristic of the new environment, therefore the use of the substantive *maahanmuuttaja* is logical.

After substantives, discourse particles are the units which are most attractive. From the bilingual speaker's point of view, they are pragmatically relevant elements. In the scientific grammar of the Estonian language (EKG I 1995: 18), the term *particle* is used as a consolidated name for all unchangeable words (e.g. adverbs, proadverbs, adpositions, conjunctions, affixal adverbs, modal verbs and interjections). In Finnish linguistics, several names and classifications have also been used (see detailed survey ISK 2004: 769). In bilingual studies, pragmatic discourse elements include discourse markers, conjunctions, routine words, words expressing modality and assessment, interjections and endings (for more detail see Keevallik 2006a:

118). Still, the occurrence of these elements in the present subject matter is limited. The dialogue particles *joo* and *kyll(ä)* are dominant in the subject matter, and to a lesser extent the performance particles *eiku, niinku, ni(i)nku(n)* also occur (for basis of the classification see ISK 2004: 770; see also Hennoste 2000: 1777–1780). Other particles occur once or twice (for instance *jahah, hei, hei kuule, juu*). In some cases, the copying of communication formulas takes place, but they only account for a marginal percentage of the subject matter. The reason for this is the situation in which the material was gathered (interviewing), which creates frames for participants' conversational behaviour (relative formality, the interlocutors' questioner-respondent roles, fixed conversational topics, etc.), and limits the speaker's activity in the conversation and affects their need to use certain elements. Therefore, in interview situations Finnish greetings, leave-taking or thanking routines are not likely to be used. The fact, however, that different pragmatic elements actually are in use is indicated by copies fixed in the participatory observation. Leelo Keevallik (2006a, 2006b) has studied borrowing pragmatics in the case of the oral speech of the Estonian population in Sweden. She explains the occurrence of pragmatic discourse words in bilingual communication as follows: they are used frequently in the other language, they are morphologically simple, short, and do not influence the syntactical constitution of the utterance (Keevallik 2006a: 120, 2006b: 129). She adds that as pragmatic discourse elements are rather automated in frequent conversational functions, keeping different linguistic systems apart can be more difficult in their case than, for instance, in the case of propositional linguistic forms (2006a: 120).

Based on the language data collected, it can be said that particles are one of the first to enter the speaker's mother tongue in a contact situation. Copying them does not require the speaker to have good Finnish language skills; copying is also supported by the closeness of the languages in contact. At this point, a good example is provided by a language informant (INF24) who has lived in Finland for two years (at the moment of interviewing), and who does not speak Finnish. However, in a one-hour interview the particles *joo* and *kyllä* occur many times in their speech. No other copies occur.

The language data gathered during participatory observations transpired to be relevant additional material for describing the Estonian-Finnish code-copying process. They complement the subject matter gathered, illuminate the speakers' language use outside the interview situation and reflect wider operation with Finnish elements. The subject matter indicates the instrumental importance of the Finnish language in everyday conversation, where Finnish performs its specifically pragmatic tasks, being a more relevant and attractive choice for the speaker for some reason. The language data gathered in the participatory observation also reveal that in reality the functions of the Finnish language are much wider than the interview situation reveals.

Three examples of the copying of pragmatic elements in everyday conversations are presented. The first describes the arrival of guests to a language informant's (INF9) birthday party (there were only Estonians present). The example illustrates the parallel use of Estonian and Finnish words for greetings and congratulations. Language informant INF9 initiates the use of Finnish elements. This can be construed as a signal to other participants in the conversation, which shows that the use of Finnish is a communication means accepted within the group:

(4)   INF12:     *Tere-tere!*
      INF9:      **No moikka**, *jõudsite ka lõpuks kohale!*
      Külaline:  **Onneksi olkoon** *sünnipäevalapsele!*
      INF12:     *Palju õnne minu poolt kah.*
      INF12:     'Hi there!'
      INF9:      '*Hi* to you too, you've finally made it!'
      Guest:     '*Happy birthday* to the birthday boy!'
      INF12:     'Happy birthday from me, too.'

The second example (5) illustrates starting a telephone conversation. Answering the call, the language informant copies the routine of starting a typically Finnish telephone conversation: construction *first name + puhelimessa* (e.g. *Tiina puhelimessa* – literally: *Tiina on the phone*). It must be said that the person who called the language informant was an Estonian familiar to them and the call had been agreed on earlier:

(5)  INF17:  /.../ *puhelimessa.*
           /.../
     INF17:  *Tere-tere. Olete tagasi?*
     INF17:  '/.../ **is speaking.**'
           /.../
     INF17:  'Hi there. Are you back?'

Now let us observe the occurrence of particles in the interview situation. As mentioned above, the biggest group of globally copied units are the particles *joo, kyllä* and *niin.* Some Estonian and Finnish particles are similar in their phonetic form, meaning and occurrence function, therefore copying them is logical. At the same time, not all Finnish particles are copied globally, only their selected properties. This can be observed, for example, with units which are identical or close in their phonetic structure, but semantically somewhat different (e.g. *kyllä* ja *küll*). As a result of copying selective properties, copies are formed whose phonetic structure proceeds from the Estonian language but which possess other properties of the close Finnish unit.

Of the above-mentioned particle, global copying of particle *joo* (ten cases of occurrence), is natural. Its frequent occurrence can be explained by the peculiarity of the conversational situation: the interviewer asked many general questions which required a "yes" or "no" answer. In oral Estonian speech, one of the possible answers would be the particle *jaa* or *jah* (Hennoste 2000: 1785).

Examples 6 and 7 describe the global copying of the particle *joo* into the Estonian language. In the first example, the language informant and the author of this study talk about language use within the family. Resuming the conversation topic the interviewer asks the language informant a question about the bilingualism of their family members. The informant answers the question with the particle *joo*, agreeing that their family is bilingual:

(6)  KP:     *Pead=sa ennast ja oma peret kakskeelseks?*
     INF11:  *No minu pere (.) **joo** on kindlalt (.) on kindlalt.*
     KP:     'Would you consider you and your family bilingual?'
     INF11:  'Well, my family (.), yes they are (.) they are for sure.'

*Joo* as a mark of agreement also occurs in example (7). The respondent agrees with other language informants' opinions that the terms used for foreigners are disdainful:

(7)  KP:  *Kuidas sa ise sellesse sõnasse suhtud?*
     INF3:  *Joo, kõik kardavad hirmsasti ja häbenevad*
            *praegusel ajal sitä või maahanmuuttaja.*
     KP:  'What do you think of this word?'
     INF3:  'You know, nowadays everybody is really afraid
            and ashamed of it or *immigrant*.'

The most interesting of the particles occurring in the subject matter is *kyllä ~ küll*. *Eesti kirjakeele seletussõnaraamat 1993* (The Explanatory Dictionary of the Estonian Written Language) differentiates nine functions for the linguistic form *küll*. *Küll* may occur when stressing a statement, confirming or stressing an answer, to help accentuate a speaker's opinion when stressing an assumption, and to show hesitation, astonishment, helplessness. Is a word for adding emphasis in various exclamations and stresses the speaker's emotion in an affirmative sentence, which actually includes a negative or doubting opinion about something.

Based on the informants' language use, it can be concluded that in the case of this linguistic form, the speakers proceed from the functions of the Estonian word *küll*. Syntactically, however, the linguistic form is in the wrong place for Estonian language speakers, that is, mostly at the beginning of the utterance. The location of the particle, which differs from monolingual Estonian language, also displays copying of Finnish intonation. To make the occurrence of the particle more expressive, two examples have been chosen. In both examples the particle occurs in a function confirming (example 8) or stressing (example 9) what has been said. In both cases, the copy is placed at the beginning of the utterance:

(8)  INF5:  *Et see on mul nagu selline, et ma isegi ei mäleta, et ma oleks seda* [soome keelt] *kunagi õieti õppinud, et see lihtsalt on minul jäänud külge ja ma olen seda lihtsalt üritanud rääkida, et ma ei pea selleks pingutama.* **Küll** *ma räägin võib-olla mingeid erandeid valesti, aga noh see ei takista mind nagu suhtlemast ja siin on ka, mul on lihtsalt nagu vene sõbrad tekkinud ja ja siis on nagu suur osa minu minu sellest elust on venekeelne.*

'It's like I don't even remember that I've ever actually studied it [Finnish], it's like simply stuck in my head and I've simply tried to speak it, it's like I don't have to think about it. *Well*, maybe I use some exceptions in the wrong way, but it doesn't prevent me from speaking, and here, again, I've, like, made some Russian friends and, and then a big part of my, my life here is in Russian.'

(9)  KP:  *Millest see* [emakeele säilitamine] *sinu arvates sõltub?*
INF14:  **Küll** *mina arvan, et see on perest kinni.*
KP:  'What do you think it [preserving your mother tongue] depends on?'
INF14:  '*Well*, I think it has to do with family.'

The occurrence of the particle *nii(n)* is also somewhat problematic. It can be seen from the subject matter that the language informants copy the phonetically close Finnish particle *niin*, which can be construed as replacing Estonian particle *noh*. This particle is generally located at the beginning of a syntactic unit and its main function is to explain and give reasons for the preceding talk or action:

(10)  INF7:  *No põhimõtteliselt nagu see on nüüd võib-olla sellest tingitud, et meil on see, et noh vanem laps on juba kolmandas klassis ja tal on nagu see keelekasutus on nagu laiem ja nii edasi,* **nii** *temal on täiesti ükskõikne asi, et mõlemad keeled on tu: ühtemoodi tugevad, aga et väiksemad on ehk veel nagu see kujunemas välja, et et nad ajavad segamini mõnikord ja.*

'Basically you know, it may be because, that we have,
that our elder kid is already in the third form and
he uses the language more and so on, *so* for him it
doesn't make any difference that both languages are
stro– are both equally strong, but maybe the younger
ones are still, like, developing, and sometimes they
mix them up and –.'

(11)  INF8:     *No ma arvan, et need inimesed, kes nagu suhtlevad
                minuga jaja on huvitatud **niin nii(n)** nendel on nagu
                see pilt olnud nagu ennemgi juba selline positiivne.*
                'I think that the people who talk to me and, and are,
                like, interested, *yes*, they have, like, had a positive
                picture before as well.'

First generation language informants move in parallel between Estonian and Finnish language circles using both languages for different
purposes and in different situations. The active use of both languages
forms the basis for contacts which induce linguistic impact in both
language directions: speaking the Estonian language the speaker is
simultaneously under the influence of the Finnish language, using
the Finnish language under the influence of the Estonian language.
Finnish acquired in adulthood as a foreign language is also influenced
by contacts – it is unavoidably influenced by the speaker's mother
tongue. Thus, in the case of the community under study, it is wrong
to state that contact induced phenomena only occur in the speakers'
mother tongue, although it is a specific feature of the oral use of a language which can be instantly noticed – the speaker's languages have
a reciprocal impact.

Let us now examine examples 12 and 13. In both cases, Finnish language informants create an analogical form from Finnish units
which differs from the units used in monolingual Finnish (Est-Fin
*liikkeenvaihtoveronumero* pro Fin *liikevaihtoveronumero* and Est-Fin
*bilettaja* pro Fin *bilettäjä*). It is possible that from the point of view
of the language informants, the linguistic forms entirely correspond
to the norms of the Finnish language. In that case, the copy would
more likely reflect the language informant's Finnish language skills.

Long-term residence in another language space and the acquisition of another language in adulthood does not necessarily mean the acquisition of perfect fluency in that language, the speakers creating their individual language variety, an idiolect, on the basis of the foreign language. However, this hypothesis has not been proved, as such speakers' Finnish language skills have not been studied:

(12) INF3:  *Meiegi oleme nagu Tampere Eesti Klubi **ärr üü** [ry].*
*See on nagu ühistu. Sellepärast, et me saime, siis*
*meil on siis nagu Soome oma selle, ma ei teagi, ärr*
*üü nagu tähendab, see on tulumaksu numbri, see on*
*nagu meil öeldakse **liikkeenvaihtoveronumero**.* (Fin
*liikevaihtoveronumero*)
'We are, like, the Tampere Estonian Club *ärr üü* [ry],
too. It's like a society. Because we got, because we
have like the Finnish, I don't know, like *ärr üü*, it's a
tax number, or as we say, *company tax number*.'

(13) INF8:  *Ei, ma ole käinud, ma ei ole selline eee **bilettaja**.* (Fin
*bilettäjä*)
'No, I haven't been, I'm not much of a, erm, *a party*
*person*.'

For this Finnish language speaker, the linguistic form differs from the monolingual standard of the Finnish language, for the Estonian language speaker from the standard of the Estonian language. In both cases, an independent form comes into being which differs from the standards of both languages.


## 5. Conclusions

The history of the Estonian-speaking population in Finland dates back to the early 20th century when there was a sizable Estonian community, approximately 2,000 persons. After World War II, the Estonian-language population in Finland decreased several fold. The work of Estonian societies and public cultural activities in the Estonian language were suspended. The political situation also meant a suspension of emigration from Estonia to Finland. The emigration of Estonians to Finland resumed after the collapse of the Soviet Union in 1991 and soared after Estonia joined the European Union in 2004. Approximately 22,000 Estonian citizens (31.01.2009) currently reside in Finland. Although Estonians have lived in Finland throughout Finland's history, large-scale immigration only commenced in the 1990s, and these different waves of immigration and emigration resulted in the emergence of new Estonian-language communities, the so-called "late-origin communities", which have no connection, and probably no contact, with the descendants of those Estonians who emigrated to Finland in the first decades of the 20th century or remained in this country after World War II. These various Estonian groups are differentiated by their historical, cultural, social and linguistic experience both in their host country and country of origin. On the basis of the latest Estonian emigration statistics, it can be concluded that Estonian-language communities in Finland are the fastest growing foreign Estonian communities in the western diaspora and these statistical data also indicate that the Estonian population in Finland is evolving into the largest Estonian community in the western diaspora.

The bilingual language use of first generation immigrants is characterised by the dominant use of unidirectional copying from Finnish into the Estonian. The bilingual speaker moves within the frames of the Estonian language until a change takes place in the conversational setting which motivates the speaker to use Finnish. At a relatively primary stage of language contacts, bilingual speech is characterised by the copying of the units, patterns or structural features of the model code as a casual, spontaneous linguistic behavioural mode for a certain purpose. The manifestation of copies can be construed as the addition of a new language tool into the speaker's mother tongue, but it is also possible that the copy produced on the basis of L2 material conventionalises and then starts replacing the linguistic form of the mother tongue completely. Although the key-words of Estonian-Finnish code-copying are spontaneous and momentary, it can be assumed that copies will grow more customary in idiolects, where they will then reach the community level and become habitualised. The Impact of the Finnish language to differing degrees, can be observed in the speech of all the language informants. Although the attributes of Estonian-Finnish bilingual speech in the relatively initial stage of contact are spontaneous and momentary, one can suppose that innovations which spread in idiolects will reach the group-level language and become more customary in speakers' language use over time, eventually finding a permanent place in the speaker's mother tongue.

## References

Appel, René & Pieter Muysken 1987: *Language contact and bilingualism.* London: Arnold.

Backus, Ad 1998: The intergenerational codeswitching continuum in an immigrant community. – Guus Extra & Ludo Verhoeven (eds), *Bilingualism and Migration.* Studies on Language Acquisition 14. Berlin: Mouton de Gruyter. 261–279.

—— 2004: Turkish as an immigrant language in Europe. – Tej K. Bhatia & William C. Ritchie (eds), *The Handbook of Bilingualism.* Oxford: Blackwell. 689–724.

—— 2006: Limits to modularity: The 'insertion' of complex 'lexical' constructions in codeswitching. – Conxita Lleo (ed.), *Interfaces on Multilingualism. Acquisition and representation.* Hamburg Studies on Multilingualism 4. Amsterdam/Philadelphia: John Benjamins. 261–279.

Berry, John W. 1992: Acculturation and adaptation in a new society. – *International Migration 30: 69–85.*

Eamets, Raul & Kaia Philips 2004: *Tööjõu vaba liikumine Euroopa Liidus ja selle mõju Eesti tööturule.* Tartu Ülikooli Euroopa Kolledži toimetised 20. Tartu.

EKG I = Erelt, Mati & Reet Kasik & Helle Metslang & Henno Rajandi & Kristiina Ross & Henn Saari & Kaja Tael & Silvi Vare (eds) 1995: *Eesti keele grammatika I. Morfoloogia. Sõnamoodustus.* Eesti Teaduste Akadeemia. Eesti Keele Instituut.

EKKS 1993 = *Eesti kirjakeele seletussõnaraamat.* Eesti Teaduste Akadeemia. Eesti Keele Instituut.

Extra, Guus & Ludo Verhoeven 1998: Immigrant minority groups and immigrant minority languages in Europe. – Guus Extra & Ludo Verhoeven (eds), *Bilingualism and Migration.* Studies on Language Acquisition 14. Berlin, New York: Mouton de Gruyter. 3–29.

Halmari, Helena 1997: *Government and Codeswitching. Explaining American Finnish.* Studies in Bilingualism Series 12. Amsterdam/Philadelphia: John Benjamins.

Hennoste, Tiit 2000: Sissejuhatus suulisesse eesti keelde IV. Suulise kõne erisõnavara 3. Partiklid. – *Akadeemia* 8: 1773–1806.

—— 2003: Keelekasutuse uurimine. – Mati Erelt (ed.), *Eesti keele uurimise analüüs.* Emakeele Seltsi Aastaraamat 48/2002. Tallinn: Emakeele Selts. 217–262.

ISK = Hakulinen, Auli & Maria Vilkuna & Riitta Korhonen & Vesa Koivisto & Tarja Riitta Heinonen & Irja Alho 2004: *Iso suomen kielioppi.* Helsinki: Suomen Kirjallisuuden Seura.

Jamin, Jérôme 2003: *Migrants and ethnic minorities in Belgium.* CEDEM. Université de Liège.

Johanson, Lars 1993: Code-copying in immigrant Turkish. – Guus Extra & Ludo Verhoeven (eds), *Immigrant languages in Europe.* Clevedon & Philadelphia & Adelaide. 197–221.

—— 2006: Turkic language contacts in a typology of code interaction. – Hendrik Boeschoten & Lars Johanson (eds), *Turkic languages in contact.* Turcologica 61. Wiesbaden: Harrassowitz Verlag. 4–26.

Jürgenson, Aivar 2002: *Siberi eestlaste territoriaalsus ja identiteet.* Tallinn: Tallinna Pedagoogikaülikooli Kirjastus.

Jürjo, Indrek 1996: *Pagulus ja Nõukogude Eesti. Vaateid KGB, EKP ja VEKSA arhiividokumentide põhjal.* Tallinn: Umara.

Keevallik, Leelo 2006a. Pragmaatiliste partiklite laenutüübid rootsieesti keeles. – Helen Koks, Jan Rahman (eds), *Mitmõkeelisüs ja keelevaihtus õdagumeresoomõ maiõ pääl.* Võro Instituudi toimõndusõq 18. Võro: Võro Instituut. 116–133.

—— 2006b. Keelekontakt ja pragmaatika. – Ilona Tragel & Haldur Õim (eds), *Teoreetiline keeleteadus Eestis* II. Tartu Ülikooli üldkeeleteaduse õppetooli toimetised 7. Tartu: Tartu Ülikooli kirjastus. 85–96.

Kovács, Magdolna 2001: *Code-Switching and Language Shift in Australian Finnish in Comparison with Australian Hungarian.* Åbo: Åbo Akademis Förlag.

Kulu, Hill 1992: *Eestlased maailmas: ülevaade arvukusest ja paiknemisest.* Tartu.

Kulu, Liina 2000: *Isikute rändega seotud probleemid Euroopa Liidu idalaienemisel.* Tartu Ülikooli Euroopa Kolledž. Võru: AS Võru Täht.

Leskinen, Jari & Antti Juutilainen 2005: *Jatko-sodan pikkujättiläinen.* Helsinki: WSOY.

Liebkind, Karmela & Simo Mannila & Inga Jasinskaja-Lahti & Magdalena Jaakkola & Eve Kyntäjä & Anni Reuter 2004: *Venäläinen, virolainen, suomalainen. Kolmen maahanmuuttajaryhmän kotoutuminen Suomeen.* Helsinki: Gaudeamus.

Muysken, Pieter 2000: *Bilingual Speech. A typology of Code-Mixing.* Cambridge: Cambridge University Press.

Mäkeläinen, Tapio 2006: *Kabböle 100.* Helsinki: Aaltojen yhteys.

Myers-Scotton, Carol 2002: *Contact Linguistics. Bilingual Encounters and Grammatical Outcomes.* Oxford: Oxford University Press.

Nigol, August 1918: *Eesti asundused ja asupaigad Venemaal.* Tartu.

Nivanka, Erika 2002: *Soome lahe kahel kaldal.* Tallinn: Faatum.

Pajusalu, Karl 1998: Kas väliseesti keel on olemas? – *Keel ja Kirjandus* 4: 286–288.

Pohjanpää, Kirsti & Seppo Paananen & Mauri Nieminen 2003: *Maahanmuuttajien elinolot. Venäläisten, virolaisten, somalialaisten ja vietnamilaisten elämää Suomessa 2002.* Elinolot 2003: 1. Tilastokeskus. Helsinki.

Poplack, Shana 1980: "Sometimes I'll start a sentence in English Y TERMINO EN ESPAÑOL": Towards a typology of code-switching. – *Linguistics* 18 (7/8): 581–618.

Praakli, Kristiina 2009: *Esimese põlvkonna Soome eestlaste kakskeelne keelekasutus ja koodikopeerimine.* Dissertationes philologiae Estonicae Universitatis Tartuensis 24. Tartu: Tartu Ülikooli Kirjastus.

Pullat, Raimo 1992: *Eesti linnarahvastik 18. sajandil.* Tallinn: Olion.

Raag, Raimo 1999: *Eestlane väljaspool Eestit: ajalooline ülevaade.* Tartu: Tartu Ülikooli Kirjastus.

Rahi-Tamm, Aigi 2004: *Inimkaotused. Teise maailmasõja järgsed massirepressioonid Eestis: allikad ja uurimisseis.* Tartu: Tartu Ülikooli Kirjastus.

Relvik, Heino 2003: *Mereväe soomepoisid.* Tallinn: Soome Mereväes Teeninud Eestlaste Gild (Tallinn: EVG Print).

Reuter, Anni & Magdalena Jaakkola 2005: Venäjänkielisten, vironkielisten ja kaksikielisten maahanmuuttajien sosiaaliset verkostot. – Seppo Paananen (ed.), Maahanmuuttajien elämää Suomessa. Tilastokeskus.

Riionheimo, Helka 2007: *Muutoksen monet juuret: oman ja vieraan risteytyminen Viron inkerinsuomalaisten imperfektinmuodostuksessa.* Helsinki: Suomalaisen Kirjallisuuden Seura.

Roiko-Jokela, Heikki (eds) 1997: *Virallista politiikkaa – epävirallista kansakäymistä: Suomen ja Viron suhteiden käännekohtia 1860–1991.* Jyväskylä: Atena Kustannus.

Sankoff, Gillian 2001: Linguistic Outcomes of Language Contact. – Handbook of Sociolinguistics. Peter Trudgill & Jack Chambers & Natalie Schilling-Estes (eds). Oxford: Basil Blackwell, 638–668.

Statistics Finland – <http://www.stat.fi>.

Statistisches Bundesamt Deutschland – <http://www.destatis.de>.

STV 1946 = Suomen tilastollinen vuosikirja 1944–45. Helsinki: Tilastollinen päätoimisto 1946.

STV 1948 = Suomen tilastollinen vuosikirja 1946–47. Helsinki: Tilastollinen päätoimisto 1948.

STV 1989 = Suomen tilastollinen vuosikirja 1989: Helsinki: Tilastokeskus 1989.

STV 2005 = Suomen tilastollinen vuosikirja 2005. Helsinki: Tilastokeskus 2005.

Talve, Ilmar 1999: Kolmas kodumaa. Tartu: Ilmamaa.

Tammaru, Tiit & Kaja Kumer-Haukanõmm & Kristi Anniste [forthcoming]: Eesti diasporaa kujunemise kolm lainet.

Tarnanen, Mirja & Minna Suni 2005: Maahanmuuttajien kieliympäristö ja kielitaito. – Seppo Paananen (ed.), Maahanmuuttajien elämää Suomessa. Helsinki: Tilastokeskus. 9–21.

Thomason, Sarah Grey 2001: Language Contact: an introduction. Edinburgh: Edinburgh University Press.

Uustalu, Evald & Rein Moora 1993: Soomepoisid: ülevaade Eesti vabatahtlike liikumisest ning sõjateest Soomes ja kodumaal Teise maailmasõja päevil. Tallinn: Olion.

Valk, Aune & Kristel Karu-Kletter 2005: Eestlaste identiteet Eestis ja Rootsis. Eri kontekstide ja põlvkondade võrdlus. Akadeemia 9: 1972–2008.

―――― 2006: Rootsi eestlase eesti-identiteet. – Kaja Kumer-Haukanõmm, Tiit Rosenberg, Tiit Tammaru (eds), Suur põgenemine 1944. Eestlase lahkumine läände ja selle mõjud. Tartu: Tartu Ülikooli Kirjastus. 147–170.

Viikberg, Jüri 2001: Väliseesti keeleprobleemid (eriti seoses tagasirändega Eestisse). Eesti Keele Instituut.

Välis-Eesti Almanak 1929 = Välis-Eesti Almanak I, 1929: Tallinn: Välis-Eesti Ühing.

Välis-Eesti Almanak 1933 = Välis-Eesti Almanak 1933: Tallinn: Välis-Eesti Ühing.

# Hilistekkeline eesti keelevähemus Soomes

*Kristiina Praakli*

Soome eestikeelse elanikkonna tekkest võib rääkida alates 20. sajandi algusest, mil Soomes elas arvestatava suurusega eesti kogukond, erinevatel andmetel u 2000 inimest. Teise maailmasõja pingelistest aegadest johtuvalt vähenes Soome eestikeelne elanikkond mitu korda. Eesti seltside tegevus peatati ja omakeelne avalik kultuuritegevus lõpetati. Poliitiline olukord peatas ka väljarände Eestist Soome. Eestlaste väljaränne Soome algas uuesti Nõukogude Liidu lagunemise järel (1991) ning suurenes hüppeliselt pärast Eesti ühinemist Euroopa Liiduga (2004). Praegu elab Soomes u 22 000 (<www.stat.fi> 31.01.2009) Eesti kodanikku.

Esimene arvukam eestlaste siirdumine Soome toimus 20. sajandi esimesel kümnendil, kui terava poliitilise õhkkonna tõttu asusid Soome mitmed Eesti ühiskonna- ja kultuuritegelased. Kui Eesti 1918. aastal iseseisvaks riigiks kuulutati, elas Soomes arvestatava suurusega eesti kogukond – eri andmetel u 2000 inimest, neist suurem osa Helsingis. Helsingi kõrval elas eestlasi ka Kabböle rannakülas (Pernaja vald, Itä-Uudenmaa maakond). Lisaks liikumissuunale Tallinn-Helsingi on erinevatel perioodil valitsenud rändeline side ka Narva ja Viiburi vahel.

Soome eestlaskonna arv oli veel 1930. alguses 1500 ringis. Soome statistika aastaraamatus (STV 1948) esitatud arvandmetest nähtub, et alates 1930ndatest aastatest on Eesti kodakondsust omavate isikute arv pidevalt kahanenud. Teise maailmasõja järel Soome jäänud eestlaste kohta on raske täpseid või tegelikke arve leida.

Soome hilistekkelised eestikeelsed kogukonnad on moodustunud Nõukogude Liidu lagunemise (1991) järgsete intensiivsete väljarändelainete tagajärjel. Uus emigratsioonilaine Eestist Soome algas 1980. aastate keskel: kui 1990. aastal elas Soomes 1394 eesti keelt emakeelena rääkijat, siis 1995. aastal oli vastav arv juba 8710 ning 2004. aasta lõpus 13 978 (andmed Tilastokeskus 2005: 116–117). Eesti Statistikaameti andmetel (Statistikaamet 1995: 77; 1999: 57) on Soome siirdumise kõrgaeg on olnud 1995. aasta, mil Soome emigreerus 1067 isikut. Soome emigreerumine suurenes hüppeliselt ka pärast Eesti ühinemist Euroopa Liiduga (2004). Erinevatel andmetel on Soomes rohkem või vähem püsivalt elavate eestlaste arv ühinemisele järgnenud aastate jooksul hüppeliselt tõusnud, ulatudes viimastel andmetel 29 000-ni.

KADRI KOREINIK

# Language Ideologies and Identity-building in the Public Discourse of South Estonian

## Abstract

A group's language ideologies play a central part in the building of categories of linguistic identity. The paper aims to present and elaborate on the examples of language ideologies which were employed in identity construction or membership building by the observers and speakers of South Estonian (SE). The data sample includes texts from local papers with the macro topic of SE. Linguistic identity is conceptualised as collective identity and a (social) constructivist approach enhanced by critical discourse analysis (CDA) is applied. Accordingly, languages, identities and memberships are understood as discursively (re)produced. While studying referential and other discursive strategies employed for identity-building efforts, further explanations and interpretations of language ideologies are offered. The results confirm Van Dijk's (2006) position that identifying memberships is not enough to interpret discourses: ingroup and outgroup discursive construction varies a lot, and earlier social practices, including discourses, should be taken into account. Both speakers' and observers' referential strategies demonstrate intra-group and inter-group polarisation; predicational strategies reveal negative other presentation. The analysis of identity-building also explains language ownership: groups who discursively construct linguistic identity do not necessarily "own" the language.

*Ethnic and Linguistic Context of Identity: Finno-Ugric Minorities.* 247–266.
Uralica Helsingiensia 5. Helsinki 2011.

## 1. Introduction

There is often disagreement between observers (usually outgroup) who present language borders as originating from linguistic differentiation and speakers (usually ingroup) who act along with perceived linguistic and other markers in their immediate language context. Indeed, those two boundaries – the static borders which follow isoglosses, and imaginary ones responsible for the linguistic behavior – rarely match (Iannàccaro & Dell'Aquila 2001). These days, languages, identities and memberships are seen as symbolically (re)produced via daily practices which build boundaries between languages, identities and memberships (Gal & Irvine 1995). Thus, both ingroup and outgroup borders, are created through different practices, including discursive practices. Many authors other than linguistic anthropologists, e.g. discourse analysts, have indicated that ideas about linguistic differences – a group's linguistic representations or language ideologies – have played an important part in the development of categories of identity. As for disciplinary orthodoxies concerning language boundaries, social scientists are held responsible for relying on linguistics to provide language categories, and linguists-dialectologists, in turn, are blamed for ignoring the perception of areal variety (Preston 1989). Nevertheless, there seem to be more subtle divisions than those of observers vs. speakers, by which (linguistic) identities and memberships are discursively maintained.

The paper first aims to present and elaborate on the examples of (language) ideologies which were employed in identity construction or membership building by the observers and immediate speakers of South Estonian in public discourse. Then, the in- and outgroup's discursive practices are followed in order to determine patterns in identity-building. By studying referential and other discursive strategies, I will demonstrate that identity-building efforts vary according to the interests the individual members of both in- and outgroup may have and the (discursive) practices they have been involved in earlier. The data sample includes a range of local papers scanned for articles with the macro topic of South Estonian.

## 2. South Estonian and the public discourse related to it

The South Estonian varieties of Finnic spoken in south-eastern Estonia, including Võru (*võro kiil*) and Setu (*seto kiil*), are conventionally considered in public and academic discourse as Estonian dialects (cf. Pajusalu 2003; see Map 1).

Map 1. South-Estonian dialect areas (marked by grey stripes).

For the sake of simplicity, SE primarily stands for South Estonian varieties of Võru and Setu here. Yet, simplicity is not the only reason to leave other South Estonian varieties aside. Given the fate "of the Tartu and Mulgi dialects of Estonian, which until recently formed

249

a bridge that united the Võro-Seto language with Estonian, but are in the process of losing this function", there is a well-grounded reason for speaking about an emerging or incipient (spoken) language (Salminen, personal communication March 26, 2004). Some outgroup linguists and ingroup language activists have also followed the naming practice of the Võro-Seto language (Atlas 2009, Eller 1999, Help et al. 1996). On the other hand, the strong group identity of speakers allows talking about the two essentialised – Võru and Setu – languages (cf. Eichenbaum & Pajusalu 2001; Koreinik & Pajusalu 2007).

Nevertheless, most observers and speakers would agree that Võru and Setu differ most strongly from standard Estonian and are not intelligible to all Estonian-speakers. Võru-speakers are literally bi-dialectual people who speak, and, indeed, switch between Estonian and Võru, but identify themselves as Estonians. The national census does not count Võru-speakers separately from other ethnic Estonians. There are about 65,000 residents in the area, and according to the results of a 1998 sample survey, 90% of residents aged 25–64 claimed frequent or occasional use of Võru (Eichenbaum & Koreinik 2008; Pajusalu, Koreinik & Rahman 2000). Given the likelihood of over-reporting, and considerable out-migration, the overall number of Võru-speakers is estimated at 50,000 active or passive users (Koreinik 2007). Their strong ethnic and national identity is iconically tied to Estonian, leaving, so far, little space for local or regional identities.

Although dialectologists consider Setu a South Estonian sub-dialect, it enjoys strong public support as a language in its own right. Contrary to Võru-speakers, whose tongue is almost completely intelligible to Setu-speakers, the Setu people maintain that they are a distinct ethnic group *vis-à-vis* Estonians (Eichenbaum 1998; Eichenbaum & Pajusalu 2001). The main ethnic difference is the Setu people's different religious background (i.e. Orthodox) and geographic position within the country. To estimate the size of Setu-speakers and the Setu people is difficult, as their habitat is divided by the state border of Estonia and the Russian Federation. Researchers estimate that the number of Setu people has decreased threefold during the last century, now numbering around 5,000 (Aun et al. 2009). According to the findings of a 2005 study, a third of the area's residents (totaling around

4,000) report the Setu language as being their mother tongue and half use it frequently.

There is empirical evidence on language naming practices from 1998 which sheds some light not only upon the perception of linguistic variance and the identity of speech communities, but also on those communities' relations with neighboring communities. Naming conventions revealed imaginary borders, which appeared when accumulated naming practices were put on the geographical map of South-Eastern Estonia. The limited spread of neologism *võro-seto kiil* ('the Võro-Seto language') within the Võru and Setu borderland demonstrates that the ideology of the language activists had only been partly successful; elsewhere in the Võru and Setu-speaking area other naming patterns (and linguistic identity too) were observable. (Koreinik & Pajusalu 2007).

The perception of linguistic borders and related (linguistic) identity may result from contesting – legitimising and delegitimising – (language) ideologies and related identity building. In my previous research (Koreinik forthcoming) I analysed the public discourse of (de)legitimation[1] from 2004–2005 by applying a discourse-historical approach to critical discourse analysis (van Leeuwen & Wodak 1999; Wodak 2003). For that reason, Estonian media texts with national coverage and small-circulation literary magazines were examined for the macro topic of the recognition of SE. From 2004, language activists have demanded that SE be recognised. This followed the linguistic emancipation which began in the late 1980s. I was looking for (language) ideologies appearing in the discourse of (de)legitimation, i.e. for what referential and argumentation strategies were used. The main result – that the *topos* of threat is overwhelmingly employed to justify keeping SE excluded from the category of "language" – shows that the discourse of (de)legitimation can be described as the discourse of endangerment. As for identity building, both the proponents and the opponents of SE recognition employed the referential strategy of

---

1.  Legitimation mostly results in the delegitimation of opposing groups and their ideologies; a group has to demonstrate that its principles are right and just, and their opponents' principles are not. In the process of legitimation the actor is portrayed as a representative or member of an institution. (van Dijk 1998.)

polarisation. The opponents used personal pronouns and collective nouns for establishing the boundary between Estonians and Estonian speakers on one hand, and South Estonian activists on the other. Also, both groups were involved in negative other-presentation: the proponents were blamed for opportunism, the opponents for ignorance.

## 3. Main concepts: (Language) ideology and (linguistic) identity

In the context of collective action, ideology is conceptualised as "a set of symbolic frames which collective actors use to represent their own actions to themselves and to others, within a system of social relationships" (Meluzzi 1996: 349). Furthermore, ideology operates to legitimate the (collective) actor and (de)legitimate the opponent and his/her identity. Legitimation is the key ideological function of discourse (van Dijk 1998). Thus discursive practices often involve (de)legitimation efforts. Language ideologies (re)produce social difference between different languages/varieties (Blackledge 2005) and "reflect the perception of language and discourse that is constructed in the interest of a specific social or cultural group" (Kroskrity 2000: 8). Hence, language ideologies may serve to legitimate the interests and identities of immediate speakers, language planners, observers, or others.

Identity, on the other hand, has been defined as a self-concept, performativity, an informed knowledge about one's group membership, and the emotional meaning attached to it (see also Niño-Murcia & Rothman 2008). Issues of identity are usually raised when memberships or group boundaries are challenged or negotiated or questioned: "(o)ne thinks of identity whenever one is not sure of where one belongs" (Bauman 1996: 19). For example, regional identity is defined as a constitutive element of localised resistance to globalisation (Castells 1997), and its narratives often refer to ideas of nature, landscape, the built environment, culture/ethnicity, dialects, economic success/recession, periphery/centre relations, marginalisation, stereotypic images of a people/community, both of 'us' and 'them', actual/invented histories, utopias and diverging arguments on the identification of people (Paasi 2003).

Linguistic identity is mostly seen either via "linguistic behavior as a series of acts of *identity*" (Le Page & Tabouret-Keller 1985: 14) or as the symbolic capital linguistic forms represent (Bourdieu 1991). As a part of everyday behavior, the use of a linguistic form can become an index of speakers' social identities. "But speakers (and hearers) often notice, rationalise, and justify such linguistic indices, thereby creating linguistic ideologies that purport to explain the source and meaning of the linguistic differences" (Gal & Irvine 1995: 972). Here, linguistic identity is conceptualised as collective identity and the construction of group/membership boundaries familiar from the (social) constructivist approach is extended by postmodern concerns regarding public discourse (cf. Cerulo 1997; Potter & Edwards 1999). In order to understand identity-building, the analysis of the discursive tools employed for creating linguistic memberships and linked group boundaries/distinctions is required:

> *Collective identity is not out there, waiting to be discovered. What is 'out there' is identity discourse on the part of political leaders, intellectuals and countless others, who engage in the process of constructing, negotiating, manipulating or affirming a response to the demand – at times urgent, mostly absent – for a collective image.* (McSweeney 1999: 77–78.)

Although, there is "(t)he shift to view collectivities more as entities in constant flux, and therefore negotiation and renegotiation of membership, does not impede members of a group from deploying an essentialist argument in order to advance a political agenda" (Niño-Murcia & Rothman 2008:15). Consequently, there will always be the question of who is involved in the construction of (linguistic) identity, by whom issues of identity are voiced (speakers, activists-custodians, planners, and other interested individuals/groups), and whose voice is hegemonic.

## 4. Data and method

The number of texts on SE in national and local papers since its institutionalisation[2] is around one thousand. My sample of 21 articles includes both media texts with national coverage and local texts from county papers, in order to study identity-building efforts and discursive practices voiced by the outgroup, including scholars, columnists, and other observers, and the ingroup, i.e. speakers and activists. Similarly to another article currently being written, where deagentialisation in the discourse of endangerment is analysed, I have picked texts where concerns over language loss or dialect extinction were brought up, as I presume this topic to be important enough to voice linguistic representations and to reveal possible polarisation on this matter.

A discourse, a text within its context, is both a social practice/action and its representation, and CDA is concerned with both aspects (Van Leeuwen 1993). Wodak (2003) holds that the discursive construction of groups, e.g. 'Us' and 'Them', and their strategic characterisation, supports the discourse of identity and belongs to the pervasive discourse. Referential or nomination strategies are used to represent memberships, to construct ingroup and outgroup. Intergroup polarisation is observable by the use of (personal) pronouns, which constructs identities and emphasises social distance (van Dijk et al. 1997; Wodak 2003). While looking for predicational strategies, stereotypical and evaluative attributions of positive and negative qualities and implicit and explicit predicates are focused on. The objective of predication is in "labeling social actors more or less positively or negatively, deprecatorily or appreciatively" (Wodak 2003: 139). In addition to the referential and predicational strategies focused on, argumentative strategies are given some consideration, to the extent that such arguments can be found in the same text samples (ibid.).

---

2. The linguistic emancipation of SE varieties started with the actions of Võru Movement ca 20 years ago (see also Kansui 1999). In the mid-1990s the movement vied for state backing and as a result the state R&D institution, the Võru Institute, was founded. The institute has been active in corpus, status, and acquisition planning. The process can be called the institutionalization of SE (Koreinik 2007; Koreinik forthcoming).

# 5. Results

## 5.1. Referential strategies

Given the vague distinction between referential and predicational strategies (Wodak 2003), the interpretation of the results under separate paragraphs would seem rather rigid as both categories may include the moves of the other discursive strategy too. The following two extracts (Extract 1, 2) demonstrate a difference activists make when talking about Võro-folks (or speakers). The difference is voiced by the personal pronoun "they". "We" refers to the whole audience of Estonian speakers. In extract 3 "we" is voiced by an activist and refers to activists too. In the case of the (de)legitimation discourse "they" represented the Võro speakers (incl. activists) too (Koreinik forthcoming). Similar – the use of the pronouns "we" and "they" – referential strategies are also employed by an outgroup language planner (Extract 4).

(1)  *Kui **me** räägime võru keelest, siis sellel puudub ainult üks
     identiteet ja see on **võrokeste** eneseteadvus, **nad** peavad ennast
     eestlasteks ja sellega tuleb arvestada. **Nad** tahavad ennast
     eestlasteks pidada.*
     'If **we** talk about the Võro language, then it lacks one identity
     only and it is the self-consciousness of **Võro-folk, they** regard
     themselves as Estonians and it must be taken into account.
     **They** want to regard themselves as Estonians.'
     (Võrumaa Teataja August 12, 1995)

(2)  ***Võrokesed** peaksid kokku hoidma, on **nad** ju omaette rahvus.*
     'The Võro-folk should stick together; they are yet a nation on
     their own. (Postimees August 7, 2000)

(3)  *"**Meie** üks ja peamine eesmärk on võru subnatsiooni säilita-
     mine."*
     '**Our** sole and primary objective is the preservation of Võru
     sub-nation.' (Postimees August 14, 1998)

255

(4)  *See ei tähenda, et **me** ei peaks jätkama kõigi lõunaeesti keele-*
     *kujude tutvustamist ja kas või sporaadilist kasutamist, et **nen-***
     ***del aladel** ei kaoks passiivne keeleoskus ja **nende keelekujude***
     *täielik mõistmine, ja et **neid keelekujusid** ei häbenetaks.*
     'It does not mean that we should not continue familiarising our-
     selves with and even sporadically using all the South Estonian
     varieties, in order that passive proficiency and complete com-
     prehension of **those varieties** in **those areas** would not disap-
     pear, and that **those varieties** would not be shamed of.'
     (Postimees November 10, 2007)

As for other discursive strategies, the argumentative strategy of theoretical rationalisation is employed. Both moves, explanation and giving a definition, are used. In this case the activists were not trying to
"hide their internal plurality" (Meluzzi 1996: 356), instead, a variety
of ideas are traceable over the years and among individual activists.
The neologism of "variety" which replaces here the familiar "dialect"
is introduced in Extract 4.

Extract 5 is drawn from an article by a teacher of Võru language
and culture and "we" seems at first to refer to membership of a group
other than just Võru-speakers, most likely to active and concerned
Võru-speakers, activists, the custodians of Võru and diversity (cf.
Muehlmann 2007). The second one (Extract 6) is voiced by an outgroup columnist and the "we" refers to Estonians and Estonian speakers.

(5)  *Praeguse süsteemitu võru keele ja kultuuri õpetamisega ei*
     *suuda **me** järgmisi võrukeelseid põlvkondi luua.*
     'With the existing unsystematic teaching of the Võru language
     and culture **we** cannot produce the next Võru-speaking genera-
     tions.' (Võrumaa Teataja December 13, 2008)

256

(6)   *Suurem jagu **meie** praegusi emakeeleõpetajaid poleks selleks
vist võimelisedki, on ju **neile** pealuu sisse taotud, et keel on üks,
püha ja normitud.*
'Most of **our** contemporary teachers of the mother tongue could
not be possibly able to do that, **they** are [=] brainwashed into
thinking that the language is single, sacred and standardised.'
(Postimees March 28, 2000)

In Extract 7 the discursive position of the inclusive, established majority and the construction of a common future in the enlarged European
Union is voiced. In the next Extract (8) the Finnic identity is built
by explanation. Explanation is a common move in the argumentative
strategies of rationalisation. The argumentation is supported by the
rest of the context, in an interview where the language loss and identity shift of some Finnic people is also discussed.

(7)   *"**ELi minejatena** tuleb **meil** oma väikekeelte ja murrete kaits-
miseks teha senisest rohkem."*
'**We as EU entrants** have to do more than before for the preservation of small languages and dialects.'
(Maaleht January 14, 1999)

(8)   *Seega on keelekeskkond **läänemeresoomlase** identiteedi säili-
miseks hädavajalik.*
'Thus the language environment is indispensable for the preservation of **a Finnic** identity.' (Sirp September 27, 2002)

In the following example (Extract 9) a local Võru-speaking journalist
opposes herself and "us" to those who have been introducing the new
standard. However the agents, who are responsible for standardisation
and thus for damaging spoken Võru, are suppressed (not mentioned).
Suppression is realised via passive agent deletion. As the way a social
action/actor is represented may shape its interpretation (van Leeuwen
2008), it is more difficult to identify with those not mentioned than
with "us" who worry about the language and set ourselves up in opposition to the unmentioned ones.

257

(9)  *Kui nii edasi läheb,* **tekitatakse** *isade-emade ja vanaisade-vanaemade* **meile** *kõnekeelena õpetatud ja veel säilinud võru keelele kasu asemel hoopis kahju.*
'If it goes on like this, instead of good harm **is being done** to the Võru taught as a spoken language by grandpas-grandmas and still preserved.' (Võrumaa Teataja December 20, 2008)

By reference to (Baltic) Germans, as legitimate others, authorisation is voiced (Extract 10). Authorisation entails references to historicity, tradition, law, religion, and people (van Leeuwen 1995).

(10)  *Üldse olid Lõuna-Eesti asja eest väljas kõige rohkem* **sakslased.**
'All in all, **the Germans** were the most active in South Estonian matters.' (Sirp September 27, 2002)

## 5.2. Predicational strategies

Both ingroup and outgroup columnists have attributed mainly negative qualities to the language activists (Extract 11–13). Extract 11 is drawn from the title of an article by an outgroup columnist, writer and translator and refers to SE activists and their activities. In Extract 12 authorisation is employed: reference to the people, to everyman is made by appealing to the taxpayer. The latter is also an example of the representation of a social actor by genericisation (van Leeuwen 2008). In general, activists are represented as groups, they are assimilated.

(11)  *Need tagakiusatud paremad eestlased.*
**'Those persecuted better Estonians'.**
(Title in Eesti Päevaleht May 17, 1999)

(12)  *Ikka ja jälle otsivad* **Võru Instituudi** *"teadurid" endale tööd, et õigustada* **maksumaksja** *miljonite kulutamist.*
'Again and again **"researchers"** of **Võru Institute** are making work for themselves in order to justify spending the taxpayer's millions.' (Võrumaa Teataja December 20, 2006)

(13) *Mind on ära tüüdanud* **murdefännide** *pidev seletamine, kui väga Nõukogude ajal keelati ja mõnitati, et õpetajad sundisid ka vabal ajal õpilastele kirjakeelt peale.*
'I am fed up with **the dialect fans'** constant explanation how much (it) was prohibited and mocked, that teachers forced the standard on pupils in their free time too.'
(Võrumaa Teataja July 26, 2008)

Moreover, an ingroup linguist and a columnist oppose the creation of a Võro-Seto language (standard) by calling it a foolish joke or a fouled language.

(18) *See Võru ja Setu liitmine on minu meelest* **mõtlematult narr temp.**
'The uniting of Võru and Setu is **an inconsiderately foolish trick** to my mind.' (Viruskundra October 1996)

(19) *(...), et ei olegi vaja osata eesti keelt, vaid* **solgitud võru keele sugemetega setu keelt.**
'(...), that there is no need to know Estonian but **the Setu language contaminated by the elements of Võru language.**'
(Võrumaa Teataja December 20, 2008)

The next predicational strategies can also be interpreted as narratives of regional identity and are employed by both in- and outgroup. South Estonia has been described as being different to North Estonia but, however, in a positive way. Extracts 20 and 21 are also examples of comparison. Comparison – "the claim that (legitimate) others have engaged in similar actions" – is the tool of authorisation and "a well-known move in several strategies of legitimation" (Rojo & van Dijk 1997: 537). Ireland was referred to as a legitimate other here. Giving a definition is voiced by an ingroup activist (Extract 22).

(20) *Lõuna-Eesti on omaette maailm, teistsugune, palavam ja poeetilisem kui Põhja-Eesti. Nende suhe on ehk nagu Iirimaal Inglismaaga.*
'South Estonia is a world apart, different, warmer and more poetic than North Estonia. Their relationship is perhaps like that which Ireland has with England.'
(Eesti Päevaleht November 23, 1996)

(21) *(...), tuleks lõunaeestlust käsitleda laiemalt elulaadina, eluhoiakuna, lõunaeesti traditsioonide väärtustamisena, umbes nii nagu Iirimaal kestab üldisest keelevahetusest hoolimata edasi iiri elulaad, (...).*
'(...), South Estonianness should be treated as something wider – as a lifestyle, an attitude, the appraisement of South Estonian traditions, approximately like the Irish way of life continues despite general the language shift in Ireland, (...).'
(Postimees November 10, 2007)

(22) *(...) teiseks on Võrumaa lõunaeestluse kontsentraat, kõik lõunaeestiline on siin esindatud oma erilisuses ja äärmuses.*
'...secondly, Võrumaa is **the epitome of (being) South Estonian**, all South Estonian is represented here in its distinctiveness and extremeness.' (Sirp September 27, 2002)

## 6. Conclusions

The referential strategies employed demonstrate multiple polarisations: both between speakers of the ingroup and between in- and outgroup. The earlier analysis of discursive positions in the (de)legitimation discourse also demonstrated implicit polarisation: the established majority (the proponents of SE recognition) vs. the endangered majority (its opponents) (Koreinik forthcoming). Some ingroup columnists refer to ingroup activists as "they" or use passive agent deletion. Ingroup activists use "we" both ways: inclusively for all Estonians and exclusively for ingroup activists. However, "they" is used for

Võru-speaking-folk too. Võru-speakers are thus constructed as being Finnic people, EU-entrants and Estonians, by turns the ethnos and a sub-nation. Although Võru-activists are constructed as a group of persecuted Estonians, as dialect "fans", sometimes their agency is hidden. The identity-building discourse runs parallel to the (de)legitimation discourse, where the proponents of SE argued from the discursive position of the established majority and with no reference to their opponents. Instead, ingroup activists are engaged in authorisation by reference to legitimate others and in rationalisation. Ingroup columnists, in turn, are involved in negative other presentation, they try to marginalise and even homogenise ingroup activists. Indeed, the Other "is often essentialised and imagined as homogeneous" (Gal & Irvine 1995: 975).

The creation of a Võro-Seto standard is opposed by ingroup columnists. Võru and Setu are represented as essentialised. The dislike of the Võro-Seto naming practice is not supported by discursive practices alone. The survey data from 2005 in both Setu and Võru-speaking communities reflect some exclusive membership or identity-building (Koreink & Pajusalu 2007: 194-5). Ingroup activists, and an outgroup columnist too, support identity-building by (re)producing (regional) narratives about South Estonia.

To conclude, the results show that it is too one-dimensional to draw ideological memberships exclusively in terms of language use: speakers as the ingroup and observers as the outgroup. Although *we* is occasionally used to refer to SE speakers, the use of personal pronouns and other referential strategies demonstrate that ideological *we*-groups are built on a narrower basis than that of speaking SE or not. Van Dijk (1998) solves the puzzle of ideology vs. group identity with dynamics in the process of identification: some principles/representations may adapt to social or political changes, some others may stay unchanged. For example, despite a shared language, other memberships, social and other resources, objectives, and interests vary a great deal, causing group identity to depend on particular situations, successful experiences, the existence of opponents, etc. Therefore, both the ingroup and the outgroup can be far more complex to define and further evidence is needed on their agendas. Data other than media texts would provide the analysis with additional depth. Nevertheless, there is reason to consider some voices who participate in identity-building in the public discourse of SE as members of ideological groups:

> *Hence, a number of social criteria about permanence, continuity, social practices, interests, relations to other groups, and so on, need to be satisfied, including the fundamental basis of group identification: a feeling of group belonging that is typically expressed by the pronoun we* (Van Dijk 2006: 119).

Taking into account their voiced interests, relations to other groups and/or group belonging, ingroup language activists and outgroup language planners undoubtedly fit into ideological groups. The position of columnists is, however, more ambiguous and requires further analysis. Yet the analysis of language ideologies and identity-building for SE also clarifies an issue of language ownership: groups who are discursively involved in the construction of linguistic identity do not necessarily "own" the language. The concept of language ownership is worth considering when it comes to the analysis of language policy and planning, an area where the discursive and other practices of SE activists and others definitely belong.

# References

Atlas 2009: UNESCO Atlas of the World's Languages in Danger, 2009 edition. – <http://www.unesco.org/culture/ich/index.php?pg=00139> 2.7.2009.

Aun, Mare & Valk, Heiki & Selart, Anti & Lillak, Anti (eds) 2009: *Setomaa 2. Vanem ajalugu muinasajast kuni 1920. aastani.* Tartu: Eesti Rahva Muuseum.

Bauman, Zygmunt 1996: From Pilgrim to Tourist – or a Short History of Identity. – Hall, Stuart & Paul du Gay (eds), *Questions of Cultural Identity.* London: Sage. 18–36.

Blackledge, Adrian 2005: *Discourse and Power in a Multilingual World.* Philadelphia, PA, USA: John Benjamins Publishing Company.

Bourdieu, Pierre 1991: *Language and Symbolic Power.* Cambridge: Polity Press.

Castells, Manuel 1997: *The power of identity.* Oxford: Blackwell.

Cerulo, Karen A. 1997: Identity construction: New Issues, New Directions. – *Annual Review of Sociology* 23: 385–409.

Eichenbaum, Külli (ed.) 1998: *Ku kavvas Setomaalõ seto rahvast jakkus?* Publications of Võro Institute 2.

Eichenbaum, Külli & Pajusalu, Karl 2001: Setode ja võrokeste keelehoiakutest ja identiteedist. – *Keel ja Kirjandus* 7: 483–489.

Eichenbaum, Külli & Koreinik, Kadri 2008: *Kuis eläs mulgi, saarõ ja võro kiil?* Publications of Võro Institute 21.

Eller, Kalle 1999: *Võro-Seto language.* Võru: *Võro* Instituut.

Gal, Susan & Irvine, Judith T. 1995: The Boundaries of Languages and Disciplines: How Ideologies Construct Difference. – *Social Research* Vol. 62, No. 4: 967–1001.

Help, Toomas & Jüvä, Sullõv & Kasak, Enn 1996: Võro-seto kiil. – Jüvä Sullõv & Marju Kõivupuu (eds), *Võrokiilne lugõmik* (2nd edition). Võru: Võro Instituut.

Iannàccaro, Gabriele & Dell'Aquila, Vittorio 2001: Mapping languages from inside: notes on perceptual dialectology. – *Social and Cultural Geography* 2, 3: 265–280.

Kansui, Akiko 1999: *Tiiki syugi undou ni okeru gengo to tisiki zin – Esutonia nanbu Voru tihou no zirei kara.* PhD Dissertation. Osaka: Sougou Kenkyuu Daigakuin Daigaku. [cited from unpublished English summary.]

Koreinik, Kadri 2007: *Võro. The Võro language in education in Estonia. Regional Dossiers Series.* Ljouwert/Leeuwarden: Mercator European Research Centre on Multilingualism and Language Learning.

—— 2011: Public discourse of (de)legitimation: the case of South Estonian language. – *Journal of Baltic Studies* x–x. [forthcoming]

Koreinik, Kadri & Pajusalu, Karl 2007: Language naming practices and linguistic identity in South-Eastern Estonia. – Roger Blokland & Cornelius Hasselblatt (eds), *Language and Identity in the Finno-Ugric World. Proceedings of the Fourth International Symposium at the University of Groningen, May 17–19, 2006.* Maastricht: Shaker. 192–204.

Kroskrity, Paul V. 2000: Regimenting Languages. – Paul V. Kroskrity (ed.), *Regimes of Language. Ideologies, Polities, and Identities.* Santa Fe, New Mexico: SAR.

Le Page, Robert B. & Tabouret-Keller, Andrée 1985: *Acts of Identity.* Cambridge: Cambridge University Press.

McSweeney, Bill 1999: *Security, identity and interests.* Cambridge: Cambridge University Press.

Melucci, Alberto 1996: *Challenging Codes. Collective action in the information age.* Cambridge: Cambridge University Press.

Muehlmann, Shaylih 2007: Defending diversity: Staking out a common global interest? – Duchêne, Alexandre & Heller, Monica (eds), *Discourses of endangerment: ideology and interest in the defense of languages.* London; New York: Continuum.

Niño-Murcia, Mercedes & Rothman, Jason (eds) 2008: *Bilingualism and Identity. Spanish at the crossroads with other languages.* Studies in Bilingualism 37. Amsterdam: John Benjamins Publishing Company.

Paasi, Anssi 2003: Region and place: regional identity in question. – *Progress in Human Geography* 27, 4: 475–485.

Pajusalu, Karl 2003: Estonian dialects. – Mati Erelt (ed.), *Estonian Language.* Linguistica Uralica, Supplementary Series 1. Tallinn: Estonian Academy Publischers. 231–272.

Pajusalu, Karl & Koreinik, Kadri & Rahman, Jan 2000: *Lõunaeesti keele kasutusest Kagu-Eestis.* – Koreinik, Kadri & Rahman, Jan (eds), *A kiilt rahvas kynõlõs... Võrokeste keelest, kommetest, identiteedist.* Publications of Võro Institute 8, 13–37.

Potter, Jonathan & Edwards, Derek 1999: Social Representations and Discursive Psychology: From Cognition to Action. – *Culture and Psychology*, Vol. 5(4), 447–458.

Preston, Dennis R. 1989: *Perceptual Dialectology. Nonlinguists' Views of Areal Linguistics*. Topics in Sociolinguistics. Dordrecht: Foris Publications.

Rojo, Luisa Martin & van Dijk, Teun A. 1997: "There was a problem, and it was solved!": legitimating the expulsion of 'illegal' immigrants in Spanish parliamentary discourse. – *Discourse & Society* 8, 4.

Van Dijk, Teun 1998: *Ideology: A Multidisciplinary Approach*. London: Sage.

Van Dijk, Teun A. 2006: Ideology and discourse analysis. – *Journal of Political Ideologies*, 11 (2), 115–140.

Van Dijk, Teun A. & Ting-Toomey, Stella & Smitherman, Geneva & Troutman, Denise 1997: Discourse, Ethnicity, Culture and Racism. – Teun A. Van Dijk (ed.), *Discourse as Social Interaction. Discourse studies: A Multidisciplinary Introduction, Vol. 2*. London: Sage.

Van Leeuwen, Theo J. 1993: Genre and field in critical discourse analysis: a synopsis. – *Discourse & Society* 4, 2: 193–223.

—— 1995: *The Grammar of Legitimation*. London: School of Printing, School of Media.

—— 2008: *Discourse and Practice: New Tools for Critical Discourse Analysis*. Oxford Studies in Sociolinguistics. Oxford University Press.

Van Leeuwen, Theo J. & Wodak, Ruth 1999: Legitimizing immigration control: a discourse-historical analysis. – *Discourse Studies* 1, 1: 83–119

Wodak, Ruth 2003: Populist discourses. The Rhetoric of Exclusion in Written Genres. – *Document Design* 4, 2: 132–148.

# Keeleideoloogiad ja identiteediloome lõunaeesti keele avalikus diskursuses

*Kadri Koreinik*

Keeleideoloogiad mängivad (keelelise) identiteedi loomes olulist rolli. Artikli eesmärgiks on arutleda nende keeleideoloogiate üle, mida kasutavad identiteediloomes üheltpoolt lõunaeesti keele uurijad-vaatlejad ning teiseltpoolt kasutajad. Tekstivalim koosneb üle-eestiliste ja kohalike ajalehtede lõunaeesti teemalistest artiklitest aastatest 1995–2008. Keelelist identiteeti mõistetakse ennekõike kollektiivse identiteedina. Seda vaadeldakse (sotsiaal)konstruktsionistlikku lähenemist silmas pidades ja kasutades kriitilise diskursuse analüüsi vahendeid, mis lubavad keelt, identiteeti ja sotsiaalseid gruppe käsitleda diskursiivselt (taas)toodetuna. Artiklis analüüsitakse mitmesuguseid identiteediloomes kasutatavaid strateegiaid, eeskätt viitavaid või nimetavaid strateegiaid (*referential or nomination strategies*). Tulemused kinnitavad Van Dijki (2006) seisukohta, mille järgi ei piisa identiteediloome seletamisel sotsiaalse grupi liikmesuse – antud konteksis keelekasutajad *versus* mittekasutajad – kindlakstegemisest-määramisest, kuna identiteediloome varieerub tugevasti grupisiseselt ja ka -väliselt, arvestada tuleb ka varasemate sotsiaalsete (diskursiivsete) praktikatega. Nii lõunaeesti keele kõnelejate kui ka vaatlejate (lingvistide, kolumnistide jms) strateegiad näitavad nii grupisisest kui ka -välist polarisatsiooni, predikatiivsed strateegiad (*predicational strategies*) lisaks ka negatiivset teise-esitlemist (*negative other-presentation*). Sarnaseid võtteid kasutati ka lõunaeesti keele (de)legitimatsiooni diskursuses (Koreinik ilmumas), mida võib ühe põhilise kasutatud *topos*'e järgi pidada ka ohu- või ohtustatuse diskursuseks (*discourse of endangerment*). Identiteediloome analüüs seletab ka keele n-ö omamise (*language ownership*) küsimust: need grupid, kes (keelelist) identiteeti diskursiivselt loovad, ei pruugi keelt "omada".

RIHO GRÜNTHAL

# Population decline and the Erosion of the Veps Language Community

## Abstract

At the beginning of the 21st century the Veps language still survives as one of the few autochtonous minority languages in northwest Russia and the northeastern Baltic Sea region. Located in geographically remote areas with little political or economic importance, some Veps communities have survived until the present day despite of the upheavals of the 20th century, which in many regions led to the total destruction of indigenous communities. However, none of the few existing Veps communities have avoided the intensive urbanisation and modernisation that has, irrespective of the differences in political systems, continuously brought about population decline in all of the traditional core areas of the Veps language.

In the long run, the breakdown of linguistic networks, which are a vital resource for language maintenance and inter-generational transmission, is the most important individual factor in the decline in the number of Veps speakers. Numerous changes and decisions have weakened the ability of originally rural communities to make the transition to modern networks, severed their connections with the wider Veps community and destroyed their vivid linguistic landscapes.

This article focuses on the reasons for the changes in Veps language communities and linguistic networks in the light of both published and fieldwork data carried out between 2006 and 2009 in Central Veps villages. Local-level changes which fragment the language community strongly affect linguistic identity and everyday language usage. After all, language shift and the loss of a unique identity are aspects of a long-term process spanning several decades.

*Ethnic and Linguistic Context of Identity: Finno-Ugric Minorities.* 267–293.
Uralica Helsingiensia 5. Helsinki 2011.

## 1. Introduction

The Veps language was first documented at the beginning of 19th century (Branch 1973: 83–92) and the following two centuries have gradually provided us with more detailed information on the language and its background. As Veps lacked a written standard until the 1930s, traditional research has focused on collecting reliable data on different Veps varieties. The historically known and documented Veps speaking areas and the Veps settlements were documented in a geographically compact area between the lakes of Ladoga (Finnish *Laatokka*), Onega (Finnish *Ääninen*) and Belozero (Finnish *Valkea-järvi*) in northwest Russia. As we might assume from their close proximity, linguistic differences between geographically adjacent varieties of Veps are not very big when compared to local variants in many other languages. However, as is often the case with language communities that have been stable for a relatively long period, there are some areal differences and isoglosses, and these account for the distinctions between the three main dialects of Northern, Central and Southern Veps (cf. Map 1).

The geographical distribution of the Veps language does not completely correspond with the taxonomy of Veps dialects, because linguistically the Northern dialect is no more distinct from the Central dialects than is the Southern one. Geographically, the Northern dialect area is isolated, found separately on the southwestern coast of Lake Onega north from the River Svir' (Finnish *Syväri*), while the two other dialects are spoken along the River Oyat' and in the region south of Lake Onega. However, some of the clearest and more numerous grammatical isoglosses appear between the geographically adjacent areas of Central and Southern Veps. The latter area used to have the closest connections with the former Russian capital of St Petersburg, as the railway connecting St Petersburg and Moscow runs just south of the Southern Veps area.

Agriculture and the rural economy used to be the main sources of living for the Veps. In the past, before the advent of modern communication and transport, the Veps regions were rather far from the urban areas. Even the capital of the Russian Empire, St Petersburg, founded in 1703, began to have a more serious influence on the Veps

Map 1. The Veps language area. 1900 based on the appendix of Tunkelo (1946) with place names in Finnish, and 2000.

territory only after the industrialisation and urbanisation of Russia began in earnest during the Soviet period, a time when its policies reached even the most peripheral areas of the empire. The cultural, economic and political changes of the 20th century reached the distant villages, and this was seen as a resource for satisfying the needs of the growing cities. Parallel with this process, peasants were violently attacked by the new communist rulers in the 1920s and 1930s.

Administratively, the historical Veps language area today belongs to three different administrative units: the Republic of Karelia (northern Veps), Leningradskaya oblast (Central and Southern Veps) and Vologodskaya oblast (Central Veps). The division of a geographically united set of villages into separate, centrally ruled administrative units was particularly disastrous for the Central Veps area, which lost its internal connections and transport routes and saw the collapse of education in the national language (Joalaid 1998, Kryuchkova 1992: 176–178, Petuhov 1989, Pimenov & Strogalshchikova 1989, Strogalshchikova 2005: 219–223). In the 1930s, the administrative structure of the Soviet Union was reorganised and several units were formed on the basis of ethnic territories. As a result many small nations gained their own administrative districts and a large number of Veps village councils were founded. In 1931 a Veps national district was established in Vinnicy (Veps *Vidl*). In this district of Leningradskaya oblast, nine out of 11 village councils were Veps. In 1936 there was a total of 24 Veps village councils in the Leningradskaya oblast (Joalaid 1998, Kurs 2001: 70, Strogalshchikova 2005: 219). However, this did not last long because the system was abolished almost as soon as it was created during Stalin's reign of terror. In 1937, school education, which had begun in 1931, was abolished and Veps along with all other nationally orientated activities were prohibited. This was followed by the suppression and abrogation of national organisations and institutions, and accelerating assimilation.

From the perspective of linguistic taxonomy, the Veps language is Finnic with around ten different varieties (Grünthal 2007, Laakso 2001, Salminen 1998, 2009). Estonian and Finnish are the two modern examples of this subgroup of Uralic languages, whereas Veps belongs to a long list of less well known and endangered languages

(Kolga & al. 1993, Salminen 2007, Wurm 2001). Karelian and Lude are geographically adjacent and linguistically most closely related to Veps. Indeed, Lude, frequently labelled Ludic dialects, is intelligible to a Veps speaker under certain conditions, although geographically these two language communities were located quite separately from one another when they were first documented. In general, however, the Veps language is clearly distinct from other Finnic languages and is not intelligible to other speakers without special training. The most prominent characteristics that diachronically distinguish Veps from other Finnic languages are the language's numerous endogenous innovations and the extensive influence of Russian.

Over the last one hundred years, two major changes have affected the Veps language community and its continuity in terms of inter-generational linguistic and cultural transfer. Firstly, the number of speakers has been in constant decline since the end of 1930s. Secondly, although there used to be regional divergence between Veps varieties, as a rule, despite the bilingualism of some individual members, the Veps language communities were dominated by fluent Veps speakers who used Veps in different sociolinguistic contexts. During the second half of the 20th century, bilingualism and the failure of Veps to incorporate modern terminology began to marginalise its usage. This sociolinguistic change occurred simultaneously with devastating cultural changes, political turmoil and wars (Grünthal 2009, Strogalshchikova 2005, 2008a, Vepsy 2007).

When a language community changes, this has a big impact on local identity, its foundations and retention. In local communities with a long history and their own individual traditions, language loss is culturally comparable to a break-down in the economy or, for instance, famine. During the 20th century, several Veps villages were wiped off the map. They were either destroyed by the stream of political decisions that forced populations to abandon their settlements, or their inhabitants became socially, culturally and linguistically stigmatised and thus these inhabitants started to look for better living conditions in the urban centres. Extensive bilingualism has made it much easier for the residents of rural communities to migrate to urban centres.

INFORMANT 1:

> *hän eläb Važinoiš. po-Vepski pagižemei. siguu narodan aigan pagižemei po-russki. erasti po-telefonuu pagižemei ka po-Vepski, mišto sekretoid ii tedaiš, midä svonib. jesli po sekretu, hän pagižeb po-Vepski, mišto vävu ii tedaiš. vävu om russkij.*

'She lives in the town of Važina. We speak Veps. In the presence of other people we speak Russian. Sometimes we talk Veps on the telephone so that we can keep the topic of our conversation secret. If it is meant to be secret, she talks in Veps so that my son-in-law will not know. My son-in-law is Russian.'

Geographically, it is still possible to identify a distinct Veps language area, since there are villages in every main dialect area that have been preserved until the present day. There has been some migration to Veps areas from other parts of Russia and the Caucasus and from other parts of the former Soviet Union. Nevertheless, the influence of the urban communities is more important than immigration to the Veps regions in terms of ethnic and demographic changes. The surrounding network of economically important Russian cities already existed in the 19th century, and it consists of such industrial and commercial entres as St Petersburg, Podporož'e, Petrozavodsk, Vytegra, Vologda and Tikhvin. These cities have considerably affected the fate of the Veps villages, most of all because the Veps have migrated there.

From the viewpoint of culture and language the changes in the past hundred years have been both extremely dramatic and irreversible. Demographic change and the conversion of previously monolingual communities to become bilingual combined with other changes, starting with the collapse of education in the national language and promotion of the Russian language in the media. During the Soviet era the social infrastructure and way of life were organised so that the central administration, with its one-party system wielding complete political and economic power could rule and dominate all actions on the local level. Ultimately, the reorganisation of society and the ubiquity of the communist party influenced everything, including interaction between the areas in whichVeps was spoken. Mutual communication was made difficult and then finally ceased to exist at all,

since the traditional routes between Veps villages had disappeared
and new roads and railways were being built to connect the villages
to the cities, rather than with one another. As a consequence, certain
villages that were located in the heart of the Veps language area were
now located at the periphery of the main road networks. As Veps identity dawned for the second time, at the end of 1980s and the beginning
of 1990s, the administrative fragmentation and the reestablishment of
mutual communication networks was one of the main concerns of the
Veps population (Vepsy 2007).

In sum, the aforementioned changes strongly affect the linguistic
identity of the Veps of today. An average Veps speaker is quite aware
of the stigmatised history of his language and its cultural and geographical context. At the same time, bilingualism and language shift
have allowed access to those services that are available in Russian and
have facilitated the creation of new networks in the modern economy.
For an average Veps speaker there is little if any need to lament the
loss of the opportunity to use the Veps language (cf. Grünthal 2009).

I shall next proceed with an overview of the demographic development of the Veps, and then discuss the influence of bilingualism
and language shift on Veps identity.


## 2. The Veps population in numbers

When engaging in research on eroding communities, official statistics and individual experience combine to form a picture of the whole
process. The life stories that are encountered and a shared background
create the history of those groups of people who belong to the core of
ethnic and linguistic minorities such as the Veps. However, official
statistics and the data from population censuses show only the tip of
the iceberg. They often reflect processes or situations that occurred
decades ago and decisions that were made in an entirely different
political context. When assessing the long-term erosion of an ethnic
group it is absolutely necessary to understand what really happened in
the past. Regarding the demographic data, the statistics we find in the
last two Russian censuses of 1989 (covering the whole Soviet Union)
and 2002 continue the tradition of earlier censuses beginning in 1897.

Interpretations of the difference between the statistics spanning several decades should start with an account of the synchronic context of a given census. Numbers and statistics are reliable only if they are embedded in a larger framework, that of a qualitative interpretation of language communities as vital and socially reproductive networks serving the interests of their members (Sarhimaa 2009).

According to Seppo Lallukka (1990: 175–287), the decrease in the number of native-speaking Mordvins (Erzya and Moksha), Maris, Udmurts and Komis presented in the census of 1989 (1959, 1970, 1979), is largely due to passive assimilation. From a more holistic perspective, the decrease of Finno-Ugric speaking populations started as early as the 1970s, although this did not occur simultaneously in every case. Migration inside the Soviet Union and an increased knowledge of linguistic and ethnic identity may have temporarily slowed down the process in 1980s, but the evidence from the censuses of 1989 and 2002 indicates that assimilation soon accelerated again (Lallukka 2005).

Russia's federal nationalities policy and legislation form the contemporary official framework that affects all minority groups in Russia. This policy therefore has a direct influence on the ethnic activity of Finno-Ugric minorities (Lallukka 2001). The most dramatic political and socioeconomic changes of the 20th century were reflections of Russian's policies as a whole. Nevertheless, local conditions, and history and an area's relations with centralised power account for some diversity in the ethnic assimilation and language shift of various groups. As with other peoples living in border areas, being on the front line during the Second World War had a direct influence on the Veps: something that makes their story more individual with a concrete connection to those events that took place at a local level in a geographically small area. The following narrative recalls the time immediately prior to World War II and the period of Stalin's repressions in the 1930s.

INFORMANT 2:

> *Pittärves eduu oli sorok semei. kaikučces oliba kanzad. i diki äjan ristituid raskulačivoiba. daže sinunke ninga pagižemei, a koumanz sid, ed ümbŕad vajeht sanun, i sindai võdas. antta desjat let. Miide elo vot mitte ol'!*

INTERVIEWER:
*a ken sanoi miše necid kanzoid tariž veda?*
INFORMANT 2:
*ken sanui? a vot oliba mugomad mehed.*
INFORMANT 3:
*ka nügüd jo mehiid ii ole, ka mejak pagižta? oma jo kolnuded kaik.*
INFORMANT 2:
*kolnuded, no satoiba tatein. vot primerom, Fen'a-t'otalein, rodnijale t'otale, Van'a tean voinas ol', a hänele stroiba sid tagaman. nu hän näge... hot oli, sanub linneb nügud jo voin. hän četko konečno tez'. linneb voin, ii linne saharanke čajud joda. ii linne, sanub, nece mugoi golod. i eläda, sanub, linneb zeml'anke. nu konečno voinan mii sorom radoimei. voin proidi ningoi, ogromnyi voin. i golodad nägiba i kaiked. i vot muga tatan, tatan miide männu. sanui saharanke čajud ii linne da joda da vot neniš vajehiš. a von sid Agafonovan Kol'a, oh sa d'ad'a, ninga ii voi pagišta. nu a kerazihesoi da podpisit paniba dei tuliba da Dimitriev arestovan da kümne vot andoiba. vot minun elo, miide elo. ni miš! a nügude hän om napravdeidud ammusei jo.*

— 'There were forty families in Pittärv. A family in every [house]. Very many people were deported. We would be talking like this, and then (there would be) a third one, you did not say a meaningless word, and you would be taken. You would get ten years. That was our life!'
— 'Who said that those families should be deported?'
— 'Who said? There were such men.'
— 'Those men do not exist any more, why talk? They are all dead.'
— 'They are dead, but they deported my father. For example, Aunt Fenya's father Vanya was in the war, but he was ordered (to go) behind the front, so he saw... he said there will be a war. He knew it for certain. There will be a war and no more tea with sugar. There won't be any, he said, this is such a starvation. And he said that you would have to live off the land. Of course we worked through the war with pain. The war ended, a massive war. People were starving and everything. And our father

was gone. He said there would be no more tea with sugar to drink and because of those words. But then K. A., "oh you!", one should not speak like that. So they arrived and signed and arrested Dimitriev and sentenced him to ten years. See, this is my life, our life. For nothing! But he was rehabilitated quite a long time ago.'

The Veps villages were immediately behind the front. The reminiscences of the older generation include tragic stories of famine, disease and poverty during and after the war. The dismantling of the pre-revolutionary economic system, the repression during the Stalin regime and the hardships of the war itself dramatically influenced the everyday life and ethnic sustainability of the Veps. All this took place within just 25 years. After the catastrophes of the 1930s and 1940s, other changes followed that suppressed the Veps language community and prevented it from regaining its vitality and retaining its language. This is the starting-point for understanding the population decline of the Veps during the 20th century (table 1).

| Year | 1897 | 1926 | 1939 | 1959 | 1970 | 1979 | 1989 | 2002 |
|---|---|---|---|---|---|---|---|---|
| Total number of ethnic Veps in Russia | 25,607 | 32,773 | 31,449 | 16,170 | 8,281 | 7,550 | 12,142 | 8,284 |
| Reported number of native speakers | [25,000] | 31,000 (94.7%) | | 7,600 (46.1%) | 2,840 (34.3%) | 2,730 [!] (36.1%) | 6,350 (50.8%) | [< 4000] |

Table 1. The demographic development of the Veps in Russia according to Russian and Soviet censuses (Kurs 2001: 71–77, Strogalshchikova 2005b: 215–218, 2008a, 2008b: 10).

The numbers and summaries of official reports that are presented in Table 1 should not be taken as absolute facts. In reality, diverse subtle interpretations are needed to understand those collective changes and individual life stories that are embedded in the statistics.

The official statistics display abundant ambiguity in reporting the number of native speakers and those who are supposed to have a command of a given language in population censuses. An important difference between the years 1989 and 2002 is that in the latter the native language was not asked of all. Indeed, many minorities such as the Veps had reached such a stage in bilingualism and language shift that almost 100% of those people belonging to a given ethnic group were reported to have a command of Russian, whereas in numerous cases the command of the minority language was much weaker. As regards the Veps, in 2002 a total of 5,753 people were reported to have a command of Veps. However, the relationship between Veps as a native language, as a second language, and different degrees of bilingualism, language shift and ethnic assimilation is too complicated to be discussed only in the light of numbers.

According to official statistics, by 1989 a notable change had occurred in the relational distribution of the Veps in the three main administrative units that comprise the geographical Veps area, namely the Karelian Republic, Leningradskaya oblast and Vologodskaya oblast. As the centrally administered political programme aimed at abolishing those villages without prospects hit most severely the Central and Southern Veps areas (Yegorov 2007, Heikkinen 2000, Lapin 2007, Petuhov 1989, Pimenov & Strogalshchikova 1989: 4–6), population loss and ethnic and linguistic change have been more rapid in these areas. At the time of the 1989 census, the largest Veps population lived in the Republic of Karelia (5,954). Their number had declined faster in the Leningradskaya oblast where there were 4,273 and in the Vologodskaya oblast, where there were 728. A hundred years earlier, at the time of the first Russian census of 1897, it was reported that roughly 25% of Veps belonged to the northern group living in what is now the Veps area in the Republic of Karelia. By 2002 the difference between the three main administrative units had further increased. According to official statistics, there were now 4,870 Veps living in the Republic of Karelia, 2019 in the Leningradskaya *oblast'* and 426 in the Vologodskaya oblast. (Joalaid 1998, Kazakevitch 2002: 17, Kryuchkova 1999: 97–99, Kurs 2001: 71–77, Strogalshchikova 2008a, 2008b: 10.)

## 3. Comparing official demographic and fieldwork data

Demographic processes do not take place in a vacuum: rather, they are part of contemporary political, social, economic and ethnic processes. From a socioanthropological and geographical perspective, the Veps of the 21st century are both a rural and an urban people, they have a multilingual and multiethnic background which operates beyond the core historical and geographical Veps area. It is often difficult to get a more detailed picture of the demographic situation solely on the basis of available official statistics. In the course of fieldwork that was carried out between 2006–2009, I had an opportunity to observe the population and the demographic situation in several Central Veps villages in the northeastern part of Leningradskaya oblast in the municipality of the Podporozhskiy rayon. It turned out that, as a rule, the official numbers exaggerated the actual number of people who lived permanently in the local villages.

In Russia, the difference between ethnic and linguistic minorities and majorities is frequently discussed at the federal level. However, the actual state-of-the-art should be discussed more concretely at the municipal level. As mentioned above, the administrative border between the Leningradskaya and Vologodskaya oblasts splits the historical Central Veps area into two with no modern connections or shared infrastructure. Furthermore, in the Leningradskaya oblast the Central Veps area is divided into two municipalities, the Lodeynopol'skiy rayon and the Podporozhskiy rayon. Here too, the villages are connected to the municipal centres without a need to cross the rayon borders, which means that the connections and networks between the Veps villages have been very weak during the past decades.

From a larger geographical perspective, the Podporozhskiy rayon is found in the periphery of the Leningradskaya oblast and does not have the same prospects for rapid economic growth as the giant city of St Petersburg, which is the centre of the entire north-western part of Russia. The population censuses make a distinction between the rural (5,600) and urban (8,300) populations. Together they totalled 13,900 in 2006, according to the statistics centre of the municipal administration. Most of the Veps population live in two volosts, Ozerskaya and Kurbinskaya. Below, the latter is used as a case study that illustrates the relationship between official statistics, their geographical coordinates and the actual number of inhabitants in the given villages in more detail.

| Administrative Unit | Households | Inhabitants |
|---|---|---|
| Kurba | 143 | 350 |
| Minickaya | 38 | 70 |
| Makaryevskaya | 6 | 9 |
| Kazyčenskaya | 43 | 87 |
| Fedorovskaya | 12 | 16 |
| Vasilyevskaya | 10 | 20 |
| Kurbinskaya *volost* (in sum) | 252 | 552 |
| Ozerskaya *volost* | 259 | 535 |
| Podporozhskiy *rayon* (in sum) | | 13,900 |

Table 2. Number of inhabitants of Kurbinskaya *volost*, Podporozhskiy *rayon* in 2006, according to the municipal statistics centre (see, NLO).

Both sociohistorically and geographically, the Kurbinskaya *volost* belongs to the Central Veps core area with the exception of the current centre, Kurba, which was founded at the end of the 1950s to supply the forest industry with labour and accommodation. Migration from other parts of the Soviet Union brought new Russian-speaking people to the area at a time when internal migration within the *volost* increased. A part of the labour force came from neighbouring Veps villages and their migration soon began to have a negative effect on local demography and the social infrastructure as schools were closed and the remaining children placed in boarding schools.

Today, villages located in the Kurbinskaya *volost* do not have any permanent local administration and, as a rule, how administration works at this local level depends on those units higher up in the hierarchy. At the grass-root level there are two old Veps villages that are located in the area, *Mäggärv* and *Ladv*. The former name corresponds to the Russian *Minickaya* on Russian maps, and the latter includes the four last units listed in table 2 above: *Makaryevskaya* (Veps *Sepän*

279

*agj*), *Kazyčenskaya* (Veps *Pagast*), *Fedorovskaya* (Veps *Ondrein agj*) and *Vasilyevskaya* (Veps *Järven taga*). This division illustrates how Veps villages have been divided into smaller parts, called *agj* 'end' in Veps. *Mäggärv* also consists of six parts (*Orgveh, Selgveh, Ostašmägi, Pagast, Birž* and *Agveh*), although they are not mentioned in the list. In addition, *Ladv* used to have at least six.

Map 2. *Ladv* village and its districts based on a contemporary Russian geographical map (VLO 43). The administrative names of the parts of the Ladv village are: Makaryevskaya (in Veps Sepän agj), Kazyčenskaya (in Veps Pagast), Fedorovskaya (in Veps Ondrein agj) and Vasilyevskaya (in Veps Järven taga). Fedotovskaya is not inhabited.

In *Sepän agj* (in the vernacular alternatively *Sep*), which today is only loosely attached to the other parts of *Ladv*, the number of permanent households has been falling for several years and in the past few years there has been an even more abrupt change, which signifies the extinction of a living language community and the loss of those family and social networks that used to be the basis of the community. According to the official census of 2002, the number of permanent households in the district (administratively *Makaryevskaya*) was six and the number of inhabitants nine. By 2006 the number of permanent households decreased to between four and five, and by 2009 there were only two left. The number of inhabitants was six in 2006 and decreased to three by 2009. Similarly the number of people living in *Järven taga* (administratively *Vasilyevskaya*), on the other side of the lake, does not correspond with the official statistics. According to a report by NLO, there were ten households and 20 inhabitants in 2006. In practice the number of permanent inhabitants was eight and the number of households four.

The number of inhabitants in other listed village parts has clearly been overestimated too, because it does not correspond to the actual number of permanently settled inhabitants. This should not be taken as a conscious attempt to provide unreliable statistical information. The mismatch rather reflects the difficulties of local authorities in collecting reliable data from the periphery and also the settling of socially displaced individuals. It must also be noted that the number of temporary residents, most notably those revisiting their home villages during holidays, is higher. Yet in terms of the language community and the maintenance of crucial vernacular networks, a temporary increase in the local population does not have a very far-reaching positive effect.

While conducting my fieldwork, I observed a similar mismatch between official data and the actual situation in other villages as well. In Mäggär'v for instance, the inhabitants were able to list those permanently settled by name, which the research team tested by visiting every house in the village. The official figure in 2006 was 70, but the number of permanent inhabitants did not exceed 40. In both Mäggär'v and Ladv the highest density was in the centre of the village (*Pagast*).

By contrast, the population is much more sparse in the more outlying districts.

We shall not discuss the demographic situation and its background at greater length here. Suffice it to say that the overall number of births is low in the health care district of Vinnicy to which all Veps villages in the Podporozhskiy rayon belong. It is highest in Vinnicy, which has roughly 2,200 inhabitants (2,158 in 2002; 2,243 in 2008). In the 21st century, the annual birth rate has fluctuated between 22 and 38 for the whole district.

## 4. Processes parallel to population decline and the reciprocal influence of change mechanisms

Population decline and demographic change always reflect other changes that do not solely affect the population structure, but have a much wider background in social, economic and political conditions. They affect the way a language community lives, maintains and transfers its culture and language, the most distinctive foundation of individual and collective identity for the next generation. For instance, age distribution directly affects the birth rate. A relative increase in the older generation means fewer families with small children and fewer young adults of childbearing age. Furthermore, there are other matters that influence the vitality of rural communities: the lack of or reduction in public services such as schools, shops and medical care that accelerate migration and increase the rate of unemployment. Both as a result of this process and of other centrally decided changes, living conditions simply become too hard for individual people and the generation which should be in charge of the intergenerational transmission of language and culture. As a matter of fact, this has been one of the major concerns of the few Veps activists who during the past two decades since the breakdown of the Soviet Union have made it their concern to discuss the future prospects of the Veps and their language more openly (Vepsy 2007).

Linguistically, the most immediate result of the erosion of traditional communities and migration from the geographically core areas is the breakdown of crucial language networks. In a rapidly changing social and economic environment, the language networks of the past do not often match the geographically large multiethnic networks that are today the basis of social networks. Consequently, the dissimilation of linguistic and social networks is an essential reason for the erosion of a language community and language shift (Grünthal 2009). The increase in bilingualism and language shift has taken place in the Veps language communities simultaneously with the aforementioned changes. As shown in table 1 above, in 1926 94.7% of Veps spoke their native language, whereas roughly sixty years later, in 1989, only 50.8% spoke Veps as their mother tongue (cf. Table 1 above). During this period, the Veps language area became fully connected to the modern media, education and communication systems, which operates in Russian. These are concerns that sixty years ago influenced the Veps language community to a far lesser extent.

In societies with a positive attitude to cultural and linguistic pluralism bilingualism is mentioned as a positive resource that should be used to enhance the parallel usage and development of minority and majority languages (Fishman 1991). Under politically, socially and economically less stable conditions, bilingualism very often serves as the path to language shift (Romaine 1995: 38–51, 2004: 56–57, Sarhimaa 1999: 195–199, Thomason & Kaufmann 1988), although, in principle, the simultaneous use of two or more languages and their parallel development in children's speech is very common. Bilingualism and multilingualism do not automatically trigger cross-linguistic interference (Auer 1984, Döpke 2000, Muysken 2000, Romaine 1995: 78–240).

Veps is a typical example of the latter case. As a rule, bilingualism has been an intermediate stage in an intensive unidirectional language shift, rather than a dynamic module of interaction used to support the adaption of a minority language and its speech community to a rapidly changing social and cultural environment. The process resembles that of many other linguistic minorities in Russia and other parts of the world. The increase of mixed marriages and the migration of individual speakers have a social motivation. Their influence on the assimilation of Finno-Ugric speaking peoples in Russia is connected with a biased promotion of bilingualism at the expense of

283

minority languages, which have no official protection. As a matter of fact, bilingualism was consciously favoured by the Soviet administration as a means of accelerating the implementation of Russian as the majority language. This policy had an extremely negative influence in those areas where minority languages used to flourish. (Lallukka 1990: 175–245.)

Where there is parallel use of two or more languages, it is necessary to distinguish between different stages and forms of bilingualism or multilingualism. According to the most classical treatment, and following Weinreich's (1968 (1953): 9–11) terminology, in coordinate bilingualism the speaker learns and uses two languages separately within separate contexts, whereas in subcoordinate bilingualism one of the languages influences and replaces the lexical and conceptual representation of the other language (Romaine 1995: 78–79). In the long run this affects the domains in which a given language is used because one of the languages increases its space at the expense of the other. At the individual speaker level it actually means that the lexical and conceptual memories are asymmetric at the cross-linguistic level (Romaine 1995: 90).

Extensive bilingualism, while there is a lack of balance between the minority and majority language, may also have consequences that cannot be controlled simply by increased awareness of the endangered situation of the minority language. There is evidence from many studies that children will not use the minority language with those who do not present a stable language system (e.g. Clyne 1997, Döpke 1992, Romaine 1995: 49–51). In the case of Veps, efforts to encourage the language at school were weakened by the fact that it was merely a school subject, a target of teaching, rather than the vernacular language of every-day communication and a model for the next generation.

## 5. Veps Identity in Change

Ultimately, language shift and its social, economic and political context, affects the linguistic identity and vernacular language choice of individual families, which is where language is learned and transferred to the next generation. Virtually all Veps villages have suffered from a constant decline in their populations since World War II, with the younger generations moving to the towns. An average family has members in both the towns and villages, speaks Russian every day and is almost fully assimilated into the Russian language community. A bilingual speaker does not often pay any attention to code-switching in an everyday speech situation. Consequently, those situations in which Veps can be used are becoming more rare.

An average family includes members who live in different parts of Russia, most often in north-western Russia but also in other parts of the former Soviet Union. In every family there are members who do not speak Veps, but who speak Russian instead as their first language. This is not only true of families in which one of the spouses comes from outside the Veps language community, but also for children and grandchildren whose parents preferred to use the majority language as their basic communication tool at home, school and in the outside world. Regarding education, in the interviews carried out between 2006 and 2009 in Central Veps villages, it came to light that there were still some elderly people who had never gone to school because of the difficult conditions at the end of 1930s and during the following years of the War. In principle, however, provision was made for education in Russian for the entire post-war generation, and those who did not learn Russian at school learned it in everyday life.The Veps identity, like that of stigmatised minorities in general, is very different to that of the monolingual, culturally strong, economically independent, politically recognised ethnic groups. Multilingualism, the extensive use of the majority language, geographical fragmentation, the erosion of earlier collective networks and attachment to social structures, which undermine earlier ethnic and linguistic borders, are all characteristic of present-day Veps identity. These generalisations illustrate the situation at the beginning of the 21st century, but as changes seldom happen overnight they also reflect changes that have occurred over several decades, beginning in the first half of the 20th century.

In his account of multilingualism in modern Russia, Haarmann (1998) claims that despite its multiethnic background, actually Russia can only be described as modestly heterogeneous. This is largely the result of the upheavals of the 20th century, the structuring of Soviet society, and Soviet language policies with their abrupt twists and turns. From this viewpoint, the revitalisation of the local identity of non-Russians at the end of the 1980s could be seen as a reaction to Russian dominance; the result of a long accumulative process (Haarmann 1998: 231).

Table 3 lists some of the most relevant facts that illustrate the weakening of the Veps language community and Veps identity both from the perspective of the present day and from a historical point of view.

### Demography

(1) The absolute and relative number of native Veps speakers has decreased significantly.

(2) The weakening of ethnic identity decreases the number of ethnic Veps.

### Administrative and political situation

(3) Administrative borders do not correspond to ethnic and linguistic areas.

(4) Economic centres are far from the core geographical area of the language communities.

(5) There is very little if any official legislation that encourages the use of the Veps language.

### The sociolinguistic situation and the state-of-art of the language community

(6) Learning and teaching at school is not based on the Veps language.

(7) The Veps language has no importance in everyday media and electronic communication.

(8) Migration and aging are accelerating linguistic erosion.

(9) Language communities have become extremely fragmented.

(10) Rural networks are connected to urban centres but not to other rural networks.

### Linguistic changes

(11) The Veps language community is completely bilingual.

(12) Abundant code-switching is characteristic of the speech of individuals.

(13) There are only limited domains in which Veps can be used.

Table 3. The Erosion of the Linguistic Identity of the Veps.

The key problem with the erosion of linguistic and ethnic identity, as with language shift or even the death of language, is that it is possible to compensate for or change negative trends only in the long run. Moreover, those effects that once initiated the acceleration of language shift and the erosion of ethnic identity will continue to affect the existing language community even after several decades have elapsed. The termination of teaching in Veps in the 1930s, the gradual closing of the vast majority of village schools during the following sixty years, the discouraging of Veps children from speaking Veps in the 1950s and 1960s, all belong to this same chain of events. Once learned, linguistic attitudes long remain. The list is far from complete. However, the point is that the current situation must be analysed within the framework of the wider array of decisions, regulations and laws that citizens are subject to, and also in terms of simple human adaptation to changing conditions.

## 6. Conclusions

The aforementioned demographic change and the decay of the Veps language community is the cumulative result of the many negative influences on Veps identity which have led to a constant process of language shift. The case of Veps is not at all an exception, rather it proves the rule and it shows us the details that cause language shift, and ultimately language extinction. In the Russian context, the most crucial factors are connected with the rise and fall of communist power in the 20th century and cultural change of a type that has long strengthened urban communities at the expense of rural ones. In this sense the Veps example is similar to others where there is an imbalance between rural life and the urban centres, and a mismatch between traditions and modernisation. In principle, the size of a given ethnic minority and the number of speakers is not as decisive in this respect as the degree to which a given minority language has gained a foothold in modern society and its speakers have committed themselves to this piece of cultural heritage.

In this article, Veps identity was mainly discussed on a general level from the perspective of collective heritage and the language community. In this context, population decline is the result of the very limited and occasional interaction with modern society of the Veps language, and the dissonance between modern social and geographically concentrated linguistic networks. In other words, the structure of the modern family looks very different from that of the traditional model in the Veps language area, because these include members in the towns and members of other ethnicities, most notably speakers of Russian. The limited use or almost complete lack of use of Veps in the modern media and in education marginalises it for those who should be transferring the language on to the next generation in the new environment. Consequently, local identity and local culture are not as important to the ethnic and linguistic identity of the Veps as they could or should be. The stigmatisation of ethnic and linguistic identity severely threatens local identity and linguistic and cultural continuity. Revitalising and rebuilding eroding language communities should simultaneously reconcile those factors that caused the dramatic weakening of ethnic and linguistic identity in the first place.

## References

Auer, J. C. P. 1984: *Bilingual conversation*. Amsterdam: John Benjamins.

Branch, Michael 1973: *A. J. Sjögren. Studies of the North*. MSFOu 152. Helsinki: The Finno-Ugrian Society.

Döpke, Susanna 2000 (ed.): *Cross-linguistic structures in simultaneous bilingualism*. Studies in bilingualism 21. Amsterdam: John Benjamins.

Fishman, Joshua A. 1991: *Reversing language shift: theoretical and empirical foundations of assistance to threatened languages*. Clevedon: Multilingual matters.

Grünthal, Riho 2007: Finnic languages and Baltic Sea language area. – *Incontri Linguistici* 30. Pisa & Roma. 29–48.

—— 2009: Kieliyhteisön rapautuminen ja kielellisen identiteetin muutos: 2000-luvun ersämordvalaiset ja vepsäläiset. – Anna Idström & Sachiko Sosa (ed.), *Kielissä kulttuurien ääni*. Tietolipas 228. Helsinki: SKS. 265–289.

Haarmann, Harald 1998: Multiethnic Russia and its Soviet heritage. – Christina Bratt Paulston & Donald Peckham (eds), *Linguistic Minorities in Central and Eastern Europe.* Multilingual matters 109. Philadelphia: Clevedon. 224–254.

Heikkinen, Kaija 2000: Metamorphosis of the Russian Baba. – *Modernisation in the Russian provinces. Studia Slavica Finlandensia* XVII. 292–305.

Joalaid, Marje 1998: Vepsäläisten asuma-alueet ja niiden hallinnollinen jako kautta aikojen. – Leena Nissilä (toim.), *Suomen kielen päivä 13. november 1997.* Tallinn: Tallinna pedagoogikaülikool. 10–33.

Kazakevitch, Olga 2002: Education of indigenous minorities of Russia in the 1930s and in the 1990s: mother tongue at school. – Kazuto Matsumura (ed.), *Lectures on Language Situation – Russia, Estonia, Finland.* ICHEL Linguistic Studies Vol. 6. Tokyo: University of Tokyo. 1–34.

Kolga, Margus, Igor Tõnurist, Lembit Vaba & Jüri Viikberg 1993: *Vene impeeriumi rahvaste punane raamat.* Tallinn: Nyman & Nyman.

Kryuchkova, T. B. 1992: Jazykovaja situatsija v Karel'skoj Respublike. – *Jazykovaja situatsija v Rossijskoj Federatsii.* Moskva. 168–197.

—— 1999: Jazykovaja situatsija v Respublike Karelija istorija razvitija i sovremennoe sostojanie. – *Pismennye jazyki Rossii i drugih stran SNG status i funktsii.* Moskva. 97–113.

Kurs, Ott 2001: The Veps: an administratively divided nationality. – *Nationalities Papers* 29. 69–83.

Laakso, Johanna 2001: The Finnic languages. – Östen Dahl & Maria Koptjevskaja-Tamm, *The Circum-Baltic languages: An areal-typological approach. Typology and contact 2.* 615–750.

Lallukka, Seppo 1990: *The East Finnic Minorities in the Soviet Union. An Appraisal of the Erosive Trends.* Suomalaisen Tiedeakatemian Toimituksia B 252. Helsinki: Suomalainen Tiedeakatemia.

—— 2001: Finno-Ugrians of Russia: Vanishing Cultural Communities? – *Nationalities Papers* 29. 9–39.

—— 2005: Venäjän suomalais-ugrilaiset: väestölaskentojen kertomaa. – Paula Kokkonen (ed.): *Sukukansaohjelman arki. Suomalais-ugrilainen perintö ja arkipäivä. Studia Fenno-Ugrica 21.9.–16.11.2004.* Castrenianumin toimitteita 64. Helsinki: M. A. Castrénin seura, Suomalais-Ugrilainen Seura & Helsingin yliopiston suomalais-ugrilainen laitos. 28–46.

Lapin 2007 = В. Лапин: Шимозеры – трагедия диалекта. – Seppo Lallukka (ed.), *Вепсы и этнокультурные перемены XX века.* Studia Slavica Finlandensia 24. Helsinki. 95–106.

MSFOu = Mémoires de la Société Finno-Ougrienne.

Muysken, Pieter 2000: *Bilingual Speech. A Typology of Code-Mixing.* Cambridge: Cambridge University Press.

NLO = Население Ленинградской области по возрасту и уровню образования. *Итоги всероссийской переписа населения 2002 года.* Статистический сборник. Федеральная служба государственной статистики. Территориальной орган ФСФСПО г. Санкт–Петербургу и Ленинградской области (Петростат) 2005.

Petuhov 1989 = А. В. Петухов: Административная разобщенность – фактор ускорения ассимиляции вепсов. – *Problemy* 1989. 55–63.

В. В. Пименов и З. И. Строгальщикова: Вепсы – расселение, история, проблемы этнического развития. – *Problemy* 1989. 4–26.

Problemy 1989 = В. Пименова, З. Строгальщикова и Ю. Сурхаско (ред.), *Проблемы истории культуры вепсской народности.* Petrozavodsk: Karel'skij filial AN SSSR.

Romaine, Suzanne 1995: *Bilingualism.* Second edition. Oxford: Blackwell.

—— 2004: Language-Contact Studies. – Ulrich Ammon, Norbert Dittmar, Klaus J. Mattheier & Peter Trudgill (eds), *Sociolinguistics / Soziolinguistik*, Part 1. An International Handbook of the Science of Language and Society. 2nd completely revised and extended edition. Berlin: Walter de Gruyter 2004. 49–58.

Salminen, Tapani 1998: Pohjoisten itämerensuomalaisten kielten luokittelun ongelmia. – R. Grünthal & J. Laakso (eds) *Oekeeta asijoo. Commentationes in honorem Seppo Suhonen sexagenarii 16.V.1998.* MSFOu 228. 390-406.

—— 2007: Endangered Languages in Europe. – Matthias Benzinger (toim.), *Language Diversity Endangered.* Berlin: Mouton de Gruyter. 205–232.

—— 2009: Uralic (Finno-Ugrian) languages. <http://www.helsinki.fi/~tasalmin/fu.html> (updated July 2009, read 3rd January 2010)

Sarhimaa, Anneli 1999: *Syntactic transfer, contact-induced change, and the evolution of bilingual mixed codes.* Helsinki: SKS.

—— 2009: Social Network Theory as a framework for studying minor Finnic languages with special reference to Karelian. – Jussi Ylikoski (ed.), *The Quasquicentennial of the Finno-Ugrian Society.* MSFOu 258. Helsinki: Finno-Ugrian Society. 161–190.

Strogalshchikova, Zinaida 2005: Päättyykö vepsäläisten historiallinen taival? – Lassi Saressalo (ed.), *Vepsä: Maa, kansa, kulttuuri.* SKST 1005. Helsinki: SKS. 211–235.

—— 2008a = З. И. Строгальщикова: Вепсы на рубеже XX–XXI веков: по данным официальной статистики и социологических исследовании. – *Вепсы на рубеже XX–XXI веков. По материалам межрегиональной научно-практической конференции «Вепсы – коренной малочисленный народ Российской Федерации: перспективы сохранения и развития.»* Петрозаводск: Учреждение Российской академии наук Институт языка, литературы и истории КарНЦ РАН. 57–109.

—— 2008b = З. И. Строгальщикова: *Вепсы.* Петрозаводск: Периодика.

Thomason, Sarah & Terence Kaufman 1988: *Language contact, creolization and genetic linguistics.* Berkeley: University of California Press.

Tunkelo, E. A. 1946: *Vepsän kielen äännehistoria.* Helsinki: SKS.

Vepsy 2007 = *Вепсы: Модели этнической мобилизации. Сборник материалов и документов.* Сост. Е. И Клементьев, А. А. Кожанов, З. И. Строгальщикова. Петрозаводск: Карельский научный центр.

VLO = *Восток Ленинградская область. Атлас.* Санкт-Петербург: Минобороны России, 2003.

Weinreich, Uriel 1968 (1953): *Language in contact: findings and problems.* The Hague: Mouton.

Wurm 2001 = Stephen A. Wurm (ed.), *Atlas of the world's languages in danger of disappearing.* Second edition, revised, enlarged and updated. Paris: UNESCO Publishing.

Yegorov 2007 = С. Егоров: Вепсы Шугозера во второй четверти XX – начале XXI века. – Seppo Lallukka (ed.), *Вепсы и этнокультурные перемены XX века.* Studia Slavica Finlandensia 24. Helsinki. 107–125.

# Снижение количества вепсов и разрушение вепсской языковой сообщества

*Riho Grünthal*

Как и у многих иных малычисленных народов России количество вепсов, несколько увеличившееся в начале 1900 годов, стал уменьшать. В случае с вепсами уменьшение количества вепсов началось уже перед второй мировой войной, как и, например, у карелов, но значительно раньше, чем у многих прочих восточных финно-угорских народов. У многих из последних рост количество продолжался еще до 1960–1970 годов.

С точка зрения языка драматизм ситуации со снижением количество вепсов и их урбанизацией сказался в разрушении языкового сообщества. Административные сведение и приведенные в данной статье в качестве примеров сведения из средневепских деревень противоречат друг другу. В деревнях уже приходят в полный упарок языковые резервы, которые смогли бы возместить урбанизацию, старение народа и снижение его количества.

Административные и политические изменения в конце 1900 годов способствовали резкому ухудшению языковой сферы. Общее социо-лингвистическое положение ускорило языковую ассимилияцию. Длительное двуязычие, связанное с этим изменение кодов повлияли на языковой идентитет вепсов.

# Vepsläiẑiden lugumäran lanktemine i vepsläiẑen kel'kundan kadomine

*Riho Grünthal*

Äjiden toiẑiden Venäman vähäluguiẑiden rahvahiden lugumär 1900-voziden lopus kazvamiẑespäi om vajehtanus lanktemiẑehe. Vepsläiẑil nece lanktemine zavodihe jo edel tošt mirun voinad, siloi-ẑo, kut ozutesikš karjalaiẑil, no aigemba mi toiẑil suomalaiẑ-ugrilaiẑil rahvahil. Erasil nimitatud rahvahil kazvamine jatkui völ 1960-1970 vozihesai.

Kelen polespäi dramatiẑen situacijan tugen oli vepsläiẑiden lidnoihi sirdämine i kel'kundan kadomine. Adminstrativiẑed tedod i neciš tedosanuteses todud sil'mnägubale tedod eroneba toine toiẑespäi. Küliš ei ole enamb kel'rezervoid, kudambad voiẑiba vajehtada situacijad parembaha polhe rahvahan lidnaha sirdämiẑen tagut. Sen liẑaks lugumäran lanktemiẑehe painab rahvahan vanhtumine.

Administrativine i politine situacii 1900-voziden lopus painab negativišesti rahvahan sulamiẑehe. Ühthine kel'sociologine i vepsän kel'kundan situacii tegeb terambaks kelen assimil'acijad. Pit'kaigaine kaks'keliẑuz' i kodiden vajehtamine, kudambad om sidotud toine toiẑhe, oma vajehtanuded rahvahan kel'identitetad.

LARISA SHIROBOKOVA

# Ethnic Identity and Udmurt people

## Abstract

The question of ethnic identity is always an important issue in multi-cultural regions when the level of contacts between ethnic groups is high enough. In the Soviet Union, however, questions of ethnic identity have been almost completely ignored, both in politics and also in research. Since the collapse of the USSR, these questions are again being discussed among minorities in Russia. Ethnic identity has particular significance in the territory of the Udmurt Republic, which is home to more than 70 different nationalities and where the Udmurts are a minority in their own titular republic, the majority being Russian.

Language is often considered one of the major factors, even the most important factor, in ethnic identity building. In this study, I attempt to discover the role of language, relative to other factors, in building Udmurt ethnic identity in modern-day Russia. A second aim is to investigate how the official status of the Udmurt language influences of the significance of the Udmurt language as a factor for identity building. My study focuses on a rural community and an internet site for social networking.

*Ethnic and Linguistic Context of Identity: Finno-Ugric Minorities.* 295–320.
Uralica Helsingiensia 5. Helsinki 2011.

## 1. Introduction

The Udmurt language belongs to the Finno-Ugric language family. The Udmurts mainly inhabit the Volga Federal District, the area between the River Kama and the River Vyatka. The Udmurt Republic, formerly known as the Udmurt ASSR, occupies 42,100 km² in the lower reaches of the River Kama, northeast of the confluence of the Kama and the Volga. The Republic borders Tatarstan to the south. Udmurts are also to be found in the neighboring republics and in other semi autonomous territories: Kirov oblast and Perm Kray in Russia, Bashkortostan, Tatarstan, and Mari El.

Throughout their history, the Udmurt people have been known as *Votyaks* in Russian, or *Ar* in Tatar. The Udmurts, however, consider the name Votyak derogatory and offensive. They describe themselves in the following ways: *udmurt, vudmurt, odmort, udmort, ukmort* (in the plural, the ending *-joz* is added, e.g. *udmurtjoz* 'Udmurts'). (Salánki 2007: 27.)

Map 1. The location the Udmurt Republic.

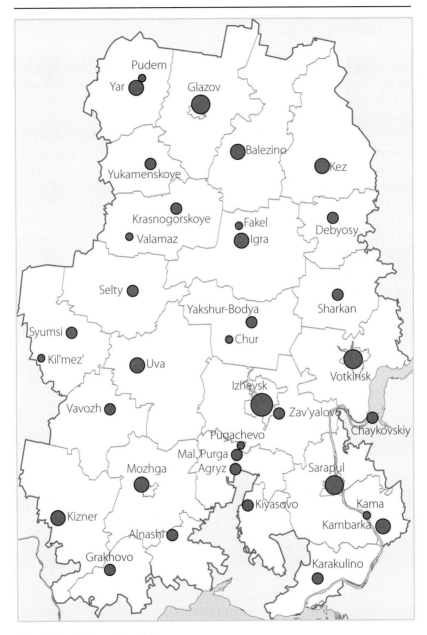

Map 2. The Udmurt Republic.

## 2. Demography

According to the 2002 national census, there are 636,900 Udmurts in the Russian Federation. Of the Udmurts 72.3% live in their own ethnic republic, where they form less than a third (29.3%) of the total population (<www.perepis2002.ru>).

Figures for the number of Udmurt people and Udmurt speakers are shown in Table 1. The number of Udmurt people both in the Udmurt Republic and in the Russian Federation as a whole reached a peak at the beginnig of the collapse of the Soviet Union in 1989. From 1989 to 2002 their number decreased (by some 35,900 in Udmurtia and 77,900 in the Russian Federation as a whole). From 1959 to 1989, knowledge of the Udmurt language decreased in the Udmurt Republic by 19.1% but then showed a slight increase of 2% between 1989 and 2002. However, 28% of Udmurts living in the Udmurt Republic did not speak their mother tongue in 2002. When looking at the Russian Federation as a whole, the loss of language speakers is even higher, because almost one third of Udmurts did not speak their mother tongue in 2002.

| Year | Number of Udmurts in the Udmurt Republic | Udmurts in the Udmurt Republic as a % of its total population | Knowledge of the Udmurt language among Udmurts in the Udmurt Republic % (and total figure) | Number of Udmurts in the Russian Federation: | Knowledge of the Udmurt language among Udmurts in the Russian Federation % (and total figure) |
|---|---|---|---|---|---|
| 1926 | 404,800 | | | 514,000 | |
| 1939 | 479,700 | | | 599,900 | |
| 1959 | 475,900 | | 89.1% | 615,600 | |
| 1970 | 484,200 | | 82.6% | 678,400 | |
| 1979 | 479,700 | | 76.4% | 685,700 | |
| 1989 | 496,500 | 30.9% | 70.0% | 714,800 | |
| 2002 | 460,600 | 29.3% | 72.0% (330,800) | 636,900 | 67.5% (429,400) |

Table 1. The number of Udmurts between 1926–2002 and knowledge of the Udmurt language (Pusztay 2006: 14; Salánki 2007: 22).

According to Lallukka (2001: 17), the past few decades provide ample evidence of how bilingual Finno-Ugrian parents have failed to transmit their mother tongue to their children. This failure has been particularly marked in the urban areas. As a result, most Finno-Ugrian language communities have decreased in size. Table 2 shows the main changes in the living areas of Udmurts between 1959–2007. There was a rapid growth in urbanisation among the Udmurts between 1989–2007, that is after the collapse of the Soviet Union.

| Year | Area of residence | |
|------|------|------|
|      | rural | urban |
| 1959 | 85.2% | 14.8% |
| 1979 | 81.5% | 18.5% |
| 1989 | 80.2% | 19.8% |
| 2007 | 55.7% | 44.3% |

Table 2. The number of rural and urban Udmurts between 1926–2007 (Lallukka 1990: 106; Pusztay 2006: 14; Salánki 2007: 23; Shkliaev and E. Toulouze 2001: 2).

The Udmurts' knowledge of the Russian language is shown in Table 3. In practice, almost all Udmurts are bilingual. Only 1.6% of urban Udmurts do not speak Russian, and among those living in rural areas the rate is slightly higher, 3.1%. While Udmurts can also read Russian, non-Udmurts are seldom fluent in the Udmurt language (Shkliaev and Toulouze 2001: 101). Udmurts use Udmurt and Russian in different areas of language usage.

| Area of residence | Number of Udmurts | Knowledge of Russian among Udmurts | |
|------|------|------|------|
|      |      | total number | % |
| Urban Udmurts | 296,976 | 296,044 | 99.7 |
| Rural Udmurts | 339,930 | 329,254 | 96.9 |

Table 3. The number of rural and urban Udmurts in 2007 and knowledge of the Russian language (Salánki 2007: 26).

There are only about 10,000 (2–3%) Udmurts, who mainly live in the countrysides and who do not speak Russian. The Udmurts can also read Russian, while non-Udmurts are not usually fluent in Udmurt (Shkliaev and Toulouze 2001: 101).

## 3. Ethnicity, identity and language

According to Crystal (2003: 51), questions of individual linguistic identity only become critical in connection with ethnicity or nationality. Ethnic identity is nothing but a sense of loyalty and attachment to the group from which a person believes (s)he originates. As Bartha (2005: 57) notes: "Thus the use of language(s) is the practice of identity: on the one hand, the various forms of language use are the signs of identity; on the other hand, identity is constructed and presented to the speaker and to others. As social values regarding the use of languages change, including language ideology, identity changes too".[1]

Identity is a category which depends on a population's or nation's attitude towards life.

John Edwards (1985: 6) suggests that a definition of ethnic identity must involve both subjective and objective considerations. From his point of view, the objective aspect includes immutable factors such as language, religion, and ancestry. The subjective aspect implies that ethnic belonging is voluntary, mutual, and a reflection of belief. Therefore, a definition of ethnic identity should combine these objective and subjective considerations with other factors as well. I shall try to show what factors are fundamental in the case of the Udmurt people.

The language situation of the Finno-Ugrian peoples, including that of the Udmurts, is discussed in the study by Pusztay (2006). Several studies in connection with the sociolinguistics of the Udmurt language have been conducted (Krylova et al 2000; Phenomenon 2001; Phenomenon 2002), and in addition some ethnopsychological and ethnosociological research has also been carried out (Baymetov et al 1999; Belorukova 1999; Shirobokova 1999).

---

1. Translated by Shirobokova.

The next two sections of my article present the role of the Udmurt language in the identity of Udmurts, the nature of which was by analysing the situation of two different Udmurt groups, one a group of internet-using urban Udmurt youths, the other a group in an Udmurt village.

## 4. Udmurt youngsters and the internet

The internet may be very useful in preserving and maintaining minority languages. The presence of a minority language on the internet gives prestige to that language and thus encourages the speaker to use it. Unfortunately, the use of the internet in rural areas is still limited and many young Udmurts do not have the possibility of chatting or browsing on it.

Consequently, today, there is a stark difference between the linguistic situation in the villages and the cities. It seems notice that Udmurt language revitalisation works better in the cities, especially in the Capital Izhevsk, than in the villages because of internet penetration. In urban communities, people are beginning to show a greater interest in the Udmurt culture and language. In Izhevsk, there are many cultural events. The annual cultural festival Etnofuturists is becoming an increasingly popular event. Held at the beginning of summer, music, dance, performances, exhibitions and installations dominate in this event, where traditional folklore and folk art are combined with elements of modern art. This event is popular mainly among the younger generation and people living in the city. The main goal is to arouse interest in Udmurt culture (Salánki 2007: 44–46). There are also Udmurt discos, which are very important for young people. In the main, these events are found in the cities.

There are only limited number of books and magazines in the Udmurt language. An average of 10 to 15 books are published in Udmurt every year, most of them by the Udmurt Republic's press. They are not printed in large numbers, usually under 10,000 copies. Normally the published books and magazines can only be bought from the publishers, directly from the authors, or through subscription.

The internet may be very useful in the preservation and mainte-nance of minority languages, given the difficulty in obtaining printed material in those languages. The application of Udmurt in the internet during the past years shows that the Udmurt language can be succes-fully adopted in the new environment. There are some official pro-jects on the internet which consist of websites for Udmurt national literature, ethnic music of different varieties, websites providing the opportunity of studying the language, online dictionaries, national online forums and news, etc.

There is also an Udmurt version of the Wikipedia Encyclope-dia, but little or no information of a commercial or practical nature is available in Udmurt.

Since 2001, there have been about a dozen websites either using the Udmurt language, or dedicated to topics of the Udmurt language and culture. These include: "Удмуртский язык"[2] ('Udmurt lan-guage'), "Удмуртские стихи"[3] ('Udmurt poetry'), "Удмуртская кухня"[4] ('Udmurt cuisine'), "Удмурт портал"[5] ('Udmurt por-tal'), scientific and cultural information portal "Удмуртология"[6] ('Udmurtologia'), "Вся наша жизнь – Игра"[7] ('All our life – the game'), the personal websites of the young poets Nadja Pchelovodova[8] and Roman Romanov[9], "энциклопедия Удмурт элькун"[10] ('Ency-clopedia of the Udmurt Republic'). All these sites have been created by individuals on their own initiative and largely at their own expense.

Between 2007 and 2008, some new websites appeared offering Udmurt language content. The Udmurt Republic's newspaper Удмурт дунне[11] (Udmurt Dunne) opened its own website, and an online liter-ary magazine for young writers and poets Инвожо[12] (Invozho), was set up (Saharnyh 2008).

2. <http://home.udmnet.ru/udmurt_kyl>
3. <http://home.udmnet.ru/kylbur>
4. <http://udmkuhnia.ru/index.htm>
5. <http://udmurtportal.info>
6. <http://www.udmurtology.narod.ru>
7. <http://smchirkoff.narod.ru>
8. <http://nadimy.narod.ru>
9. <http://www.kazak-of-sky.ru>
10. <http://www.suri.ee/entsik/entsik.html>
11. <http://udmdunne.ru>
12. <http://www.invozho.ru>

The Hungarian Finno-Ugrist and linguist, Kata Kubinyi (2008) commented on the situation thus: "Due to the new forms of writing (online forums, text messaging, etc.) Udmurt language use is increasing among the urban Udmurt youth; however, where there are adverse conditions, such as the lack of an internet connection, it is difficult to increase Udmurt language use. It would be very important in the future to inform professionals involved in language planning and language policy of this fact. As we can see from the experience of the past ten years, the only way to revitalise the language is through daily communication in Udmurt."

I would like to present a Russian variant of the well-known American social networking site Facebook. Vkontakte[13] is a much more up-to-date and reliable source of information for young people living in Russia than the traditional media.

Udmurt youths, in particular, have been using it very actively, and they are not afraid of expressing their opinions in public on the current problems, which are not only cultural and linguistic, but also political. The role of this site is very important, since it has given a new impetus to the Udmurt language. We can even talk about a "new golden age" for the Udmurt language, because on this website we can see that Udmurt youngsters enjoy writing and debating in Udmurt.

They have created a group named Удмуртлык[14], which can be roughly translated as 'Udmurtness'. For one year the slogan of this group was: "Быдэс дуннеысь удмуртъёс, ойдолэ огазеяськоме! Удмуртлык но удмурт кыл понна висисьёслэн огазеяськонзы" ('Udmurts of the world unite! The union of followers of the Udmurt language and culture'). In Summer 2009, it changed to: "Быдэс дуннеысь удмуртъёслэн кусып возён интызы" ('Virtual contact area of Udmurts all around the word').

When I started writing this article, I decided to turn to the Udmurt youths on this particular social network for help. I developed a survey asking young Udmurts to list some factors that in their opinion form ethnic identity.

In the survey, I used Levkovich and Min's (1996) factors for distinguishing one nation from another: the uniform myth about the

---

13. &lt;http://vkontakte.ru&gt;
14. &lt;http://vkontakte.ru/club644235&gt;

origin of people, common territory, collective memory, the common historical destiny of minorities (heroes, historical events), a uniform religion, traditions, language, and, finally, partial togetherness within the group (Levkovich & Min 1996).

The diagram below was made using data from a survey conducted in February, 2009 to which there were 90 respondents.

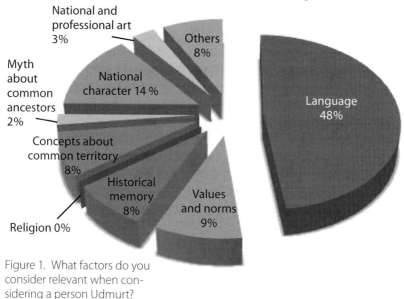

Figure 1. What factors do you consider relevant when considering a person Udmurt?

Figure 1 shows the results of the internet survey, where Udmurt people answered the question: "What factors do you consider relevant when considering a person Udmurt?" As we can see from the diagram, the language itself was seen as being the most intrinsically related to identity.

In her thesis, Kardinskaya (2005: 100–105) reveals the ethnic identity of Udmurts by analysing the opinions of Udmurts. Kardinskaya examines such factors as national character, origin, birth parents, traditions, customs, religion, and language. She points out that the main characteristic of "Udmurtness", the national language, is losing its practical meaning, but it is still the most important factor for ethnic identification. The Udmurt language is considered of value in the historical "past" but of less importance in the present, and this reveals the incompleteness of "Udmurt Ethnicity". Many informants have a positive attitude to opening Udmurt classes and schools, and they consider the national language to be an integral part of Udmurt identity. The respondents thought that Udmurt Ethnicity could be rounded out through the teaching of Udmurt at school.

However, my survey also shows that while language is the most important factor in the Udmurt identity, it was chosen by less than 50% of respondents. Some other factors, therefore, also play a role in creating Udmurt identity. The second most important factor, according to Udmurt informants in the internet survey, was "national character", which was chosen by 14.1% of respondents.

In her survey, Kardinskaya's (2005: 103) respondents explained the Udmurts national character in the following ways:

1. *"Удмурты мягче, что ли, гораздо сговорчивее."*
   'Udmurts are softer, perhaps, and much more tractable.'

2. *"У удмуртов простой, более мягкий характер."*
   'Udmurts have a simpler, gentler nature.'

3. *"Мы же... стеснительные", "простые".*
   'We are ....shy', 'simple'.

4. *"Наша нация чем отличается – скромностью, застенчивостью."*
   'Our nation differs due to our modesty, shyness.'

Consequently, the respondents in Kandinskaya's survey considered the characteristics of the Udmurt people positive in comparison to other peoples (tractable, gentler, modest; simple and shy might also be mentioned as positive values).

Figure 1 also shows that other important factors were: "values and norms" (9%), and "historical memory" and "concepts about the native common territory" (both 8%). "National and professional art" (3%) and "the myth about common ancestors" (2%) were seen as less important. For the youngsters in the internet survey, religion was not one of the characteristics of Udmurts.

## 5. The de jure and de facto status of the Udmurt language, and language use in an Udmurt village

Bilingual language use is very common in the world today; in fact more people in the world are bilingual than monolingual (Myers-Scotton 2008: 2). However, bilingualism is often misunderstood by non-professionals. The education system in the Udmurt Republic, and certainly in other schools in the Russian Federation, is often ignorant of the advantages of bilingualism.

Russian has been replacing Udmurt for many years – in practically all walks of life, including in the home, which has demotivated the younger generation to learn their native language. The Udmurt value system has been shattered. As a result, many young Udmurts strive to assimilate themselves into the Russian culture (Salánki 2007: 39).

A language act (Pusztay 2006: 112) was passed in the Udmurt Republic in 2001, giving the Udmurt language the status of an official language alongside Russian. The law states that in the Udmurt Republic there are two official languages: Udmurt and Russian. Consequently both languages should have equal status. However, the prestige of Russian plays a very important role. Law and practice are two different things.

Even if Udmurt is an official language in the Republic, the language situation in Udmurt villages is very complex. Education in the Udmurt Republic is only in Russian. In rural primary schools, Udmurt is taught three times a week, and Udmurt literature twice a week. Udmurt is taught throughout the first nine grades, but Udmurt literature is only taught in the 10th and 11th grades. In higher grades students may opt to continue studying Udmurt. Often parents decide whether or not their children need Udmurt. Parents are often afraid that bilingual children are at risk. One common belief is that children's brains will not be able to cope with the task of mastering two languages, which will cause them to fall behind. Another misbelief is that the teaching of Udmurt language and literature at primary school places extra strain on the child when there are a lot of other subjects to concentrate on, and when it is difficult enough already. (Kelmakov 2002: 55; Salánki 2007: 39.)

That is why, to date, there has been a strong emphasis on mastering Russian in the countryside. School teachers also put pressure on parents, continually telling them to speak to their children solely in the language of the school. As a result, Russian is given priority in mixed Russian-Udmurt families (Phenomen 2001: 119).

Kardinskaya (2005: 104) quotes the opinions of her respondents on the Udmurt language in the rural areas of the Udmurt Republic:[15]

> *The majority of respondents recognise that "children don't know the Udmurt language", "in most cases, somehow children don't speak in Udmurt anymore, everybody tries to speak in Russian", "now we rarely hear conversations in Udmurt between children. Children speak more in Russian, as they go to school and learn mostly in Russian".*

Teachers require students to speak among themselves in Russian, even outside class, in order to improve their future prospects.

For instance, in my home village, where 98% of inhabitants are Udmurt, the Udmurt language is used in public. However, the teachers at the kindergarten teach everything in Russian. That means that children only learn numbers, colours and other basic vocabulary in Russian.

Consequently, children have problems with vocabulary at primary school, since there Udmurt is spoken instead of the Russian they learnt in kindergarten.

In 2007 I collected the data on language use in my home village, which has a population of 400 people, 98% of whom are Udmurt. The results show that Udmurt is not always the main medium for spoken and written communication among the Udmurts.

I asked informants in the village about the language of SMS messages. The results are shown in Table 2. Almost half the informants (48%) did not write text messages at all. The majority of those

---

15. „Большинство респондентов признают, что «дети-то уже не знают удмуртский язык», «в большинстве случаев дети почему-то по-удмуртски уже не разговаривают, все стараются по-русски говорить»; «сейчас редко услышишь разговор на удмуртском языке. Дети больше на русском разговаривают, так как в школу идут и изучают, в основном, русский язык»." (Kardinskaya 2005: 104.)

informants who did write SMS messages wrote them entirely (42%) or mainly (3%) in Russian. Nobody wrote messages entirely in Udmurt. The other options – mixing the two languages or alternating between Russian and Udmurt – were also rarely used.

Similar to the case of SMS messages, calculating money is predominantly in Russian (Figure 3). 64% of informants always used Russian when calculating money, 12% often used Russian (12%).

Figure 2. Language for SMS messages.

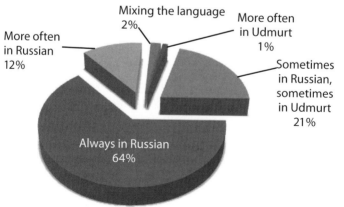

Figure 3. Language for calculating money.

Nobody calculated money exclusively in Udmurt, and those who often used Udmurt amounted to only 1%. This might be because numbers are taught to children at primary school only in Russian.

When I asked kindergarten teachers in my village the reason they did not read fairy tales to children in Udmurt, they answered honestly that the idea had never even occurred to them.

There is, however, no evidence to suggest that either bilingual education or a bilingual upbringing confuses children. In fact, there is much evidence that there are cognitive advantages for bilingual children and that children who are educated in more than one language develop better literacy in both languages, as well as deeper content knowledge. (Bialystok, 2001.) Unfortunately, there are not enough language experts in Udmurtia who could speak about the advantages of bilingualism and using the children's mother tongue.

## 6. The paradoxes of Udmurt language use

Many inhabitants of Russia do not consider native language knowledge an important matter, which could be the result of the historical oppression of the nationalities (Lallukka 2001: 1–2).

There was a fiery debate between Udmurts who spoke the Udmurt language and those who did not over the factors of ethnic identity on the discussion board at <http://vkontakte.ru> (<http://vkontakte.ru/topic-644235_16759189>).

First I quote the opinions of Udmurt people who are able to speak their mother tongue:

1.  *"Мон уг валаськы кызьы удмурт кылэз тодытэк астэ удмуртниманы луэ (in Udmurt). По-моему только зная язык, ты можешь прочувствовать народ до конца – разговаривать, как удмурты, делать, как они. А удмурт, который не знает кроме умоесь и зечбур, все-равно в среде удмуртов не будет таким же. НЕЛЬЗЯ стать 100% удмуртом не зная язык! Как можно воспринять те же ценности и нормы? Без знания языка формирование национального характера невозможно!"*

'I do not understand how they can call themselves Udmurt without a knowledge of the language? I think that only with a knowledge of the language can you feel really one of the people: talk like an Udmurt and act like an Udmurt. An Udmurt who knows nothing but Hi and Hello in Udmurt will not be the same person in an Udmurt-speaking environment. It is impossible to become Udmurt without a 100 per cent knowledge of the mother tongue! How is it possible to abide by the same values and norms? The establishment of a national consciousness is impossible. Without knowledge of the language it is impossible to build a national character!'

2. *"Для удмуртов язык – ведущий признак в сохранении этнич-ности. Язык – главный стержень, к которому прибавля-ются все остальные этнодифферинциирующие факторы и из которых складывается удмуртский менталитет!"*
'For the Udmurt people, language is the main factor in the preservation of ethnicity. Language is the core from which other factors evolve and from which the Udmurt mentality can develop.'

3. *"Нет языка – нет возможности для внутриэтнического дис-курса, нет средств для передачи опыта и ценностей и т.п..*
   *Всё же, в случае с удмуртами язык, безусловно, веду-щий признак в сохранении этничности."*
'No language means no opportunity for intraethnic discourse, there is no basis for the transference of experience and values and so on.
   Nevertheless, the Udmurt language, of course, is a key feature in the preservation of ethnicity.'
(<http://vkontakte.ru/topic-644235_16759189> 2.3.2009.)

We can see that, today, most urban Udmurt youths have discovered that the language they speak defines their place in society, marks their ethnic identity, and even their political affiliation. More importantly, they want to speak their native language, both in the cities and on the internet.

In the opinions quoted, Udmurt values and norms and the national character can only be built with the help of the language. The language was also seen as one of the main means of preserving the Udmurt identity.

However, there are also young Udmurts who do not speak their mother tongue. They see the role of the language very differently from those quoted above:

1. *"Язык далеко не основной этнодифференцирующий признак. Можно знать 2–3 слова по удмуртски, но тем не менее причислять себя к удмуртам. И наоборот, человек вырос в удмуртской деревне, но впоследствии намеренно дистанцируется от всего удмуртского. То же самое с признаками родители, корни, происхождние. Родители-удмурты могут намеренно "русифицировать" своего ребенка, но впоследствии у этого ребенка проснется интерес к удмуртскому. И, наоборот, у удмуртговорящих родителей вырастает, придерживаясь открытого безразличия к удмуртской культуре."*

'Language is not the main factor when considering a person Udmurt. One can know 2–3 words in Udmurt, but, nevertheless, one can be reckoned among the Udmurts. On the other hand, someone who grew up in an Udmurt village, but who later intentionally distanced himself from the Udmurt-speaking environment might not be considered Udmurt. The same with such things as parents, roots, descent. Udmurt parents may intentionally Russianise their children, but later those children can start to take an interest in the Udmurt language and culture. On the other hand Udmurt parents may have children growing up who are indifferent to the Udmurt culture, or who denigrate it.'

2. *"Основной этнодифференцирующий признак на мой взгляд – это сопереживание той или иной общности, стремление помочь ей, интерес к перспективам ее развития."*

'In my opinion, the main factor in building identity is sympathy towards the fate of one's nation, the desire to help it, and interest in the prospects for the development of the nation.'
(http://vkontakte.ru/topic-644235_167591891.3.2009.)

311

For young Udmurts who do not speak their mother tongue, the major factor in building Udmurt identity cannot be the Udmurt language, in which they lack proficiency. For them, Udmurt identity is symbolised by sympathy towards the fate of their nation, the aspiration to help it, and an interest in the prospects for its development.

## 7. Discussion

The result of turbulent and diverse cultural contacts is a feeling of instability respecting one's world view. When the world ceases to be clear, people begin to search for what would help to restore the integrity and orderliness of the world, protecting it from difficulties. Nowadays, in these circumstances, more and more Udmurt people (especially youngsters) are beginning to seek support in the time-honored values of their ethnic group, which seem to be the most reliable and understandable. As a result, we can see that through the awareness of belonging to ethnic groups the Udmurt people are seeking a way out of a state of social powerlessness in order to feel part of a community that will provide them with values in a dynamic world, and protect them from adversity.

Language is a reflection of mentality, which characterises the national culture and mutual human relations; moreover it is one of the most essential factors for building a national identity. Consequently, an alarm must be sounded if the ongoing decline of the Udmurt language is to be halted.

According to national census figures, the number of Udmurts living in the countrysides is on the decline, for which reason the number of Udmurts who know their native language is decreasing, too.

The mass migration of population, rapid urban growth, ethnic contacts, the influx of Western culture make the ethno-cultural environment weak. It is increasingly difficult to bring up children who higly respect their own culture and language. This is especially case with smaller ethnic groups, including the Udmurts. In this situation, there is an urgent need for more active and focused involvement in the process of ethnic socialisation, modern social institutions, such as the national media, educational institutions, public organisations, special government authorities, which are responsible for the preservation of national cultures, languages, traditions and ethnic identity in a satisfactory manner.

One of the most important social institutions for arousing interest in language and culture at this stage of revitalisation of the Udmurt language has become the internet. The possibility of using the internet in Udmurt has already produced some results. In fact the first step in revitalisation must begin from a motivation to study and read, although another essential step in this process would be to write texts in all possible contexts in Udmurt. In the urban communities people are beginning to show a greater interest in the Udmurt culture and language.

The Udmurt language use is increasing among the urban Udmurt youth; however, any adverse condition such as the lack of an internet connection in the countrysides makes it difficult to increase the use of Udmurt.

The main problem in Udmurtia is that children living in villages have no interest in learning and mastering their mother tongue. There is a strong aspiration toward mastering Russian in the countryside. My experience shows that in the villages the children have no interest in their mother tongue, and that parents and teachers do not even try to motivate children in this respect, because they think that the most import concern is to master Russian, in order to provide for the future. Thus despite the official status of the Udmurt language, the prestige and practical use of the language fall short of what should be desired. Accordingly, the using of the native language is limited to the most close, intimate spheres of life.

It is important to note that the future of every ethnic group depends on its youth. That is why attention to the Udmurt language as a major element of national culture should be raised during the preschool years, when children learn the spoken language associated with the domestic sphere of communication and with surrounding reality, as well as the language of amateur and folk arts.

What can we do in order to boost the social motivations for bilingualism, especially in the villages? How can we help to show the parents that there are several advantages that children might obtain from being bilingual and being educated bilingually?

Fortunately, the current positive changes in Russia concerning people having a minority status are beginning to be seen. We can say with assurance that the Finno-Ugrian peoples are becoming more and more accepted, and this can also be thanks to those Hungarian and Finnish linguists and active participants who are supporting talented young Finno-Ugrian people. This all raises the hope that ultimately the status of the language will improve.

I would suggest that now the most important goal must be to train sociolinguists – including native linguists and specialists – who will be able to instruct school teachers and the school teachers will be able to explain to parents how they can deal with the specific language situation in the family, in other words with the problems of bilingualism.

It might be argued that it is more efficient to start with the parents, but, in order to do this, good native language teachers would be needed to help and play an important role in the language revitalisation project.

As I have already mentioned, there are a number of myths which often emphasise the negative aspects of minority languages, thus influencing the attitude of people towards these languages. Consequently, I think teachers should help dispel popular misconceptions about bilingualism.

University teachers, school teachers and parents should be given an opportunity to work side by side and cooperate in order to improve the language situation of the Udmurt village. In addition, this would give the Udmurt youth ample opportunities for self-realisation and understanding their own culture's true value.

# References

Bartha, Csilla 2005: Nyelv, identitás és kissebségek. A nemzeti/etnikai identitás fogalmának értelmezései a szociolingvisztikában és egy országos kutatás tükrében. – *Érték és valóság. Egység a különbözőségben. Az Európai Unió és a nemzeti kisebbségek.* Hetedik füzet/2006: 53–85.

Baymetov et al. = Байметов, В.А. & Ишмуратов, А.В. & Разин, А.А. & Радевич, А.Ф. 1999: Удмурты и русские (сравнительное психологическое исследование). – *Вестник Удмуртского Университета* 1999.4: 3–7.

Belorukova = Белорукова, Г.П.: Обучающаяся молодёжь Удмуртии в период реформирования российского общества (Опыт этносоциологического изучения). – *Вестник Удмуртского Университета* 1999.4: 22–31.

Bialystok, Ellen 2001: *Bilingualism in Development: Language, Literacy, and Cognition.* Cambridge: Cambridge University Press.

Crystal, David 1998: *The Cambridge Encyclopedia of Language.* Cambridge: Cambridge Univesity Press.

Edwards, John 1985: *Language, Society and Identity.* Oxford: Blackwell.

García, Ofelia 2008: *Bilingual education in the 21st century: a global perspective.* Ofelia Garcia, with contributions by Hugo Baetens Beardsmore. Malden MA.: Blackwell Publishing.

Kardinskaya 2005 = Кардинская, С.В. 2005: Удмурты об этнической идентичности (опыт пилотажного исследования). – *Социологические иссделования* 2005 № 5. С: 100–105.
– <http://www.ecsocman.edu.ru/socis/msg/270180.html> 15.02.2009.

Kelmakov, Valej K. 2002: Udmurttien nykytilanteesta. – Marja Lappalainen (ed.), *Sukukansapäivien satoa. Kirjoituksia ja puheenvuoroja suomalais-ugrilaisuudesta.* Castrenianumin toimitteita 57. Helsinki: M. A. Castrénin seura, Helsingin yliopiston suomalais-ugrilainen laitos & Suomalais-Ugrilainen Seura. 49–58.

Krylova et al 2000 = Крылова, А. & Бехтерев, С. & Бехтерева, Л. 2000: *Удмуртская Республика. Модель этнологического мониторинга.* Москва: РАН.

Kubinyi, Kata 2009: Diákkonferencia az ELTE Finnugor Tanszéken.
– <www.renhirek.blogspot.com/2009/05/diakkonferencia-az-elte-finnugor.html> 22.04.2009.

Lallukka, Seppo 1990: *The East Finnic Minorities in the Soviet Union.* Helsinki: Suomalainen Tiedeakatemia.

—— 2001: Finno-Ugrians of Russia: vanishing cultural communities? – *Nationalities Papers* Vol. 29, No. 1: 9–39.

Levkovich & Min: Левкович В.П. & Мин Л.В. 1996: Особенности сохранения этнического самосознания корейских переселенцев Казахстана. – *Психологический журнал* Т.17. № 6. С: 72–81.

Myers-Scotton, Carol 2008: *Multiple voices: an introduction to bilingualism.* Malden, MA.: Blackwell Publishing.

Phenomen 2001 = Губогло, М.Н. & Смирнова, С.К. (ed.) 2001: *Феномен Удмуртии. Парадоксы этнополитической трансформации на исходе XX века.* Москва: РАН.

Phenomen 2002 = Губогло, М.Н. (ed.) 2002: *Феномен Удмуртии. Том 5. Национальное строительство и межэтнические отношения.* Москва–Ижевск: Удмуртия.

Pusztay, János 2006: *Nyelvével hal a nemzet.* Budapest: Teleki László Alapítvány.

Saharnyh 2008 = Сахарных, Денис 2008: Новое в развитии удмуртского национального интернета. Зима–осень 2008 г. – <http://udmurt. info/pdf/texts/udmurtnet-zima-osenj-2008.pdf> 25.04.2009.

Salánki, Zsuzsanna 2007: *Az udmurt nyelv mai helyzete.* Doktori disszertáció. Kézirat. [Unpublished.]

Shirobokova = Широбокова, Н.Ф. 1999: Отношение студентов к национальной культуре и некоторые вопросы их национального самосознания (по материалам вузов Удмуртии). – *Вестник Удмуртского Университета* 1999.4: 39–42.

Shkliaev, Aleksandr & Toulouze, Eva 2001: The mass media and the national question. – *Udmurtia in the 1990s nationalities papers* vol. 29, no. 1: 97–108.

www.perepis2002.ru = *Всероссийская перепись населения 2002 года.* Официальный сайт Всероссийской переписи населения 2002 год. – <http//:www.perepis2002.ru> 15.02.2009.

# Этническая идентичность и удмурты

*Лариса Широбокова*

Вопрос этнической идентичности всегда был актуален для поликультурных регионов, где уровень межэтнических контактов достаточно высок. В Советском Союзе этнические вопросы были закрытой темой на уровне политики, а также в научных исследованиях. После распада СССР эти вопросы стали важными среди национальных меньшинств, появился интерес к своим корням у народов России. Этническая идентичность имеет особое значение на территории Удмуртской Республики, где проживают более 70 национальностей. Численность населения Республики – 1,6 млн. человек, из которых 460 тыс. составляют удмурты.

В данной работе делается попытка рассмотреть важный параметр этнической идентичности для национальных меньшинств в современной России, а именно язык. Данный фактор сравнивается с другими факторами, играющими также немаловажную роль в жизни народов. Во всей обширной литературе, так или иначе рассматривающей вопросы этничности, считается аксиомой, что язык является одним из важнейших, а, может, и самым важным этноконсолидирующим признаком идентичности. Так ли бесспорно это утверждение, если мы рассмотрим реальные факты удмуртской языковой ситуации? Важно также выяснить, каким образом официальный статус удмуртского языка влияет на фомирование и сохранение этнической идентичности. В нашем исследовании мы уделяем внимание интернет-страницам социальной сети, делаем попытку сравнить сельские и городские общины, особенно настроения и мнения молодых удмуртов.

Мы должны отметить, что на индивидуальное речевое поведение оказывают воздействие и социокультурные установки говорящего, и его самоидентификация.

1. Так, интернет может быть весьма плодотворным в достижении общих целей в сохранении и развитии удмуртского языка, а также в укреплении этнической идентичности удмуртской молодежи. Наличие электронной сети на языке меньшинства

дает престиж языку, мотивирует пользователя писать на своем родном языке. Необходимо создать как можно больше возможностей использования удмуртского языка в интернете, особенно важно создать такие условия для деревенской молодежи. Мы можем отметить новую форму и период в развитии языков национальных меньшинств – это создание национального интернета.

2. Важно отметить противоречивый характер понятия «удмуртскость»: большая часть удмуртской молодежи в городах открывают для себя, что язык, на котором они говорят, определяет их место в обществе, их этническую принадлежность, и даже их политической взгляды. Они хотят говорить на своем родном языке в городах и в виртуальном мире интернета. При этом в деревнях, где, казалось бы, находится источник удмуртского языка и культуры, чувствуется ослабление «удмуртскости». В деревнях исчезает понимание важности родного языка, немаловажную роль в котором играет роль школы, поскольку именно в школе начинается социализация детей.

# Этнической идентичность но удмуртъёс

*Лариса Широбокова*

Этнической идентичностен герӟаськем юанъёс котьку но туж мечкыт сылӥзы но сыло сыче интыосын, кытын одӥг дыре трос пӧртэм йӧскалыкъёс нуналысь нуналэ кусып возё, пумисько. Советский Союзын этникаен герӟаськем юан-валэктонъёс политикая ёзъёсын кемалы пытсамын вал, озы ик научной институтъёсын. СССР куашкам бере пичи лыдъем калыкъёс куспын та юанъёс туж важноесь луизы, Россиын улӥсь калыкъёс асьсэ выжыосынызы тунсыкъяськыны кутскизы. Этнической идентичность Удмурт Элькунын туж бадӟым инты басьтэ, угось элькунын 70-лэсь трос пӧртэм йӧскалык улэ. Элькунын улӥсь калыкъёслэн лыдзы нош ваньмыз чош 1,6 миллион, соос пӧлысь 460 сюрс удмуртъёс.

Та ужын пичи лыдъем калыкъёслэсь этнической идентичностен герӟаськем юанъёслы валэктон шедьтыны тыршиськом, уката но бадӟым саклык идентичность кылын герӟаськем ужпумъёсты сэрттыны-пертчыны дэмласьком. Та фактор эскериське но чошатӥське мукет факторъёсын но, кудъёсыз озы ик бадӟым гинэ инты басьто пичи лыдъем калыкъёслэн улоназы. Та темалы сӥзем литератураын воштонтэм луэ одӥг малпан: кыл – идентичность валанлэн огез самой кулэ луись тодметэз.

Зэмзэ но, сыче ик споръяськыны луонтэм меда та валэктон, эскероно ке удмуртъёслэсь кыл ситуацизэс сэрттон-пертчонын кылдӥсь зэмос луись фактъёсты. Та ужын ми саклык висъяськом интернет-бамъёслы, чошатыны тыршиськом гуртъёсын но городын улӥсь адямиослэсь, уката ик егитъёслэсь мылкыдзэс, этнической юанъёсын герӟаськем малпанъёссэс.

Одно ик пусйыны кулэ, адямилэн вераськемез, кыл кутэмез вылэ мерлыко-чеберлыко условиос влиять каро, озьы ик адямилэн асшӧдонэз.

Кылсярысь, тани интернет туж емышо луыны быгатоз удмурт кылэз утёнын но азьланьтонын но озы ик удмурт егитъёслэсь этнической идентичностьсэз, асьсэды удмурт луэмзэс юнматонын. Электронной вотэс пичи лыдъем калыкъёслэн кылзылы престиж сётэ, интернетын пукисьёслы анай кылынызы гожъяськон мылкыдзэс лопыртэ. Соин ик одно ик тросгес луонлык кылдытоно удмурт кыллэн интернетын кутйськемезлы, update но гуртъёсын улйсь удмурт егитъёслы но пиналъёслы асьсэ кылзэс интернетысь адӟыны луонлык сётоно. Туннэ нуналлы пичи лыдъем, пичи кылъем калыкъёслэн улоназы выль вамыш но вакыт адӟиське – йöскалык интернет кылдытон.

Одно ик пусйыны кулэ «удмуртлык» валанлэсь пумит луись сямзэ: тросэз городын улйсь удмурт егитъёс валаны кутско, кыл, кудйныз соос верасько, мерлыкысь интызэс возьматэ, кыче йöскалык пöлы пыремзэс пусъе, озьы ик политикаен герӟаськем малпанъёссэс но шарая шуыса. Удмурт егитъёслэн каръёсын но интернетлэн бамъёсаз удмурт сямен вераськыны мылкыдзы нуналысь нуналэ бадӟыма. Нош гуртъёсын, кытын, малпалод кадь, отын удмурт кыллэн но культуралэн кутсконэз, пöзись интыез луыны кулэ, «удмуртлыклэн» лябӟемез шöдйське. Гуртъёсын ышыны кутскиз валан, анай кыл котькуд удмурт адямилэн улоназ туж кулэ луись инты басьтэ шуыса. Одйгез муг талы – школа, угось школаын кутске пиналлэн мерлыко улонэн тодматскемез, отчы вамыштонэз.

OUTI TÁNCZOS

# Identity Construction
# in an Udmurt Daily Newspaper

## Abstract

The aim of this article is to examine how methods of critical discourse analysis (CDA) can be utilised in studying representations of linguistic identities and the role of minority media in defining minority identity. It is a case study on the only Udmurt-language daily newspaper, the government-owned *Udmurt Duńńe*. According to sociolinguistic surveys, language is considered the core element of being Udmurt. Nevertheless, a language shift is rapidly taking place among the younger generations. This development creates the need for a redefinition of the concept of being Udmurt. The results of a text analysis on *Udmurt Duńńe* articles illustrate this ongoing process. Text analysis shows that the newspaper dedicates much attention to the question. It emphasises the role of language as a central constituent of being Udmurt and takes a rather optimistic view of the present state and future prospects for the Udmurt language. Some problematic linguistic issues are discussed in *Udmurt Duńńe*, but not all: for instance, the growing group of Russian speakers of Udmurt ethnic origin is ignored, and being Udmurt or Russian are presented as mutually exclusive categories. The answers the newspaper provides to the question of who is Udmurt are to some extent contradictory to the prevailing linguistic situation and development.

*Ethnic and Linguistic Context of Identity: Finno-Ugric Minorities.* 321–340.
Uralica Helsingiensia 5. Helsinki 2011.

# 1. Critical discourse analysis in tracing identity construction

A nation is a system of cultural representations. As Stuart Hall (1992: 292) puts it: "We only know what it is to be 'English' because of the way 'Englishness' has come to be presented ... by English national culture". Thus, knowing what being a member of a nation means requires constant participation in creating such representations and interpreting them. This article focuses on the representations of being Udmurt in an Udmurt newspaper. Methodologically, the study is based on critical discourse analysis, starting from the premise that language ideologies and attitudes, as well as elements of group identity construction, can be discovered by examining newspaper texts. The results are valid only for the particular newspaper in question, but even so they shed some light on the current situation in the language community.

Critical discourse analysis (CDA) has proven to be a useful tool, especially for scholars operating with an interdisciplinary approach. "Critical" refers to the goal of enhancing our understanding of power relations and ideological processes behind the texts (Fairclough 1989: 109). CDA stresses the reciprocal nature of the relationship between texts and society. As a scientific framework it goes beyond the linguistic features of the text by linking them to their larger context, in this case to the surrounding community. (Fairclough 1995: 33–34.)

One of the focuses of the critical analysis of media discourse is the representation and constitution of relations and identities. In the modern world, representations spread by the media play a significant role in constructing identities. Also, for minorities news coverage is an important means of gaining attention and a chance to make their voices heard (Pietikäinen 2003: 583). The minority media construct their readers' identity and self-image both intentionally and unintentionally. It is rewarding to investigate the strategies used in representing the minority: What factors and features are emphasised? How explicit is the strategy of representation? Does it attempt to transform the assumed image of the minority or does it focus more on tradition and preservation? Does it allow for several identities and fuzzy borders?

Seppo Lallukka (2001: 10) points out that many Finno-Ugric societies are internally divided by administrative, dialectal, religious and linguistic boundaries. Moreover, large sections of these societies seem indifferent to their nationality. In such an environment the minority media need to choose whom to address and whom to include and exclude. This selection is particularly interesting, as this is what many readers of a minority paper come to see as a possible definition of the minority group. It is also a definition that carries the weight of official printed media and may thus control the identification of individuals.

Minority media also provide readers with ideas about the status of the language and the community. According to Martin Ehala (2009: 128), an individual speaker's linguistic behaviour is greatly affected by her evaluation of the vitality of the linguistic community. Minority media need to be taken into consideration as an actor in this evaluation process. Perhaps it is no exaggeration to say that investigating the representations of a minority in the media can shed light on issues regarding the future prospects of the community envisaged by the authors of that media and also their reactions to these prospects.

Representations of identity in a text can be found at all levels of language, and therefore a comprehensive description can only be achieved by a thorough examination of the whole text. This exhaustiveness, however, limits the number of texts examined and thus reduces the possibility of making generalisations from the study. Therefore, with the aim of extending the data, only a few features were selected for review. The study focuses on the use of the ethnonym *udmurt*. It rests on the assumption that the frequency of the ethnonym roughly corresponds to the centrality of the topic in the paper, and that examining the head nouns it modifies gives an insight into what concepts Udmurtness is most often associated with. One of the objects of this study was to find out whether the head nouns show any clear co-occurrence tendencies, and what these reveal about the perception of Udmurtness. To complete the picture, more general representations of Udmurtness in the texts were also analysed, and the observations placed in their sociolinguistic context.

## 2. Sociolinguistic situation among the Udmurts

As Larisa Shirobokova (see pp. 295–320 in this volume) gives an overview of demographic development among the Udmurts during the last century in her article, this topic is not discussed here in depth. In the following, just the main sociolinguistic changes will be presented briefly.

Demographic developments among the Udmurts follow the general tendencies of the Finno-Ugric peoples of Russia. The census of 2002 shows a significant decline in the proportion of Finno-Ugrians in the population of the Russian Federation. This decline is mainly the result of assimilation. (Lallukka 2005: 31, 42–44.) Assimilation tendencies, natural and forced, have existed among the Finno-Ugrian peoples of Russia since the Tsarist Era (Lallukka 2001: 9–10). Linguistic assimilation plays a salient part in the assimilation process.

During most of the Soviet regime the use of the Udmurt language in public and administrative contexts was very limited. After the collapse of the Soviet Union, the legal status of the Udmurt language altered significantly: in 1990 it was declared equal to Russian inside the Udmurt Republic. Later legislation has also confirmed this status. (Salánki 2008: 28, 61.) Nevertheless, there is a wide disparity between the legal status of Udmurt and the actual use of the language. In practice, Udmurt remains the language of private life. Access to, for instance, Udmurt-language education or media does not measure up to the legislation in force. (id. 204.) This is in accordance with the traditional image of Russian as the language of prestige and public life, and of Udmurt as the language of the backward countryside (id. 69).

Zsuzsanna Salánki's (2008: 37–39) overview of the current linguistic situation among the Udmurts is not encouraging to read. Less than 50% of Udmurt children receive instruction in the Udmurt language. Schools only provide instruction in Udmurt if requested by the parents. Many parents neglect this, as the attitude of both parents and teachers is often negative towards minority language learning and bilingualism at school. Russian is also the language of instruction in institutions of higher education, with the exception of the Faculty of

Udmurt Philology at the Udmurt State University (id. 41–42). Thus, the development of Udmurt towards the position of an acknowledged language in society has already been gravely hindered by the educational system.

Other factors contributing to linguistic assimilation include mixed marriages (due to lack of knowledge and negative attitudes towards bilingualism) and urbanisation, which transform the linguistic networks of the individual and often lead to increasing use of Russian. Practically all Udmurts are either Udmurt-Russian bilingual or Russian monolingual, which results in Russian being preferred in contact situations with speakers of Russian, who, as a rule, are monolingual (id. 26–27). It is noteworthy that only around 73% of ethnic Udmurts speak Udmurt. Especially among young adults has language shift already taken place to some extent and Salánki (id. 81) describes this as "massive". She relates this phenomenon to the previous generation's fluency in Russian. This demonstrates that in the case of Udmurt bilingualism has not been a stable linguistic condition but just a stepping stone in the process of language shift. This can partly explain why bilingualism has not gained popularity among minority activists even though the Udmurt population is in fact bilingual.

As mentioned above, the media do not publish sufficiently in the Udmurt language. The whole republic is covered by just one Udmurt-language daily, the *Udmurt Duńńe*. In addition, a local newspaper, some supplements in Russian local papers and a few magazines are published in Udmurt. However, their scope is modest and they are published more infrequently. Despite the designation "daily", *Udmurt Duńńe* also only appears three times a week. (Salánki 2008: 44.) The fact that the popularity of the internet is constantly growing, especially among the young, (cf. Shirobokova) can, in my opinion, be partly explained by the biased content in and poor availability of the traditional media. The unrivalled position of *Udmurt Duńńe*, nevertheless, makes it an influential actor in shaping the attitudes of those reading newspapers in Udmurt.

## 3. Ethnic self-identification of the Udmurts

Under Soviet rule, ethnic pride, or even the application of an ethnonym determining a minority people, could be interpreted as nationalism, which did not fit in with the official ideal of internationalism. After the collapse of the Soviet Union, questions of ethnicity, nationality and minority rights started to attract attention. Until then the image of the Udmurts had mainly been that of a primitive peasant nation, but now this image was questioned. The beginning of the 1990s was a time of active societal debate on the question of ethnicity. The sombre past, however, had left its imprint on the Udmurt community, and the discussion was not welcomed by all Udmurts. (Shkliaev & Toulouze 2001: 97–101.) Discussion of the issue seems to have abated, but not all the questions have been answered.

As to the question of who is Udmurt, the usual answer seems to be "one who speaks Udmurt" (cf. Shirobokova). According to Salánki (2008: 81) the Udmurt language is the most significant constituent of the Udmurt group (national) identity. She also mentions "being Finno-Ugrian" as an important factor (id. 46). She states that "if someone is Udmurt but does not speak Udmurt, this fact is regularly mentioned when describing them"[1]. The quote ("is Udmurt but does not speak") proves that in spite of the significant role of the language, it is possible to define someone as Udmurt by other factors. This view is supported by the fact that only 72.8% of those who declare themselves Udmurt speak the language (id. 81).

## 4. Udmurt in *Udmurt Duńńe*

In order to extract from the data as much information as possible about identity construction and perception, quantitative and qualitative methods are combined in the following analysis. Quantitative methods give a broader idea of the subject, whereas qualitative methods provide a more focused view.

---

1. Author's translation

## 4.1. Data

My data sample consists of 64 articles published in *Udmurt Duńńe* in January and February 2007. *Udmurt Duńńe* is published by the government, and its editorial office is situated in the capital city Iževsk (Salánki 2008: 44). The content of the paper is restricted to local news from Udmurtia and neighboring areas. It does not report foreign news, and even news from other parts of Russia is rare. Interviews are a common story type, which possibly reflects the paper's intention to express opinions without committing itself to those opinions (Shkliaev & Toulouze 2001: 101). This makes the selection of interviewees an important ideological act.

## 4.2. Frequency of the ethnonym udmurt

I scanned the 64 articles for the ethnonym *udmurt*. Other variations of the ethnonym also exist, but in standard language *udmurt* is used. According to Grünthal (2009: 267), ethnonyms can be considered extremely evident manifestations of linguistic identity, which is why I chose the ethnonym as the means of demarcating the data. This selection reduced the data to 27 articles, more than 40% of the original material containing the ethnonym. The frequency of the ethnonym *udmurt* in the texts was high: it occurred 130 times. On average there were 4.8 occurrences per article. These figures give the impression that Udmurtness is a central topic in *Udmurt Duńńe*.

Considering the relatively modest size of my data, I wished to confirm my results by contrasting the frequency of the ethnonym *udmurt* with the ethnonym *žuč* 'Russian'. I searched for these words throughout the whole *Udmurt Duńńe* web archive, and *udmurt* produced 2340 hits and *žuč* less than a third of this figure, only 686. This, for its part, seems to confirm the assumption of a more central role for 'Udmurt' in comparison with 'Russian'. (Pynnönen 2009: 28.)

## 4.3. Attributes and head nouns

In most occurrences, the ethnonym functioned in the texts as an attributive adjective. I found it interesting to observe what kind of head nouns it was connected with and if recurrent combinations could be detected. My hypothesis was that the attribute not only modifies the meaning of the head noun, but that a reoccurring head noun can also project its meaning onto the attribute, that is, if we repeatedly see the ethnonym *udmurt* together with concepts like 'song' or 'choir', our interpretation will be that being Udmurt is closely connected with music. I searched the data for cases where *udmurt* functioned as an attribute, and divided the head nouns into eight thematic groups. The figure below shows the division of the head nouns between these groups.

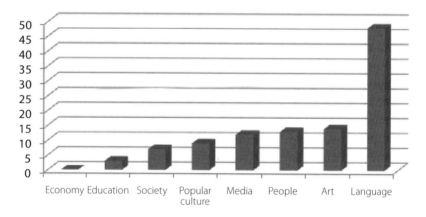

Figure. Head nouns divided into thematic groups.

The thematic group "Language" stands out strikingly in the graph. The head noun belonged to this group in 48 instances. In most cases the head noun was *kyl* 'language'. This means that in most cases when 'Udmurt' is mentioned in *Udmurt Duńńe*, it appears in a context dealing with the language. If we continue with the idea that the head noun may modify the meaning of the attribute, this brings us to the conclusion that 'Udmurt' is mostly defined by the Udmurt language. This corresponds with Salánki's views on language as the foundation of Udmurt identity.

## 4.4. Selection of topics – partial views of the world

Objectivity is a feature often connected with the news, but the news, as well as all other texts, are filtered through the author, in this case the journalist, who chooses the perspective from which to write. The news item may reflect the journalist's personal views or it may reflect the societal position of the medium he works for. This position also affects the selection of news: not all events become news stories but they are selected according to the interests of the medium. This inclusion and exclusion of events results in a partial view of the world. (Fowler 1991: 10–11.) In the following, I shall give some examples of narratives concerning the Udmurt language to illustrate the view of the world *Udmurt Dunńe* transmits. These samples are particularly interesting from the point of view of selection and evaluation. I have translated the excerpts into English, but my analysis is based on the original text.

## 4.5. Visibility of the Udmurt language

The visibility of the Udmurt language in everyday life is a recurring topic in the texts.

(1)  *Лыдӟисьёсмы адӟизы ни, луоз: бадӟым сюресъёс вӧзысь тросэз гурт но шур нимъёс удмурт кылын но гожтэмын.*
     'Our readers have probably already noticed that along the main roads many of the names of villages and rivers are already written in Udmurt, too.'

The example reveals the author's assumption that the readership is interested in linguistic issues and pays attention to the visibility of Udmurt. The use of the possessive suffix (*-мы*, 1Pl) produces the impression of a community that shares the same interest. Examples (2) and (3) share the same tone as they present new forms of Udmurt media, such as the internet, and encourage readers to take part.

(2) *Удмурт кылэз вӧлмытонын интернет туж бадӟым луон-лык кылдытэ.*
'In spreading the Udmurt language the internet represents a great opportunity.'

(3) *Озьыен, аслэсьтыд удмурт сайттэ усьтыны секыт уз луы.*
'So, opening your own Udmurt website is not difficult.'

Examples (4), (5) and (6) are taken from an interview with a prominent young state official, himself of Udmurt origin, dealing with linguistic issues. As regards the selection of interviewees, this is a telling example of the highlighting of the "ideal Udmurt". Among *Udmurt Dunńe*'s interviewees there are many intellectuals, especially linguists and language teachers, but also others who have succeeded in life and yet maintained their ties with Udmurt language and culture. The young official suggests practical solutions for improving the visibility of Udmurt and also criticises the absence of Udmurt in the streets, for instance on non-official signs wishing customers a Happy New Year.

(4) *Туэ городысь одӥг магазин азьысь ӟуч но удмурт кылын «Выль арен!» гожтэмез адӟи.*
'This year I [only] saw one shop in the city that had the text "Happy New Year" in Russian and in Udmurt in front of it.'

The context reveals that all the other signs were only in Russian. In examples (5) and (6) the interviewed official suggests solutions to the problem of the poor visibility of Udmurt.

(5) *Калыклэсь та ласянь малпанзэ чутрак воштоно ӟечез пала, мед луозы удмурт нимо печення-конфетъёс, колбаса, тортъёс...*
'People's notion of this subject needs to be upgraded in a determined way: let there be biscuits and sweets, sausages, cakes etc. with an Udmurt name.'

(6) *Удмурт кылын лыдӟиськон мылкыдэз, тужгес но*
*егитъёс пӧлын, бурдъян понна капчи литература борды*
*басьтӥськоно.*
'One must start to produce popular literature in order to stimu-
late the young, especially, to read Udmurt.'

The official's appeal does not address the readers directly, as it is
expressed by the use of impersonal structures (optative mood *мед*
*луозы* 'let there be', necessive participles *воштоно* 'has to be changed',
*басьтӥськоно* 'has to be undertaken'). By using these structures the
speaker somewhat blurs his/her responsibility and the responsibility
of her/his background community, those people whose task it is to
encourage a broader use of Udmurt. It is not clear who is expected to
realise the launching of these products – the manufacturers, the state
or the consumers. The baton is not really passed to anyone, and thus
the issue can easily be ignored.

## 4.6. The Udmurts and the others (the non-speakers)

The writers of *Udmurt Dunńe* are concerned about those Udmurts and
Russians who do not encounter the minority language in their daily
life and also about the Russian majority's negative attitude towards
the language. This is shown by examples (7)–(11).

Examples (7)–(9) are taken from a text reporting on a language
camp for Udmurt children. It is written in the form of a dialogue in
which an Udmurt university student tries to convince the Russian
children of the value of the Udmurt language.

(7) *Нош школаос удмурт кылэз воксё но валасьтэм ӟуч пиналъ-*
*ёссэс ыстӥллям.*
'But schools have also sent [to language camps] children who
don't understand a word of Udmurt.'

Example (7) provides interesting information on the problems of language preservation: minority language camps are organised, but those
who select the participants are either deliberately trying to undermine
their activities or have not fully understood the function of these

camps. The presence of Russian monolingual children in these camps is likely to hinder the use of Udmurt, as all young Udmurts know Russian and are accustomed to communicating in Russian.

(8)   *Одӥг пол ӟуч пиналъёс шуизы: «Лагерьын туж ӵем чузъяське удмурт кыл.*
      'Once the Russian children said: "You hear Udmurt very often in the camp".'

This quote proves that the representatives of the majority do not usually have much contact with the minority language. The next sentence in the text reveals the negative attitudes of the majority children towards the minority language: *Ми ум валаське сое, валаммы но уг поты!* ('We don't understand it and we don't even want to!').

(9)   *Нош удмурт кылэз дышетӥмы ке, милемыз школаысь эшъёсмы серекъялозы, - кылӥськиз куара.*
      '"But if we study the Udmurt language, our school mates will laugh at us", a voice said.'

In (9), Russian children are talking about the possibility of learning Udmurt at school. It is not clear who would laugh at them – the Udmurt children, the Russian children or both? One possible interpretation is that the status of Udmurt is so low that studying it is considered absurd. Another interpretation is that the whole idea of members of a majority learning a minority language is alien to school children in Udmurtia.

Excerpt (10) is a quote from the young Udmurt official mentioned above in (4), (5) and (6).

(10)  *Зэм, Лановоез удмурт кылын нокин уз вераськыты.*
      'Indeed, no one is going to make Lanovoy speak Udmurt.'

Vasiliy Lanovoy is a popular Russian actor. The official is envisaging a poetry evening where Lanovoy recites Udmurt poems. However, he finds it impossible to conceive that Lanovoy could read them in Udmurt. His complete disbelief is expressed with the modal adverb *зэм* 'indeed'. It reveals not only the attitude of the speaker towards the Udmurt language, but also his assumption concerning the attitudes of the linguistic majority. His proposal is that Lanovoy read the poems in Russian and an ethnic Udmurt actor read them in Udmurt.

Examples 11–14 deal with the responsibility of Udmurts towards their language.

(11) *Мукет ласянь, удмурт кыл отын-татын сокем уг кылӥськы-адӟиськы бере, сое тодӥсьтэмъёс кызьы чебер-лыксэ валалозы?*

'On the other hand, if the Udmurt language cannot be heard and seen, how can those who are not familiar with it realise its beauty?'

(12) *Малпасько, кылмес, культурамес азинтон понна огдыре ик ужано солэсь данзэ будэтон бордын (удмуртъёс пӧлын гинэ ӧвӧл, мукет выжыос пӧлын но).*

'I think that in order to foster our language and culture they need to be promoted at the same time (not only among the Udmurts but also among other peoples).'

(13) *Асьмеос ке ӧм, кин удмурт кылмес узырмытоз?*

'Who is going to enrich our Udmurt language, if not we ourselves?'

(14) *Эн вунэтэ: удмурт кылмы жильыртӥсь ошмес кадь пыдэ-стэм но али ӝужась сяська кадь чебер!*

'Do not forget: our Udmurt language is as clear as a rippling spring and as beautiful as a flower bursting into bloom!'

In examples (11) and (12) the "others" are not named as Russians, but considering the sociolinguistic background this is the most likely interpretation, as the Russian-speaking community affects the situation of Udmurt the most. The indifference of the Russians to Udmurt is explained by their lack of knowledge. The Udmurts are left with the task of maintaining their language (13), promoting it and convincing the Russians that it is worth knowing and preserving. However, the speaker in (14) does not have full confidence in Udmurt speakers. He needs to remind them of the value of the language. In (11) and (14) beauty is mentioned as a major attribute of the Udmurt language and also as a reason for the majority to respect and help preserve it. This hints at a perception of language in which a language as such is not automatically valuable. Its value depends on its qualities, which is why the author feels the need to convince the Udmurts and the Russians of the beauty of Udmurt. Examples (12)–(14) stress the unity of the group with the use of the 1st and 2nd Person Plural (i.e. *кылмы* 'our language'). The language is presented as shared cultural heritage. These examples are appeals to the readership and contain affective vocabulary and metaphors: *жильыртӥсь ошмес кадь пыдэстэм*, 'clear as a rippling spring'. These features may be connected partly with a tradition of ceremonious rhetoric, but they still reveal the need to appeal to the public for the preservation of language.

## 4.7. The Udmurt language as a part of identity

The following examples present the Udmurt language as a salient part of the national and personal identity.

(15)  *Удмурт сямен вазисько: «Я, кенаке, мар тонэ сюлмась-*
      *кытэ?»*
      'I address her in Udmurt: "Well, auntie, what is it that worries you?"'

(16)  *Адямилэн тусыз ик воштӥське, мылкыдыз бурдъяське,*
      *удмурт кылын ваньзэ тупен-тупен маде ни.*
      'Even the appearance of the person changes, his/her spirits rise, he/she shares everything in detail in the Udmurt language.'

The examples above are quotes from a psychiatrist of Udmurt nationality describing how his patients react when they are given the chance to use Udmurt with him. It hints at a notion of language as a central factor of identity, a component of the "true personality" and a means of communicating one's innermost feelings. The vocabulary is affective and informal (*кенаке* lit. 'my aunt'; *сюлмаськытыны* 'worry').

The seemingly positive sentence nonetheless reveals a linguistic situation in which speakers of Udmurt usually need to communicate with their doctor in the majority language.

Examples (17) and (18) underline the stability of the language. The first one, however, incorporates the message that Udmurts who move away from their birthplace tend to go through a language shift. Example (18) is about a Russian teacher in an Udmurt environment who has learnt Udmurt. Sociolinguistic background information reports that this is not a usual phenomenon. Over all, the newspaper seems to have selected encouraging examples of individuals who behave contrary to the dominant tendency.

(17) *Дас ньыль ар вордскем палъёсызлэсь палэ¬нын улыса но, Александр Васильевич удмурт кылзэ ӟеч тодэ.*
'Even though Aleksandr Vasilyevich has been away from his birthplace for fourteen years, he still speaks Udmurt fluently.'

(18) *Покчи классъёсын пиналъёс ӟуч сямен ваньзы пыр-поч уг валало бере, Викторлы аслыз шаплыгес дышоно луиз удмурт кыллы.*
'As the children in first grade did not understand everything in Russian, Viktor himself had to actively learn the Udmurt language.'

Examples (19) and (20) are also particularly interesting as the journalist connects knowing Udmurt with being Udmurt. Both of examples refer to Russians learning Udmurt.

(19) *Семьяязы ӟуч кылын верасько вал, нош татын со удмурт луэ.*
'In his family he had spoken Russian, but here he became Udmurt.'

(20) *Узей-Тукляе вуэмзы бере лач-лач удмуртъёс луизы.*
'Having arrived in Uzey-Tuklya they became Udmurts with ease.'

Through the adversative conjunction *нош* 'but' in (18) the reader is given assurance that the latter part of the sentence will be the opposite of the former, that is, it will tell the reader that the person started to speak Udmurt. Instead, the journalist has taken a step further in his interpretation – to him, speaking Udmurt and being Udmurt means the same thing. This probably reflects a sociolinguistic background of biased bilingualism, in which ethnic Russians hardly ever speak Udmurt. It is noteworthy that, to the writer, the language is superior to all other markers of identity. In this sense, "Udmurt" is not a closed category, but outsiders can become insiders by adopting the language. The adverb *лач-лач* 'smoothly' emphasises the naturalness of this process. The importance of a local, homogeneous Udmurt community is also elicited: arriving in the dominantly Udmurt village triggers the process. According to Wixman (1993: 423), the Russian ethnic system has always been an open one. It has given non-Russians the opportunity to join in, provided they adopt the Russian cultural norms and language. The presented openness of the Udmurt system can be interpreted as a counterpart of the Russian assimilative model. However, it would be most interesting to carry out a survey of Udmurts' opinions about the degree of openness in their community and whether it is theoretically possible to accept new Udmurts from outside the community.

## 5. Evaluation of the results and the methods applied

Examining texts from one newspaper does not give precise information on the constituents of Udmurt identity, but it does illuminate the way in which it is searched for in *Udmurt Dunne*. Very much effort is put into building group identity. What makes this particularly interesting is the fact that *Udmurt Dunne* is a government-owned paper and, as such, it is creating an image of the "official way of being Udmurt". Whether this identity-building is intentional or not remains unclear. It reveals, nevertheless, that for the authors it is not self-evident what it means to be Udmurt. In their texts they constantly deal with this question in an almost programmatic way. In my opinion this can be interpreted as a signal of insecure national identity.

The analysis of the presented data shows that in *Udmurt Duńńe* texts the narrative of being Udmurt stresses the importance of the language, the most obvious feature when distinguishing between Russian and Udmurt culture. This focus on language and art does not allow for a flexible image of being Udmurt. It excludes the growing group of Udmurts who do not speak or do not want to use the language. In the texts, being Udmurt and being Russian are often placed in opposition to each other and there are no allusions to possible multiple identities. These tendencies are similar to reactions described by Stuart Hall (1992: 310). Hall speaks about "cultures of hybridity", by which he refers to new Diasporas created by post-colonial migrations, but many of the features of these cultures relate to other minorities as well. People belonging to these cultures are bearers of several identities and they need to be able to combine several cultures without assimilating completely into either one. Their cultural identities are in transition. One reaction to this phenomenon is to turn to tradition, and unity and purity are emphasised as elements of the national narrative (id. 294, 309). Most likely this is the situation many Udmurts find themselves in.

The evaluation of the sociolinguistic situation is a recurring feature in the texts I examined, but what catches the eye is the directing of that evaluation towards detailed, smaller-scale issues, such as the absence of Udmurt in the everyday linguistic landscape. Among other significant sociolinguistic trends, language shift is touched upon, and so is the prestige of Russian, but, for example, bilingualism and diglossia are not much discussed. Martin Ehala (2009: 136) states that opposition and resistance often derive from a situation in which the community finds the prevailing linguistic situation illegitimate. Nonetheless, another possible consequence of the perception of injustice and illegitimacy is the acceleration of assimilation. Active engagement in enforcing linguistic rights was not characteristic of *Udmurt Duńńe*. One possible explanation is that there is no perception of the linguistic situation as illegitimate. However, the historical background argues for assuming that there has been a perception of injustice, but that it has led to assimilation rather than opposition.

I would like to underline the role of *Udmurt Dunne* as the only Udmurt-language daily. On account of its position, it functions as a showcase for the Udmurt media, which lends importance to the representations it contains. The image spread by *Udmurt Dunne* is encouraging, and the positive tone it takes is a natural choice for enhancing the readers' appreciation of being Udmurt. Presenting Russians learning Udmurt and Udmurts maintaining their native language in a foreign environment serves this purpose. Its abstention from societal discussion and criticism may seem alarming from the outside, but it is also possible that this policy caters to most readers' needs. A minority media is not necessarily involved in politics; often its role is just to consolidate the solidarity of the community (Pietikäinen & Laihiala-Kankainen & Rynkänen 2007: 155).

In all, I find the method applied in my thesis suitable for obtaining information on linguistic identities and attitudes. However, the scope of this study covers a rather limited area of language use. Because the importance of the internet is growing, an analysis of internet texts, perhaps informal discussions, would complete the picture. A similar analysis of Russian newspaper texts would be essential for comparing the views and attitudes found in the minority- and majority-oriented media. The scope should be further broadened by carrying out sociolinguistic interviews concerning the readers' interpretations of the texts and contrasting these with the results of a text analysis.

# References

Ehala, Martin 2009: An Evaluation Matrix for Ethnolinguistic Vitality. – Susanna Pertot & Tom Priestly & Colin Williams (eds), *Rights, Promotion and Integration Issues for Minority Languages in Europe*. Palgrave Macmillan Ltd. 123–137. <http://lepo.it.da.ut.ee/~ehalam/pdf/Evaluation%20matrix%20published.pdf> 14.10.2009.

Fairclough, Norman 1989: *Language and power*. London: Longman.

—— 1995: *Media discourse*. London: Edward Arnold.

Fowler, Roger 1991: *Language in the News. Discourse and Ideology in the Press*. London – New York: Routledge.

Grünthal, Riho 2009: Kieliyhteisön rapautuminen ja kielellisen identiteetin muutos. – Anna Idström & Sachiko Sosa (eds), *Kielissä kulttuurien ääni*. Helsinki: Suomalaisen Kirjallisuuden Seura. 265–289.

Hall, Stuart 1992: The question of cultural identity. – Stuart Hall & David Held & Tony McGrew (eds), *Modernity and its futures*. Cambridge: Polity Press. 273–325.

Lallukka, Seppo 2001: Finno-Ugrians of Russia – Vanishing Cultural Communities? – *Nationalities Papers* 29 (1): 9–39.

—— 2005: Venäjän suomalais-ugrilaiset – väestönlaskentojen kertomaa. – Paula Kokkonen (ed.), *Sukukansaohjelman arki*. Castrenianumin toimitteita 64. Helsinki: M. A. Castrénin seura, Suomalais-Ugrilainen Seura & Helsingin yliopiston suomalais-ugrilainen laitos. 28–46.

Pietikäinen, Sari 2003: Indigenous identity in print. – *Discourse & Society* 14 (5): 581–609.

Pietikäinen, Sari & Laihiala-Kankainen, Sirkka & Rynkänen, Tatjana 2007: Медиа меньшинства в контексте гражданского общества – опыт русскоязычных в Финляндии. – *Ethnicity Studies 2007 (2)*. 151–173. <http://web.ebscohost.com/ehost/pdf?vid=3&hid=116&sid=a360f7fa-a0d1-47b5-952c-174ffd781ada%40sessionmgr109> 15.10.2009.

Salánki, Zsuzsanna 2008: *Az udmurt nyelv mai helyzete*. Doktori disszertáció. Eötvös Loránd Tudományegyetem, Finnugor Tanszék.

Shkliaev, Aleksander & Toulouze, Eva 2001: The mass media and the national question in Udmurtia in the 1990s. – *Nationalities Papers* 29 (1). 97–108.

Wixman Ron 1993: The Middle Volga: Ethnic Archipelago in a Russian Sea – Ian Bremmer & Ray Taras (eds), *Nations and Politics in the Soviet Successor States*. Cambridge: Cambridge University Press. 421–447.

# Identiteetin rakentuminen
# udmurttilaisessa päivälehdessä

*Outi Tánczos*

Medialla on merkittävä rooli identiteettien muotoutumisessa. Median tuottamia representaatioita voidaan tarkastella kriittisen diskurssianalyysin keinoin. Kriittinen diskurssianalyysi ottaa huomioon tekstien ja ympäröivän yhteiskunnan vastavuoroisen suhteen ja pyrkii löytämään ja analysoimaan teksteihin kätkeytyvien valintojen arvo- ja asennetaustoja. Artikkelissani tarkastelen udmurtinkielisen päivälehden, *Udmurt Duńńen*, teksteissä esiintyviä tapoja representoida udmurttilaisuutta. Tarkastellut tekstit ovat ilmestyneet alkuvuonna 2007. Analyysin tulokset antavat lisätietoa siitä, kuinka vähemmistökielinen päälehti suhtautuu kielellisen tilanteen muutokseen ja sen synnyttämään tarpeeseen määritellä udmurttilaisuutta uudelleen. Udmurtin kieltä on pidetty udmurttilaisuuden tärkeimpänä rakennusaineena. Kielenvaihto on kuitenkin viime vuosina huomattavasti kiihtynyt udmurtinpuhujien keskuudessa. *Udmurt Duńńe*ssa udmurtin kieli on keskeinen ja toistuva aihe. Kiihtyvästä kielenvaihdosta huolimatta lehden tekstit korostavat edelleen udmurtin kielen merkitystä udmurttilaista identiteettiä luovana ja udmurttilaisuutta säilyttävänä tekijänä. Lehden näkökulma kielellisiin kysymyksiin, ennen muuta udmurtin kielen nykytilanteeseen ja tulevaisuuteen, on yllättävänkin optimistinen. Udmurtin kielen näkyvyyden merkitystä korostetaan, mutta monet udmurtin puhujia koskevista kielellisistä ilmiöistä, kuten kaksikielisyyden vaikutus kielelliseen käytökseen, jäävät käsittelemättä.

MÁRTA CSEPREGI & SOFIA ONINA

# Observations of Khanty Identity: the Synya and Surgut Khanty

## Abstract

In this study we deal with two groups remote from each other geographically and different in their language and ethnic identity: S. Onina examines the situation of the Synya Khanty and M. Csepregi the Surgut Khanty.

The traditional way of life and settlement structure has survived right up to the present along the Synya River. The Khanty, originally from along the Synya, can be divided into three groups on the basis of their language skills: the first group comprises those where all generations speak the language fluently; they live in small villages beside the river. The second group is composed of families living in the central villages. Here the parents actively use the language, the children only understand it. The third group is made up of educated Khanty who have migrated to the towns. In these families the parents still speak the Khanty language but the children no longer do.

Since the 1960s there has been intensive oil and gas production in the lands of the Surgut Khanty, bringing with it a large influx of Russian-speaking industrial workers. In the last twenty years, use of the Khanty language has been steadily declining, even in Khanty families living in the traditional way. In addition to language use, the study also examines the use of ethnonyms, costume, customs and religion in the experience of identity. We also touch on the situation where the fear of exclusion and being treated as inferior lead to the abandonment of self-identity.

*Ethnic and Linguistic Context of Identity: Finno-Ugric Minorities.* 341–358.
Uralica Helsingiensia 5. Helsinki 2011.

# 1. Introduction

The question of identity, and in particular that of the Finno-Ugrian peoples, has been the subject of a number of scholarly forums, conferences and publications. We quote from a recent study on the Shuryshkary Khanty as an introduction to our own study: "The territory inhabited by the Khanty is very large and there are substantial linguistic and cultural differences. The Khanty cannot be examined as a culturally uniform group and information collected within a single Khanty group cannot characterise the entire community. For centuries the economic and social changes have been influencing the culture of the various Khanty groups in different ways."[1] (Siikala and Uljashev 2008: 149–150).

The Khanty live in Russia, in northwest Siberia, along the Ob and its tributaries. Their lands belong, for the purpose of public administration, to the Tyumen oblast, and within this to two autonomous districts. According to the census of 2002 they number 28,678 persons in the Khanty-Mansi Autonomous Okrug Yugra and 8,760 in the Yamal-Nenets Autonomous Okrug. The easternmost Khanty, 873 in number, live in the Tomsk oblast and the 88 westernmost Khanty in the Komi Republic. In other regions of Russia a total of 1,829 persons declare themselves to be Khanty. Probably slightly less than half of the Khanty, around 47%, speak their native language.[2] Even the majority of those who speak the language are bilingual. At the very latest, by the time they begin school all Khanty learn Russian and in time this becomes the dominant language with Khanty restricted to use within the family.

A number of dialects differing considerably in phonology, morphology and lexicon have emerged within the Khanty linguistic territory, which covers over half a million square kilometres. These are generally divided geographically into northern, southern and eastern

---

1.  Hantien asuma-alue on hyvin laaja ja sen kielelliset ja kulttuuriset erot merkittäviä. Hanteja ei voikaan tarkastella kulttuurisesti yhtenäisenä ryhmänä eikä yhden hantiryhmän keskuudesta koottua tietoa voi pitää hanteja kokonaisuudessa kuvaavana. Taloudelliset ja yhteiskunnalliset muutokset ovat muokanneet eri hantiryhmien kulttuuria jo vuosisatojen ajan.
2.  <http://www.gks.ru/PEREPIS/tabs.htm>

Map 1. West Siberia.

Map 2. The
Khanty-Mansi
Autonomous
District in
Russia and
the main
living areas of
Khanty and
Mansi.

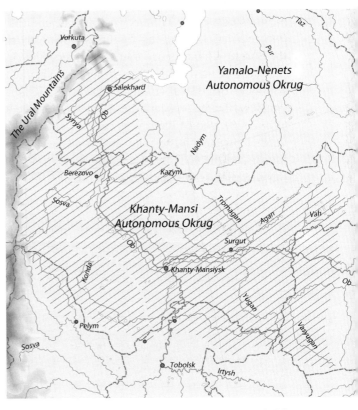

343

groups. The northern dialect region extends from the mouth of the Ob to the confluence of the Ob and the Irtysh. It seems likely that speakers of the southern dialects switched language around the mid-20th century so that Khanty can no longer be heard spoken along the Irtysh and its tributaries, the Demyanka and the Konda. The eastern dialects are spoken along the tributaries of the middle Ob.

In our study we deal with two groups remote from each other geographically and different in their language and ethnic identity: the Synya and the Surgut Khanty. The River Synya flows through the Yamal-Nenets Autonomous Okrug, so the Synya Khanty dialect belongs among the northern dialects. The town of Surgut is located in the Khanty-Mansi Autonomous Okrug and the dialect known as Surgut is one of the eastern Khanty dialects. The differences between the northern and eastern Khanty dialects are so great that it would be more correct to speak of separate languages. One of the authors of our study, Sofia Onina, was born beside the Synya while Márta Csepregi has been doing linguistic and folkloristic research among the Surgut Khanty since 1992. Another study in this volumeby Zoltán Nagy deals with the third group, the Vasyugan Khanty. There are a number of general studies of the whole Khanty-speaking territory that describe the present linguistic situation (see: Csepregi 1997, Sipos (ed.) 2006), two of them very recent (Salo 2009 and Csepregi 2009). Table 1 presents basic information on the two Ob-Ugric groups, the Mansi and the Khanty, according to the population censuses of the Soviet Union (1989) and Russia (2002).

| Ob-Ugrians | 1989 | | 2002 | |
|---|---|---|---|---|
| | persons | language speakers % | persons | language speakers % |
| Mansi | 8,474 | 37.1 | 11,432 | 24.1 |
| Khanty | 22,521 | 60.5 | 28,678 | 47.3 |

Table 1. Total Ob-Ugrian population and the percentage speaking their native tongue based on data of the 1989 and 2002 censuses.

## 2. The Synya Khanty

The Synya is a western tributary of the Ob, close to the Arctic Circle. It arises in the Urals and flows into the Little Ob south of Muzhi. Because this region, lacking mineral resources, has escaped industrialisation, the traditional way of life, based on fishing, hunting, gathering and reindeer herding, has been preserved along the Synya. The settlement structure has remained unchanged too. There are eight small villages along the river, each consisting of a few houses, with all of their inhabitants belonging to the same clan. The Synya people live in these houses from autumn till spring. The reindeer herders drive their animals into the Urals for the summer while the others move down to the Ob to fish. Ovgort, the central village, has a population of around 1,500, of whom 1,200 are Khanty (Ovgort 2009). However, some of those who declare themselves to be Khanty of the Synya now live elsewhere and so they differ from each other in language behaviour and self-identity. The Khanty of the Synya can be divided into three groups on the basis of their language use (Onyina 2006: 57–61, Onina 2008): the first group comprises those where all generations speak the language fluently, the second group families where the parents actively use the language but the children only understand it, and the third group parents who still speak Khanty but whose children no longer do. In the following we take a closer look at these three groups.

### 2.1. Both adults and children fluent in their native tongue

These people live in the traditional villages and are engaged exclusively in traditional occupations. Part of the community moves to the Ob for the summer to fish while the other part herds reindeer. The reindeer herders live a nomadic life in the Urals for most of the year. Families move around together but their children only spend the school holidays with them. They communicate among each other solely in Khanty. They use traditional means of transport – boats and sleds – the women wear folk costume and also make their own winter clothing and footwear from reindeer skins.

Their children attend boarding schools in the central village, Ovgort. Accommodation in a hostel is arranged so that children with the same family name, meaning that they are all from the same village, are placed together in the same room. Professional child-care workers who speak Khanty work in the hostel, so the children are able to use their native tongue. In their free time they learn Khanty crafts. They are often given traditional Khanty food: boiled, baked or raw fish, frozen meat, or raw reindeer meat.

## 2.2. Parents speaking Khanty and with little proficiency in their native tongue

These are the Synya Khanty who live in the central village, Ovgort. The parents have completed secondary or higher education and work in institutions such as kindergartens, schools or the fish processing plant, where communication is exclusively in Russian, the language understood by all nationalities. Those over 25 years of age are able to speak their native tongue. They use the language only in the home environment, within the family, or if they are speaking with older people who do not speak Russian. Young Khanty parents from the traditional culture, although fluent in their native tongue, only speak Russian with their children so that they will do better at school. As a result, the younger generation only speaks Russian. The young people understand the Khanty language and respond to it, but they always reply in Russian, even if their elders address them in Khanty.

In the recent past, the majority of elderly Khanty moved into the village. They are fluent in Khanty and understand Russian but do not speak it. They understand what their Russian-speaking grandchildren say, but most of them reply in Khanty.

The Ovgort Khanty do not make their own tools and very few of them wear traditional dress. Some of the women may wear Khanty dress, tie their shawls in the Khanty way and wear the winter cloth or reindeer skin coats, but their footwear is always factory-made. They do not make their own clothes but buy them or barter them from women who still practise the traditional craft. In the barter trade, a reindeer skin coat can be worth a motorbike or motorboat.

## 2.3. Parents speaking Khanty and children not familiar with the language

These are the groups of Khanty who live in towns and have completed secondary or higher education. All occupations are represented here. They work in education, culture, health care, commerce and public administration, in jobs that can impose a big psychological strain on the northern peoples. Many of them live in Khanty–non-Khanty mixed marriages and do not attach importance to the nationality of their partner.

There is no communication in the Khanty language within these families, even if the parents speak Khanty. As a result the children do not learn their parents' native tongue. The Khanty language is rarely spoken, most often in the presence of members of the older generation. Even those familiar with the native tongue speak and think in Russian.

These people do not wear Khanty dress at all, although it is important for the women to possess a Khanty folk costume. They do not sew clothing or practise crafts, but buy the Khanty clothing and objects or receive them as gifts and use them to decorate their homes. They are familiar with the Khanty customs and religious traditions but do not practise them.

## 2.4. Low prestige of Khanty language and culture

The circumstances described above determine the sense of ethnic and linguistic identity. Today the young generation of Khanty simply do not want to be Khanty. Children of kindergarten age say: "I'm not Khanty, I'm Russian". More and more young people want to resemble the majority nation.

It is not easy to integrate into the majority population. It is Onina's experience that Russians are irritated if a Khanty wants to be of equal standing with them. And the Khanty, especially young people who have moved from the countryside to a town, feel awkward and are ill at ease among Russians. They are ashamed to wear folk costume and speak in their native tongue. But there are also encouraging phenomena. Students studying at the Khanty-Mansiysk State University clearly showed increased self-esteem after they took Sofia Onina's course in the "Ethnology of the Ob-Ugrian peoples". As they got to know their own culture they realised that they are inheritors of valuable traditions that they can embrace with pride.

The natural process of the transmission of culture and language has been broken over the past decades. The generation of 40–50 year-olds or older possess all the skills of the traditional economy and culture, but under the new conditions are unable to pass on their knowledge to their children. In the past this transmission took place on weekdays, as they worked together. But today's youth, who spend most of their time in boarding schools in a Russian-speaking environment, have lost contact with the way of life and traditions of their people. As a result they not only fail to learn the language, but also lack a sense of perspective for the traditional way of life. Nowadays the occupations of reindeer herder, fisherman and hunter have very low prestige among the young generation. The youth department of the Yamal-Nenets Autonomous Okrug is trying to change this situation by organising ethnological expeditions for Khanty and Nenets youths who have lost contact with their roots (Sipos 2006).

It can be seen from the above classification that, as is to be expected, the language and Khanty identity are preserved mainly among the Khanty living a traditional way of life; a way of life that is becoming increasingly rare in the entire Khanty-speaking territory. The Synya valley is a special case because here the prerequisites still exist for that way of life. The second and third groups in Onina's classification can also be found elsewhere in the region of the Ob. In the mixed population central villages built in the 1950s, the Khanty language can be heard less often, and in the absence of work and meaningful occupations there is a great danger of lumpenisation. Khanty afflicted with alcoholism and forced to the fringes of society can do little to preserve their language and culture. Indeed, the low prestige of the Khanty language depends to a considerable extent on the image majority society has formed by observing these unfortunate people. The Khanty who have learnt a trade or earned a diploma and live in the towns switch language.

## 3. The Surgut Khanty

The Surgut dialect is spoken along the tributaries of the middle Ob. These rivers are to the north of the Ob, the Pym, the Tromagan and the Agan, and to the south of the Ob the Great Yugan and the Little Yugan. The majority of Surgut Khanty live in the territory of the Surgut rayon, but there are also Yugan Khanty in the Nefteyugansk rayon, while most of the Agan Khanty live in the Nizhnevartovsk rayon.

It is difficult to estimate the exact number of speakers. According to official data, in 2005 there were 2,800 indigenous people in the Surgut rayon, 98% of whom were Khanty and 2% Forest Nenets and Mansis. About 500 families, that is more than 2,000 persons, live in the tribal lands (KhMAO 2009). In our experience those Khanty who lead a traditional way of life, breeding reindeer, hunting and fishing, do use their language: only those who have moved to the towns abandon it and switch to Russian – even within the course of a generation. The number of Surgut Khanty is greater by about 800 when those kinfolk who live on the banks of the Agan River and belong administratively to the Nižnevartovsk rayon are added (Nizhnevartovsk 2009).

Geographically this territory lies on the border of the forest tundra and the taiga. North of the Ob the traditional economy is forest reindeer herding, that is the Khanty families follow their reindeer and change their place of dwelling each season. Further south around the source of the Yugan, in the taiga zone, they do not keep reindeer but only engage in fishing and hunting. The traditional way of life has been in decline since the 1960s when the extraction of oil and gas began. Big industrial towns have been built along the main waterway, the Ob, and the Khanty have been forced back to the tributaries and their headwaters.

The Hungarian co-author of this article, Márta Csepregi, did her first fieldwork in the region in 1992 among the Tromagan and Yugan Khanty, and since then has been closely following changes in language use and ethnic identity. In the following we present a few case studies to illustrate the ethnic situation and state of the language.

## 3.1.   The language situation since the early 1990s

In 1992, in the seasonal quarters of the reindeer herding Khanty – as they called it: in the forest – all generations only spoke Khanty. At that time there were still monolingual Khanty, members of the oldest generation, who had sufficient prestige to declare that only Khanty can be spoken in the forest. However, the educated members of these families, who lived in towns or villages, did not pass on the language to their children. In the second half of the 1990s family members who had lost their jobs in the towns moved out to the forest quarters. Some of them only spoke Russian and so for their sake conversation was more and more often in Russian. Now practically all native Khanty speakers are bilingual and the children learn both languages simultaneously. Both languages are present in the forest quarters too and code switching is very frequent even within a sentence. The local people say that they do not even notice whether they are speaking Khanty or Russian. Even the dogs understand command words in Russian. The reindeer is the only being that they only address in Khanty. Nevertheless, there are some young people who grew up in the forest and went on to attend university who preserve and actively practise the traditional culture (Csepregi & Sosa 2009).

Industrialisation came earlier to the region along the River Agan that Csepregi visited in the early 2000s. The story of the traditional lands of the Khanty writer Yeremey Aypin is a good example of the changes. After the death of the writer's father in 1995, everyone thought that the settlement would become depopulated. But a few years later three families moved there to try forest life. The young heads of the families – Aypin's cousins – had lost their jobs in the town and so decided to live in the forest. However, the linguistic-cultural continuity had been interrupted. While the men had been in state employment they had forgotten the traditional way of life. At the beginning of the school year the families live in the village so that their children do not have to stay in boarding school. They use the forest quarters more as a summer home and fishing place. The men speak a mixed language, the children only speak Russian and know only a few expressions in Khanty.

## 3.2. A few markers of identity

### 3.2.1. Ethnonyms

Identity is the distinction between *us* and *them*, and this distinction is most easily made at the linguistic level with the help of ethnonyms. It was found that the Surgut Khanty do not have an ethnonym applying to all the Khanty people. They do not feel either the ethnonym *Ostyak*, which was used in Tsarist times, or *Khanty*, which was first used to designate them in Soviet times, to be their own. This is because the Russian word *ханты* reflects the pronunciation characteristics of the northern Khanty dialects. In the eastern Khanty dialects it has the form of *ḳăntəγ*. But expressions with the prefix *ḳăntəγ* do not only designate the Khanty. *ḳăntək ḳo* means not only 'Khanty man', but also 'man' in general. Accordingly the construction *ḳăntəγ jåγ* also has two meanings: 1. 'Khanty people' 2. 'people of traditional culture'. If a Surgut Khanty wishes to refer to the whole of mankind living on the earth, he says: *rut'-ḳăntəγ jåγ*, literally: 'Russian-Khanty people'.

At the beginning of the Soviet period the authorities tried to get rid of the pejoratively used external ethnonyms and therefore began to use their own internal names to refer to the nationalities of the Soviet Union. In the case of the eastern Khanty this aspiration was not realised. As Yosif Sopochin, a Tromagan Khanty, commented in August 1996: "We are Khanty only in Russian[3]. In Khanty our name is *ḳăntəγ jåγ*, but we don't use that either, but refer to the different groups of our people on the basis of the rivers. We say: *tŏrəm jăwən jåγ* 'Tromagan people', *åwən jåγ* 'Agan people', *jăwən jåγ* 'Yugan people', *kasəm jåγ* 'Kazym people', and so on."

The situation is even more complicated along the Agan. There Khanty live side by side with Forest Nenets. Intermarriages are common and in the ethnically mixed families Khanty-Nenets bilingualism and dual identity is taken for granted. As a Forest Nenets declared with a touch of self-irony: "If I get up in the morning and wash, I'm a Khanty. If I don't wash, I'm a Nenets."[4]

---

3. "Мы ханты только по-русски."
4. Oral communication by Elena Perevalova, October 2009.

## 3.2.2. Dress, ethics

Yosif Sopochin, quoted above, said that women's nationality was always visible because they wore Khanty costume all the year round, but men could only be seen to be Khanty in winter when they wore their reindeer skin coats. Is a person who lives in a town and speaks Russian a Khanty? Is (s)he a Khanty as long as the ethnonyms Khanty and Mansi figure in the name of the autonomous district?

According to a communication from Lyudmila Kayukova, the urban Khanty, who have become Russified in their language, differ from the Russians in that the women hang out their washing so that their underwear is lower than the men's and children's clothing and in a place where strangers cannot see it. In the forest environment they take care not to wash men's and women's clothes together, but they are unable to do this in the town. The rules of cleanliness and avoidance determining Khanty identity are outliving the language even if not in every minute detail.

## 3.2.3. Religious traditions

From the 1990s, religious traditions have also played an important role in the expression of identity. Although religious observances of all kinds were banned in Soviet times or at least qualified as a sign of backwardness, animism, respect for the forces of nature is still very much alive among the Khanty. They regularly visit the sacred places and hold their regular communal feasts where they can experience a sense of belonging together. Some ceremonies are held in public and they can be used by the Khanty to express their difference from the Russians and also allow the Russians (and Ukrainians, Tatars and migrant workers of other nationalities) to become acquainted with Khanty culture. Traditional Khanty feasts, such as the Crow Feast, which greets the arrival of spring, and other celebrations inherited from the Soviet era (e.g. Fishermen's Day, Reindeer Herders' Day) are now unimaginable without a ceremonial sacrifice. These events, which are a combination of a carnival and a sporting event, have largely contributed to the fact that the Khanty are now more willing to declare their identity to the majority society and also that non-Khanty now acknowledge the existence of the Khanty and recognise the value of their culture.

### 3.2.4. The opposition between outside and inside, tradition and modernity

It has already been noted that even at the level of ethnonyms the Khanty do not define themselves as a single people. Accordingly, their identity is not Khanty identity either, but – to take an example from the Surgut territory – Tromagan, Agan, Yugan, etc. The Tromagan Khanty knows exactly how her/his dress, way of life, customs, language, etc. differ from those of the Agan Khanty. In addition, he also experiences the difference between the people of the forest and the town, or as he puts it, between Khanty and Russian. The Khanty living in the forest live in the traditional culture. An urban Khanty communicating in Russian increasingly sees her/his people and their culture from the outside and in that comparison barbarism and civilisation are opposed.

The formulation of self-identity is a process in which similarities and differences to other peoples must be constantly assessed. In their fear of being regarded as inferior and excluded, the Khanty do not dare to differ greatly from the Russians. This is the cause of a phonetic change that occurred in a number of dialects that have since become extinct. Yugan Khanty who have moved to the region of the River Salym pronounce the voiceless lateral fricative *ł* very characteristic of the Surgut Khanty dialect, as *t*. Lyudmila Kayukova, who comes from this group, explains this by saying that they are more civilised than the other Yugan Khanty, and they do not wish to differ greatly in their speech from the Russians. In a situation where two languages are in contact, sometimes the minority language adapts to the phonetics of the prestige language. Lauri Posti believes that this was why the palatal consonants in the languages of the Baltic Finns became depalatised – in that case the influence was Germanic (Posti 1954), although there may be another explanation for the change (Kallio 2000).

A book on the Tromagan Khanty living in their traditional culture published in 1995 in Hungary (Winter, et al. 1995). This book contains photos depicting their life and culture, as well as poems by

353

Agrafena Pesikova inspired by the photos. These poems are actually the first example of Surgut Khanty literature. This album came to be used for an interesting survey: Agrafena Pesikova showed it to many people. Those who had not yet broken away from their culture looked at it with pleasure, tried to identify the places, compared the implements with their own and copied the ornamentation on the fur coats for themselves. In contrast, the Russified Khanty living in towns found the images to be rough, shameful and hurtful. "What is all this blood? Why did they take photos of dirty children? Why did they have to shame the Khanty before the whole world?" they asked. Some of them were not even prepared to take a second look at the book. They did not understand the verses and considered the publication of the book insulting (Peszikova 1998).

## 4. Conclusion

In our study we outlined a few typical characteristics of the Khanty linguistic and ethnic identity, but we did not deal with all aspects of this complex question. Among others, we did not discuss the problem of literacy and the literary language, which is the subject of much debate among the Khanty too. We only touched upon the question of education, although it has an important role to play in shaping a healthy self-identity. Further research and joint efforts are needed if the Khanty wish to survive and if this aspiration is also to find support in the majority society.

# References

Csepregi, Márta 1997: General information about the Ostyaks (Khantys). –
Acta Ethnographica Hungarica 42: 275–284.

—— 2009: The very highly connected nodes in the Ob-Ugrian networks. – Jussi Ylikoski (ed.), The Quasquicentennial of the Finno-Ugrian Society. Mémoires de la Société Finno-Ougrienne 258. Helsinki: Suomalais-Ugrilainen Seura. 9–32.
<http://www.sgr.fi/sust/sust258/sust258_csepregi.pdf>

Csepregi, Márta & Sosa, Sachiko 2009: Comparable sample texts of Surgut Khanty in 1996 and 2008. – Journal de la Société Finno-Ougrienne 92. Helsinki: Suomalais-Ugrilainen Seura. 193–208.
<http://www.sgr.fi/susa/92/csepregisosa.pdf>

KhMAO 2009 = Официальный веб-сайт органов государственной власти Ханты-Мансийского автономного округа – Югры.
– <http://www.admhmao.ru> 10.10.2009.

Kallio, Petri 2000: Posti's superstrate theory at the threshold of a new millenium. – Johanna Laakso (ed.), Facing Finnic. Some Challenges to Historical and Contact Linguistics. Castrenianumin toimitteita 59. Helsinki: Suomalais-Ugrilainen Seura & Helsingin yliopiston suomalais-ugrilainen laitos. 80–99.

Nizhnevartovsk 2009 = Официальный сайт Нижневартовского района ХМАО – Югры. – <http://nvraion.ru> 10.10.2009

Onyina, Szofja 2006: A hantik identitásának kérdéséhez. – Folia Uralica Debreceniensia 13. 55–63.

Onina = Онина София 2008: К проблеме национального самосознания народа ханты. – Bereczki A. et al. (eds): Ünnepi írások Havas Ferenc tiszteletére. Urálisztikai Tanulmányok 18. Budapest: ELTE Finnugor Tanszék. 588–604.

Ovgort 2009: <http://www.admmuji.ru/sp/ovgort.php> 10.10.2009

Peszikova, Agrafena 1998: A „Szibériai rokonaink" című fotóalbum fogadtatása a szurguti hantik körében. – Márta Csepregi & Péter Domokos (eds): 125 éves a budapesti finnugor tanszék. Urálisztikai Tanulmányok 9. Budapest: ELTE Finnugor Tanszék. 49–52.

Posti, Lauri 1954: From Pre-Finnic to Late Proto-Finnic. – Finnisch-Ugrische Forschungen 30: 1–91.

Saarinen, Sirkka & Herrala, Eeva (eds) 2008: Murros. Suomalais-ugrilaiset kielet ja kulttuurit globalisaation paineissa. Uralica Helsingiensia 3. Helsinki: Helsingin yliopiston suomalais-ugrilainen laitos & Suomalainen Tiedeakatemia & Suomalais-Ugrilainen Seura.

Salo, Merja 2009: Hantin kielen historia ja tulevaisuus. – *Idäntutkimus* 2/2009: 57–69.

Siikala, Anna-Leena & Uljašev, Oleg 2008: Hantien monet maailmat – paikalliskulttuurit globaalistuvassa maailmassa. – Sirkka Saarinen & Eeva Herrala (eds). *Murros. Suomalais-ugrilaiset kielet ja kulttuurit globalisaation paineissa.* Uralica Helsingiensia 3. Helsinki: Helsingin yliopiston suomalais-ugrilainen laitos & Suomalainen Tiedeakatemia & Suomalais-Ugrilainen Seura. 149–170.

Sipos, Mária 2006: On the Possibilities of Revitalizing Synya Khanty. – R. Elangaiyan, R., McKenna Brown, Nicholas D.M. Ostler & Mahendra K. Verma (eds), *Vital Voices. Endangered Languages and Multilingualism.* Central Institute of Indian Languages publication no. 572 Bath: Foundation for Endangered Languages & Mysore: Central Institute of Indian Languages. 95–99.

—— (ed.) 2006: *Obi-ugorok a 21. században.* Budapest: MTA Nyelvtudományi Intézete. <http://fgroszt.nytud.hu/publikaciok/obi-ugorok>

Winter, Erzsi – Szopocsinova, Agafena & Kerezsi, Ágnes 1995: *Szibériai rokonaink.* Budapest: Vízió Művészeti Alkotóközösség.

# К проблеме языковой и этнической идентичности народа ханты – на примере сынских и сургутских ханты

*Марта Чепреги – София Онина*

В зависимости от степени владения хантыйским языком выявляются три группы:

1. Владеют языком старшее и младшее поколение. Общаются между собой исключительно на родном языке. Ведут только традиционный образ жизни. Изготавливают сами и пользуются не только традиционную одежду, но и средства передвижения. По роду своей деятельности: оленеводы, охотники и рыбаки. Дети фактически круглый год находятся в интернате. Соблюдают многие традиционные обряды.

2. Владеют языком взрослые и дети, но чаще живут в сельской местности. Реже общаются на родном, чаще общаются на русском языке. В меньше степени изготавливают традиционную одежду, утварь и средства передвижения, но чаще не для удовлетворения собственных нужд, а для продажи. Предпочитают профессии воспитатель, санитарка, кочегар, охранник, доярка и т.п. Дети с родителями проживают дома и из дома посещают школу. Соблюдают не все традиционные обряды.

3. Владеет языком часто старшее поколение, дети фактически не владеют родным языком, но очень хорошо владеют русским. Общаются между собой исключительно на русском. Живут часто в крупных населенных пунктах, городах. Традиционных изделий не изготавливают и не носят, но предпочитают иметь их в качестве сувениров. Это своего рода класс современной интеллигенции. Для них привлекательны сферы образования, культуры и искусства, здравоохранения, коммерции и органы управления. Они осваивают те виды нетрадиционных занятий, которые для народов Севера считались психологически трудными. Традиционные формы занятости для них утрачивают привлекательнось. Не соблюдают традиционных обрядов, но знают многие традиции своего народа.

# Щӑньа па сургут хӑнты дыпи хӧрасэд па йасӈед элты

## *Марта Чепреги – София Онина*

1. Хӑнты йасӑӈӑн йӑма хошдӑт ун ӧтдад элты ай ӧтдад унты. Ӱды сӧх тӑйдӑт. Хӑнты пӧрмас верты хошдӑт. Щит вой-хӱд ведты йох па тащӑн йӑхты йох. Ньаврэмдад арпелӑкӑн интернатӑн улдӑт, туп кӑньикулы пӧрайӑн йӧхи йӑӈхӑдыдӑт. Хӑнты йӑмӑӈхӑтдӑт арпелӑкдад уйӑтдӑт.

2. Хӑнты йасӈед щикуш уйӑтдэл, лый кӱтдадӑн арпелакӑн рӱщ йасӑӈӑн пӧтӑрдӑт. Тащ хотӑн ӑт йӑӈхдӑт, хӱд туп дэты кемӑн улдӑт. Ай вошӑтӑн улдӑт. Ньаврэмдад йӧдта улдат па ӑшкудая йӑӈхӑдыдӑт. Мӧдты вош рупатайӑн рупитдӑт, хӧй садикӑн, хӧй кӧчегаркайӑн, хӧй ӑшкудайӑн. Унанѣидад-унащидад ӑт кепа верӑтдӑт ищипа рӱщ йасӑӈӑн талдӑт. Хӑнты пӧрмас хошдӑт верты, верлӑт-ки, арпелакӑн тыныты кеша.

3. Хӑнты йасӈед арпелакӑн ӑт уйӑтдэл. Ун ӧтдад ньань кемӑн верӑтдӑт, ньаврэмдад щӑх йасӈед ӑт уйӑтдэл. Хӑнты пӧрмас вӧдаӈ ӑт верлӑт, туп мойдӑм хӑнты пӧрмасӑт шавиман тӑйдӑт. Тӑм мӧхет ун вошӑн улдӑт. Уншӑк тӑхайӑн рупитдӑт: леккарӑт, утӑдтӑты нэӈӑт, утӑдтӑты хуйӑт, кущайа рупӑтдӑт. Ньаврэмдад рӱщӑт иты тӑйдӑдад. Лый кӱтдадӑн туп рӱщ йасӑӈӑн пӧтӑрдӑт. Унанѣидад-унащидад щикуш йасӈед уйӑтдэл, лыйӑл ищи кеншӑк рӱщ йасӑӈӑн пӧтӑртыйа. Хӑнты щирӑн ӑт улдӑт. Хӑнты йӑмӑӈ хӑтӑлдад щикуш уйӑтдӑлад нэпекӑт элты, щи щирӑн ищипа ӑт улдӑт.

ZOLTÁN NAGY

# The Invisible "Ostyaks":
# The Khanty people
# in the Tomsk Oblast

## *Abstract*

In this study I deal with the ethnopolitical position of the Khanty living along the river Vasyugan. After some initial dilemmas I decided
to take the example of the village of Novy Vasyugan and analyse how
the name "Ostyak" works as an "invisible", concealed social category:
how they are excluded from the historical canon on both levels, the
village's and the oblast's. I examine the mode of representation (1) of
the memory of the recent and even more recent Russian conquests, the
civilisation of the taiga, represented in the official memory; (2) of the
cult of the archaeological cultures in "ancient culture" discourse; (3)
of the Evenkis and the Khanty from the Khanty-Mansi Autonomous
Okrug in the discourse of exoticism; (4) of the relocated people in the
process of making the Moscow-periphery conflict visible. I will point
out the fact that the "Ostyaks" only have a place in the local academic
discourses, with hardly any place in the local cultural scene and no
place at all in local economic and political life. I will also discuss
how the category of "Ostyak" works as a "race" or lifestyle category
and how lumpenisation, criminalisation and extreme poverty become
ethnic markers. Finally I will show how – due to the aforementioned
points – the Vasyugan Khanty became a dissolved community void
of all meaning, without any interest in identifying themselves as a
distinct community.

*Ethnic and Linguistic Context of Identity: Finno-Ugric Minorities.* 359–384.
Uralica Helsingiensia 5. Helsinki 2011.

## 1. Introduction

This article concerns of people called Vasyugan Khanty in the Finno-Ugric and Ethnographic literature.[1] The area along the river Vasyugan is the southernmost region where the native Khanty population can be found (See Map 2 in Csepregi's & Onina's article in this volume, p. 343.). Administratively, the river Vasyugan belongs to the Kargasok township of Tomsk oblast. Vasyugan Khanty (actually it's Vakh-Vasyugan) is one of the sub-dialects of the Eastern-Khanty dialect. The cultural regions of "traditional" Khanty culture are more or less the same as the dialect regions. The Vasyugan-Vakh Khanty, who speak the same dialect and who were endogamous before the 20th century, count as a characteristically distinct ethnographic group and there has been a long tradition of its study. (See primarily Kulemzin and Lukina 1977.)

Due to the demographic changes of the past hundred years it is quite difficult to give a precise picture about the number of the Khanty along the Vasyugan. Ever since the 1930's there have been continuous political relocations: from 1931, within a few years, the Khanty, who had accounted for 95% of the population, were reduced to being a 10% minority amongst the relocated Russians. This tendency increased when, in the 1940s, more political refugees were relocated there, mainly from the Baltic States, and also from the end of the 1960s, when exploration for new crude oil fields and economic immigration began. The Vasyugan Khanty practically dissolved into the newcomer Russian or non-Khanty population.[2] Today – even according to the most optimistic calculations – there are not more than 100–200 Khanty living along the Vasyugan river[3] and most of them do not speak the Khanty language; there are only few elderly people who are

---

1.   The River Vasyugan is the western tributary of the Ob River, approximately a thousand kilometres from the mouth of the Irtiš river.
2.   Jordan (2003: 46) also admits that the Khanty along the Vasyugan had been under the most powerful Russian influence after the regions of the river Ob and Salim.
3.   According to the statistical data of Kargasok rayon there were altogether 1,116 natives living in the rayon in 1998, 799 of whom were identified as Selkup in their identity cards. A smaller part of this group are Vasyugan Khanty, who are normally named as Selkups in the statistics of Tomsk oblast.

fluent in Khanty (see e.g. Bromlej 1976, Gumilev 1989, Shirokogorov 1923).

In this paper I deal with the question of how the Vasyugan Khanty have been excluded from local and national-discourses in Tomsk oblast due to the aforementioned facts; how, instead of using interpretations based on ethnicity, the Khanty are interpreted in various categories and, as a result, how they are becoming a "dissolved community".

## 2. Initial dilemmas

I started my article with a slightly uncertain sentence, saying that I am going to write about a group of people who, in the ethnographic literature, are called Vasyugan Khanty. The main reason for my uncertainty was my not being convinced that it is absolutely correct to call that group an existing group or community. This dilemma is closely connected to the debate in the literature on ethnicity, about what we can consider as an ethnic group, or whether we can call these groups of people actual groups. According to widely accepted viewpoints in Finno-Ugrian studies and Soviet-Russian ethnographic literature, ethnical identity means deep, ancient attachment to the group and culture. This is an objectivist theory that puts a real, actual thing behind ethnic identity, which says that ethnic identity is a ready-made thing, that it is predestined at birth and lasts a lifetime.[4] According to another approach, ethnicity is the result of the creative imagination, a social construction typical of a definite moment in time which is actually based on the interests of the elite and also on a reconstructed or invented tradition (see e.g. Anderson 2006). Ethnic culture is not regarded as a ready-made, precisely defined range of cultural tools, but it is acknowledged that the differences always present between groups are sometimes interpreted by the individual and also the community as ethnic differences. Here there is a shift in attention from the differences of actual cultures to the attributed cultural elements. In other words, in accordance with Frederik Barth's theory (Barth 1969),

---

4.  See for example Shirokogorov 1923 and Bromlej 1976.

ethnicity is in fact maintained by the border phenomena of human groups, the continuous processes of creating distances and differences. The similarity of these two viewpoints is that both of them regard ethnic groups as groups, but according to many other experts they should be regarded as categories. They should be considered categories that mainly work in cognition, "in perception, interpretation and representation" thus meaning a worldview essentially (Brubaker 2005). An ethnic group then is not an actual group with group cohesion but a performative category of the social classification that we use to interpret and constitute these groups, thus the ethnic group is a category that comes about while being used. As a result, a social researcher has to study not the group but existence in the group. (Brubaker 2005 and 2006.)

The other reason for my uncertainty is the question of whether the category of Vasyugan Khanty works as a category that constitutes a social group. In connection with this there is another question that of how and how much the Khanty category is used in Tomsk oblast, and more precisely along the Vasyugan, and whether it occurs in public, political and cultural discourses at all. To present this subject, I have to use sources that look at the Khanty 'from outside'. I analyse the picture Russian society has of the Khanty and also themselves in order to understand why the Khanty have the role which I am going to describe in this paper, in public discourses.[5]

A third reason for my uncertainty can be found in the discrepancy indicated in the title: looking at it from the river Vasyugan, it is not at all easy to meet the expectations both of the Finno-Ugrian academic literature and "political correctness" and sharply divide the terms "Ostyak" and "Khanty".[6] It is a well known fact that, in the beginning, the literature – concerning the term lifestyle – referred to the Selkups, who live near the Khanty, as Ostyaks[7]. Today modern

---

5. In Russian history Slezkin (1994) analyses the ethno-politics of Russia and the situation of the so called northern minorities with the same method.

6. Khanty are one of the Finno-ugric speaking people, along with the Mansis. In earlier academic writings they were referred to as "Ostyaks", while we could read about the Mansis as "Voguls". About this see also below.

7. In the Russian Empire, as well as in the early ethnographic literature, Kets were called Yenisey Ostyaks, Selkups were termed Ostyak Samoyeds or Narym Ostyaks while Lyapin Mansis were referred to as Lyapin Ostyaks (Etnografiya 1958).

Russian technical literature calls them Khanty and Selkups. The official state administration's categories are different: most of the Vasyugan Khanty have been called Selkups in official statistics since the 1970s,[8] which state that since the Selkups are the biggest group in the native population in Tomsk oblast everybody who lives there should be labelled as Selkups to make things simple. Before that, both the Khanty and the Selkups were referred to as Ostyaks. At the same time, when non-Khanty people living in this region talk about these ethnic groups they call them Ostyaks. It is also important to note that the Vasyugan Khanty call themselves *kantay jəy* in Khanty (meaning Khanty people), but when they speak Russian they never use this name, neither do they use Khanty, but they clearly define themselves as Ostyaks. Unlike the scientific literature, they use this name self-consciously and don't think of it as dishonest. They do use the name Khanty when speaking in Russian, but then they mean exclusively those who live in the Khanty-Mansi Autonomous Okrug, therefore they are not usually just called Khanty but Khanty-Mansi. I have adapted to this chaotic local practice of using names by not using the names of ethnic groups as 'scientific' categories. I use quotation marks when talking about "Ostyaks" including the Vasyugan Khanty and the Selkups, "Khanty" including the Khanty of the Khanty-Mansi Autonomous Okrug, "Russians" including the local non-Khanty and non-Ostyak population. (Cf. Nagy 2002.)

---

8.    According to the statistics of the administration of Kargasok township 1,116 natives lived in the rayon in 1998 out of whom 799 were called Selkups on their Identity Cards.

## 3. Visible and invisible categories

Novy Vasyugan[9] had its 70th anniversary 2003. A great celebration took place with cultural programmes, sports events, high-ranking guests, people of whom the place is proud and those famous individuals who used to belong to the region. The cultural part consisted of showing the history of the village in ten year sections with speech and music. The historical tableaux were introduced with a short talk. In this talk,[10] which was actually the prologue of the whole programme, the indisputable fact that this region was inhabited before the relocations was not even mentioned.[11] Beside the motif of Ermak conquering Siberia (for the first time), only the Bronze Age Tukh-Sigat people were remembered as forerunners of the "real" (*настоящий*) history, which started with the relocations. No thought was given to the fact that Khanty settlements had been in existence for a long time in this region. Only the extremely remote past was acceptable for the official history of this community; beside that, only the Russian discoveries, however tenuous and incidental, were accepted into this historical

---

9.   The village next to the river Vasyugan is the furthest, the "uppermost" settlement today, above it there is no more officially registered inhabited place with a local government. The village lies where the 19th century Vasyugan Khanty culture had its centre: even in the beginning of the 20th century several Khanty temporary settlements could be found near the village including the rather densely populated village of Aypolovo that used to be one of the centres of the river. According to its website Novy Vasyugan has 2541 inhabitants today, and based on the legal data only 86, which is 3,4 %, belong to the northern minorities. (PASPORT 2008). The existence of the village depends exclusively on the crude oil fields and oil processing plants nearby. (See also: NOVVAS).
10.   "The history of Novy Vasyugan is full of mysteries. The archaeological works carried out in the 1980s tell us that there were human settlements around Ozernoye even in the Bronze Age. In some historians' opinion in the dark 16th century the pioneers discovering Siberia including the troops of Cossack Ataman Ermak Timofeevich reached these ancient places. (...)
   The *real* [highlighted by me] history of Novy Vasyugan started in the 20th century. 1930–40s. Collectivisation and industrialisation are going on in the country. And here, in May and June in 1933 the first tows appear on the Vasyugan with people labelled as kulaks. Our fathers and grandfathers who were directed here with all their families without equipments to survive: without tools, clothes and everyday utensils; and they did survive. (...)"
11.   According to Plotnikov's (1901) data in 1898 Vasyugan District (уезд) had 680 inhabitants altogether, out of whom 640 were "natives".

canon. In the programme both the relocated and the oil miners were presented as conquerors, explorers like Ermak.

The official history of the village, then, can be interpreted as the appearance of humans (primarily Russians) in the uninhabited taiga, the unmanageable marshland. This was the appearance of the ideologically neutral Bronze Age culture, Ermak, whose figure is not at all ideology free, and the two waves of settlement in living history: the relocations and the beginning of oil mining. The untouched and uninhabited terrain (forest and marshland) waiting to be conquered appears in the classical literature on relocation. Here I cannot produce a large number of examples – there is only one text I want to refer to, not only because of its content but also because its place of appearance and way of use is worth paying attention to. In 2008, the local government of Novy Vasyugan created a multimedia presentation beginning with the following poem from Sergei Dorofeyev, representing the official interpretation:[12]

| | |
|---|---|
| *Край тайги, край болот,* | *The taiga, the marshland,* |
| *комары да туман* | *mosquitoes and the fog,* |
| *Где извилистой лентой течет* | *Where the VASYUGAN runs* |
| *ВАСЮГАН,* | *as a meandering ribbon,* |
| *По тропинке пойти –* | *On a path, if you went,* |
| *далеко не уйдешь,* | *you would not get far* |
| *Областком по реке* | *In an oblasok[13] you go* |
| *в никуда приплывешь.* | *into the nothing.* |
| *Пролетели столетья,* | *Centuries flew by,* |
| *затаился урман,* | *the forest kept its secret,* |
| *Череда лихолетий обошла* | *Hard times did not reach* |
| *Васюган,* | *Vasyugan,* |
| *А в 30-м году,* | *But in the '30s* |
| *нарушая покой,* | *by breaking the silence,* |
| *Заревели гудки* | *There were horns screaming* |
| *над таежной рекой.* | *from the taiga river.* |

---

12.   The (non literary) translation is the work of the author. The poem is not only about populating places along the river but also about these places becoming empty: the fate of the villages is being closed down by the centralising politics.

13.   Traditional gouged Khanty boat

| | |
|---|---|
| *Баржи летней порой* | *Tows went up on the river* |
| *плыли вверх по реке* | *in summertime,* |
| *И плескалась волна* | *And waves splashed* |
| *на прибрежном песке.* | *on the sand.* |
| *В трюмах барж тех – народ,* | *In the belly of the tows there were* |
| *в трюмах – люду полно.* | *people, the belly was full of people.* |
| *Знать куда их везут,* | *Nobody knew* |
| *никому не дано.* | *where they were going.* |
| *Из степей да в урман* | *Kulaks from the steppes were taken to* |
| *завезли кулаков.* | *the deep forest,* |
| *Васюган их встречал –* | *The Vasyugan received them,* |
| *горемык мужиков.* | *those miserable people.* |
| *Запылали костры по ярам* | *Fires were flaming on the bank from* |
| *вдалеке –* | *the distance,* |
| *Стон и плач разнеслись* | *The silent river carried the sighs* |
| *по притихшей реке.* | *and tears.* |
| *Сколько силы мужицкой здесь* | *How much manpower* |
| *крестьянин вложил,* | *the peasants used* |
| *Чтобы край Васюганский* | *To fill the country of Vasyugan* |
| *проснулся, ожил.* | *with life.* |
| *Сколько русских погостов* | *How many Russian graveyards were* |
| *прибавилось вновь.* | *filled again,* |
| *Только вспомнишь об этом –* | *It chills your blood* |
| *стынет в жилушках кровь.* | *just to remember.* |
| *Пронеслось лихолетье над* | *Hard times have reached you,* |
| *тобой Васюган,* | *Vasyugan,* |
| *Где деревни стояли –* | *The sites of the villages are covered* |
| *стеною бурьян.* | *with weeds.* |
| *Все рассыпалось прахом,* | *Everything is scattered like ashes,* |
| *все быльем поросло,* | *Everything is grown over with grass,* |
| *И людские страданья* | *And the human suffering is taken* |
| *волной унесло.* | *away with the waves.* |

The other significant group of the Russian settlers, the oil miners, has the same kind of approach to this land. They also consider themselves pioneers, first settlers (*первопосетител*) who have had to work bravely in the cultureless forest in extreme conditions day in day out. This pioneer enthusiasm ignores the fact that a group of people regarded these forests as their homes when they – the miners – appeared, and they still do. A beautiful example of Novy Vasyugan oil-miner romanticism is a poem "My Vasyugan" by Yuriy Zonov, a local bard (Zonov 2008: 3).[14]

| | |
|---|---|
| *Наш край таежной глухомани* | *This is our place in the taiga, behind God's back.* |
| *Земля геологов, нефтяников, болот* | *The world of geologists, oil man and the marshland,* |
| *Одних она романтикою манит,* | *One of us is attracted by the romantic,* |
| *Других она работой позовет* | *The other one by the work.* |
| *Здесь буровые вышки кочуют по тайге,* | *Oil drills are walking in the woods here,* |
| *Ближайший ресторанчик в далеком Каргаске,* | *The nearest inn is in far away Kargasok,* |
| *И вести редкой почты как праздник для души,* | *And the rare news by post is festivity for the soul.* |
| *Наш адрес – Васюганье, окраина глуши,* | *Our address is Vasyugan, the edge of the wilderness,* |
| *Наш адрес – Васюганье, сюда нам и пиши* | *Our address is Vasyugan, write us here.* |
| *Припев: Васюганье мое "наказанье" мое,* | *My Vasyugan, "my punishment",* |
| *Мы с тобою давно уж на ты,* | *We've been on first name terms for a long time,* |
| *А назад оглянись – там ведь целая жизнь:* | *But if you look back – there's a whole life behind you:* |
| *«Средь болот нефтяные кусты»* | *"Oil drills amongst the marshes".* |

As I have already mentioned, this village has made its official history, its historical canon, several times. Neither the multimedia self-portrait nor the brief summary of the website mention that the Khanty population had lived here before the relocation. This same reticence can be

---

14.   The (non literary) translation is the work of the author.

found in the history of naming the village. In 1933 it was given the name *Могильный Яр* ("Cemetery-side") for it was built on the site of the cemetery of the neighbouring village of Okunsigatskoe. In fact, the present day high street is exactly above the former cemetery. In 1934 due to the "glum" tone of the name (sic!) the local commissar named the place *Смирновка* (Smirnovka) after himself. But this name was not set to last either because soon – again for a short time – it was given the name *Путь Севера*, that is the 'Way of the North', and finally the name *Новый Васюган* ('Novy Vasyugan') was established. The Khanty past was viewed as a bad memory then, a "glum" fact to be silent about, certainly not something that should represented in the name of the village.

In the official memory of the village, the basic symbol of thinking about the region is the taiga, the uninhabited deep forest, the "*глухомань*". The forest (and the marshland) represents remoteness from the world, the exclusion of the people there and its uninhabited state. This forest must be conquered, taken over and made habitable for the people (the relocated ones); the forest can be seen as the opposite of civilisation. The forest appears in the same way in the memories of the founding of the village, of the relocation. Every survivor has the same description of the relocation: families were transported on an ark going up the river and left at the riverbank at every few kilometres saying they should live there from then on. The first few years were about creating the possibilities for civilisation, clearing the forest; everybody thinks of that as the most important and difficult episode.

These examples show clearly that the "Ostyaks" are not present in the public discourse of the village (and in a broader context of the whole township of Kargasok and Tomsk oblast). There's no trace of the Khanty in the discourses of the "homeland", the "motherland", they remain unnoticed, unrecognised. The Khanty past is not part of the community's past, Khanty memories are not part of official memories, they have been lost in favour of the memories of the majorities;[15] the Khanty are not part of the memory-community of the village of

---

15.   To "the competitive memory" see: Burke 2001.

Vasyugan, not part of the value system represented in public talks, thus they are not part of the community either.[16]

Similarly, the "Ostyaks" are missing from the official oblast memory too. The history of the region before Russian colonisation belongs not to the local "native" people but to archaeological cultures such as the Tukh-Sigat. The most famous of these is the so-called Kulay culture of which there are regular presentations and exhibitions (about this see e.g. Chindina 1994). This culture has an outstanding artistic heritage, even by today's aesthetic standards, and it inspires the alternative intellectuals in Tomsk who, instead of accepting official (Russian) cultural ideals, try to find their roots elsewhere, in an ancient culture. The most well known art community is the society of *Сомона КуКуН* (Somona KuKuN), who are staunch representatives of Siberian purism. The name carries artistic and ideological roots: "*Сомона*" is the female form of the word shaman (formed according to the logic of the Russian language), and "*КуКуН*" is an acronym meaning "*Кулайское Культурное Наследие*", that is Kulay Cultural Heritage. According to their artistic credo, they would like to use ancient local cultural elements in an avant-garde way, distancing themselves from the falsity of consumer society and getting back to the "сердцебиение вселенной" ('heartbeat of the universe'; see: IDEJA). This art group,[17] with its desire to get back to the "ancient", the "local", looks only at the archaeological cultures, just like the official Novy Vasyugan memory does. They too ignore the local "native" minorities, but they do, however, accept them as the mediators of the Kulay culture.

As we can see, the "Ostyaks" have no role whatsoever in the process of national self-interpretation, official memory – and the avant-garde art group – represents discontinuity, not the continuous past. They make that past a memory which cannot be lived now, which they cannot be part of. This idealised presentation makes them lieux de mémoire according to Pierre Nora's words (Nora 1984–1992, in Hun-

---

16. To the relation between collective memory and collective identity see: Assmann 2004.

17. The group chiefly consists of artists of fine arts but the representative and reformer of the imagined Kulay music culture, Natalja Neljubova, the local underground singer also belongs here. For more details about them see: KUKUN.

garian Nora 1999). It is easy to identify oneself with this past for there is a huge time gap, there is no direct connection to it at all and it is firmly set in the past, so it means no responsibilities for the individual. In contrast, if they were to choose the past with the "Ostyaks" it would be more difficult to take on board. This past is unpresentable because the "Ostyaks" are not humanising pioneers but a barbaric, historically stagnent, lumpenised layer of society with very low prestige. If they were put in the story, the Russians could not avoid facing the colonist past. (See also Leete 1999.)

Interestingly enough, it is in the attachment to these archaeological cultures that the official, communal memory and the Vasyugan Khanty memory work alike. This past is an integral part of both of these memories and both sides try to expropriate it for themselves. The majority "Russian" memory, as we have seen, connects to these cultures via the myths of the first conquerors; while expropriating memories is also a kind of conquest: this legendary Bronze Age is the beginning of history, taking it over is actually extending the rather short history of Russians in Siberia and by doing so they build up their (not only) symbolic power over this territory. At the same time the Vasyugan Khanty connect these "ancient" cultures with their own mythic history. In their historical memories there were three world-periods, historical periods before the present day ("the time of this age") (Cf. Nagy 2006a). The "time of fire of the sky and earth" is the first era when the world was being formed, when Gods populated it with humans, animals and plants. The second era is the "time of song and tale" when the local guarding spirits lived their earthly lives; in this period heroes who guided the lives of humans became Gods. The third and longest era is the "time of wars" when only humans lived in the world; humans who were not able to turn into either animals or gods and who were in a continuous state of war with each other. This period, the "time of wars" is identified with the golden age of the ancestors of today's Vasyugan Khanty and based on that they tie the archaeological sites to their memories of their ancestors, their forefathers, and they build direct references to the archaeological works, to the practice of telling tales about that era.

As a result, of the aforementioned the "Ostyaks" are invisible in the official public discourses of Tomsk oblast. The thing that might, however, make them visible is the delicate and double-edged notion of exoticism. The Khanty shamans could be well known if they didn't wear such ordinary clothes and if there were, indeed, shamans today. The oblasok would be an excellent cultural symbol, and indeed it was the subject of a film made by the researchers of the Tomsk State University,[18] but today this boat is often made by Russians. Thus the "Ostyaks" don't live up to the expectations of urbanites interested in exoticism because Khanty culture hardly differs from that of the "Russians" living nearby. To the majority of people the prototype of being a "Siberian", a "native" – something which is also presented in the national media - was represented by the Evenkis, who lived there in very small numbers. The Evenkis seemed much more archaic than the other native peoples due to their lifestyle, which was nomadic reindeer herding[19], and also their distinct, "unique" outfits, which they kept much longer than the Khanty, who abandoned their traditional clothing earlier. It is important here to note that to the Vasyugan Khanty the Evenkis were the representatives of freedom, "the real forest life" and their shamans enjoyed great respect amongst them (in details: Nagy 2006b and 2007a.).

In spite of all this, in public, in the public knowledge of Tomsk oblast, there are "Khanty" living next to them in Western Siberia. "Real Khanty", according to them, wear traditional clothing, furs, have bear-festivals and have significant apparatus to represent their interests. They cannot reconcile this knowledge – which is strongly exaggerated by the media – with the culture of the Vasyugan Khanty. Therefore they sharply distinguish the local "Ostyaks" from the "Khanty" living in the Khanty-Mansi Autonomous Okrug. There is an exhibition on the Khanty in the local history museum in the northernmost city of Tomsk oblast, in Strezhevoy, but the material exhibited there was not collected along the Vasyugan in Tomsk oblast but in the region of Nizhnevartovsk and Megion in the Khanty-Mansi Autonomous Okrug. Thus neither in Strezhevoy are the "local Ostyaks", a minority living there amongst the other inhabitants, considered worthy of an exhibition. (MUNICIPAL.)

---

18. „Хантыйский обласок". A film of A. Mihaylov, expert N.V. Lukina (1992).
19. Reindeer herding was practically unknown amongst the other native minorities in Tomsk oblast.

In spite of the aforementioned facts, the Khanty culture does appear in the region of Tomsk oblast, but almost exclusively in scientific discourses. Tomsk ethnographers, primarily N.V. Lukina and N.V. Kulemzin, carried out extremely thorough studies on the Vasyugan Khanty (Kulemzin and Lukina 1977), there were archaeological works carried out in the area and the Department of Indigenous Languages of Siberia (*Кафедра Языков Народов Сибири*) founded by A. P. Dulzon is already an independent department of the Tomsk State Pedagogical Institute.

The "Ostyaks" are invisible in the political arena too: the Kolta Kup, the association representing the small peoples of the north, has little political influence and their problems and demands are only accepted in the field of culture. This is demonstrated by the fact that any decisions to be made in connection with them are dealt with by the local government's cultural department even when they concern economic questions such as minority co-operatives (*общчина*).[20]

It is also important to note that the association of Kolta Kup has taken up the cause of the Vasyugan Khanty, however, originally it was founded as a society for the local Selkups' interests. The reason for this collaboration is the fact that both groups realised they could not work effectively without getting together. In the name of effectiveness they accepted the homogenizing tendency of the oblast's minority politics, according to which, for example, all the "Ostyaks" were labelled as Selkups in the nationality section of their passports during the 1970s, when a general passport change took place. Referring to this, one of the leaders in Kolta Kup who, according to ethnographic research, should be called Khanty, calls himself Selkup.

This invisibility of the Vasyugan Khanty might be surprising for those who know that in the Khanty Mansi Autonomous Okrug regional politicians deliberately choose the (festive) culture of the Khanty and

---

20. Their rather restricted latitude is shown by the requirements the local government raises when setting up obščinas (communes). Every obščina wanting to pursue any economic activity has to have a considerable vehicle park (amphibious vehicle, motor sledge, motor boat), moreover each of them has to provide an individual forester status. It is only a poetic question how much these absolutely necessary conditions are part of the "traditional way of life"! (To the connection between lifestyle and ethnicity see Xanthaki 2004.)

Mansi as an emblem to emphasise its distinctiveness in the Moscow-region debate, although the number of titularly ethnic people is only 1,5% in that region. The Khanty have their own museum, journal and radio station there, which is an achievement unthought-of in Tomsk oblast. In 1992 a presidential decree came into force that accepted the right of the Khanty to their national territories,[21] as opposed to the Vasyugan people, where there was no acceptance of their rights whatsoever, that is, they received no compensation for the oil drills set up in their territories. It would seem obvious that in the triangle of nationalism[22] the Khanty living in the territories of Khanty-Mansi Autonomous Okrug fill the role of (1) a supportive motherland along-side the role of (2) the nationalising state (Tomsk oblast in this case), and the role of (3) the national minority (the Vasyugan Khanty here). However, Khanty intellectuals in Khanty-Mansi Autonomous Okrug also ignore the Vasyugan people, sometimes there is slight academic interest but this is very marginal[23] for indeed they look on the Vasyugan Khanty as extinct. (Cf. Szalnyikova 1992.)

The relation between the Khanty-Mansi Autonomous Okrug and the Vasyugan Khanty can be understood when we look at it from the perspective of the Soviet minority politics. Nationalism was already controlled in the multinational Soviet Union but below the Soviet state level there were two other levels where ethnic links were institutionalised. One of them was the theory of ethno-culturally and individually based ethnicity, which made inheritable ethnicity indicated in personal documents both a category of social-statistics and of law. The other was the theory of ethnicity based on territories that principally defined the organising logic of the Soviet member states, republics, autonomous republics and autonomous areas. The theories of individually and territorially based ethnicity "matched neither legally nor conceptually": the territorial differences between the actual place of

---

21.  About the policy and the economic and political situation of the Khanty-Mansi Autonomous Okrug see Novikova 2008.
22.  The three-sided relations of nationalism see Brubaker 1994 and 2006.
23.  The scientific programs are organised strictly according to administrative units, the finance for science hardly makes research outside the Khanty-Mansi Autonomous Okrug possible.

the ethnic groups and the designation of the ethnically based administrative units were the result of a deliberate strategy (Brubaker 1994 and 2006). This centrally generated anomaly was part of the power-play of the Soviet government and it caused the territorial division of the Khanty, although they were centrally labelled as homogenous on an individual basis.

The existence of the "Ostyaks" as an invisible ethnic group is very likely connected to the fact that the social group chosen by Tomsk oblast as their emblem in the center-periphery debate was the group of the relocated. This oblast, the infamous Narym Kray, was already a well known place for relocation in the Tsarist era and was the focus of one of the biggest waves of relocations in the 1930s–40s (Krasilnikov 2003). Accordingly the oblast of Tomsk constructs its own modern self-portrait according to these harsh measures *"репрессия"*[24] not giving any room to the "Ostyaks" who due to their well developed assimilation cannot be shown off as distinctively as the Khanty in Khanty-Mansi Autonomous Okrug. Thus, for example, in Tomsk the political relocations have their own museums – moreover there is a similar museum in Narym, where Stalin used to be in exile – while the "Ostyaks" only appear in temporary exhibitions. The same shift in emphasis can be observed in the local media programmes, in the local press and, getting back to the opening scene of this study, in the anniversary celebration[25] of Novy Vasyugan. The relocation also takes centre stage in the official memories of Novy Vasyugan.

## 4. The meanings of the category of "Ostyak"

It would be wrong to think that local "Russian" society entirely ignores the "Ostyaks" living among them, being different from them. The strongest evidence for this is the concept of "race": in local discourses

---

24.    In Russia the term *репрессия* is used for sanctions and retributions against the so called enemies of the people under the Stalinist era.

25.    I say this not only because of the content of that programme but also because the privileged guest, the excellent writer from Tomsk, Vadim Makseev, who is of Estonian origin, was also present in this role.

the name "Ostyaks" means a distinct race based on their physiognomy just like the Caucasians or the Turks. (Cf. Nagy 2002, 2005.)

In the term "Ostyak" there is a reference to language difference, in spite of the fact that the "Russians" cannot distinguish the "Ostyak" languages, so cannot tell the Khanty and Selkup apart. It is also noteworthy that language as a differentiating factor has no importance to the Vasyugan Khanty either, they themselves think of the Selkups as "Ostyaks", who "только говорят по другому" ('simply speak differently'). (Cf. Nagy 2002, 2005.) Although we must not forget that none of these languages work in daily communication today, both the Khanty and the Selkups use Russian in everyday life. To the "Russians" the term "Ostyak", as a language, has some obscene connotations and this feature is recognised by the youngsters with Khanty ancestors too. (Cf. Nagy 2002, 2005.)

The term "Ostyak" also means a kind of lifestyle. The way of life that is based primarily on fishing, hunting and other ways of using the forest is strongly connected to life in the taiga. (Cf. Nagy 2002, 2005.) It is even applied to others when they have similar fishing and hunting equipment and methods, hunting cottages and diet.[26] The evidence of how much the "Ostyak", as a lifestyle category, is not ethnically based is in the fact that in Novy Vasyugan the descendants of the 19th century settlers are sometimes called "Ostyaks" just like the Ukrainian man who though born in Ukraine and with a distinct "khokhol" dialect, has, because of his wife, lived amongst the "Ostyaks" for a long time.[27]

In local discourses "Ostyak", as a lifestyle category, is often understood as a lumpenised, poor culture. This interpretation is enhanced by the everyday sight of the "Ostyaks" living in the villages but being unable to integrate.[28] Strongly connected to this is the widely-held opinion that most crimes and all murders are com-

---

26.  It also true to the Selkups of Tomsk oblast. See Shahovcov 2006.
27.  To the lifestyle based ethnic-definitions, its historical side and to the Russians listed among the natives see Znamenski 2007.
28.  In Kargasok township that Novy Vasyugan is affiliated to in 2001 out of 842 people, who belong to the northern minorities, 775 were unemployed, that is 92%. (Shahovcov 2006: 161.)

mitted by "Ostyaks" (For interpretation see Nagy 2000). The picture of lumpenisation is intensified by the fact that the former Khanty settlements – which are practically deserted today – often become places of refuge for the marginalised, down and out, or families who cannot stay in Novy Vasyugan and are wanted by the police; these villages are becoming ghettos. The Khanty temporary settlement – Ozernoye –, for example, which, in the 1960s, Kulemzin (1993) called the last paradise of the Vasyugan Khanty culture is now the place of outcast. Or take the former Khanty centre, Aypolovo, next door to Novy Vasyugan. It is the home of three Khanty all together, the rest of the population are from Novy Vasyugan, all marginalised down and outs. They maintain their relationships, groups of friends and lifestyle in Aypolovo too, thus the place has become a hotspot for wild parties: people from Novy Vasyugan go there for the night or even for a few hours taking a huge amount of alcohol with them, drink it all and share it with the locals who can hardly afford to buy any on their own. The perception of the "Ostyak villages" as "criminal and alcoholic villages" no doubt creates the concept of the "Ostyaks" as "criminals and alcoholics". That is, deviance and lumpenisation become markers that help to distinguish the "Ostyaks" from the "Russians", ignoring ethnic content based on descent.

It also adds to the notion of a poor culture that the "Ostyaks" enjoy certain legally provided privileges: they get firewood with some discount, in the case of building or renovating a house they get a permission to use the forest for free, they are given priority regarding permits, to shoot certain animals they get a permit at a reduced price or for free up to a certain numbers of those animals, they get permission to carry arms earlier in the season than other locals and they are also supported with grants to get into higher education (cf. Shahovcov 2006). These benefits reach them most of the time, but often the money sent to the "Ostyaks" is spent on the villagers' social interests – if everything goes well – or it goes to provide official residences for young intellectuals who would hardly stay there otherwise. These privileges are well known and in order to get them many children from so-called mixed marriages have begun to call themselves "Ostyaks". These benefits are so important that Shahovcov (2006) suggests regarding them as ethnically distinguishing marks.

Representing the life of the "Ostyaks" as denoting a poor and deviant culture makes it impossible for them to put their own lives and problems into an ethnic discourse. This is partly the reason why Vasyugan Khanty "ethnopolitical entrepreneurs"[29] – if there is such a thing at all – have no real ammunition and hence cannot succeed in the local political arena.

## 5. Dissolved community

Now the question emerges as to whether the Khanty or Ostyak category constitutes a social group, whether there are people who identify themselves with these terms or, if the politics of suppression have been successful and, there's no such identification. The answer is very complicated and cannot be discussed fully here. Among the ethnic identities available to the people described as Vasyugan Khanty in the ethnographic academic literature there is a kind of "Ostyak" identity, but there is also a *"россиянин"* 'Russian' identity, that can be understood as a special Slavic character, which results in a strong identification with the motherland and the Soviet system. (Nagy 2002, 2004.) The "Ostyak" identity seems rather amorphous (Nagy 2002). On the one hand they think about their ethnic identity as a unpresentable, on the other hand there is a group solidarity in operation amongst them which values the idea of descent and also common memories in the case of the older generations. Many of the younger generations do not accept this ethnic identity, they do not think lineage is that important, their lifestyle hardly differs from the Russians'. They certainly do not work as a memory-community. If instead of looking at the settlements separately, we consider the whole social framework in the Vasyugan region then the community of the Vasyugan Khanty can rightly be called a disintegrated, dissolved community. Péter G. Tóth calls this phenomenon a "community without meaning" where "we can find the disappearance of structures, acculturation, lumpenproletariat, dismantling of traditions and finally dismantling and falling to pieces of a society" (Tóth 2002: 29–31).

---

29.   The term is used by Brubaker (2006).

This disintegration is the reason why N. V. Lukina and V. M. Kulemzin only carried out a retrospective study of the Vasyugan people for they thought that only some traces of their culture could be found anymore (Kulemzin and Lukina 1977). The scope of their research included cultural phenomena regarded as so archaic that they were the remnants of a lost "Khanty world". Another colleague from Tomsk who makes ethnographic films was of the same opinion, he said: "if you go to Yugan you'll understand why we only go there. Things in Vasyugan are nothing compared to the Yugan region. You still can find real Khanty culture there."[30] Due to the perception of a lack of authenticity no researcher has been to the Vasyugan since the time of N. V. Lukina. This lack of authenticity also results in the exclusion of the Vasyugan region from all research done by institutions dealing with the Khanty culture. In addition, the recently begun studies by Westerners are concentrating on the places regarded as more archaic.[31] For this reason a presentation about the Khanty can seem new and exotic at a conference organised by Khanty in Khanty-Mansiysk. Paradoxically, due to the lack of research on them a field not special and not exotic enough has now become a special and exotic one.

The Vasyugan region is a research field that has not been traditionally open to ethnologic researches. As Anna Losonczy was told when she announced her research plans among black people in Columbia: "They are not cultures, it is not a subject of ethnography" (Losonczy 1999: 107). The reasons for the lack of research, according to Losonczy, are the following: "Probably the slightly theological definition of culture blocked the understanding of this field as an ethnological subject. That is to say, if the theory is that culture must raise a kind of religious adhesion amongst people, and that the basic existential merit against culture is the absolute desire to maintain things and loyalty in the Christian sense then this loyalty and reproduction has only one alternative: cultural emptiness, forgetting everything, cultural lumpenproletariation. According to this idea these fields seem completely uninteresting." (Losonczy 1999: 106.)

---

30.   Personal discussion with A. Mikhailov
31.   Cf. Jordan 2003, who was influenced by this when choosing the research field.

Besides, in the value-orientation of Ob-Ugric studies, connecting the questions of culture and language in a dogmatic way also plays a large role. According to researchers who base their studies on language-families, and also the "native researchers" taught by them, that losing the language practically means losing the culture as well is a historically understandable process. The Vasyugan Khanty dialect is indeed nearly extinct, so based on this fact academic attention is fading too.

The culture of the Vasyugan Khanty is in many respects different from the black culture in Choco studied by Losonczy (2001). For there "the ritual work tries to put down a kind of territoriality for the people living in the suburbs, in rootless district and at the same time it tries to re-create some possibilities for remembering, some continuity in the constant discontinuity where violence penetrates everything" (Losonczy 1999: 111). There are no works for community or shared memories, the remote groups become memory-communities on their own. For the Vasyugan Khanty are dissolved not only geographically among the great numbers of relocated, among the local "Russians", but their ways of communication are also dissolved. Consequently they do not operate as an interpretive community, that is, they have no interpretive capital in common, nor competence[32] to be able to interpret things together. (Cf. Nagy 2007b.)

Therefore the Vasyugan Khanty, the "Ostyaks", are invisible not only in the high-level discourses of Tomsk oblast but in many ways they are also invisible to themselves. There are no interests or motivation for which the Vasyugan Khanty would make an effort to maintain the integrity of their culture or try to display it to the world or revive it. The Vasyugan Khanty have no interest in identifying themselves as a distinct group, there are no new cultural symbols being made to replace the old ones and to create distinction.

---

32.   To the interpretive community see Kálmán 2001 and Fish 1980.

# Bibliography

Anderson, Benedict 2006: *Elképzelt közösségek. Gondolatok a nacionalizmus eredetéről és elterjedéséről.* Budapest: L'Harmattan – Atelier.

Assmann, Jan 2004: *A kulturális emlékezet.* Budapest: Atlantisz.

Barth, Frederik (ed.) 1969: *Ethnic Groups and Boundaries. The Social Organization of Culture Difference.* Boston: Little, Brown and Company.

Bromlej, Julian Vlagyimirovics. 1976: *Etnosz és néprajz.* Budapest: Gondolat.

Brubaker, Rogers 1994: Nationhood and National Question in the Soviet Union and Post-Soviet Eurasia: An Institutionist Account. – *Theory and Society.* 1994/1: 47–78.

—— 2005: Csoportok nélküli etnicitás. – Kántor Z. & Majtényi B. (szerk): *Szöveggyűjtemény a nemzeti kisebbségekről.* Budapest: Rejtjel.

—— 2006: *Nacionalizmus új keretek között.* Budapest: L'Harmattan – Atelier.

Burke, Peter 2001: A történelem mint társadalmi emlékezet. – *Regio.* 12/1: 3–21.

Chindina 1984 = Чиндина, Людмилла Александровна. 1984: *Древняя история среднего приобья в эпоху железа: кулайская культура.* Томск: Изд. Томского Университета.

Etnografiya 1958 = Этнография народов СССР. Народы Сибири и Севера. Малые народы Севера. Москва: Издательство Московского Университета.

Fish, Stanley 1980: *Is There a Text in This Class? The Autority of Interpretive Communities.* Cambridge, Mass. – London: Harvard University Press.

Gumilev 1989 = Гумилёв, Лев Николаевич. 1989: *Этногенез и Биосфера Земли.* Ленинград.

IDEJA = Идея проекта. – <http://www.kukun.ru/html/n_idea.html> 12.9.2009.

Jordan, Peter 2003: *Material Culture and Sacred Landscape. The Anthropology of the Siberian Khanty.* Walnut Creek – Lanham – New York – Oxford: Rowman & Littlefield.

Kálmán, C. György (ed.) 2001: *Az értelmező közösségek elmélete.* Budapest: Balassi.

Krasilnikov 2003 = Красильников, Сергей 2003: *Серп и Молох. Крестьянская Ссылка в Западной Сибири в 1930-е году.* Москва: Росспен.

KUKUN = <http://www.kukun.ru> 12.9.2009.

Kulemzin and Lukina 1977 = Кулемзин, Владислав Михаилович & Лукина, Надежда Василевна 1977, *Васюганско-ваховские ханты.* Томск: Издательство Томского Университета.

Kulemzin 1993 = Кулемзин, Владислав Михаилович 1993: Сто лет спустя ... Из полевых матерналов. – Е.В. Осокин (ред.), *Северная книга.* Томск: Томский региональный отдел по социльно-экономическому развитию районов Севера. 116–127.

Leete, Art 1999: Ways of Describing Nenets and Khanty «Character» in 19th Century Russian Ethnographic Literature. – *Folklore* 12. <http://www.folklore.ee/Folklore/vol12/charactr.htm> 8.9.2009.

Losonczy, Anna 1999: Szinkretizmus az elméletben, a terepen és a múzeumban. Földessy Edina interjúja Losonczy Annával. – *Tabula* 2/1: 105–115.

——— 2001: *A szentek és az erdő.* Budapest: Helikon.

MUNICIAPAL = Муниципальный историко-краеведческий музей г. Стрежевого. <http://www.museum.ru/M613> 10.9.2009.

Nagy, Zoltán 2000: "Fél méterrel repülni a föld felett". A vodka a vaszjugáni hantik kultúrájában. – *Tabula* 2000/3(2): 284–315.

——— 2002: "Miféle hantik vagyunk mi?" A vaszjugáni hantik és a világ. – Pócs Éva (szerk.): *Közösség és identitás.* Studia Ethnologica Hungarica III. Budapest: L'Harmattan – PTE Néprajz Tanszék. 33–77.

Nagy 2004 = Надь, Золтан 2004: Родина и родная власть. Один из сегментов взсязы хантами и русскими. – Т. В. Волдина (ред.), *Сохранение традиционной культуры коренных малочислеенных народов Севера и проблема устойчивого развития.* Материалы Международной научной конференцнн. Москва. 546–552.

Nagy 2005 = Надь, Золтан 2005: Хантыйско-селькупские межэтнические связы в бассейне Васюгана. – Wágner-Nagy, B. (szerk.): *Mikola-konferencia 2004.* Szeged: Dep. of Finnougristics. 63–74.

Nagy, Zoltán 2006a: Az isten és az ördög huzakodása. A megrontott teremtés és a hanyatló idő gondolata a vaszjugani hantiknál. – Andrea Ekler & Éva Mikos & Gábor Vargyas (szerk.): *Teremtés. Szövegfolklorisztikai tanulmányok Nagy Ilona tiszteletére.* Studia Ethnologica Hungarica VII. Budapest: L'Harmattan. 62–80.

381

Nagy 2006b = Надь, Золтан 2006b: Об однм шаманском бубне васью-
ганских хантов. – *Вестник Томского Государственного Университета. Серия: Гуманитарные науки (История, этнология).* 2006/1.
вып.1 (52): 123–126.

Nagy, Zoltán 2007a: On a Shamanic Drum of the Vasiugan River Khanty. –
*Shaman* Vol. 15. Nos. 1–2, 27–46.

—— 2007b: *Az őseink még hittek az ördögökben. Vallási változások a
vaszjugáni hantiknál.* Budapest: L'Harmattan.

Nora, Pierre (szerk.) 1984–1992. *Les lieux de mémoire I–III.* Paris: Gal-
limar.

—— 1999: Emlékezet és történelem között: A helyek problematikája. Ford,
K. & Horváth, Zsolt; lektorálta, jegyz. Benda Gyula. – *Aetas* 1999 3:
142–157. <http://www.aetas.hu/1999_3/99-3-10.htm> 12.9.2009.

Novikova, Natalia I. 2008: Khanty and Mansi. – L. Sillanpää, *Awakening Siberia. From Marginalization to Self-Determination: The Small
Indigenous Nations of Northern Russia on the Eve of the Millennium.*
Acta Politica 33. Helsinki: Department of Political Science, University
of Helsinki. 173–192.

NOVVAS = <http://www.novvas.tomsk.ru> 10.9.2009.

PASPORT 2008 = Паспорт муниципального образования „Нововасю-
ганское сельское поселение".

Plotnikov 1901 = Плотников, А. Ф. 1901: *Нарымский Край.* Записи
Русского Географического Обшества X/1. СПБ.

Shahovcov 2006 = Шаховцов, Кирил. Г. 2006: Льгота ли быть
селькупом? – Д. Функ & Х. Бич & Л. Силланпяя (ред.), *Практика
постсоветских адаптаций народов Сибири.* Москва: Институт
этнологии и антропологии РАН. 157–172.

Shirokogorov 1923 = Широкогоров, Сергей. 1923: *Этнос, Исследование
основных принципов этнических и этнографических явлении.*
Sanghaj.

Slezkin, Yurij 1994: *Arctic Mirros. Russian and the Small Peoples of the
North.* Ithaca.

Szalnyikova, Ljudmila, 1992: „Vége lesz az egész hanti népnek". – *Valóság*
1992/2: 118–124.

Tóth, Péter G. 2002: A „közösség". Egy fogalom megalkotása, kiteljesedése,
széthullása és felszámolása. – Pócs Éva (szerk.), *Közösség és identitás.*
Studia Ethnologica Hungarica III. Budapest. 9–31.

Xanthaki, Aleksandra 2004: Indigenous Rights in the Russian Federation: The Case of Numerically Small Peoples of the Russian North, Siberia, and Far East. – *Human Rights Quarterly* Vol. 26: 74–105.

Znamenski, Andrei A. 2007: The "Ethic of Empire" on the Siberian Borderland. The Peculiar Case of the "Rock People", 1791–1878. – Nicholas B. Breyfogle & Abby M. Schrader & Willard Sunderland (eds), *Peopling the Russian Periphery. Borderland Colonization in Eurasian History.* Routledge 106–127.

Zonov 2008 = Зонов, Юрий: *Ммое родное Васюганье.* Power Point prezentáció, 2008.

# A láthatatlan „osztjákok",
# vagyis hantik a Tomszki megye területén

*Nagy Zoltán*

Tanulmányomban a Vaszjugán folyó menti hantik nemzetiség-politikai helyzetével foglalkozom. E kérdésről írva szembe kell nézni azzal a problémával, hogy mennyire tekinthető a csoport az etnicitásdiskurzus alapkategóriájának, hogy mennyire tekinthetők egységesnek a vaszjugáni hantik, illetve hogy mi a kapcsolat a szaktudomány és a helyi névhasználati gyakorlatok között. Novüj Vaszjugán település példájából kiindulva elemzem, hogyan működik „láthatatlan", elhallgatott társadalmi kategóriaként az „osztják" elnevezés: hogyan szorulnak ki a történeti kánonból mind a település, mind pedig a megye szintjén. Bemutatom, hogy az őshonos népek emlékezete helyett hogyan szerepel (1) az újabb és újabb orosz hódítások, a tajga civilizálásának emlékezete a hivatalos emlékezetben, a kitelepítések narratívájában és az olajbányász-romantikában; (2) a régészeti kultúrák kultusza az „ősi" kultúra diskurzusban; (3) az evenkik és a Hanti-Manysi Autonóm Terület hantijai az egzotizmus diskurzusában, (4) a kitelepítettek a Moszkva – periféria konfliktus láthatóvá tételében. Rámutatok arra is, hogy az „osztjákok" csak a helyi tudományos diskurzusban kaptak helyet, alig van helyük a helyi kulturális színtéren, és nincs helyük a helyi gazdasági és politikai diskurzusban sem. Elemzésemben arra is kitérek, hogy az „osztják" kategória hogyan működik „rassz" és életmód kategóriaként, illetve hogy a lumpenizálódás, a kriminalizálódás és a mélyszegénység hogyan válik etnikus markerré. Végezetül azt mutatom be, hogy a vaszjugáni hantik mindezek hatására hogyan váltak felolvadt, jelentés nélküli közösséggé, amiben nem fűződik semmi érdekük ahhoz, hogy önmagukat önálló csoportként határozzák meg, nem termelnek az eltűntek helyett új, az elhatárolódást érzékeltető kulturális szimbólumokat.

SÁNDOR SZEVERÉNYI &
BEÁTA WAGNER-NAGY

# Visiting the Nganasans in Ust-Avam[1]

## Abstract

The aim of this article is to illustrate the socio-linguistic situation of the Nganasans in the village of Ust-Avam (Taymyr Peninsula) in regard to their ethnic and cultural identity over the last 40 years, namely since the establishment of Ust-Avam.

After a short introduction, we present an overview of the demography, distribution and language use of the Samoyedic peoples in the second part of the article. In the third part of the article, we also describe the village of Ust-Avam by giving its location and providing a brief overview of its history and the ethno-demographic characteristics of its population.

In the fourth section, we portray in brief the Samoyedic peoples in the light of the newest official data, and will then focus on the Nganasans, especially those living in Ust-Avam. We illustrate their demographic tendencies, use of languages, and current ethno-cultural situation. In the fifth section, we present some of the results of our short interviews and questionnaires conducted in Dudinka during fieldtrips in May 2008 and in Ust-Avam in July and August of the same year. In addition to language use, this section also focuses on the natives' opinions on the future of their language and the importance of ethnic identity and the role of the language.

In the sixth section, we discuss about the fieldworker's responsibility. In the final chapter we will present our conclusions.

---

1.   Supported by OTKA (National Scientific Research Fund, Hungary), K60807 project.

## 1. Introduction

This article is primarily based on the following important sources. Firstly, fieldwork material collected in May and July-August, 2008 (linguistic documentation, supported by OTKA – National Scientific Research Fund, Hungary). Unfortunately we were not permitted to survey the current administrative data on the village. This was possibly due to an article on Ust-Avam that was published in the weekly periodical *New Times* and the regional periodical *Taymyrka* (Masyuk 2008). It accurately portrayed the present social and economic situation in the settlement and hence the people of the village did not respond well to it. A second important source is John Ziker's work, *Peoples of the Tundra* (2002). The American cultural anthropologist spent more than a year in Ust-Avam in the second half of the 1990s, mostly working with the Dolgans. Thirdly, Krivonogov's (2001) work on the peoples of Taymyr is also very important to our article. Krivonogov and his colleagues conducted comprehensive research on the sociolinguistic situation on the Taymyr Peninsula in the 1990s.

## 2. The demography and geographical location of the Samoyedic peoples

Before addressing Ust-Avam in detail, let us briefly present the most recent statistics on the Samoyedic peoples as they exist today (see Table 1). First, it is worth noting that all Samoyedic languages and cultural traditions are endangered. However, while all groups have this in common, there are significant differences between Samoyedic peoples concerning their way of life and identity. However, there are considerable similarities, too. The groups living in Taymyr villages (Nenets, Enets, Nganasans), for instance, share similar characteristics. Our current example and the data on Ust-Avam can consequently be regarded as valid for the whole Taymyr Peninsula and similar groups that are not dealt with in this case study.

Samoyedic peoples are among those small ethnic groups who have never had titular republic. Nowadays they all live as minorities in autonomous areas in Russia. With the exception of the Nenets, these peoples comprise up to 1–2% of inhabitants in their titular autonomous areas. There are also groups that are scattered in different administrative units, such as the Selkup people who live in three autonomous areas, so they are geographically fragmented and show considerable dialectal differences. Map 1 presents an overview concerning the geographical distribution of West Siberian peoples including the Samoyeds (Nenets, Enets, Nganasans, and Selkups).

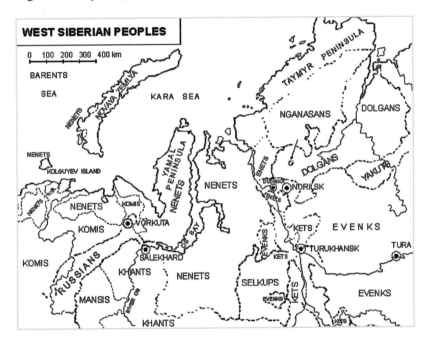

Map 1. West Siberian people
(<http://www.joshuaproject.net/peopctry.php?rop3=107700&rog3=RS>).

Historically, there used to be several less numerous ethnic groups in West Siberia that lived in a wide geographical area as can be seen in Map 1. The Nganasans, the focus of the current study, belong to the northernmost ones. The demographic development can be followed in the official censuses that were carried out in the Soviet Union and Russia. The official results concerning the Samoyedic peoples in the latest census (2002) are summarised in Table 1.

Demography, language status (2002 Census)

| | Nenets | | Enets | | Nganasan | | Selkup | |
|---|---|---|---|---|---|---|---|---|
| Ethnic population | 41,302 | | 237 | | 834 | | 4,249 | |
| | urban | rural | urban | rural | urban | rural | urban | rural |
| | 7,844 | 33,458 | 51 | 186 | 165 | 669 | 786 | 3,463 |
| Total number of speakers | 29,052 | | 84 | | 391 | | 1,230 | |
| Native speakers | 27,977 | | 66 | | 380 | | 1,127 | |
| Use of state language (Russian) | 89 % | | 97 % | | 98 % | | 99 % | |
| Other languages spoken | Enets, Dolgan | | Nenets, Dolgan | | Nenets, Dolgan | | Nenets, Khanty | |

Table 1. The population size and the languages used by Samoyeds (Duray et al 2007).

The data drawn from the 2002 Russian census are unreliable in relation to language use because the question on respondent's mother tongue was omitted, thus the data should be taken as results of estimations based on earlier censuses and other available information on speech communities. Comparing to earlier data, the estimated number of Samoyed languages speakers dramatically decreased between 1989 (the date of the previous census) and 2002: Nenets: −2%, Selkup: −10%, Nganasan: −23%, Enets: −3%.

Around West Siberia the indigenous people have been compelled to leave their homeland and move to the villages and towns, giving up not only their traditional culture but also their language. The current linguistic situation resulting from this change is that the people who still speak these four Samoyedic languages mostly belong to the older generation. Nevertheless, the case of Nenets, the biggest Samoyedic language by number of speakers, is somewhat different from that of other Samoyedic languages. In general, most members of these ethnic groups are not balanced bilingual speakers but monolingual Russian speakers. They have a very limited knowledge of the language of their parents and grandparents. Due to this fact intergenerational transmission of the Nganasan language has practically stopped.

The linguistic situation of the four Samoyedic minorities under review according to Fishman's Graded Intergenerational Disruption Scale (GIDS; 1991, 2001) is extremely alarming. Enets and the southern Selkup dialects are at Stage 8 at which the number of fluent speakers is so low that the community needs to re-establish language norms, which requires external experts, such as native speaker linguists, if available. Nganasan and some Nenets and Selkup dialects and groups are at Stage 7 on Fishman's scale as the older generation uses their language enthusiastically but children do not learn it. In the best case L1 is taught as L2. Some reindeer herding Nenets communities are the only ones who represent Stage 6 on Fishman's scale as the socialisation (in terms of language and identity) of children takes place both at home and in the community (Duray et al. 2007).

## 3. The past and present of Ust-Avam

### 3.1. History of Ust-Avam

Map 2 below illustrates the location of Ust-Avam, and shows the entire Taymyr Peninsula. The vast majority of the peninsula is lowland tundra. Its population is about 13,000 – excluding Dudinka with its 25,000 inhabitants – scattered over 900,000 km² of harsh terrain.

From the middle of the 20th century, most Nganasans have lived in permanent settlements in three villages. The largest population can be found in Volochanka consisting of ca. 300–400 people. Compared to it there is a smaller community in Ust-Avam with ca. 250–300 people, while the remaining Nganasans live in the eastern part of the peninsula in Novaya and their number is significantly smaller than that of the community living in Ust-Avam. In addition to these three main groups the Nganasans are also scattered among other settlements and can be found in Dudinka. The history of Ust-Avam illustrates the background of ethnic and linguistic relations in the region and provides insight into the processes of a period, covering nearly half a century, which has dramatically altered people's lives and accelerated their linguistic, cultural and ethnic assimilation. The first collectives were established in the Avam tundra in the 1930s by the Soviet government. From the 1930s to the 1960s, the main centres of the Soviet administration were Old-Avam, Novorybnoe and Kresty. These collectives shared the responsibility to control the route between Dudinka and Khatanga. Ust-Avam began to take on its present form in the late

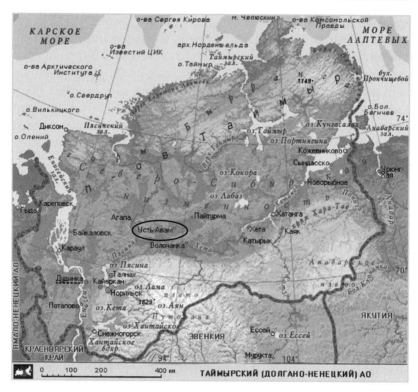

Map 2. The location of Ust-Avam (Усть-Авам) in the Taymyr Peninsula.
(<http://planetolog.ru/map-rus-oblast-zoom.php?oblast=TAY&type=1>.)

1950s, when the government began to close its administrative centres along the Dudinka-Khatanga reindeer trail. Ust-Avam and the Taymyrskiy Gospromkhoz were created in 1971. At the same time Novorybnoe and Old-Avam were closed and services in Kresty were restricted. The social services moved to Ust-Avam, and Dolgans and Nganasans, who had never lived together so closely before, were settled there (for further details see Ziker 2002: 63–83).

The disappearance of domesticated reindeer at the end of the 1970s was an important event, since it significantly decreased access to hunting and fishing grounds. The Nganasans used reindeer for transportation – they have not had any other since – and when they disappeared their hunting and fishing grounds shrank to around 80–100 km².

They have been living on the most northern edge of Russia for centuries, almost completely isolated from Russian colonialism for a long period of time. They were engaged in fishing, hunting and trapping (reindeer and fur animals), they bred reindeer and mainly used them for transport. The Soviet authorities had already started nationalisation, the organisation of kolkhozes, the buying or appropriating of domesticated reindeer and the execution of tribal leaders, i.e. shamans and "kulaks", in the 1930s, but none of this radically changed the Nganasans' semi-nomadic lifestyle. Five collectives were running in the Avam Tundra in 1938. However, at the beginning of World War II, the vast majority of native inhabitants already belonged to one of these collectives (Ziker 2002: 80).

Ust-Avam was founded in 1971 and everyday life there is hard. The village is about 330 km from Dudinka, and the closest sizeable settlement is Volochanka, which is 90 km away. Helicopters are the only means of transportation. Normally, there are 3 flights a month (only on Wednesdays) and they are very expensive, around 200 Euros in local money (ca. 8000 Roubles). Ust-Avam has approximately 700 inhabitants. They live in brick apartment buildings shared by 2–4 families. A single apartment contains a kitchen and a living room. After the centralisation of the 1970s essential social services were also moved to Ust-Avam: in addition to local administration, a school, a nursery, a hospital, a post office and two shops were built, as we observed during our fieldwork.

The local government solely consists of Russians and the principal of the village, the doctor and the policeman are all Russians. Of these the village policeman gets replaced on a regular basis. Doctors serve for 2–4 years and receive higher wages than their colleagues elsewhere. They usually return to more densely populated areas after their service. In our experience, and according to other sources, the few shops are owned by Russians and the shop assistants are Russians as well. In our experience, this has a major effect on the choice of language.

Picture 1.
Ust-Avam
from the air.

Picture 1 shows structural planning of the settlement and how it is organised in a geometrical way. The most important buildings are the school, the municipal headquarters, the post office and the hospital. There are also two cemeteries and the power generator, which constantly supplies the village with electricity.

## 3.2. Subsistence today

We adopt Ziker's term "survival-economy model" (Ziker 2002: 17) to describe the current subsistence situation in Ust-Avam. The main goal of the Gospromkhoz enterprise, established in the early 1970s, was to provide wild reindeer meat, fish, fur pelts, and crafts for Norilsk. In the last decade, however, Norilsk has begun to import from abroad. Its workers have become superfluous, but the settlements have remained. During the 1980s, Taymyr Gospromkhoz had up to 1,800 employees, but now it has only 220. Furthermore, Ust-Avam has only 32 professional hunters and fishermen (Molgonec 2009). Due to the long distances and harsh climatic conditions, the little settlements have become increasingly isolated from the mainstream economy since the breakup of the Soviet Union.

It is therefore unsurprising that the rate of unemployment is extremely high, and deaths from unnatural causes are relatively common. This is partly caused by the high rate of alcoholism. Although no exact figure is available, according to what we saw during the fieldtrips, the number of attempted suicides seems to be extremely high, corresponding with tendencies around the whole arctic area (see e.g. Penney et al. 2008, Tester & McNicoll 2004, Wexler 2006).

The fundamental reason for these statistics is the human sense of desperation. In the case of the younger generation the problems are caused by segregation: the traditional relationship with the elder generation has been irreparably broken and this may be the result of linguistic difficulties. They are also unable to adapt themselves to the new "capitalist" order, which in fact hardly even exists. The Nganasans are a nation whose cultural, linguistic and ethnic identity is nearly lost and they do not have any realistic possibilities to affect their situation due to a lack of money and proper education and because there are very few jobs and very little accommodation available in Dudinka. Therefore, they are virtually trapped in the settlements.

The streets are usually empty, even during the daytime. Working men toil on boats and ships or go fishing, the unemployed stay at home and watch television. Women usually stay at home as well. However, there is no television broadcast in Nganasan and only a few radio programmes are broadcast and then for just 10–15 minutes a day. There are Nganasans who would like to listen to these programmes but do not have a radio. Almost every family has a TV set and more and more apartment buildings are equipped with satellite dishes. Watching satellite TV strengthens their desperation as they are confronted with pictures of life in the outside world, which most of them cannot be a part of.

The everyday living conditions are narrow as seen in Picture 2. The housing is shared by a married couple and their five children. Not only have the nomadic tradition of the whole family sharing a single tent, but also the harsh conditions and a lack of money, forced these people to crowd into a tiny flat. The traditional cloth, *parka* (Picture 3), is rarely used.

Picture 2. Interior: Kitchen and living room.

Picture 3. The traditional cloth, *parka*.

# 4. Demography, language use and traditions – Statistics and fieldwork experience

## 4.1. Age distribution and language use among Nganasans

We shall next return to demographic characteristics. It must be noted that there may be some differences in the present-day situation, because our conclusions are based on data provided by Krivonogov and his research group (Krivonogov 2001). It was mentioned earlier that the data are fairly old, because they were collected in the mid-1990s. The trends described by the data are definite processes as they are still on going and were confirmed by our experiences. Moreover, no one else has been able to conduct such a comprehensive study since. The standard of living has been constantly falling. Below, we will present some of the most significant figures. The ethnic breakdown of

Ust-Avam is the following: there are approximately 300 Nganasans (approximately 40% of the population of the village), approximately 350 Dolgans (respectively 50%), and approximately 40 Russians (respectively 6%), approximately 30 others (respectively 4%).

These figures have not changed much over the years. The vast majority Russians immigrated to the settlement after its completion, between the end of the 1980s and the early 1990s. Many of the non-local construction workers settled in the village. Since then, the number of Nganasans has slightly decreased.

| age | male | female | age | male | female |
|-----|------|--------|-----|------|--------|
| > 80 | 3 | 3 | 35–40 | 16 | 33 |
| 75–80 | 1 | - | 30–35 | 29 | 39 |
| 70–75 | 10 | 3 | 25–30 | 39 | 42 |
| 65–70 | 6 | 3 | 20–25 | 39 | 41 |
| 60–65 | 4 | 4 | 15–20 | 42 | 40 |
| 55–60 | 7 | 7 | 10–15 | 65 | 51 |
| 50–55 | 11 | 20 | 5–10 | 58 | 66 |
| 45–50 | 5 | 24 | < 5 | 65 | 82 |
| 40–45 | 21 | 19 | | 421 | 477 |

Table 2. The Nganasans in the 1990s, divided by age (Krivonogov 2001: 140).

Today, life expectancy is only 40–42 (Masyuk 2008). This number is based on the drastic decrease in the number of people over the age of 40, especially men. In our personal experience, men over 60 are hardly to be found in Ust-Avam, and hence, the elderly women are mostly widows, and not really that old either. The oldest generation is between 60 and 65 years old. There are very few people over this age, the overall population size is dramatically decreasing.

| age | fluent | slight difficulties | great difficulties | understands but does not speak | none |
|-----|--------|--------------------|--------------------|-------------------------------|------|
| +70 | 100 | – | – | – | – |
| 60–69 | 100 | – | – | – | – |
| 50–59 | 95.6 | 2.2 | – | 2.2 | – |
| 40–49 | 88.2 | 2.9 | 5.9 | 1.5 | 1.5 |
| 30–39 | 78.3 | 7.0 | 6.9 | 6.9 | 0.9 |
| 20–29 | 39.2 | 16.5 | 17.7 | 18.4 | 8.2 |
| 10–19 | 7.6 | 3.1 | 15.2 | 41.1 | 33.0 |
| 0–10 | 5.2 | 0.7 | 5.6 | 16.7 | 71.8 |

Table 3. Level of language use among Nganasans by age (Krivonogov 2001: 155).

Table 3 very clearly shows the dramatic pace of the switch from Nganasan to Russian within a span of just two generations. The figures show a clear and irreversible process; a process which, in two or three generations, has led to fluency in the Nganasan language falling to below 10%. What is also clear is that this process has only accelerated over the past 20 to 30 years. As is shown in the fifth column, the number of those who do not speak the language at all has increased nine fold. Although this survey was conducted more than ten years ago, the trends it describes are equally true for the situation today.

The following chart (Figure 1) illustrates the same trend in the use of Nganasan language use but in more detail. It becomes evident that people under 40 barely speak the language (marked with the dark area) today and that Nganasan and Russian as mother tongues seem to be mutually exclusive.

Under the ascribed circumstances, it is unsurprising that Russian is the dominant language and a further shift towards the Russian language is to be expected.

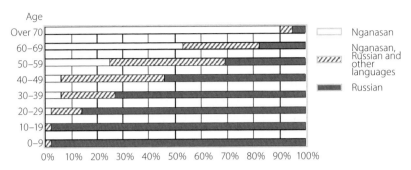

Figure 1. Language use among Nganasans in the different age groups (Krivonogov 2001: 156).

## 4.2. Marriage and Ethnicity

As Krivonogov observed, mixed marriages between Nganasans and Dolgans and Nganasans and Russians are a fairly new phenomenon, despite the fact that Nganasans have lived next to Dolgans for several centuries. Only marriages to Nenets or Enets were common in the past. (Krivonogov 2001: 196.)

The following chart presents data on the rate of mixed marriages entered into the 1990s (Krivonogov 2001: 182). This period saw a dramatic increase in the number of marriages between Russians and Nganasans, and between Nganasans and Dolgans. These mixed families exclusively speak Russian, even if neither of the parents is Russian. Furthermore, children in such families do not learn either of the ethnic languages.

| spouse | Nganasan | Dolgan | Russian |
|---|---|---|---|
| Nganasan | 16 | 7 | — |
| Dolgan | 9 | 36 | 1 |
| Russian | 11 | 9 | 3 |

Table 4. Marriages of Nganasans by ethnicity in Ust-Avam in 1994 (Krivonogov 2001: 182).

397

An important factor in the acceleration of language loss is the ever increasing blending of the Nganasan, Dolgan and Russian ethnicities that has been occurring since the 1970s, when these peoples settled in Ust-Avam. Table 4 shows that the number of pure Nganasan marriages is far below the number of mixed marriages.

The impact of mixed marriages is indicated by the figures for the ethnic affiliation of children's parents. The parents of 75% of children born in the district between 1971 and 1975 were both Nganasans, however, within 15 years this figure had decreased to 30%, as a result of mixed ethnic settling (Krivonogov 2001: 184).

The figure and charts we have selected for section 4 show the most prominent tendencies – Krivonogov's research contains further revealing charts. They suggest a connection between the language loss and the vanishing of ethnic and cultural values.

## 4.3. Where have the "traditions" gone?

The statistics presented here can be compared with cultural changes, most notably those concerning the ancient traditional way of life. In practise this means the rapidly increasing extinction of the cultural identity of the Nganasans. Additionally, although little solid, up-to-date information can be found on this topic, the following related facts should be noted:

1.    It has long been known that shamanism is no longer practised: the last shaman died in the 1990s and his costume and its accessories are exhibited in a museum in Dudinka.

2.    The *Ngamtusuo* folklore group, has an even decreasing number of members. Most of its members are deceased or very old and there is no new generation coming up. We managed to take part in festivities celebrating the settlement but only three old members of this group performed at the event.

3.    The presence of *Kojkas* (three-dimensional carved wooden idols) is one of the last signs of the ancient religion in the house. Ziker mentions never having seen one in Ust-Avam (Ziker 2002: 108). However, we succeeded to see one, but also witnessed a young family simply selling it to researchers.

Concerning folklore, the native speakers we worked with, who were supposedly capable of telling folk tales, told us that most of their stories had already been recorded. On the one hand this is a credit to the researchers and fieldworkers, on the other hand it shows how desperate the situation is. However, not being able to tell folk tales should not be interpreted as a clear sign of language loss.

## 5. Cultural and Ethnic Identity

Let us now turn to some of the results of the five interviews (with 60–65 year-old local women) we made in Ust-Avam and the questionnaires filled out in Dudinka by six young Nganasans (born between 1986 and 1991).[2] Unfortunately we were unable to talk about the ethnic situation with young Nganasans in Ust-Avam as it would have required more money and time. Furthermore, in recent years, ethnic disputes have arisen between Nganasans and Dolgans in Ust-Avam, and, therefore, we did not dare to ask questions on this topic. The customs of language use dominated the interviews we had with the young people. In the following we would like to highlight some significant findings concerning the connection between language and identity.

We observed some interesting contradictions in the answers we received from the young people. The second question we asked, for instance, was about the interviewees' mother tongue and here all informants chose "Nganasan". Later, reaching the 19th question we asked, "When did you acquire the Nganasan language?" Two of the interviewees answered, "Never" and all of them gave Russian as their first language. At an even later stage, the 60th question was as follows: "Is the Nganasan language important for you?" The following answers were given:

---

2.   The survey in Dudinka is based on a standard sociolinguistic questionnaire. The applicability of the questionnaire in Ust-Avam turned out to be problematic. In Ust-Avam we tried to work in less official circumstances relying on free conversation and participating observation. In fact, this method would have required a considerably longer stay among the native speakers.

*–Yes, we want to give knowledge of the Nganasan language to our children.*
*–Yes, in order to not forget my mother tongue.*
*–Any language knowledge is useful.*
*–Yes, but we cannot speak Nganasan.*
*–Yes. (without reasons)*
*– "A big minus." (without reasons)*

The young interviewees communicated in Russian with the older generation and only spoke Russian at home, even though their parents could speak Nganasan. They claimed that the quality and quantity of Nganasan books and dictionaries was not sufficient. Furthermore, all Nganasan children had not learnt Nganasan as a mother tongue at the boarding school in Ust-Avam (1 hour a week, age 6–8), but now they can learn Nganasan at the boarding school in Dudinka (2 hours a week).

It was also difficult for the young to keep in touch with relatives in the villages. This had an effect on the loss of language and culture. The young could only visit them in the villages once or twice a year and all of them said that this was insufficient. One of the informants had no relatives in the villages.

The older generation was very uncertain about the future of the Nganasan language. All of them claimed that knowledge of Nganasan was important, but they used Russian at home, even with their children. When asked why their children were addressed and spoken to in Russian, even though they considered Nganasan important, one of them replied: "I told them to pay more attention at school…".

However, they said that both languages should be used in teaching and that both should be taught. However, even a former Nganasan teacher preferred teaching in Russian, although she spoke Nganasan well, because it is "easier and more profitable".

The questionnaire included a question about being Nganasan, more precisely about which factors defined a genuine Nganasan person. Most of the older speakers did not understand the question, they simply answered: "I am a Nganasan", "Nganasan is Nganasan". They were not even able to determine their ethnic identity through factors such as clothing, way of life or language use. Terms such as nationality or ethnicity bore little significance because of the immense mestisation of the last 40 years.

One of the women, when asked about the meaning of Nganasan identity, finally asked a question, epitomising the whole situation in Ust-Avam: "My mother is an Enets, my father is a Nganasan, my husband is a Dolgan, my sons speak only Russian. So, who am I supposed to be?"

This corresponds to an utterance from one of Ziker's informants (Ziker 2002: 153): "We are not Dolgan and Nganasan anymore. We are peoples of the former Soviet Union".

## 6.  Appendix: the fieldworker's responsibility

As far as we know, paying native informants for their work was not the only practice ten years ago. The fieldworker did not pay money, as a fee, to the native speakers and according to informal sources, it was not the custom in other areas or with other peoples/tribes either. In many other areas it still isn't. Native speakers usually work with fieldworkers for gifts in kind. In Ust-Avam this has recently changed. Today in Ust-Avam native Nganasan informants expect to be paid for their assistance and this has its pros and cons.

The most important advantage is that fieldworkers can have expectations about certain tasks to be provided by their speakers, for example, in a detailed analysis of available language data. The informants profited of the collaboration as well because the financial benefit is sometimes much higher than their monthly pension.

However, there are other interesting consequences. First, informants realise that their native language knowledge has worth. They also become conscious of the value of their native language, that it is precious not only for the researchers but for them too. For example, we conducted some interviews and tests on some grammatical problems – the woman who was a former Nganasan teacher at the local school was often surprised by the seemingly forgotten linguistic intricacies of the language.

Second, news of their work with the researchers spread rapidly in the village. Consequently, our informants gained more respect in the community. However, it is doubtful that this would have strengthened their ethnic identity, since the questionnaires suggest that native language does not play an essential part in their ethnic identity.

Furthermore, conducting research with one ethnic group exclusively, in this case with Nganasan, might provoke conflicts. For instance, several Dolgans have felt insulted by the special attention paid to Nganasan in recent years, which has meant the almost annual presence of researchers bringing with them money.

The number of *"chistye Nganasanki"* has increased. The word *chistye* means ethnically pure referring to their origin and they are usually the first to offer their services to fieldworkers. However, it is no use asking questions about their "racial purity" or their knowledge of Nganasan since they are practically incapable of providing sensible answers. Their identity is different from those who have been raised and educated in a traditional Nganasan environment, coexisting peacefully with the other ethnic groups. A new form of identity seems to exist bereft of substance, an identity which, on ethnic grounds, often results in bitter disputes and conflicts.

## 7. Conclusions

Our experience confirms Krivonogov's statement that the term "ethnicity" has no real significance and function without real cultural values. Their weakening is a result of a long-term process and the assimilation of the Nganasans and Dolgans to Russians (mestisation; Krivonogov 2001: 199, Ziker 2002: 153). Ethnicity is becoming more important for the younger generation, but their identity seems to be bereft of almost any significant meaning. They express these values (e.g. the importance of language, way of life), but they do not live according to them.

# References

Duray, Zsuzsa & Sipos, Mária & Sipőcz, Katalin & Várnai, Zsuzsa & Wagner-Nagy, Beáta 2007: *The Current Sociolinguistic Situation of some Uralic Peoples*. ICML 11, Pécs. Poster handout.

Fishman, Joshua A. 1991: *Reversing Language Shift. Theoretical and Empirical Foundations of Assistance to Threatened Languages.* Clevedon, UK: Multilingual Matters.

—— (ed.) 2001: *Can Threatened Languages Be Saved? Reversing Language Shift, Revisited: A 21st Century Perspective.* Clevedon, UK: Multilingual Matters.

Helimskij = Хелимский, Е. А. 2002: *Языки народов России. Красная книга.* Москва: Academia.

Krivonogov = Кривоногов, В. П. 2001: *Народы Таймыра. Современные этнические процессы.* Красноярск: Красноярский педагогический университет.

Masyuk=Масюк, Е. 2008: Таймыр: как живут там, куда только вертолетом можно долететь. Да и то три раза в месяц. – *New Times* 14. <http://archive.newtimes.ru/magazine/2008/issue074/doc-55571.html> 29.07.2009.

Molgovec = Молговец, Сергей 2009: Антикризисный флагман. *Заполярный вестник.* I: 25. <http://www.norilsk-zv.ru/articles/antikrizisnyy_flagman.html>, II: 2. <http://www.norilsk-zv.ru/articles/antikrizisnyy_flagman_2.html> 27.07.2009.

Penney, Christopher & Senécal, Sacha & Guimond, Eric & Bobet, Ellen & Uppal, Sharanjit 2008: *Suicide in Inuit Nunaat: An analysis of Suicide Rates and the effect of Community-level Factors.* Position paper for the 5th NRF open Assembly, September 24th – 27th 2008. <http://old.nrf.is> 22.09.2008.

Tester, Frank James & McNicoll, Paule 2004: Isumagijaksaq: mindful of the state: social constructions of Inuit suicide. – *Social Science & Medicine* 58: 2625–2636.

Wexler, Lisa Marin 2006: Inupiat youth suicide and culture loss: Changing community conversations for prevention. *Social Science & Medicine* 63: 2938–2948. Ziker, John P. 2002: Peoples of Tundra. Northern Siberians in the Post-Communist Transition. Illinois: Waveland Press.

# Нганасаны в Усть-Аваме

*Шандор Северени – Беата Вагнер-Надь*

В настоящей статье ставится цель описать социологическую и языковую ситуацию людей, живущих в Усть-Аваме. Используя данные ранних описаний (Ziker 2002, Кривогонов 2001), авторы публикуют результаты собственного «маленького» социолингвистического исследования, проведенного в 2008-ом году в Усть-Аваме и в Дудинке.

При исследовании языкового, этнического и культурного сознания нганасан очень важно учитывать процессы, произошедшие на Таймыре в последние 40-50 лет, т.е. основание посёлка Усть-Авам, переход долган и нганасан на оседлость.

В начале 1990-х гг. почти все нганасаны были уже расселены в посёлках со смешанным населением (Усть-Авам, Волочанка и Новая). Этот факт ускорил ассимиляцию. Нганасанам не удалось сохранить традиционные промыслы. Люди, которые родились и выросли в тундре (т. е. старшее поколение), владеют языком и всем комплексом культурных навыков, но у них нет возможности передать это наследие молодым поколениям. Еще одним негативным фактором оказалась гибель всего поголовья домашних оленей в конце 1970-х гг. Оленеводство у нганасан почти прекратило своё существование. Жизнь на Таймыре в новой ситуации (т.е. после распада СССР) не стала лучше и легче, даже наоборот.

# List of Contributors

Csepregi, Márta (ELTE University, Budapest)
Csepregi.Marta(at)btk.elte.hu

Grünthal, Riho (University of Helsinki)
Riho.Grunthal(at)helsinki.fi

Koreinik, Kadri (University of Tartu)
Kadri.Koreinik(at)ut.ee

Kovács, Magdolna (University of Helsinki)
Magdolna.Kovacs(at)helsinki.fi

Laakso, Johanna (University of Vienna)
Johanna.Laakso(at)univie.ac.at

Nagy, Zoltán (University of Pécs)
Nagy.Zoltan(at)pte.hu

Onina, Sofia (Yugra State University, Khanty-Mansiysk)
OninaS(at)yandex.ru

Praakli, Kristiina (University of Tartu)
Kristiina.Praakli(at)ut.ee

Raag, Raimo (Uppsala University)
Raimo.Raag(at)moderna.uu.se

Scheller, Elisabeth (University of Tromsø)
Elisabeth.Scheller(at)uit.no

Seurujärvi-Kari, Irja (University of Helsinki)
Irja.Seurujarvi-Kari(at)helsinki.fi

Shirobokova, Larisa (ELTE University, Budapest)
larisza.shirobokova(at)gmail.com

Straszer, Boglárka (Uppsala University)
Boglarka.Straszer(at)moderna.uu.se

Szeverényi, Sándor (University of Szeged)
Szevers(at)nytud.hu

Tánczos, Outi (University of Helsinki)
Outi.Tanczos(at)helsinki.fi

Tánczos, Vilmos (Babeş-Bolyai University, Cluj-Napoca / Kolozsvár)
Tanczosvilmos(at)yahoo.com

Wagner-Nagy, Beáta (University of Hamburg)
Beata.Wagner-Nagy(at)uni-hamburg.de

CW00690093

# TIME
# BUBBLES

*Junction of Realities*

Thomas Trimble & TJ Trimble

Time Bubbles   Copyright © 2020 by Thomas Trimble & TJ Trimble

All Rights Reserved.

All rights reserved. No part of this book may be reproduced in any form or by any electronic or mechanical means including information storage and retrieval systems, without permission in writing from the author. The only exception is by a reviewer, who may quote short excerpts in a review.

Cover designed by Thomas Trimble

This book is a work of fiction. Names, characters, places, and incidents either are products of the author's imagination or are used fictitiously. Any resemblance to actual persons, living or dead, events, or locales is entirely coincidental.

Thomas Trimble & TJ Trimble

Visit my website at www.ttrimble.com

Printed in the United States of America

First Printing: Sept 2020
Kindle Direct Publishing

TT7

# CONTENTS

Introduction ........................................................1

What is Time? ......................................................4

The Basics ..........................................................12

Research Commitment...........................................20

Finding a Bubble ................................................27

Think Tank..........................................................34

Horace Finds a Bomb ..........................................50

Explorer .............................................................74

Steven's Lab........................................................86

The Walkthrough.................................................93

The Big Test........................................................100

The Next Steps .................................................................114

A Trip to the Other Side.................................................140

Changing Time ................................................................157

Time Goes On ..................................................................171

# INTRODUCTION

Dr. Alfred Mershon Ph.D., MD is a Physicist and Medical Doctor. Years of study have made him an expert on the theories of time travel and alternate realities, but it wasn't until 10 years ago that an event made him an expert on alternate histories as well. During a research project he was doing with the United States Navy, Dr. Mershon experienced all these theories firsthand.

Although the Navy quickly classified the events of his mission that had occurred in 2025, stories leaked out and were turned into a book. Not wanting to make a big deal of the fact that the book contained some classified materials, the Navy allowed it to be published and simply debunked the information that it contained. The author, Thomas Trimble, published Surprise Battle: A Different Outcome. The story contained within the book brought a sci-fi spin on the events that Dr. Mershon had experienced first-hand.

After he retired from the Navy project, the good doctor started doing research into the events that he had experienced at sea. His theories based on his research of alternate realities, alternate histories, and time travel lead to his finding Angel investors to support his mission to find the truth about what he had experienced. While Dr. Mershon's reasons are pure as a snowflake, who knows what lurks in the minds of those supplying the money? Do they want to visit the past in hopes that they can change that one event in their life that may have altered their future forever? Do they want to go back and buy that IBM stock as a penny stock? Do they want to visit the future and learn what the human race may evolve into? The scariest option of all is that they want to alter history for the entire planet by changing a major occurrence in history. No matter their motivations Dr. Mershon's money coffers are now full, and he may complete the research that has driven him since his incident.

My name is Randolph Ebb, I am the scientific documentarian for Dr. Mershon's team, and I will be telling you this story as I saw it unfold before my eyes. Please sit back and enjoy this scientific search for the truth.

# WHAT IS TIME?

**D**id you ever ask yourself the question what is TIME? The simplest answer is the clock. The giant round face of a classic grandfather clock, the hour, minute, and second hands spinning around the center spindle in a never-ending race in a single direction. Each tiny movement of the second hand pushes us forward in time like the raging waters of a flooded river. Unable to control its movement, direction of flow, or its speed, we merely exist stuck in the never-ending control of its grasp. No matter how much we fight it, 60 seconds will become one minute, 60 minutes will become one hour, and finally, 24 hours will become one day. Try as we might time is a living breathing unbreakable stallion that follows its own path.

The myriad of theories on time travel is as many as there are colors in the spectrum of light. Some say traveling at extreme speeds will allow you to break free from the bondage of time. Some say that if you could only fly around the sun backward at a fast-enough speed you will be able to travel back in time. Theories have stated that time is like a switchboard and all you have to do is dial the correct number and you will travel to that time and reality. Time travel theories are like opinions everyone has got one and they all stink in their own way.

The year is 2035, and the light from a tiny desk lamp dimly illuminates the room. Sitting in front of his powerful computer workstation, Dr. Horace Main looks over the data as it pours from the mind of the computer. Although he is just thirty-five years of age, his shaggy long white hair and bushy eyebrows make him look like Einstein to some people. Pushing his thick glasses back up his bulbous nose, Horace as he likes to be called, punched more information into his computer.

Dr. Horace Main, Ph.D. has degrees in Quantum Physics and Mathematics. Currently, he is part of a team studying the concept of time travel, specifically the concept of Time Bubbles and how they influence the ability to move between the realities contained within.

While Horace continues to type copious amounts of data into his supercomputer a look around the room reveals that not much was spent on decorations. Hanging on the wall is a large electronic smart frame. The picture displayed contains two giant images that appear like soap bubbles those children play with on a beautiful summer day. The prismatic color display is shining across the outer perimeter of the bubbles as they move around on the screen. Suddenly two bubbles collide in the center of the screen, but the bubbles don't burst they meld into each other. The two bubbles form a new unique prismatic shape in their center as they hang in the air.

Some people might look at this as an interesting screen saver, but the scientist in this lab know that these pictures represent years of their hard work. The team's leader calls this theory, Time Bubbles.

Dr. Alfred Mershon Ph.D., M.D. is the genius mind behind the Time Bubble theory. Having been born in Germany 65 years ago, his life had seen its ups and downs. Receiving a Ph.D. in physics and an M.D. Dr. Mershon has always been an extremely intelligent man. With his lab assistant Horace, they are trying to do what has never been done before, officially.

Speaking in unofficial terms and using the most ambiguous language possible due to the Top-Secret nature of the events, Dr. Mershon has traveled thru time. The year was 2025, the place the south Pacific Ocean. Onboard a United States Naval Vessel an incident that would change history as we know it was about to occur. Without going into detail, let's just say that Dr. Alfred Mershon's experiences changed his viewpoint on the theories of time travel.

Dr. Mershon's experiences lead to his personal mission to build the Mershon Laboratories for Time Research (MLTR). Looking around the world to find the best possible team of scientists, Dr. Mershon's first hire was Horace. Although he was young at the time his scientific acumen allowed him to become Dr. Mershon's second in command. The rest of the team was selected from various organizations and schools, each one providing expertise that would benefit the research. By the time he pulled his initial team together, twenty specialists were working at MLTR, and still growing in number.

Standing in the large conference room of the laboratory Dr. Mershon looked over his team before he gave them their introduction to his unique theory of time travel.

"Ladies and, Gentlemen welcome to day one at MLTR. We are about to go on a journey beyond anything that you have ever experienced. Using my theories along with all of our combined IQs we shall be able to complete the tasks before us.

First, let me explain the theory that is the culmination of my life's work. Like most of you, I grew up reading and watching Sci-Fi, the many stories of the time paradox, and how things that changed in the past will affect things in the present. The main theory being that the slightest change in the past would cause ripples that would change the future as a stone dropped in a lake the waves would be dependent on how big the change was. If you took a doughnut from a café in France in 1942 the ripples would be small, but if you killed Hitler the ripples would be enormous. The best way to describe the ripples would be a sunami 100 ft tall hitting Los Angeles.

Einstein's theory of Time Dilation has influenced me in some ways, but I have made my own intuitive leaps. He had the idea of time slowing and speeding up based on relativity.

All of this research and there still was no actual proof that time travel was even possible until an event that occurred Ten Years ago. The details of the event are highly classified. However, this single event opened my eyes to the fact that all of these theories *might carry with them a grain of truth. Leading me to the theory that we will be trying to prove.*

*The basics of my theory are the idea of a myriad of Alternate Realities. As we stand here today we are in our reality, which is a single bubble of space and time. Floating around us in the multiverse are many more bubbles floating around each other. The scene would look like a giant bubble machine blowing millions of bubbles inside the Superdome. Each bubble floats along containing its own reality timeline. Every bubble looks identical from the outside but on the inside, the range of differences could be astronomical. If you think about these bubbles like frames of a movie being viewed one at a time, there is a very small difference between one bubble and the next. Their timelines could be the same up until what we call a POD or Point of Divergence. A place where the timelines alter from the previous reality or similar realities. Some PODs could be small like the grass is no longer green to dinosaurs still walking the Earth. Another possibility would be that Japan won WWII while defeating the USA, England, France, Russia, and even Germany leaving them as the superpower of the new world order.*

*My theory is that when these Time Bubbles touch each other they allow you to shift between realities like they opened a doorway and all you have to do is walk through it.*

*However, if there is one of you in both timelines when they cross with each other you can replace yourself in the new reality. One result could be that your memories no longer apply in the reality you are in. This would most likely only occur if the two timelines align with each other but if they are further divergent from each other this would not be a problem.*

*Therefore the following tasks are what we will be working on so that we may travel between realities with a limited amount of danger.*

*First, we will need to find a way to read the information from a Time Bubble to determine where on a timeline the bubble currently resides as compared to our Time Bubble. These forms of measurements will allow us to move forward with the second item on our agenda.*

*Secondly, we will need to create some form of device that will allow us to move back and forth between the bubbles safely and securely. This device must maintain a stable connection between the two bubbles. Thus allowing us to return home after we explore an alternate reality.*

*Finally, we will have to actually move between these realities to prove the theories correct and thusly prove to the world that travel between realities is possible.*

*I leave you with this final thought experiment. Have you ever been standing in a crowded room when someone walks up to you? They weren't there a couple seconds ago when you last looked but suddenly there they are like they materialized from the ether. What if it weren't a simple blind spot in your vision that allowed this person to sneak up on you, but a Time Bubble opening a doorway that was hidden in your blindspot? What if it weren't the person behind you, but you who accidentally stepped through the Time Bubble and into an alternate reality? These are just a few of the questions that we will need to answer. So Ladies and Gentlemen good luck and may we succeed on our mission."*

Applause filled the room as all the scientists cheered to show their excitement about what the future might hold for them.

# THE BASICS

Looking back in the large computer lab where Horace is sitting in front of a massive computer center. The big room contains many other computer workstations where scientists are frantically working on the mathematics required to complete Dr. Mershon's quest of proving the Time Bubble theory. Tucked away in a dark corner of the room stands a massive almost seven-foot-tall shiny aluminum robot with a NASA logo on each arm. The lettering across the solid chest reads, "A.M.B.R.O.S.E." which stands for (Autonomous Martian Bot to Run Observation and Scientific Experiments). Like all government projects there needed to be an acronym, otherwise, the government couldn't build it. Although the robot stands like a man, it wasn't built like a man. The long solid metal legs don't end in feet, but a sophisticated track system that would've allowed the robot to maneuver across the surface of the red planet unimpeded by any obstacle. The three arms give AMBROSE the abilities of a Swiss army knife, providing every tool he may require during his mission. Along the head a series of antennae allow the robot to communicate with Earth faster than any other communication system which was currently available. The onboard Artificial Intelligence or AI that AMBROSE carries can run thousands of scientific experiments, while autonomously exploring the surface for any signs of life. Additional features on the robot include multiple cameras, two full color, two black and white, and a full night vision camera.

Although NASA paid over $10 million for the Cadillac of robots, Dr. Mershon got it at the bargain price of $1 million thanks to the government's shut down of NASA. Those wonderful Congressmen and women that voted to close the greatest scientific organization in the United States did him a favor when they caused a garage sale.

AMBROSE is under the purview of Dr. Steven Allen, Ph.D. His degree from MIT in Robotics makes him especially qualified to turn AMBROSE from a Martian explorer to a Time Bubble explorer. Dr. Allen's current mission is to adjust

AMBROSE's programming to allow him to travel through time and still be able to communicate with the scientist in this Time Bubble. The other problem that he is experiencing is how do you make a robot blend into the alternate reality that he will be sent into. In the future, it would not be a problem, but if they send him into medieval times a robot would stick out like a sore thumb. So, camouflage is one of the big challenges for Dr. Allen.

The most important item in the entire lab, the heart of MLTR, is the Time Portal. The massive golden oval standing 12 ft tall and 10 ft wide appears to be attached to the wall or is it physically embedded in the wall? Contained within the golden frame, a dark blue-green pool of swirling mystical water-like substance defies gravity by not leaving the oval. This portal is a totally proprietary design of Dr. Mershon from several years ago. This strange swirling effect is a by-product of the observation process. While it is still not a perfected science, the lab is confident that they will be able to view adjacent time bubbles through the portal soon.

Located about 15 feet away from the golden oval a large four-person computer control console is located. This console will be used by four people to control the time portal so that they will be able to see into the Time Bubble. Using proprietary software designed by MLTR the four scientists will be able to do what only Sci-Fi writers have been able to achieve in their writings.

◆ ◆ ◆

The laboratory doors slid open like something from a science fiction movie. Standing behind them, Dr. Hilda Adolfsson an expert in computer programming in the time travel field. Dr. Adolfsson is the total package, not only does she have a 170 I.Q. at six feet tall, but she also has legs for days. Her white lab coat could barely contain her ample cleavage and her long blonde hair makes her look more like a supermodel than anyone you would normally see in a laboratory like this.

The clicking of her high heel echoes through the lab as she approaches her computer console in the middle of the lab. Looking at Horace, she gave him a coy smile and a friendly wave before starting her work. Over the five years, she has worked with Dr. Mershon and Horace, she has advanced the time observation technology more than any other scientist.

The computer terminal jumped to life as she began to type her access code into the fields on the screen. Clicking on the icon on her screen the system began to run her Virtual Probe software.

The Virtual Probe is a multiple platform dynamic AI software system that can utilize R.T.S.S. to record visual images from around the world in real-time while also being able to identify the time and GPS coordinates of the visualizations. The R.T.S.S. or Real-Time Surveillance System is a government system of 150 geosynchronous satellites that not only provide real-time GPS location down to one square foot but also provide high-definition video coverage of the entire planet. I personally believe that a more proper name would be "Big Brother" after George Orwell's descriptions in his novel 1984. Of course, the government wouldn't want to admit that this multi-billion-dollar equipment system was actually used for spying on the entire planet, that would be wrong. They also would not admit that with the extreme cameras on the satellites the system can read your Driver's License in your hand from outer space.

The Virtual Probe utilizes the R.T.S.S. to scan the area within our Time Bubble to take snapshots of areas. It is also used to feed real physical information to the Quantum simulator that Horace is working with. Then the software analyzes the image and retrieves data from the database to provide the situational information for each of those images in the current setting. That data is then cross-referenced with the historical database that is stored in the cloud computer memory banks to provide any available historical snapshots of the area. All of that information should provide scientists with an accurate portrayal of the significance of any area.

Hilda's monitor lit up with an array of photos playing across the screen like a PowerPoint presentation. The dizzying array of photos fanned across the entire timeline of existence and the entire globe.

The flashing from the screen caught Horace's attention as he turned towards Hilda, "Is that your Virtual Probe? Did you finally get it working?"

"Only took five years of my life, but it appears that I finally have this beast dialed in," said Hilda with a victorious smile on her face.

"Is that our time bubble or have you finally breached another Time Bubble?"

"It's still our Time Bubble but I can scan the entire timeline, not just the current location. Pretty damn good if I do say so myself."

"Looks like you made a giant leap forward for the project. We are now one step closer to achieving our goals. You are the best, Hilda."

"Thanks, Horace. You always say the sweetest things to me."

Horace and Hilda watched the screen as the images continue to change as more images were captured by the software. Suddenly an image unlike any they had seen appeared on the monitor and before they could take a closer look it vanished and was replaced by another. They continued to watch as the software continued to extrapolate photo images both live and from historical archives and display them across the screen. Then once again another strange image appeared on the screen, this time they were able to see the image was not of a location on Earth but what seemed to be outer space itself. A dark background with tiny glimmers of light.

"Hilda, what was that?"

"Horace, I really don't know. The Virtual Probe is supposed to only extrapolate images based on terrestrial positions on the globe, looking down. The imaging system doesn't even look out into space, so I am not sure how those images appeared. I am wondering if perhaps this is a variation on the Time Bubble or maybe it was merely a mishap. For now, all I can say is we will have to continue to investigate this as our work continues."

"Hilda, I can't agree with you more. That is the standard problem with venturing into uncharted territories. You don't know what the destination looks like until you get there." With that, Horace walked off and returned to his desk to dive back into his own work, while Hilda looks over her results trying to find the variation.

# RESEARCH COMMITMENT

After MLTR had been in operation for about 6 months, Dr. Mershon called a technical staff meeting to discuss their progress. Standing in the large technical conference room Dr. Mershon looked down the long conference table at all the brilliant minds that he had collected to complete his dream project. As the wise older gentleman paced back and forth, he wondered if his project would ever come to fruition.

Dr. Mershon opened the meeting, "Welcome fellow scientists. Let me start by saying that I know we have undertaken a massive project, but I believe in my heart that we shall be able to accomplish our goals. Over the years I have undertaken several projects such as this one and I know it is hard for all the departments to communicate their progress. The point of this meeting and the several more we will have as the project progresses is to have all departments aware of the progress on all fronts. Today I want you all to share your successes and failures within each of your projects over the last six months. Horace, why don't you start?"

"Dr. Mershon, as you know I have been working on the detection software for the interaction of Time Bubbles. We are currently working on the theory that a Quantum signature is produced when two Time Bubbles interact. This signature should be able to show us how the interaction between the Time Bubbles affects the individual timelines within the bubbles. Currently, we don't have a monitoring system that is working but we are trying to get one together soon."

"Sounds like you are making some progress on the monitoring system. Please keep everyone up to date on your progress and should you need any assistance let me know."

"I have everything that I need at this time, Dr. Mershon. However, if something comes up, I will let you know, sir."

"That is the kind of progress report I want to hear. Clean, concise, and positive. Steven, your team is up next."

"Doctor, as you know my team has been working with AMBROSE to get it up and working for our purposes. The original design of the software has been updated to work on a terrestrial level rather than on Mars. We have the robot working in a fully autonomous mode and have started using simulations to ensure that he has the full capabilities we require. Our latest set of simulations has involved the software placing AMBROSE in random locations on the planet while feeding it information on its location from RTSS and on the timeline to see if the robot's software can extrapolate the information. So far, the software seems to be effectively interpreting the data it gathers and the robot can explore autonomously. The only concern I have is whether or not the communications system will work between two Time Bubbles. We should be able to set up a simulation for the interference problems that might occur once we know those parameters. When do you think we will be able to have that information since without it I will not be able to proceed with the communications system?"

"Unfortunately, we don't have that data for you at this time. I have traveled between Time Bubbles and I can't even tell you much about their make-up. Hopefully, we will have that information soon and you will no longer be delayed."

"Up next I would like to hear from Hilda about your progress."

"Dr. Mershon my team has had some early success on running the Virtual Probe through our Time Bubble. The visualization system can circumnavigate the globe and retrieve images that are not only live but historical in nature. The system allows you to input a place and time, then the software will retrieve any images from the RTSS database library as well as live images of the location from the current timeline. The problem comes when the computer tries to visualize the place on a different section of the timeline. For example, if I put the date and time for the landing of the Pilgrims at Plymouth Rock the software will show a picture of Plymouth Rock and then will broadcast images from historical archives but it will not show the actual landing. If all we are looking for is the location where the two Time Bubbles are intersecting that information will be fine but if you need to know the specific time and what is occurring, we will have to improve the resolution some more. Also, we have noticed that some areas of the scans are out of bounds for the software. These areas leave blind spots where the Virtual Probe cannot extrapolate the data. This leads us to the final mystery that we are working to solve. The probe appears to be randomly viewing images of outer space. This is not part of the software as the probe is focused on the terrestrial areas of the planet. This software glitch may not actually be a glitch but it might, and I mean might be the convergence of two Time Bubbles, and we are looking into the overlap. The computer might be interpreting that as outer space."

"That sounds like an intriguing hypothesis Hilda. It sounds to me that you have possibly made a leap forward in the viewing of Time Bubbles. Keep working hard on it and we will provide any assistance that you may require."

Dr. Mershon continued to pass around the room as he listened to his technical teams continued to explain their processes. Once he had taken in all the information from them, he decided that it was time to talk to the whole group and give them a pep talk of a sort.

"In 1961 President John F. Kennedy stood before the entire country and told them that we would land a man on the moon within a decade. At the time he didn't know what type of heroic feat he had set us upon as a nation. The total cost of which would not just be measured in dollars but in human lives. I know that we have what it takes to achieve our goals just like Kennedy believed they could. So, I now state that as of this time one year from now, November 1, 2037, I challenge us to send AMBROSE into another Time Bubble and return him safely."

The silence of the group would make the most secure person nervous. The silence was broken by grumbles of disbelief at the statement that the doctor had just made.

"My fellow scientists, I know that this is a major dedication of our time and effort, but I have gathered enough financial support from our investors to make this a reality. They have sought us out to support our mission now we have to return the faith they have in us by showing a giant leap in this new field of science. Remember nothing is impossible to achieve if you focus all your energy on achieving the goal. The only thing I want to hear from you is that it can be done. If you need more people or special equipment to achieve it, I will get it for you. My final word is, 'Get it done no matter what the financial cost.'"

With that, the Doctor walked out of the room as the stunned scientist tried to figure out what had just happened. Time was now not only the premise of the science they are working on, but it was also the fickle master standing over their shoulders as they worked.

# FINDING A BUBBLE

Almost three months had passed since Dr. Mershon had given his passionate speech to his team. Judging from the massive amount of work that has been accomplished his speech worked. The entire team has been burning the proverbial midnight oil ever since then and all that work seems to be paying off. Horace has been running the supercomputer to the limits of its computational power trying to find the convergence points for Time Bubbles. His theory that convergences leave behind a Quantum signature that can be traced has yet to be proven but don't tell the computer that it might get mad with the amount of information it has processed to date.

Horace's use of Quantum mechanics, the basic theorem upon which time travel is based, has him looking for tiny variations on an atomic level that would show a difference between Time Bubbles. His hours of work on the supercomputer have allowed him to construct a model of the Quantum world contained inside a Time Bubble. Using that model, he has been able to study the minute shifts of atomic particles. It's these shifts that Dr. Mershon has theorized occur at an atomic level when exposed to high-level radiation fields that cause a convergence point between two Time Bubbles. The excited state of these atomic particles creates a rift between the shells of the two Time Bubbles. The rift would temporarily allow someone or something to pass through thus entering an adjacent Time Bubble.

Using Dr. Mershon's theory, Horace has applied this information to his Time Bubble Quantum Model and upon feeding the software real-world variables it can ascertain the general location of the rift between bubbles.

Horace was reading over some of the data printouts from his simulations when his software sounded the detection alarm, the screen lit up with red flashing letters, "Quantum Disturbance Detected." Horace spun around in his chair and frantically typed on his keyboard launching the location subprogram in an attempt to locate the disturbance.

After what seemed like an eternity to Horace the location appeared on his screen. "Quantum Signature detected. Location: New Mexico."

A smile passed across Horace's face as he knew that his software had begun to move to the next phase of development. Although, Horace was elated that his software had started to read and locate these Quantum events in his mind all he could think about was the fact that the Virtual Probe that Hilda was working on wasn't ready yet. If we only could see into that disturbance, he thought to himself before he took off across the lab to talk to Dr. Mershon about his discovery.

As he jogged through the massive research facility all he could think was, I finally detected another Time Bubble. This is a massive leap for my team's work and the project as a whole.

Horace knocked on the door and then walked into the office. "Dr. Mershon I believe that I have finally detected a collision of Time Bubbles."

"That explains the big smile on your face. Tell me how you came to this conclusion."

29

"My software has been scanning the Quantum Model that I created to pin-point disturbances of atomic level conditions around the world. The atomic noise or yelling as I like to call it notifies me that the atoms have been stimulated due to contact with something beyond their normal experiences. Today the software indicated that a massive circular area of atoms, approximately two miles in diameter formed over a location in New Mexico. The atomic synchronizations within the circle were incongruent with the atoms outside the circle. I believe that the circular formation of atoms was the border of another Time Bubble crossing into our Time Bubble. This would indicate that their movements are similar to the photo of the soap bubbles on my wall."

"Horace, it sounds like you have made great strides in perfecting the detection of Time Bubble convergences. Now the target will be to enhance your software to be able to jump into the area of the other bubble."

"That sounds like a logical next step that needs to be accomplished, Doctor. I also feel that it is important to come up with a way to determine the length of time that the convergence of the bubbles will continue and how stable the connection between the two bubbles is."

"I knew you were a great hire, Horace. Sounds like you have everything under control for now. Although you seem to be handling everything by yourself, I still would like you to hire some fresh minds to help you out. The more minds working on the project the easier it is to solve the problem. Remember group thinking works. Also, if you could let other people use some of the computing power, I would appreciate it, we are a team after all."

"No problem, sir."

Walking from Dr. Mershon's office Horace could feel the excitement grow in his heart. I wonder if my location software could integrate with Hilda's Virtual Probe, he thought to himself as he wandered across the large laboratory. As if by fate he found himself standing in front of Hilda's office although it was not his conscious destination. Never wanting to look a gift horse in the mouth, Horace knocked on Hilda's door.

"Come in." he heard Hilda say from behind her closed door.

Horace walked in with a big smile on his face and looked at Hilda as she sat in her nicely decorated office behind her fancy walnut desk. The walls of her office are covered in awards from every major group you can imagine. Finally, Hilda looked up from the paperwork she had been working on to look at Horace.

"Hello, Horace. You look extremely happy today. How may I help you?"

"Hilda, I wanted to talk to you about how we might integrate my Quantum detection software with your Virtual Probe, that way we can view the specific area where Time Bubbles converge. I mention this because today I was finally able to make a clear detection. I figure if I pass along the GPS and time coordinates to you, your Virtual Probe should be able to investigate the area of convergence and tell us the information on the location in our Time Bubble."

"That sounds exciting Horace. I am sure that my Virtual Probe will be able to locate the position of the convergence but I am not sure if it will be able to cross over into the adjacent bubble and see anything about the timeline of that bubble. My software still hasn't cracked the timeline issues yet, but I am certain that it will happen shortly."

"Hilda, from my point of view, I believe I will start with a software update that will be able to interact with your software allowing the data to be transferred."

"If you take care of that I will upgrade the targeting software within the VP to accept your information that way it will be able to view the location in real-time and hopefully it will eventually look into another Time Bubble. That is going to take building the database with whatever surveillance systems they have or we can build. Let's hope the bubbles are so similar that they will have RTSS or something similar that we can build on."

# THINK TANK

After a couple days of toiling night and day, Hilda and Horace's team had not been able to determine the way they could figure out the time in an adjacent bubble that has made contact with their own. Time always being the key factor affecting their investigations they still could not find a way to quantify the place along a timeline where the bubbles intersect. For the two of them, the problem would just not show a solution, so they decided to call on Dr. Mershon to see if he could assist them with the problem.

Later that day they found themselves standing in front of Dr. Mershon asking for assistance.

"Dr. Mershon, Hilda, and I have been working on the integration of our two systems to be able to determine the precious location on the timeline within the bubble. To date, we have been unable to get the software to calculate this information for us. We were wondering if you had any ideas that might send us down the correct pathway," asked Horace.

"You know that I am always here to assist in any way I possibly can. As for your problem, I don't believe I have anything to offer as far as guidance. However, we do have a staff of 25 MENSA candidates out there. Why don't I call a meeting of the entire staff and we can use what they call the Think Tank approach to problem-solving? We got that fancy conference room might as well use it occasionally," replied Dr. Mershon.

"Thank you for the assistance, Dr. Mershon. We will see you at the meeting later today," said Hilda with a smile.

The multi-departmental conference room at MLTR was like the bridge of an intergalactic space station. Along the wood-paneled walls hung eight large LCD displays that attach wirelessly to the network within the room. The massive conference table down the middle contains 30 high-end computer workstations that are connected to the company's main servers as well as the extreme high-speed internet connection that allows for secure off-site searches in the massive AI Cloud computer. At the end of the conference table, a tall podium with a computer workstation stands in front of another two LCD displays. Whoever is in charge of the conference stands at the podium and has control of all the large displays to keep the discussion in line and allow everyone to participate in the presentation. Today Dr. Mershon would be leading the discussion.

Standing behind the podium he watched as the scientists in their white lab coats walked into the room like students on the first day of school. While they each found their seats, Dr. Mershon typed onto the screen the large words, "Think Tank."

"Ladies and Gentlemen. I have called you all together because we have hit the proverbial roadblock on some of the projects we have been working on. It is my hope that if we use the Think Tank method of problem-solving, we may overcome these shortfalls and move our entire project forward. I have been in communications with most of you so I know where we currently stand on all the projects but as we progress around the room, I want each department head to present the information in their own words.

I know that this is a daunting task to try and solve all the possible problems we have encountered today but if we put the questions before the group someone may be able to use some free time to solve the problem. I have great faith in the minds that I have recruited for this project and our combined intelligence will be able to overcome anything. First off, I would like to have Horace explain to you the issues that he has encountered to date."

## Horace's Issue

"First off, I would like to thank Dr. Mershon for his idea that we have this meeting to assist each other with the pitfalls we have encountered. I certainly have encountered a large pitfall and could use all your help. As you know I have been working on creating a computer simulation of our Time Bubble to look for Quantum disturbances that might indicate the interaction of our bubble with another one close by in the multiverse.

To date, I have been able to get the detectors to find the location of a possible interaction point within a ten-mile radius. I am currently working to get the algorithm to shrink the radius to something more workable for our purposes. Hilda and I have also been working on the integration of my Quantum Simulation software with her Virtual Probe software. This would allow us to accurately place her probe and investigate the interaction as it pertains to the timeline. The final step would be for us to send information to her probe from the new Time Bubble to do an investigation of their location and time coordinates.

# TIME BUBBLES

My question for the group to ponder is the idea of using something akin to Radiocarbon dating to determine the section of the timeline where two Time Bubbles have converged. You probably already know that the rate of decay of radiocarbon can be used to determine the age of an organic object. I was wondering if we could do something similar to that with the atomic energy readings that I have been getting from the convergence points. Is there any type of mathematical equation or detection system that could be used? Hopefully one of you will have a good idea to solve this problem.

Dr. Peter Balm, a renowned Nuclear Physics specialist, spoke up, "From my point of view Horace it would be possible to use multiple radiation readings from the same location to determine the amount of time that had elapsed. Imagine if you will a plane flying over the Nevada Test Site in 1951, you watch the B29 drop the 1 Kiloton bomb from its bomb doors. The massive mushroom cloud fills the air with billions of radioactive particles. You would need to extrapolate an initial exposure reading at that moment, based on what we now know about the result of that bomb, and then a radiation reading from that same location that you are currently detecting to determine the amount of decay. The mathematical equations will be hard to set up since the half-life of Plutonium Pu-239 is 24,100 years so the minuscule amount of decay would have to be calculated in the eighth or ninth decimal place. I can't say the programming would be fun, but it could be done by the supercomputer.

"I have to say that your idea might work to help determine the age of the radiation that I am detecting in our Time Bubble, but that still leaves the question of how do we determine the age of the adjacent Time Bubble. Also, those mathematical equations are going to take a long time to figure out since we are looking at something as small as a 0.3% amount of decay. We also have the need to make those same calculations without the large nuclear hot spot. However. It certainly is a start."

Dr. Mershon interjected, "That sounds like an interesting piece of the puzzle there, Dr. Balm. I think you have given Horace some good information that he can work on for a while. Does anyone else have anything to add to Horace's dilemma?"

Dr. Mickey Allen, another Nuclear Physicist, and the wife of Dr. Steven Allen, raised her hand to take her turn in the discussion. "Horace, I was wondering how many atomic anomalies you have been able to detect and the general area that they are located near."

"Mickey, I have found three anomalies located across the United States so far. The first one is in southern Nevada, the second one is located over central New Mexico and the final one is in Tennessee somewhere near Knoxville."

"Those locations make sense when you are looking at the amount of radiation being detected since those were some of the original locations for atomic testing in America. The Nevada Testing site, the site of the Trinity Test in New Mexico, and Oak Ridge, Tennessee one of the original facilities built for the Manhattan Project to manufacture plutonium. All these locations have been exposed to extreme amounts of radiation over the years so they would be easily detected."

"Looking at those locations from the historic standpoint really makes sense to me. Now that I see they all had major atomic disturbances that explain the readings I have been getting on the computer."

Dr. Mershon spoke up, "I think we have made some good strides here. I always believed that the Time Bubble I experienced had something to do with the radioactive nature of the location. This discussion has led me to believe that my hypothesis is correct."

Horace said, "I must agree Doctor. I think I have gotten enough information to keep me going for a couple months. Thanks to all of you for these ideas."

Dr. Mershon looked around the room before he spoke, "I am extremely excited at how we have come together on this set of issues. Up next, I would like to hear from Dr. Steven Allen on his progress with AMBROSE."

## Steven's Discussion about

## AMBROSE

Dr. Steven Allen stood up from his chair and looked around at his fellow colleagues. "My fellow scientists I have been working with AMBROSE to improve his capabilities for our purposes. So far, the advancements that we have made on having him run through his missions in autonomous mode have been spectacular. The navigation and research aspects of the software are working great. You may have noticed him strolling around the building observing different areas of the project.

The first technical problem I encountered is the communication system. Without knowing the parameters of the convergence of Time Bubbles I have been unable to determine a way to communicate back to our control room after he has been launched on a mission. The second question arises when we discuss his ability to move back and forth between the bubbles without sustaining any technical failures that might lead to a problem or more importantly losing him. Lastly, once he has passed through the point of convergence and landed within the diameter of the other

Time Bubble how do we disguise him so that he doesn't look like an alien trying to invade the Earth? These are my current issues; does anyone have any ideas as to how we might tackle these questions?"

The next to speak was the very young, Dr. David Petrov, a brilliant Electrical Engineer and a computer whiz who holds a Ph.D. from MIT. When I look at him, he reminds me of Chekov from Star Trek movies, young and full of energy but sometimes hard to understand. Rising from his chair he decided to add to the discussion, "Dr. Allen, if I remember the specs on AMBROSE correctly, he was supposed to use short burst communications that would be transmitted to 25 orbiting communications Drones, which he would deploy from a launch station. The rocket-propelled Drones would insert themselves in orbit at about 38,000 kilometers above him and then forward the information. Couldn't we deploy the same kind of Drones that would work similarly to a communication satellite? The Drones could also provide a GPS-type location system and an RTSS-type surveillance system. That Drone network would feed detailed information to Hilda's Virtual Probe."

"That plan might just work. It might take some time to develop the Drones and we still don't know what other communications issues might arise from the transition point. However, I think you may be onto something. Do you have any ideas about the other two problems?"

"Actually, I do. Our system will be moving him to a specific location. If we use that information and cross-reference, it with a database of cultural information. Then we can have a holographic projector create a simulation of the indigenous people. Using special clothing styles, we can hide the fact that he has three arms and no legs. We might also look into a more realistic voice synthesizer with more human speech patterns to blend in better in different languages."

"That might just work, we will have to start testing on that right away. You are definitely smarter than you look, kid. Now can you solve the transfer issues?"

"Without the variables on hand, it is almost impossible to calculate what will be needed to ensure a safe and secure transfer between the two bubbles. I got nothing for you."

Dr. Mershon spoke up, "Now David remember our Prime Directive. We shall always believe that it is possible."

"Right sir."

"We have made some great strides on the AMBROSE front. Now I would like to hear from Hilda on the Virtual Probe," said Dr. Mershon with a smile on his face.

## Hilda's Discussion

The beautiful Dr. Hilda Adolfson stood from her chair with a cheerful smile on her face. "Greetings, my work on the Virtual Probe has been progressing nicely but we are still running into a few problems.

Several years ago, a company named Wilson Applied Dynamics came up with a creation similar to the 'Transporter' from the 1960s show on TV, Star Trek. It is a matter to energy converter and re-converter. Except this one works. A person or object would enter the transporter and the system would convert their matter signature into an energy signature. Using the Virtual Probe that energy signature would be transmitted anywhere the probe was aiming including into the connected Time Bubble. Once it had been received on the other side of the portal the Transporter would then turn the energy signature back into a state of solid matter. This would then allow the person or probe to begin their work in the adjacent Time Bubble with a minimal number of stresses.

My team has been working with some scientists from Wilson which we have on a very tight contract. They are helping us build an extremely tight interface between the Virtual Probe data resources and the targeting system of the Transporter. Their scientists believe we will greatly exceed the current capability of the Transporter by itself. In fact, they have made the statement that they believe it might actually support time travel when driven by our AI system and simulations.

Horace and I have almost completed the interface system between our two programs which would allow the probe to instantaneously access the location of the convergence within our Time Bubble. Using the location and the data obtained the computer can extrapolate the historical information for the area and display photos and pertinent information to the control consoles. The main problem we are having is how to determine the timeline of the adjacent bubble. The concept we discussed orbiting Drones might provide us a large amount of baseline data about the neighboring bubble if we could also deploy them into that bubble. That network would allow us to work out a way of detecting information that will help us to determine the location and the timeline of the other bubble. The problem is similar to the one that Horace and Steve have encountered. Horace, is there any way that you can use your readings of the area to extrapolate the borders of the adjacent bubble where it penetrates ours so that we would be able to tell where the crossover occurs? This might allow us to visualize the boundaries thus giving us the information that we would need on all three fronts."

Horace perked up at the idea, "Theoretically it is possible to do that, I just think that the mathematical equations will take some time to create since no one has ever tried this before."

Dr. Steven Allen smiled at the idea and said, "You may be onto something. If I had that information, I might be able to determine the number of stresses that AMBROSE will experience when he crosses through the convergence."

Doctor Mershon then spoke up, "This has been an excellent session. We will do this once a month so if you come across something you can present it then. Thanks, people let's get back to it."

# HORACE FINDS A BOMB

After three months of arduous work by Horace and Hilda's teams they had started to improve the cohesion of their software along with the Time Portal and the Transporter. The late nights of eating cheap takeout and drinking energy drinks were about to pay off. They were all in the time laboratory where the Time Portal and the control consoles were. This is the first time this control room had been used. The team leaders were all at their stations on the console monitoring their operation. Steven was there even though AMBROSE would not be involved, because of his involvement with the Drones.

The first test run of the combined software systems was prepared. Horace pulled his global simulation up on the large screen above his workstation. Hilda's Virtual Probe began to control the display in the Time Portal. It changed from dark blue to a very bright light blue display. It was also displayed on all of their control monitors as they waited for Horace to transfer the location information.

Horace stood and turned to the team, "As you know, yesterday we deployed the test version of the Drone network in our reality bubble. It has been feeding us a large amount of data in addition to the government's RTSS system data. So, the simulation is now working using mostly current data as the highest time level and extrapolating down through time.

I hope that you are ready because I am about to launch the scanner to find us an atomic hot spot and hopefully another Time Bubble."

Horace reached down to his keyboard and hit the enter key launching his software out to the global network of sensors trying to locate the atomic anomaly. As the ones and zeroes, flew through the global network on their mission, the team sat breathlessly waiting for the results. Suddenly the screen flashed, "Energy Bubble discovered. GPS coordinates 37.1347° N, −116.0417° W. Estimated age 99 years ago."

The data from the Quantum simulation was transferred to the Virtual Probe within seconds. The main screen of the VP lit up with, "Location Received." The powerful software went to work looking across its massive database of information and began to print out its findings.

Current Location of Disturbance: Nevada Test Site, Nye County, Nevada.

Date of initial Radiation disbursement:

*July 5, 1957, 11:40 A.M. PST*

*Nuclear Bomb Test - Hood*

*Nevada Test Site*

*Southeastern Nye County, Nevada*

*About 65 miles (105 km) northwest of the city of Las Vegas.*

*Yield: 20-22 Kilotons*

The Time Portal for the first time displayed an image. The liquid-looking display showed a historical picture of that instant in time at that location based on the database

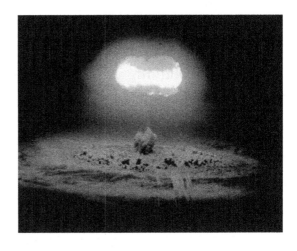

contained within the supercomputer.[1]

The first test of the Quantum Simulator combined with the Virtual Probe was a total success. For the first time, these two powerful pieces of software worked together perfectly using the location data from the Drone network.

The whole team yelled and applauded as their months of work had finally paid off. The fact that the software was able

---

[1] "Nuclear weapons test in Nevada in 1957" by International Campaign to Abolish Nuclear Weapons is licensed under CC BY-NC 2.0

to determine that the atomic signature was located over a previous nuclear explosion and was able to locate the time parameter all help to reinforce the fact that Dr. Mershon's theory of radiation is involved in the convergence of Time Bubbles was correct.

While the rest of the team celebrated their success, Horace was pounding away at his keyboard trying to launch his latest innovation, he called it "Look Back." Look Back is a software upgrade that is based on looking in the opposite direction from where the sensors located the Quantum disturbance. Like turning around to see what is behind you. This should allow the sensors to find the exact location of the convergence between the two bubbles and allow the computer to estimate the dimensions and the radioactive particle level within the adjacent bubble. As he completed his final preparations the software reached out to the sensors.

Horace's main display showed the message, "Look Back: detecting variations among the radiation signatures within the field. Exact readings are undetectable due to interference." At that moment, the display on the Time Portal went to the slow-moving outer space visual they had seen during testing. Nothing there that was understandable.

Horace looked at his teammates, "That is my new software 'Look Back', its goal is to see the area of convergence between the two bubbles. However, it appears that the area is inaccessible to the probes due to the difference in quantum signatures. I'm afraid that without physical contact I don't think we will be able to determine what lies within the other bubble."

Hilda replied, "Horace, even that much is great. We know something is there and now we can move forward using the information as a guide. I want to start working with Steven towards penetrating the shell of the adjacent bubble to deploy another set of Drones and determine what is on the other side."

"Sounds good to me. While we work on that I will have my team continue to adjust the Look Back software to identify additional information."

Hours turned into days, and days into weeks as the research team slaved over the software incessantly. As the weeks turned into months the team finally got the breakthrough that they were looking for.

One of the biggest remaining tasks for Steven's team is to figure out how to activate the Time Portal to allow AMBROSE or any physical object to cross the barrier out of our Bubble and into the other one. They have no information on what the bubble is to know how to cross its boundary.

Using the Transporter as a basis for their project Horace collected the mechanical engineering team to build an all-in-one unit that would not only work as the energy to matter converter within the other Time Bubble but could also work as the home base for AMBROSE and launch the Drones on the other side, hence the projects name, "HOME BASE." The unit which stands around five feet tall with dimensions similar to that of a four-draw filing cabinet sits on a track drive system link an army tank. Upon arrival in the adjacent Time Bubble, 'HOME BASE' would launch its system of Drones into the atmosphere to establish communications and facilitate scientific research to determine that timeline location.

Additional purposes for the station would be to work as the Transporter's energy to matter converter within the Time Bubble to allow other mechanical Drones or AMBROSE to arrive. The onboard communications and data storage capabilities would allow it to store all the knowledge gained by AMBROSE and the Drones during their time in the bubble. The final requirement for the HOME BASE was that it would transport all equipment and data back to its original Time Bubble

Horace and his team had been working on getting HOME BASE up and running with all of the detection software and the Transporter. Steven's team was creating the Drones that would do all of the research work once inside the Time Bubble. Using an existing military small format Drone, Steven's team modified it for use in both communication and investigation. Getting the Drone up and running was not easy, but they had finally achieved their goal. While his crack team loaded the single Drone into the HOME BASE unit Steven checked in on one of his top software engineers Martin Beswick.

Martin Beswick, a young guy, the newest keyboard jockey to join the team, had spent the last three months trying to break the proverbial bubble. Using HOME BASE to launch the single Drone, he hoped that his software would allow the Drone to penetrate the adjacent Time Bubble without any problems.

"Martin are we ready to light the tires and kick the fires? Wait a second reverse that, you know what I mean."

"I think we are there Steven. I have run this thing thru every simulation that I can think of and it handled everything fine. Like they always say though, reality is another problem. All I can say is that if the Drone survives entering the other Time Bubble it will definitely do its job of investigating the area and transmitting that information back to HOME BASE. Just remember my caveat."

"I won't hold it against you if something goes wrong with the transportation. However, if you crash the Drone on the other side, it will totally be your fault."

"It won't happen so I will be fine. Good luck."

"Good luck to you as well."

# TIME BUBBLES

Their three-month journey towards piercing the Time Bubbles was about to come to an end. Hours of tedious software integration and building devices no one had ever thought needed to be in existence until right now, were coming to fruition.

Horace stood before the combined project teams once again, "Ladies and gentlemen, today we finally break through the barrier of an adjacent Time Bubble and see what mysteries lay within. I give you HOME BASE." Pointing to the side as the large unit rolled across the floor towards the Time Portal. "This magnificent device is the culmination of all of our hours of hard work. Thanks to Steven's team we have loaded the first of many future Drones into HOME BASE. This crucially important piece of equipment carries our hopes and dreams into another Time Bubble. This Drone guided by Martin's brilliant software is about to go where no one has gone before. Sorry, I always wanted to say that. If everything works the way that it has on the software simulations, I have seen over the last few months we should all be in for a treat. Good luck to us all." With the completion of his rousing speech, the entire team gave out roaring applause.

Horace lifted his hand into the air to calm down the normally silent group of scientists before he looked towards his computer screen as he prepared to launch HOME BASE on its initial mission.

With that Horace hit the enter key and started his software on its quest to find another atomic disturbance. You could feel the excitement build in the room as their collective heartbeats seemed to combine into an audible thumping sound. As the data moved across the network of detection devices flying around the planet at impressive speeds, finally one of them found the target they desired. The large screen above Horace's workstation indicated the discovery, "Energy Disturbance discovered. GPS coordinates 51°23'13.19"N 30° 05' 33.60" E. Estimated age 50 years ago."

Quickly the information was transferred over to the Virtual Probe. The software flashed across the screen, "Location Received." The hum of the computers filled the air as they searched the enormous database for the information required. What is at those coordinates and at what time on the timeline? The Time Portal came to life turning a much lighter color, still just a swirling image. Then Hilda's monitor showed:

Current Location of Disturbance: Pripyat in the north of the Ukrainian SSR.

Data from initial Radiation Disbursement:

> *April 26, 1986*
> *Explosion in No. 4 Nuclear Reactor*
> *Chernobyl Power Plant*
> *Pripyat, Ukrainian SSR.*
> *Radiation exposure not recorded.*

The Time Portal displayed this historical image of the place and time of the original atomic exposure for the area. This image was from our Time Bubble and

the historical archive. It showed the totally destroyed No. 4 reactor an event that no one alive at the time will ever forget.[2]

The radioactive cloud that traveled the Earth made the news in even the tiniest of countries.

Horace jumped into his chair and pounded away at his keyboard like a pianist playing at top speed. Moments passed like a snail on a salt bed as the Look Back software searched the area for the convergence of the Time Bubbles. The screen flashed up, "Look Back has detected a similar energy field with a variance in atomic energy levels. Estimating location based on current global structure: 51°23'13.19"N 30° 05' 33.60" E."

Horace transferred the new coordinates into the Virtual Probe. Once it found that location Hilda's monitor and the Time Portal displayed the mysterious outer space image they had seen during testing. However, now in that very large image, it didn't look like outer space, but the actual inside curvature of a bubble. Similar to the way it is represented in the picture on Horace's wall. The coordinates must be in the overlapping area between the two bubbles. Nothing can be recognized by the Virtual Probe and nothing can be seen looking in either direction from our drones.

---

[2] "ORNL History" by oakridgelabnews is licensed under CC BY 2.0

Horace said to the Doctor, "Do you agree that this might be that actual junction between our bubble and another one?".

The Doctor looked very puzzled for a couple minutes, "Horace, I do not have any other way to explain it. Team any other input from anyone?"

Hilda said, "I agree with Horace. This is the image we saw on a smaller scale during the test. We had no way to see that curvature and the fact we were in the junction between two spheres. I think I understand why the Virtual Probe has not got enough reference data to find anything. It is as if the walls of the time bubble are not transparent like you would think of a soap bubble.".

Steven then spoke up, "Doctor, I think the only way we can get a look is to get a Drone to go through that wall. The only way to do that is to send HOME BASE there and have it launch the Drone. None of us can assure that it will be safe for HOME BASE and we will be able to bring it back but isn't that what scientific research is about, the big IF? I think we try transporting HOME BASE there."

The Doctor said, "Horace, you are the team leader, but I think I agree with Steven. This is the leading edge of science.".

Horace then announced, "It seems that we have proposed transporting HOME BASE into these coordinates, let it launch a Drone through the wall, and see what we have. Then pray we can bring it back. Does everyone agree?"

He looked around at the other teams and everyone signaled they agreed with the plan.

Horace said, "Alright here we go.".

Horace began to type on the keyboard to tell the Transporter's software to lock on those coordinates. A green light displayed on the monitor signified that the destination had been located and locked on. Horace reached towards the large red button on his screen and activated the Transporter.

Like a bolt of lightning from above a horizontal tube of blue electrical energy surrounded the space between the Time Portal and HOME BASE. The team watched as the system began to break down the molecular structure of the large black device. A few seconds seemed to take forever as each atom of material broke down and was recorded into the system's buffers. The flashing blue beam of light disappeared into the Time Portal and HOME BASE was gone.

Steven requested HOME BASE's current location the response was, "HOME BASE is at 51°23'13.19"N 30° 05' 33.60" E." Horace verified that those were the proper coordinates and then he proceeded towards the launch of the Drone.

The telemetry signals from HOME BASE indicated that they had full communication and telemetry with it. Steven activated the cameras on it. The image on the Time Portal was again the image that appeared to be the inside of a bubble, except now far closer. It appeared that HOME BASE was in that junction area between bubbles.

Horace made some queries into the Look Back software data to be sure how HOME BASE was oriented in that junction. He told Steven, "Rotate HOME BASE sixty degrees to the right." Steven did that and the image in the Time Portal turned. The same view but you could see it turning. Then Horace said, "Ok, HOME BASE is facing the wall of the other bubble. Steven, please launch the Drone.".

Steven typed some commands, and a message was displayed on the main screen, "HOME BASE: Drone Launched as Directed.". One of HOME BASE's cameras showed the Drone leaving a port at the top of the unit and disappearing into the dark wall.

Back at MLTR Hilda began to receive data packets from HOME BASE's software. "HOME BASE is already forwarding information on the area of the convergence. Virtual Probe is currently analyzing the data to determine the Drone's current location along the timeline.", Hilda explained.

Using a parallel timeline as the basis for comparison, per Dr. Mershon's observations, the Virtual Probe armed with this mass of reconnaissance data brought up this evaluation.

Based on the Drone data, the Virtual Probe AI analysis, the second Virtual Probe screen reported:

> *Dec 2, 1986*
> *Sarcophagus Completed*
> *Chernobyl Power Plant*
> *Pripyat, Ukrainian SSR.*
> *Radiation exposure not recorded.*

Hilda processed the images from the Drone. Suddenly, the image was displayed in the Time Portal. It appeared to be an image of the same location except in the other bubble. The entire team was in shock as they realized that they had finally taken the first great step.

The Time Portal showed a dark dank looking cloud hanging just above the ground surrounding the area of the Chernobyl Nuclear Reactor. However, this was not a rain cloud, it was a cloud of highly radioactive steam. The dark grey skies hung ominously above the area in a foreboding manner. The now desolate location looks like a post-apocalyptic nightmare.

The Time Portal displayed this image. This was the result of the data retrieved from the Drone, the radioactivity readings in that bubble, the Virtual Probe analysis of their timeline, and all the processing this massive AI system could assemble all used to target the Transporter.

After watching for a minute, Horace yelled out, "That is a live video from the Drone, not just a still picture. Could the transporter, controlled by all of this Artificial Intelligence actually have succeeded in transporting HOME BASE back into an earlier time in the timeline of that bubble? Trying to match the image that the Virtual Probe was displaying from the archives?".

The image displayed showed the No. 4 reactor at the Chernobyl power plant after they had covered the radioactive core in a concrete and steel Sarcophagus. [3] Horace turned back to his software and ordered the Drone to proceed to the area of the reactor to verify that the images from our timeline database are similar to this reality in the adjacent Time Bubble.

The Drone banked in the air and headed to an observational height above the destroyed reactor. The cameras focused down on the area and sent the images to the

---

[3] "04710017" by IAEA Imagebank is licensed under CC BY-SA 2.0

screen. The Drone's screen and the Virtual Probe's screen were identical except for the addition of the sarcophagus.

Horace yelled in excitement as he realized what the system was telling him. "Ladies and Gentlemen, we have achieved our first successful visit to an adjacent Time Bubble. Not just a basic reading but a historical live picture.

According to the readings that we have received from the Drone we are looking at the exact same location approximately 51 years minus 220 days EARLIER than our timeline. The 220 days was apparently the time to assemble the sarcophagus.

This all means that where the two Time Bubbles have meshed there is a variation on the timeline of 220 days and we have been able to transport HOME BASE back to that time. This however is not a true determination of the timeline position relative to our timeline, but it does give us the indication that the timelines in adjacent bubbles are moving along a separate path. We have made the first step in being able to find out the actual time in another Time Bubble. Of course, this is all based on Dr. Mershon's theory from his personal experience and not on actual hard science at this point."

Horace then said, "Ok that was great. Let's shut down and bring HOME BASE back."

In a minute of Horace typing on the command console, the Time Portal returned to the wavy image and HOME BASE appeared through it and was sitting at the entrance. Horace said, "Alright shut everything down.".

Hilda spoke up, "Well Horace, I have been working on the theory that adjacent time bubbles are truly just slight variations from each other's timeline. Like when you watch an old 35mm movie print frame by frame. Each frame is similar to the last one, but there is a minute difference that can be detected. Maybe Time Bubbles work the same way. If you compare ten or fifteen Time Bubbles next to each other you would see the timeline move along its own path, but each change could be traced back to a specific point of divergence along the path that created each change. Something in the past moved the timeline on this adjacent bubble by 220 days. That actually is a tiny change?"

Thomas Black, who reminded me of Kevin Hart with his short stature and slight attitude, was brought onto the team because of his years of illegal work hacking government programs which have given him knowledge of various computer systems. "I may look small, but my computer skills are big," is one of his catchphrases.

Thomas stood up and said, "The adjacent bubble theory using the cinematic frame-by-frame analogy might just work. However, how would you be able to see anything other than the adjacent bubble if they are all chained together like DNA? If your theory is correct, then we will only ever have an encounter with two adjacent bubbles in the chain. That would mean that the other bubble could well be the one that Dr. Mershon experienced. Using that knowledge, we would be able to detect a variation following his arrival in the past."

Horace responded, "That would be one possible solution but I think that if we focus more on the present instead of the past it might be simpler to detect the variations. The only problem is if the AI programming can find a variation on both timelines in the present since it currently looks at the entire timeline at once scanning for minute details."

Hilda chimed in with a new idea, "Why don't we look at this from a reverse engineering method? We want the system to find a variation between two adjacent Time Bubbles, but we can't search both of them simultaneously. Why don't we reverse the data flow between the two software systems? The Virtual Probe can locate a current large-magnitude event in our bubble and send the location information to your software. That way the computer can scan just a specific area and time. Now that I say that it really sounds simple."

Horace said, "It doesn't sound anywhere near simple to me. From my standpoint, we would need to find an event in the present that has a major energy release. Send that information to my simulation so it can locate it in our reality. Then we would have to hope that somewhere along the timeline in the adjacent bubble they are doing the exact same thing at some unknown time. Then somehow my computer simulation would have to evaluate all those events going on in both bubbles and calculate the difference on the timeline scale between the two of them. Did I miss anything? Maybe you would like us to create world peace or put on a man on Neptune while we are at it."

As Horace stood there ranting away, Dr. Mershon slipped into the laboratory to check on the progress of his team. He listened in silence as the tension in Horace's voice echoed around the room. Deep in his mind, Dr. Mershon wondered if he was pushing his team too hard. Was his passion for the project driving them over the edge?

Finally, Horace's rant came to the end and Dr. Mershon decided to speak up on the matter, "Horace, those are some extremely interesting points that you have brought before the team this afternoon. While your theories seem valid you might want to lay off the energy drinks a little, they seem to be making you edgy."

Horace replied, "I am sorry Hilda, but I think that much of a change in direction would be too much right now. You are so right Dr. Mershon. Team, I think we have been pushing ourselves pretty hard in the last few months. Why don't we call it a day and we can move forward later in the week? After we work on the problems in our separate teams for a while, we can get together for some more brainstorming next week."

# EXPLORER

O ver the next week, Hilda and Horace pushed their teams hard because they were driven to complete the next phase of advancement on the project. Hours and days of coding the new software and brainstorming ways to improve upon them with each test run were beginning to pay off. The easiest change they had made all week was giving the simulation system an acronym of RealSim, which stands for Reality Simulation since all research projects can't survive without an annoying Acronym. Scientists say that they make it easier to hold conversations if they use acronyms, but in reality, they just want to sound cool when they're talking.

The additional software that the team had created was named Explorer. I know it is not very original but scientists don't have the greatest imagination when it comes to naming things, hence all the acronyms. Explorer is a multilayer AI program that works in conjunction with RealSim and Look Back. As Horace had described its goal is to go to the place in time and space where RealSim finds the 'Hot Spot', grab information from the Look Back program as to what it is connected to. Now that they know they can see the junction of the bubbles, then use that data as a target to transport HOME BASE. Once HOME BASE is positioned at the junction. It will launch the Drones and effectively take the RealSim and the Virtual Probe with it into the other bubble.

They all think about these AI programs as physical things so they can grasp the concepts. Actually, we are talking about four major AI systems running on a massive supercomputer in the Cloud. Almost a computer's dream or is it a nightmare?

The Virtual Probe was going to be placed in some kind of digital reality representation that it would have no data about. It would have to become a detective and an information sponge to understand where and when it was. The assumption that the two bubbles are so similar may not hold up. This analysis will be done by the combination of the powerful AI programming and the information Drones placed in orbit in the attached bubble.

If the theory that it will be a very similar reality to ours is true, then the Virtual Probe will be very successful in gathering information from the Drones and their Internet if they have one then feeding it to RealSim. If the other reality Bubble, is more like the other side of Mars or the planet Purple Emptor from some other galaxy, it would not find much of anything that it could define and make useful.

That analysis by the systems will then be used to determine if AMBROSE should be sent in.

It took the whole development team about two months to code all this. Once that was done, they were very close to trying to do it physically by sending in AMBROSE.

Two months passed too quickly but this high-power scientific team did their amazing magic and now they had the entire technical part of the company in the Time Portal room to observe and brainstorm as this test was conducted.

Dr. Mershon stood up and got everyone's attention. "Team, I want to thank you all for dragging this project along so quickly. This test will be a major step forward. Let me summarize what Hilda, Horace, and I have planned. We are going to launch RealSim and let it search for a Hot Spot. Horace's team has given it a temporary rule that will make it keep only the latest incident it finds. It will most likely run for some time to do this search and filtering. We are guessing for ten minutes. To a massive supercomputer that is an eternity.

The RealSim will then pass the information to the Virtual Probe which will display the details of space/time location and any visuals possible in the Time Portal. The Look Back system will try to look to identify if there is an attached Time Bubble. Then the new Explorer system will control the attempt to 'look' into the other Bubble and establish coordinates for the Transporter to send HOME BASE. Once those coordinates are obtained, HOME BASE will be transported there. It will then launch five Drones to orbit above it in the other bubble. That will effectively bring in RealSim and the Virtual Probe to research that reality. We really have no idea how long that will all take.

If like our theory, it is the same as our Bubble on a different timeline, the response should be fast. If as Horace put it in a meeting, it is the planet Purple Emptor from some other galaxy. Then we may not get any usable information. Now let me turn the meeting over to the Ringmaster Horace... Sorry, Horace just trying to lighten it up. Take it away!".

"Alright, everyone ready?" The teams all signaled thumbs-up. Horace typed on the keyboard and RealSim started up. This search was a slower process. The main screen was scrolling location coordinates. Each one is being eliminated by a more recent time indication.

Suddenly it stopped displaying the coordinates as 44° 38' 8" North, 70° 45' 6" West. The Virtual Probe took that information and then displayed

Reference Resolved:

Jan 14, 2037, Time 11:04
Launch of the Vector Martian
Andover, Maine
Large heat excitation.

The Time Portal came alive and displayed this reference picture:

The text display explained the Vector Martian is a much large version of a Space Shuttle vehicle. It was created by a private company named Vector Sciences. Owned by the very wealthy Michael Exeter. Vector is a very large and scientifically progressive company working on things from improving our autonomous vehicles, to new house robots, and much more topped by the Vector Martian. As the name implies it was launched today heading for Mars. It is lifted into space and pushed on its way by a vehicle called the SLT (Space Launch Tug). The SLT uses 15 Scram Rocket Jet engines to take off from a runway with the Vector Martian on its back. It accelerates to Mach 7 and climbs out into space. The propulsion then switches to a Scram Rocket pushing the vehicle into space and accelerating to Mach 15 and throwing the Vector Martian on its way to Mars. Then the SLT returns and lands autonomously.

The point here is that all of that caused a very large field of atoms excited by heat and motion through the atmosphere. That is what the RealSim detected to bring it here.

Then the simulation screen displayed, "Look Back detects a similar energy field with almost matching atomic energy levels. Based on energy levels that region seems to be at a synchronized time. No more data available."

Then the AI system took over running the operation. The transaction messages were displayed, "

- Explorer activated and in control!
- Time Bubble Outer Boundary located
- Adjacent Bubble Outer Boundary located
- Boundary interior space modeled
- Proceed to transport HOME BASE?

Horace confirmed the request.

- Explorer continued
- HOME BASE Transported (as the blue flash made it disappear into the Time Portal)
- HOME BASE communication checks good.

Thomas Trimble & TJ Trimble

Confirm HOME BASE is ready to launch?

Again, Horace responded.

- HOME BASE Launch Drones
- Drones 1 – 5 launched
- Virtual Probe Activated, gathering data.
- Internet Wi-Fi type network accessed
- *(About ten minutes passed)*
- RealSim Activated
- Simulation indicates a very close match in reality
- Time is synchronized

Then the report was:

Coordinates at 44° 38' 8" North, 70° 45' 6" West. The Virtual Probe took that information and then based on the other bubble's network data displayed this message on the control console:

Reference Resolved:

> *Jan 14, 2037, Time 11:08*
> *Launch of the General Science Saturn Explorer*
> *Andover, Maine*
> *Large heat excitation.*

Hilda spoke up, "What does that mean? As far as our software can simulate the point in the Bubble overlapping ours is a very, very similar reality. Time is in synchronization. Obviously, from the data, there are some small differences showing. The name and goal of the ship are different. The launch place is the same and the atomic level excitation is the same.".

Then shocking everyone the same picture of the vehicle was displayed in the Time Portal. Hilda did some typing on her keyboard and the same picture came up again. She explained, "Because we are looking at an almost identical reality, the Virtual Probe was able to connect to their version of the Internet. It found this image of the General Science Saturn Explorer. The same design by a different company is in a different reality. I would say that the change from the POD (point of diversion) is tiny at this point in time. Other things may be greatly different. Even this huge supercomputer will take weeks to compare those differences. There may well be millions of those differences. However, this particular point is in very close synchronization with us. Does this say something about flexibility in the timeline?"

Doctor Mershon spoke up, "As I have told you I cannot discuss my experience in time travel. However, I think I can totally agree with Hilda and this even sounds like it might be the reality I left behind. Hilda, can we have the Virtual Probe focus on researching a specific time period in that reality?".

"Yes, I believe we can, what are you interested in?".

"How about the history of Bikini Atoll?"

"Alright, let me see if I can do that."

After gliding over the keys on her keyboard, the display was:

> "Requested History: Bikini Atoll
>
> Bikini Atoll is a coral reef in the Marshall Islands consisting of 23 islands surrounding a 229.4-square-mile central lagoon. It was used for nuclear weapons testing before and during World War II. The Bikini Atoll program was a series of **23 nuclear devices** detonated by the United States between 1946 and 1958 at seven test sites."

"Thanks, Hilda, that's enough. For fear of saying too much. That does sound like it may be the reality I am actually from!"

The whole group kind of gasped and started a lot of chatter on hearing that revealing statement. They all knew better than to ask any more questions of the Doctor.

Doctor Mershon got a bit choked up and forced out, "These are amazing results. We need to get as much history from there as possible and we need to get prepared to send in AMBROSE. Sorry I have to leave!"

Everyone just sat there in shock. There was a hum of chatter around the whole room. Horace just sat there for a few minutes, not really knowing what they should do. Then he composed himself and said:

"Ladies and gentlemen, I don't know what to make of that any more than any of you do. The Doctor has experienced something that we are all just dealing with, in our minds. We have no physical reference. However, this was a very successful test. Great teams make things seem simple. I know how much it is really the opposite.

Hilda let's, leave everything processing as long as it all stays linked together. We have no idea how long these junctions last. Grab all the history you can so we can compare. The system will return HOME BASE automatically.

In the meantime, the Doctor is right, we need to move to send AMBROSE in as quickly as possible. Steven, it is mainly on your back. Just ask for any help you need. Let's do a progress demo in a month. Thanks, everyone."

# STEVEN'S LAB

Down on the first floor in Steven's Lab, he is sitting at his workbench with AMBROSE the Martian exploration robot close by. Steven and his team have rewritten about 80% of the AI rules that control AMBROSE. He is now far better at navigating a Time Bubble. Based partly on the general assumption that the next Bubble is very similar to ours physically. AMBROSE can navigate roads, curbs, sidewalks, stairs, doors, elevators, escalators, and he can kind of fake the rest from camera and sensor input and his AI processing. Three mechanical arms, two tracks, and a very high level of hydraulic strength make it work.

One of the most recent additions is something like the ancient fairy tale Emperor, we have AMBROSE's new clothes. Paul Swartz one of Steven's team coders is a recently hired,

Hologram expert. He has added a series of Hologram generators to AMBROSE. He has programmed its controller with a library of clothing information since the early 1200s. The Virtual Probe will be able to pass AMBROSE a specific time frame and part of the world. The Hologram controller will create a complete set of clothes and project them around AMBROSE's body and allow him to blend into any environment which is similar to our world. It also adds facial features like hair, beards, eyes, skin tone, and many other very convincing items.

One day about a week ago, Steven was running a full-dress test on AMBROSE. He was using his favorite look a 2035 computer geek type. He was standing next to Steven's work table in his MTRL blue coverall and Dr. Mershon walked in. Now admittedly he was a bit preoccupied with some questions for Steven, but he looked up from the papers he was carrying and then said totally seriously, "Steven who is this, I don't think we have met?"

Steven could hardly keep from cracking up laughing, but he managed to say with a straight face, "Yes you have met him, his name is AMBROSE.".

Dr. Mershon was totally shocked. He said, "Damn Steven that is good. Looking really close I can tell, but from two feet it looked absolutely real". As he stuck out his hand to disrupt the Hologram to be sure. "Damn Good!"

"Thank you, Doctor, I think it will do for our needs quite well."

"I agree, good job."

The next day, Steven was running some tests with a program generating random locations and time frames, so he could check how well AMBROSE responded. The computer screen showed Location: Lancaster, PA; Time: April 1963; Gender: Male; Age: 14. The outfit suddenly changed to a 14-year-old boy who was dressed as an Amish young man with a wide black hat, billowed shirt, pants with suspenders, and black shoes. Perfect selection.

In about two months, Steven was ready to give this all a try. Hilda's team had built all the required interfaces between the Virtual Probe, the HOME BASE, the Transporter, and AMBROSE himself. Horace's team had tuned in the RealSim to keep improving the accuracy and the algorithms to screen what it decides to focus on. They decided to call a meeting just to be sure.

The next day in the conference room the entire staff was ready. Dr. Mershon started off the meeting:

"Ladies and Gentlemen, we are meeting today to do a final walkthrough of the plan to find a connected Time Bubble link to it and insert AMBROSE into it, collect all the data possible then bring him back and close the connection. Sounds simple, doesn't it?"

That gathered a round of applause and cheers. Everyone knew that it was far from simple. In fact, it was one of the most complex Quantum experiments ever attempted. This team at MTRL had now grown to 125 of the smartest scientists in the world. They were about to attempt the achievement that Dr. Mershon had challenged them to do. Heck, it was only September 1, 2037. They were running early if it works? Extremely good teams like this are never willing to plan on failure. They plan how to deal with possible problems, but they totally believed everything will work as planned. Previous tests had given them no reason to doubt that.

Dr. Mershon went on, "Hilda before we go on could you give us a report of the historic analysis from the adjacent Bubble?"

"Yes sir. As you know we had the supercomputer working on this for over a month. For those not into computers. A month for a gigantic AI supercomputer like this is like a lifetime. Generally, we had it comparing the timeline from our Bubble with the timeline in the adjacent Bubble. We started to see at least one POD (Point of Divergence) in 1942 at or near the battle of Guadalcanal in the Pacific. In our Bubble, that was a relatively insignificant battle. However, there are records of a Japanese fleet being destroyed by a totally unidentified warship. Most likely a submarine of some type. It was never sighted and eight Japanese warships were mysteriously destroyed.

In the timeline, from the adjacent Bubble, there was a major battle near Guadalcanal. A location called Savo Island. That battle was given the nickname the **Battle of Five Sitting Ducks**. It was given that name because of the loss of five Allied warships in the very rapid Japanese attack.

As I mentioned, we found that to be at least one POD. From that point on the histories are different. Maybe not all major differences but different. In both timelines, World War II against the Japanese was ended by the use of the nuclear bombs on Hiroshima and Nagasaki. It ended a year later in our timeline. That mysterious battle in the other Bubble caused the Battle of Guadalcanal to be a swift Allied victory. The Japanese surrender was signed by the Japanese on a Heavy Cruiser named USS Quincy. Our flow had the war lasting a year longer with a similar ending on the battleship, USS Missouri. There are thousands of other changes. Many people seem to be different in their histories, some people are in one or the other, not both timelines. Some died earlier and some later as impacted by the timeline changes.

Dr. Mershon, suddenly got choked up. He stood and said, "Excuse me for a few minutes and he left the room.". Everyone just kind of stared at each other. No one knew the internal secrets that were attacking the Doctor. To help cover up, Horace stood and said, "I think we should take a thirty-minute break. Thanks, Hilda.".

# THE WALKTHROUGH

Horace walked out to see if he could help Dr. Mershon. "Doctor, are you, all right?"

"Yes, Horace. That just got to me. I really wish I could explain, but you know that what happened to me is Top Secret. All I can say is that the research hit it right on the head. As far as I know, it is totally accurate. I will be back in there in a minute, just need some water."

Horace went back to the conference room. In a few minutes, the Doctor followed. He walked over to Hilda and asked to talk to her privately.

"Hilda, I want you to do a search for me, keep it very private. I need you to research four things; I want to know in both histories what you can find about Navy Admiral Henry S.

Anderson, Jr? What you can find about the submarine USS Joseph Kane? What you can find about me in the other Bubble?"

"Alright Doctor, I will check right after the meeting."

"Thanks, let's get to it."

The Doctor walked back to the podium and started off the meeting.

"People, let's get on with the subject of the day. I want to walk through the test we are going to do. I want everyone to feel free to jump in with any status or information that applies. Alright here are the steps I see happening:

1. Horace will start by activating the RealSim. It will search for a Hot Spot. His Look Back will determine if there is another Bubble in contact with ours.

2. Hilda's Virtual Probe will investigate and report the details it can find.

3. If another Bubble is in contact, the Explorer will take control and start by locating the edges of that Bubble.

4. Those coordinates will be used by the Transporter to send HOME BASE into the junction through the Time Portal.

5. Steven will then allow Explorer to activate HOME BASE and we will verify communication with it.

6. HOME BASE will launch 15 Drones into the other reality.

7. That will effectively take the RealSim and Virtual Probe into that Bubble and create a simulation.

8. RealSim will determine the location in the Bubble and share it with the Virtual Probe.

9. After we get the report on what time and where they are in the other Bubble, we will decide if we should continue. There may be dangers and we don't want to risk AMBROSE or HOME BASE.

10. If we vote to go ahead, AMBROSE will be prepared for blending into the environment.

11. After we review the findings, we will again vote on a Go to send AMBROSE in.

12. If yes, the Transporter will send him into that reality. It will be using the HOME BASE for the base location coordinates to calculate where to send him.

13. Steven's team will do a system and communication check with AMBROSE.

14. If it is a Go, then AMBROSE will be free to move into the bubble and explore and report.

15. We will observe. Allowing him to go as far as we feel safe. This is the first trip anything that does not look right we should send him immediately back to HOME BASE for recall.

16. Recall is just the reverse of the procedure.

17. AMBROSE moves close to HOME BASE in the junction area to be transported back.

18. The HOME BASE is then transported back.

19. The data from HOME BASE will be uploaded to the cloud and the computer will be allowed to process all the historical data it can locate.

All right does anyone have any problems with that plan? Steven spoke up, "No problems with the plan, just wish I knew there were no problems with the functioning of everything."

"Steven, I sure wish I had that guarantee too. As you all know, this represents a lot of our investor's money. A good test will go a long way to get us more funding and settle our investors. However, not at the cost of risking any very expensive hardware. Wave the white flag as soon as you think something is wrong so we can try to save it. I think we should take one more day for you all to be sure your pieces are right. Thursday at 8 A.M. we will run the test. Thanks for the great work."

The Doctor turned and left the room.

A couple hours later, Hilda called the Doctor, "Doctor, I have the result on that search you wanted.

<u>In Our Bubble</u>

- Admiral Henry S. Anderson, Jr. was promoted to a five-star Fleet Admiral and retired in 2030.
- The submarine USS Joseph Kane continued to serve in the Navy and was retired from active service in 2034.
- You obviously are here in 2037.

<u>In the Other Bubble</u>

- There was never an Admiral or anyone named Henry S. Anderson, Jr. There was a Henry S. Anderson. He was Captain of a World War II Heavy Cruiser named USS Quincy. It was sunk during the battle at Savo Island near Guadalcanal. He and most of the crew were killed.

- The submarine USS Joseph Kane was reported missing in the Pacific in 2025 and has never been found.

- You were reported to have been on the USS Joseph Kane when it vanished.".

"Thanks, Hilda, the information about the Admiral was what I suspected. Hilda, I wish I could tell you more but it appears that jumping from one bubble to another causes a knife-edge space in the timelines. This causes both timelines to be shifted from their original. As for me, I look pretty good for a man who vanished 12 years ago. Thanks, Hilda," and he hung up the phone. Hilda thought, "I sure wish I understood that. Just part of his secrets.".

The Doctor was thinking that there are some strange combinations of changes that happened. There may have actually been three bubbles involved. The original story of the war at Guadalcanal, the story left behind by the Kane which branched off that one and now has KANE missing, and the bubble where he, Kane, and the crew ended up and are still living. I wonder if the KANE that visited 1942 will ever come back? This certainly is complex!

# THE BIG TEST

Thursday morning came and the whole team was in the Time Portal room, making final preparations. At about, 7:50 A.M. the Doctor walked into the room. He walked quietly over to a row of chairs beside the control console. This was for all the people who were observing but not controlling any of the tests. As he walked over, a young man in a blue MTRL jumpsuit was moving by, and the Doctor kind of snapped out of his daze and said, "Oh excuse me.".

Then a very good voice simulation said, "Oh, excuse me, Doctor Mershon. Go ahead.".

The Doctor obviously had his thoughts somewhere else. Steven cracked up in laughter and yelled over, "Doctor, I got you again!".

The doctor kind of came out of the fog and he said, "Damn, that's AMBROSE, isn't it?".

Steven yelled over again, "That's two for AMBROSE!".

The whole crew broke out in a laugh.

The Doctor said laughingly, "Ok, that's enough out of all of you. Horace, get this show started!".

The Doctor thought about telling the team about what Hilda's research had found, but he decided to wait until this test was completed because it has no impact here. He did believe it redefined the POD and what it meant and the possibility of connections with three bubbles at once. But that can wait.

At the console, there was Horace, Hilda, Steven, and a couple of people from their teams. They were all in their groups kind of bunched around each terminal position. Their terminals were displayed on the three very large LCD screens on the wall surrounding the Time Portal. The Time Portal was kind of glowing a brighter blue than normal. It looked like looking into a wavy ocean on a sunny day.

Now that so many people were involved, there was a PA system at the console, so into the microphone, Horace said, "Are we Go for this test? Hilda?"

Hilda responded, "GO!"

"Steven?"

"GO!"

"All of my systems are ready too. Here we go!"

Horace typed on his keyboard and one of the display screens showed the RealSim searching for Hot Spots. Horace had provided some control rules to prevent the selection of extremely dangerous areas, so it took some searching. The display screen was scrolling location coordinates. Each one is eliminated by the new control rules.

Suddenly it stopped displaying the coordinates as 4°14'12.4"S  152°09'05.7"E.

The Virtual Probe took that information and then displayed it.

*Rabaul, New Guinea*
*Japanese Naval Base*

*Time Location: August 10, 1942, 02:05*

The Doctor who was watching very closely yelled out, "No, reject that selection!".

No one knew why but Horace typed a command and the search started again.

The next search stopped with 51°14'46.7"N 5°32'35.5"E.

The Virtual probe said:

*Hamont Station, Belgium,*
*Train Explosion*
*August 3, 1918*

# TIME BUBBLES

> *"The disaster of August 3, 1918, in Hamont in Belgium was caused by an ammunition explosion which was very common at that time. The ammunition was triggered inside the trains carrying them, setting off a huge fire and destruction."*

Then the Virtual Probe displayed this historic photo in the Time Portal.

Horace spoke up, "Alright, we have a location in our Bubble. Look Back has reported that there is a linkage with another Bubble.

The Doctor said, "Horace, please pause the operation."

Horace typed on his keyboard and everything stopped.

The Doctor said, "Help me understand this. These indications are saying that there is a Time Bubble in a junction with ours and in their reality, everything is exactly the same in terms of Time and Location as your 'Hot Spot'? Is that true?"

Hilda said, "Doctor, I believe so.".

"Hilda, with this being back in 1918, do you believe it is possible that the two realities have not had a POD to make their timelines separate?".

"Doctor, I think that is as good an explanation as any, at this point."

"Horace, I thought you had rules to prevent selecting a dangerous situation. I feel an exploding train is pretty dangerous."

"Doctor, I must agree. However, AI software makes value judgments. I had not set any specific parameters to define the term dangerous. Remember, it finds things like Hiroshima when the bomb went off. So, I guess in comparison, this is calm."

"Horace, how can we handle it? I would like AMBROSE to cross over, but can we protect him?"

"Doctor, what we could do is change the coordinates in the other Bubble. That way we can have AMBROSE enter a quarter-mile away from the explosion."

"Ok Horace, remember that robot is now worth a few million dollars."

"Ok, Doctor he will be safe."

Steven spoke up, "Sounds alright with me. Look he is ready.".

AMBROSE was dressed in a very stylish black suit, an above-the-knee-length topcoat, and a Fedora hat. Just like a tourist catching a train in Belgium circa. 1918.

The Doctor spoke up, "Horace, you are the lead, are we ready?"

"I think so, Doctor. Let's Go!"

Horace attacked his keyboard as did Steven. The Time Portal got very bright as the power was increased. Two of Horace's team directed the HOME BASE, about the size of a four-drawer file cabinet, and steered it on its track drive up next to the Portal. The main display said, "HOME BASE Initial Communication check complete.".

Steven said, "Horace, HOME BASE is ready."

Steven then asked, "AMBROSE are you ready?"

He responded with a computer-generated Dutch accent, "I am a ready Steven.".

"AMBROSE, move into position at the Time Portal.". So, AMBROSE rolled over in front of the Portal, next to HOME BASE.

Horace announced, "I am going to run the Explorer to see if we can get coordinates for the Transporter. Explorer took the lead in the simulated trip into the other Bubble.

The Explorer reported:

- Explorer activated
- Bubble outer edge detected
- Adjacent Bubble edge detected
- Coordinates resolved.
- Junction has been modeled
- Permission to activate Transporter?

Horace quickly asked, "Everyone alright to go?". They all signaled yes. So, Horace responded to the Explorer to go ahead.

# TIME BUBBLES

The Explorer said:

- Coordinates passed to Transporter
- Transport commencing
- HOME BASE disappeared in the blue light into the Time Portal.
- Explorer reported. HOME BASE Transported.
- HOME BASE: Communication check is good.

Steven's team said transport was successful, and communication with HOME BASE is excellent.

Horace typed a few commands.

The Explorer reported:

- HOME BASE, ready to launch Drones.
- Drones 1–5 launched and reporting properly.
- Drones 6–10 launched and reporting properly
- Drones 11–15 launched. Drone 13 is not reporting.
- Permission to continue?

Steven told Horace, "Let's just go without it."

Horace answered Explorer's question on the keyboard.

Explorer reported:

- Operation continues.
- Coordinates calculated based on the location of HOME BASE.
- Ready to Transport AMBROSE?

Then Horace asked Steven, "Is AMBROSE Ready?"

Steven replied, "AMBROSE is good to proceed with Transport."

Horace typed a couple commands and AMBROSE vanished into the Time Portal as Explorer reported:

- AMBROSE transport successful
- Communication check with AMBROSE successful.
- Permission to proceed?

Steven yelled out, "We are good, go ahead!".

A few commands on Horace's keyboard and Explorer reported:

- AMBROSE authorized to continue exploration.

Utilizing the coordinates of HOME BASE, AMBROSE was transported directly into the other bubble allowing for the change in parameters to take him a quarter-mile away. Suddenly three big-screen monitors showed the pictures from the primary cameras on AMBROSE.

Steven explained, "It appears that there is a problem with the camera transmission. The cameras are not able to transmit live streaming video. However, it is being recorded in HOME BASE. The cameras defaulted to a mode where they send a frame every 900 frames of video as a still picture. That is about a minute apart".

On the second big monitor, the messages were displayed:

Explorer: Initial simulation complete. The attached Bubble has been accessed.

RealSim: The location is 51°14'46.7"N 5°32'35.1"E.

Horace said, "That matches our current position allowing for the quarter-mile we added."

On the second screen the Virtual Probe showed the same historic summary:

> *Hamont Station, Belgium,*
> *Train Explosion*
> *August 3, 1918*
>
> *"The disaster of August 3, 1918, in Hamont in Belgium was caused by an ammunition explosion which was very common at that time. The ammunition was triggered inside the trains carrying them, setting off a huge fire and destruction."*

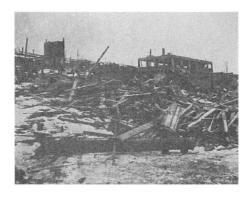

Then from his long-range camera, AMBROSE sent this still picture to the Time Portal. But in a second, the explosion occurred just as a train pulled in. AMBROSE sent another still image which was very similar to the one the Virtual Probe

had displayed. That is curious how it got in the Probes archive before this mission when it was actually AMBROSE's picture? Time is a very complex and mysterious thing. However, the team had accomplished an amazing task. They sent a robotic probe into another Time Bubble and witnessed a historic event. Now the critical part. Bringing him back.

Horace began typing and the big display said, "AMBROSE, recall order received." AMBROSE had not gone very far so he turned around and went back near HOME BASE which was still in the junction. The message displayed:

"AMBROSE, at HOME BASE."

Horace activated Explorer again:

- AMBROSE in position to transport
- Confirm Transport order?

Horace responded.

- Transport initiated
- AMBROSE returned.

In a second AMBROSE was standing just inside the Time Portal and he rolled away over to Steven. Then he said with a mechanical chuckle, "I am back.". Everyone started to cheer.

The Doctor yelled, "Calm down we are not done!"

Steven reactivated Explorer:

- Starting HOME BASE return sequence
- HOME BASE moving into position

- HOME BASE in position
- Confirm Transport Order?

Horace again responded.

- Transport initiated
- HOME BASE returned.

In a flash, HOME BASE was back just inside the Time Portal. Steven's team went over to check and reported, that everything was fine. The Doctor said loudly, "Now you can cheer. Horace shut it all down.".

# THE NEXT STEPS

The Doctor had ordered some adult refreshments and snacks in hopes of this successful trial. The whole team took the rest of the day off to celebrate and relax from the tension of making this all work. Many of them were chatting about what might be next for AMBROSE. They also wanted to look into the other Bubble after the POD when the timelines shifted.

The next morning the Doctor called an All Hands meeting in the conference room. He greeted and congratulated everyone, then he kicked off the meeting.

"Team that was great. You met my prime directive. However, it was not at all what many of us expected. The fact that the other Bubble was in Time and Location synchronization with ours is not something we expected. Are there any theories about that?"

Hilda spoke first, "Doctor, I believe that as we mentioned it might be because that Time Bubble was spawned off ours or ours off it. The result is they are the same but running on their own timeline. Until we reach a Point of Diversion, the timelines and evolution of the reality could be the same. As a status update, my systems are all fine and ready to go ahead.".

Horace spoke up, "I totally agree with that theory.".

Then the Doctor said, "I believe that is a solid theory. Even to some degree confirmed by my experience. That seemed to indicate that the main flow of reality stayed the same. What was changed by the POD was the many timelines that makeup reality. So, like my experience, if we look further along the timeline than the POD, we may see the same basic reality with historical differences in people, places, dates, and physical things. I had Hilda do a little private research, which confirmed that too. I also believe that there are far more Time Bubbles than we initially believed. Not like Horace's two bubble picture, I think there may be many more.".

"Steven, is AMBROSE alright after his trip?"

"Yes Doctor, I think we fixed the video problem. The video was fine the communication broke down it was too much of a load on the HOME BASE. We have added more processors and memory to both AMBROSE and HOME BASE to at least capture it all. We may still have to be satisfied with real-time still pictures, and video after it all gets home. We will see when we try it again. We downloaded the video and other than a spectacular picture of the actual explosion, AMBROSE was not there long enough to explore. He is ready to go again."

Steven put one very dramatic still picture on the big screen. That generated kind of a team WOW and gasp.

Steven said, "That major explosion was rated as one of the twenty worst explosions in history, killing over 1500 people.".

"Horace, how is all the rest of the system?".

"Doctor, a few minor bugs we have corrected but generally everything went as planned. I am ready to go again.".

"Thanks, people. Now I think we need to have a serious discussion about this technology.".

The doctor displayed this list on the big screen. "I have these questions, not in any specific order:

1.  What can this be used for?
2.  Should we keep repeating these trips?
3.  Can we find intersections with the other Bubble which are not caused by High Energy sources?
4.  Should we even think about sending AMBROSE to change something in the other Bubble?
5.  Could we hold AMBROSE in the other Bubble and then bring him back to a different Time/Location in our Bubble from where he left?
6.  Can we control with extreme accuracy where he would go in our Bubble's timeline? For example, if we sent him into our Bubble at Dallas on November 22, 1963, at 12:30 P.M. he would witness President John F. Kennedy being shot.

Could we then bring him back, reset the time and return him on the same, date and location, but one hour earlier? Do we have that accuracy?"

Horace spoke first, "Well on your question about what this can be used for. I think investigation or changing time are really the only two things. In the example you just used. He could be sent to investigate details in the last hour before the shooting. But then what good is that if you don't change anything? Bringing evidence back to our time would not mean much, another conspiracy theory or updating some history books. He could investigate and leave new evidence that would change the timeline anyway. He could take physical action to change time by let's say taking out, the killer. What was his name, Oswald right? Now that would certainly change the timeline and thousands of things from there on.".

"Horace, you are right. We are no closer to knowing what that would do. I never really believed in the wave time paradox theories. But what if I am wrong? A person standing beside you could vanish."

Hilda said, "We really have no facts to go on about that Paradox concept. Doctor, nothing you experienced gave you any incite about that?"

"No Hilda, we caused a change and then left that Bubble with no idea of what we may have caused. Oh sorry, forget I said that."

Then Hilda said, "As for if we should keep doing this, I think at least a couple more passive trips. Work on the time controls and then experiment with the idea of holding AMBROSE in the other Bubble and then bringing him back to a different time. I recommend the first couple tries of that with some basic little camera Drone, not AMBROSE till we are sure.".

Steven said, "I have a little Drone I used for testing, it has the communication of HOME BASE and is self-mobile, just far less memory and processing power. We could try to hold it in the Junction of the Bubbles, open another portal and then send it there. If it got lost, well that's science."

Horace said, "As for number 3, I have been able to send RealSim to a specific place by location and time or just let it find areas where there is or was a junction. I have been looking closely at the data. When RealSim is running without specific rules. It finds thousands of those locations. Remember it is three-dimensional. Each location has an earth location or GPS coordinates an x and y, and then a z depth to find the particular time. The search finds a place where today nothing is happening. Then it digs down through time and might find something in any other year. I believe the RealSim can now find that spot, no Hot Spot required.

"Ok team, let's prepare for a test the day after tomorrow. We will pick a spot in history, Steven's call. We will Transport the Drone there and have it wait at the junction. Then we will find another spot in time and send it back toward our Bubble. That is just enough to see if we have that control in location and evaluate the power of the Transporter. The result should be the Drone moving from our current place and time to another place and time in our own Bubble. Using another Bubble as the media. Then see if we can reverse it. Does that sound workable?"

Horace looked around the room and saw approval. He said, "Doctor, we are good with that. The day after tomorrow, Friday."

◆ ◆ ◆

All the scientists worked on their own individual parts of the plan. Friday came and at 8 A.M. everyone met in the time laboratory. The lead people were all at their control stations in front of the Time Portal.

Steven's little Drone was sitting in front of the portal. It was a cute little thing. About three feet tall. It had two drive tracks, two cameras mounted on swivels on the front, and one on the rear. It had a couple antennas for communication and two lights on the front that looked like eyes and one light in the rear, that looked like. Well, forget it. It was painted bright yellow to be easily seen.

Horace announced, "Everyone a go for this?". He looked around the room and got approval from everyone. Alright, the Doctor said the destination is Steven's call. What will it be Steven?".

"I am going to pick something I always wanted to see. I remember reading about this in a history class. The first controlled, sustained flight of a powered, heavier-than-air aircraft. Flown with the Wright Flyer. At 10:35 A.M. on December 17, 1903, Orville Wright flew the Flyer for 12 seconds over 120 feet of the ground. This flight was conducted on Kill Devil Hill just outside of Kitty Hawk, North Carolina. So that is what I choose.".

Horace said, "Does sound interesting. Being outside and some distance away, the Drone should not be visible to anyone. We need to set the time for about 9:30 A.M. That way everything will be completed before the flight. I was just pulling up a map of that area and found a location near the flight but out of the way. So, target coordinates are 36° 3' 52.597" N 75° 42' 20.645" W, the day December 17, 1903, the time 9:30 A.M. local time.".

Hilda said, "The Virtual Probe has recorded that as the ultimate destination. First, we need to send the Drone to the next Bubble and then come back to Kitty Hawk."

Horace said, "Ok, start the search."

The big-screen displays started to show, locations, and times as they examined possible locations. It really does not matter where it is as long as it is a junction to the other Bubble. So, the search stopped.

Hilda said, "It can be any location for this test, but it happens to be the Three Mile Island Nuclear Power plant. Another junction from nuclear energy run wild.".

Horace said, "We are only going into the junction.". Then he started Explorer:

- Explorer activated
- Coordinates received
- Bubble Wall located
- Bubble junction modeled
- Transporter programmed and ready
- Drone communication checks excellent
- Confirm Transport?

Horace asked, "Steven is the Drone ready?".

"Horace it is good, let's go."

Horace typed on the keyboard and told Explorer to proceed.

- Transport Approved
- Drone Transported

The Drone vanished into the Time Portal to the coordinates of the Junction.

Just my observation, it is interesting that it makes no sound at all, except a hum from the power equipment. The item is just disassembled by the Transporter and sent off on the journey.

Hilda said, "Virtual Probe is reporting that the Drone is located in the Junction between Bubbles.".

Horace started typing again.

- Explorer Activated
- New Coordinates received
- Transporter programmed and ready
- Drone communication checks excellent
- Confirm Transport?

Horace gave approval.

- Transport Approved
- Drone Transported

The Drone was transported back to a specific location in our bubble. The Drone could then communicate using the RTSS system.

- Drone telemetry and communication excellent
- Drone coordinates verified

The big screen displayed, Virtual Probe Reports:

*Kill Devil Hill*

*Kitty Hawk, North Carolina*

*First sustained powered flight.*

*December 17, 1903, Orville Wright pilot*

*"The first controlled, sustained flight of a powered, heavier-than-air aircraft. Flown with the Wright Flyer. At 10:35 a.m. on December 17, 1903, Orville Wright flew*  *the Flyer for 12 seconds over 120 feet of the ground."*

Horace read the screen and made the comment, "It is interesting that the Virtual Probe can match up the incident even though the Drone has arrived an hour before it happened. I am not going to try to explain that right now.".

The Drone rolled about 5 feet into the historic location in our Time Bubble. The video cameras on the Drone were not able to transmit streaming video, but it was sending still shots about every 600 frames of the video as it was recorded from the three cameras and streaming audio from its directional microphone. The Time Portal showed the Wright Flyer sitting on the launch track. The audio from the drone was connected to the PA system so all could hear. The portal showed several men walking around checking various parts. This went on for about 5 minutes. Then the man whom they suspected to be Orville Wright said something to them and they all shook his hand and he climbed into the Flyer. He lay in the middle of the bottom wing of the bi-plane configuration.

In a few minutes, the man they thought to be Wilbur and another helper, grabbed the pusher propellers and gave them a healthy pull downward. They could hear on the audio track the engine sputtered but didn't start. The next pull did it and the engine fired up. There was a man at each end of the lower wing and one in the center holding the Flyer from taking off. Orville revved up the engine a couple of times to make sure it was running right. Then he waved the signal to go. The engine sped up to full speed and the three men started to push the Flyer into history.

About 25 feet later, it lifted off the track and began to fly on its own. The flight was sustained for 120 feet and history was made. The flyer returned to earth safely.

Steven said, "That was great, I can't wait to watch the videos. They would be very educational for a history class. Alright, let's bring the Drone back. He turned it around and it rolled the five feet back to the Junction.".

Horace reset the RealSim to find their own location in time and space. Now still connected to the other Bubble and the Drone.

After it reported the proper time and coordinates, Horace activated the Transporter and the Drone popped in through the Time Portal. It came by way of the other bubble acting as a media.

It was a bit more complex, but the Drone had just traveled from our time and location in 2037 back to 1903 and returned.

Doctor Mershon who had been intently watching the whole process while leaving it to the experts, now jumped up and applauded the team. He yelled, "Congratulations to All. This has now graduated from exploring Time Bubble theory to Time Travel. Now it is getting to be fun.".

Steven said, "Wow, that was great. We are good!

Hilda said, "Steven doesn't get too big a head about this."

Steven then said, "Fans, how about we try one of those with AMBROSE?".

Doctor Mershon interrupted, "Steven, you know how much money that robot has cost us. No taking chances with it."

"Doctor, it works, we are good, I am ready to give it a try."

The doctor explored the feeling of the whole team, "Team leaders are you all in agreement with Steven that we are ready to try a Time Travel with AMBROSE?".

Horace answered, "Yes, I guess I can't see any reason not to try it.".

Hilda said, "I am not sure. Oh well, we are scientists and they experiment with things. Let's go for it."

Steven said, "Well you know I am for it."

The Doctor summed it up, "Well you all feel like we are ready to try that. It scares me a bit, but I guess we give it a try. How about Tuesday, two days from now?".

Everyone appeared to agree so that was their plan. They were not at all sure but based on the history they researched; AMBROSE may be the first object to intentionally travel through time. Second, counting the object, the Doctor traveled in unintentionally.

Tuesday Morning at 8 A.M., the team was all in their places in the Time Portal control room. AMBROSE was standing over to the side in his holographic dark blue MTRL jumpsuit, with his blond hair and blue eyes he was looking very sharp.

The Doctor stood up and started, "Ok Team are we all still good to go ahead with this?".

Everyone signaled they are already to go ahead.

Then the Doctor said, "Hilda, I think you should make the call this time. Where and when is AMBROSE going?".

Hilda was a bit shocked. She was rubbing her hands together trying to focus on a point in history to have as a target. She sat there thinking for a few minutes. Finally, she said, "I think the target should be the General Art and Industrial Exposition of Stockholm in 1897. I think it would be amazing to see what they thought was the future then. Maybe on this trip, we could let AMBROSE explore some?".

The Doctor said, "Well you heard her call. Let's get set up for it.".

Everyone was heads down getting ready. Then Horace said, "Looks like we are ready?".

Everyone confirmed that.

"Ok, here we go then."

Again, the first search of the RealSim was just to find a junction between the Bubbles where HOME BASE could set up and AMBROSE could wait so Horace was letting the search just look for the Bubble. The RealSim when left alone still tends to find high-energy locations. This time it stopped displaying the coordinates, 28.455557° N, -80.52778° E. The Virtual Probe quickly determined what that was and the time. The resulting display was:

> April 11, 1970
> Launch of Apollo 13
> Cape Kennedy LaunchPad
> Saturn V Rocket
> "Apollo 13 was a space mission scheduled to land on the moon until it was interrupted by a sudden explosion of an oxygen tank, forcing a return to earth."

Horace said, "Interesting, history in this Bubble? Maybe we should come back there later and watch?". As he recorded the location for reference. Alright, Steven we ready?".

As AMBROSE moved to the Time Portal, his image changed to a basic Victorian men's outfit starting with high waist pants held up by suspenders in a dark stripe. Next, a loose Victorian men's shirt in white. A Victorian suit with a matching vest with an ascot in place of a necktie. Button-up boots on what was made to look like his feet and a bowler hat on top of his blond hair and Swedish-looking face. He was again looking very dashing. There was something to be said for holographic dressing, you could lead the style all the time. Steven kind of chuckled looking at AMBROSE and said, "Go ahead, Horace."

Horace typed on the keyboard to activate Explorer. Explorer's powerful AI was now able to run the whole show.

First HOME BASE and then in a few seconds AMBROSE was grabbed by the Transporter and moved through the Time Portal to the Junction between the Bubbles.

Steven verified communication with AMBROSE and received a message on the big screen, "AMBROSE system status is good!"

Then he said, "Ok Horace, find where he is going."

The RealSim began a search for the coordinates that Hilda has selected. The display showed coordinates, 59°19′38″N 18°05′52″E.

The Virtual Probe did its instantaneous search and displayed:

> *May 15, 1897*
> *General Art and Industrial Exposition*
> *Stockholm, Sweeden*
> *"This event was praised as the first World's Fair"*

Then the Time Portal displayed this photo:

Hilda spoke up, "That is the place."

Horace said, "Steven, send AMBROSE in."

Typing on his keyboard, Steven issued the command to Explorer to send AMBROSE from the other Bubble back into ours in the year 1897. As soon as he moved in, his video came active sending still frames every few seconds and recording three video channels, and storing it in HOME BASE.

The Doctor said, "Should we let him explore?".

Steven answered, "That is what he was built for. Stockholm, Sweden in 1897 has got to be a lot milder than Mars. Let's do it."

Steven issued the command to AMBROSE to explore autonomously. The still pictures every minute started to show his movement.

Hilda closely watching the images said, "The exhibition site was located on the island of Djurgården. AMBROSE is crossing the Djurgårdsbron, the main bridge to the island. Many of those things are still there today.

As AMBROSE was crossing the bridge, the rear video took a still frame of a horse-drawn tram used to move visitors at the Exposition coming right at him. Then nothing!

◆ ◆ ◆

AMBROSE had gone dead! Steven typed frantically on his keyboard trying to establish communication again with AMBROSE. He got no answer. The video feeds were dead, no audio could be heard and AMBROSE would not answer the paging call from Steven.

Horace asked, "Nothing Steven?".

"No nothing coming back at all."

Horace said, "Have you tried the backup channel?"

"Yes, nothing there either."

The Doctor asked, "Steven anything on the telemetry channels?"

"Doctor, apparently the transmitter is still working it is sending me a battery level. Unfortunately, that does not give us any control and the other 5 telemetry signals are dead."

Steven kept working on the keyboard and nothing was improving.

The Doctor asked, "Steven is there any way we can help?".

"Doctor, I don't believe so at this point I have nothing. I am not sure we can even bring him back. He must get to the Junction for the Transporter to grab him."

The Doctor said with a little chuckle trying to break the tension, "Steven did you lose my robot?"

"I hope not sir, that will be coming out of my pay for a long time." Everyone had a good laugh at Steven's expense.

William Lentz, an MIT robotics engineer on Steven's team yelled over, "Steven, try the emergency homing signal on HOME BASE.".

"Thanks, Bill, I hadn't thought about that."

Steven typed a command to HOME BASE. The big screen echoed the command, "HOME BASE, received Emergency Recall."

"Command Issued, Emergency Recall. Is this Confirmed?"

Steven typed in, "Confirmed.".

The screen echoed, "Emergency Recall Command Confirmed... Command sent..."

Everyone watched the screen. Steven was fixed on his telemetry screen. Still nothing but the battery level. Then in a couple of seconds, Steven yelled, "OK AMBROSE! He has gone into an emergency reboot."

Just as the big monitor showed, "AMBROSE: Emergency Reboot Started."

Then the display showed a string of messages that no one except Steven could read. Much like the messages, people saw in historical training films about old home computers when they restarted way back in the 1970s on what they called 'Green Screens'.

The big screen displayed, "AMBROSE: Emergency Reboot Completed. Status Nominal."

Two of the video channels sent still pictures. One picture was a very close image of cobblestones, the other a clear blue sky. Steven said, "He is lying face down on the road."

Bill Lentz said, "Give it a minute Steven and let the self-righting protocol kick in.".

Suddenly, there was a green indication on Steven's Telemetry screen. The next set of still images where showing AMBROSE had gotten back to the normal position and the cameras were looking forward and backward.

The big-screen monitor displayed, "AMBROSE: Emergency Homing Signal Acknowledged. Command being executed."

The next still picture showed AMBROSE facing over the bridge. In a couple more frames, he had reached the HOME BASE unit. AMBROSE went back toward the Junction. Explorer took control, and the Transporter moved both AMBROSE and HOME BASE, back into the junction with the other Bubble.

Horace yelled, "Great save Steven and Bill." As he commanded RealSim to move to their point in time and space. Once the messages confirmed that location, he activated the Explorer to control the Transporter and AMBROSE and the HOME BASE unit popped out of the Time Portal.

The Doctor stood up and yelled, "You all did it. I thought he was gone for a time. Great job all of you."

Horace said, "Shut Down all Systems".

AMBROSE popped back into his MRTL Jumpsuit and shut down.

# A TRIP TO THE OTHER SIDE

I n about a month everyone had been cleaning and polishing their programs and AMBROSE himself. They made a couple more trips back in time in their own Bubble. AMBROSE had no more problems with the environment. His AI learned from the experience with the tram. He was able to take some great historic videos. Maybe the system could be used to rewrite a history textbook?

One of the Doctor's favorites was the surrender at Appomattox Court House, in the American Civil War, the site in Virginia of the surrender of the Confederate forces to those of the North on April 9, 1865. Now the strange part. The historic photos in the cloud computer archive showed that AMBROSE was there back in 1865 when the photo was taken, looking like a proper Confederate Officer. Time is a scary thing to study. Some things we are just not going to try to understand and that is one of them.

At a team status meeting, Horace made the suggestion, "We have gotten fixated on moving AMBROSE to other places and times in our Bubble. We have not let him explore the adjacent Bubble."

Hilda said, "That is far less predictable. We did get a lot of historical data from their version of the Internet. But actually, we don't really understand their timeline. We suspect that one POD is in 1942 but we have no information about what changes were made to the timeline and how it differs from ours. Besides, the big computer located something I have no explanation for at all.

I had asked the computer to locate the Doctor. The cloud computer has found Dr. Mershon in the adjacent bubble. It found two critical facts. First, he was reported missing with the submarine USS Joseph Kane in the Pacific in 2025. Then apparently, he did return several months later and we located him again in late 2026 living in Maine. Then we found that he was killed in 2027 in a car accident. That seems to show that we may not have been looking at the same bubble each time and there may well be three bubbles involved."

The Doctor said, "Let's do one probing trip into that Bubble to do a historical comparison. Hilda, it appears that you may have collected historical data from two different bubbles which contacted ours.".

Hilda spoke up, "Doctor, I hate to say this but one very obvious difference is you. You or at least someone by your name died in a car accident in 2027, yet here in this bubble, you are alive in 2035. There was also a young man, Michael McDow who caused the accident and was also killed.

The Doctor said, "Alright let's do some research in that bubble and see what we might be getting into. Now I want to share a fact. I am going to say this in a way not to disclose classified information, so don't ask. I can assure you that in that bubble at least one POD is in 1942. The changes made impacted hundreds of people there at the time and thousands when that expands out to the rest of the world's timelines. I don't know if that helps at all, but I can't say any more.".

The doctor paused for a minute with obvious emotion on his face. Then he said, "Horace, can you send RealSim off to try to find me in 2027?".

"Doctor, the system has gotten pretty sophisticated I believe I can ask it to search for that. It might take a while to find the right junction between the bubbles. But I think it will find it."

"Ok, team! That is the goal. Find everything you can about me in 2027 in the other bubble. Most importantly find a linkage we can use to get there. I propose we first send AMBROSE in. Maybe even to communicate with 2027 me."

With that, the entire team left to work on the problems that were created and they are many. The Doctor was thinking about one classic sci-fi theory which has always asked the question, "What if you went back in time and changed your own life, would you still be there when you tried to come back? Well, we may get to the edge of that.".

Hilda was very concerned because she knew of the other problem with the timeline. One search showed the Doctor, KANE, and the crew all still missing at the end of 2025. The latest history access showed the Doctor dying in a car accident in 2027. Are these the same bubbles and the Doctor returned somehow or is there a third bubble involved?

In three weeks, Horace told the Doctor that they would like to have a review meeting. The doctor agreed, so early the next day they all met in the conference room to check the status.

Horace spoke up first, "Team, I wanted to hold this meeting because I have heard from some of you that some progress has been made on this challenge. I would also like to propose a change in our protocol. To prevent confusion, we will call the Doctor in the other bubble, Blue Doctor. First, Hilda and I have located the Blue Doctor in the other bubble and a linkage we might be able to use.

Hilda said, "Yes, we have found a linkage, it really is pretty good because it takes us to 2027, two days before the car accident on August 12, 2027. The accident happened at 9:22 A.M. on the 14th.".

Horace asked, "Steven, have you completed the modifications to the AI in AMBROSE?".

"Horace, we have done the best we could. We bought some more voice simulation software and we have him talking naturally. He should be able to communicate with Blue Doctor. Before we go, I think the Doctor needs to coach him on some key things to say to use as a mental linkage to the Blue Doctor based on the information before the POD. We will need to make him believe what is happening rather quickly.".

"Steven, I totally agree, if he does not buy into it quickly, he could grab a shotgun and blow AMBROSE away! I think I might do that in those circumstances."

Horace then said, "Hilda, have you been able to use the Virtual Probe function to find any more details?".

"Yes Horace, we have. The Blue Doctor lives alone in a house which is a year 2024 recreation of what they called a Craftsman Style house. Actually, a beautiful home compared to the steel and glass buildings most people are confined to now or even in 2027. Today it would be almost impossible to build a home like that. Even in 2027, having the land to build it when every square foot of ground is being used for massive buildings. I found that this house was rebuilt in 2024 on the site of a house the Blue Doctor had owned since the 1950s. Eventually, it deteriorated too much to be repaired. So, he had it recreated using more modern materials but preserving the Craftsman look. Most likely one of a very few still existing.

I found some articles about our Blue Doctor. Apparently, he is in excellent health but has become a total hermit, confining himself to his house. He has published a couple of books, listed as science fiction on the subject of time travel. People believe he has been doing some research on that subject in the basement of the house, but there are no details.

As for the accident, in 2027 they had adopted a majority of autonomous vehicles. The occupant merely sets a destination and the vehicle takes them there. There are very few traffic accidents because of the greatly reduced number of human drivers to make mistakes. Unfortunately, for the Blue Doctor, he had the misfortune to meet up with one. The person failed to yield to the autonomous vehicle at a stop sign. Their vehicle impacted the Blue Doctor's vehicle causing it to roll over and off the road. Killing the Blue Doctor.".

The Doctor asked, "Hilda, any way of determining where he was going? Maybe we could change the circumstances slightly?".

"Doctor, I think we would have to send AMBROSE in to get that level of detail. Might not be until we actually make contact with the Blue Doctor.".

The Doctor asked, "Horace, what do you think the plan should be?".

"Doctor, I believe we need to give it another two weeks to polish the entire program from all aspects. Then we send AMBROSE in maybe just for a reconnaissance mission. Review again then and prepare for actual contact with the Blue Doctor. Does everyone agree with me?".

Horace looked around the room and seemed to get complete agreement. Then the Doctor said, "Alright then that will be the plan. In two weeks, we send AMBROSE in. Thank you all."

After the meeting, Hilda walked up to the Doctor and asked, "You alright hearing all of that?".

"Yes, it is fascinating to hear. I was always kind of a revolutionary/pioneer type. I would sure love to see what is happening in his basement. Maybe AMBROSE can check it out.".

"Yes Sir, we can try to do that."

In two weeks, the first thing in the morning the whole team was in the Time Portal room, making final preparations. AMBROSE was dressed in his 2027 holographic look. The Doctor walked into the lab and seemed very excited. This time he went over and grabbed a visitor's chair and dragged it over next to Horace. He said, "Mind if I join you?".

Horace with a laugh said, "Nope, it's your show, Doctor".

Horace took control of the room with a quick PA announcement, "May I have your attention!"

After everyone had focused on him, he said, "Ok, final check. Hilda, go?". She gave him a thumbs-up. "Steven?". Steven waved and said, "Ready!".

"AMBROSE, ready?".

AMBROSE answered in his newly improved AI voice synthesizer speech, *"Yes Sir, I am ready to go!"*.

Horace said alright here we go, as he fired up the RealSim software for the search into 2027 in the other bubble. The Doctor watched intently as the screen in front of Horace flashed information about each bubble junction it was discovering. After checking each one it would reject it and continue the search.

The Doctor asked Horace, "How long?".

Horace answered, "It depends how many hot spots it finds on the way. They kind of distract the search because it has to evaluate and reject it. Maybe 15-20 minutes.".

In only about 10 minutes, the screen said, "Junction found, starting the Explorer function.".

Horace announced, "The system is running the Explorer to see if we can get coordinates for the Transporter.".

The Explorer took the simulated trip into the other Bubble.

The Explorer reported:

- Bubble outer edge detected

- Adjacent Bubble edge detected

- Coordinates resolved.

- Junction modeled

- Permission to activate Transporter?

Horace quickly asked, "Everyone alright to go?". They all said yes. So, Horace responded to the Explorer, "Continue!".

The Explorer said:

- Coordinates passed to Transporter

- Transport commencing

- HOME BASE Transported. As it disappeared into the Time Portal
- HOME BASE transport successfully.
- Communication test with HOME BASE is excellent.

Horace typed a few commands.

The Explorer reported:

- HOME BASE, ready to launch Drones.

- Drones 1-5 launched and reporting properly.

- Drones 6-10 launched and reporting properly.

- Drones 11-15 launched and reporting properly.

- Operation continues.

- Ready to Transport AMBROSE?

Then Horace asked Steven, "Is AMBROSE Ready?"

Steven replied, "AMBROSE is good to proceed with Transport."

Horace typed a couple commands and AMBROSE vanished into the Time Portal as Explorer reported:

- AMBROSE transport successful

- Communication check with AMBROSE successful.

- Permission to proceed?

The system activated AMBROSE in autonomous search mode. The cameras began to send images. Apparently, the location was perfect because as soon as AMBROSE left the junction, he transmitted this image:

The Virtual Probe reported, "This image is Dr. Mershon's residence taken in 2025."

The Doctor, quietly said, "I would like that house.".

Horace said, "Ok, everyone ready to send AMBROSE in closer?". Everyone gave him approval to move on.

AMBROSE's new software was now reporting status both in a text message to their displays and by audio. He was also accepting commands verbally. Through the speakers, they heard, "*Transfer complete. All systems are reporting excellent status. Ready to proceed please provide instructions?*".

Horace said, "AMBROSE, please carefully approach the house. All cameras reporting please."

Several additional monitors flashed on showing all the views for the cameras in AMBROSE. Now able to transmit streaming video, his forward camera began to show a slow motion toward the house moving up the driveway. All other cameras were clear no one was nearby and no hazards were detected.

As AMBROSE got beside the house, the Doctor said, "Look there are lights on in those basement windows."

Horace said, "AMBROSE, slowly approach the basement window. Remove your chest camera and hold it and give us a video feed."

AMBROSE moved over close to the basement window. The window was crusted with dirt and mud from rain splashing on the gravel driveway. AMBROSE did his best to scrape off some of the crud with his hand. Titanium is not great for cleaning windows, but he was able to make a hole to see through. As instructed, he removed his miniature body camera to hold in his hand and transmit a picture looking in the window. There he was the other Doctor Mershon, Blue Doctor. Considering he was over 10 years younger than the Doctor sitting at the console, he looked older. Like something had caused a stressful life and it took a toll on his body. He seemed healthy, but just older.

He was working on some electronics on his workbench. Steven said, "Ambrose, zoom in on those circuits." He could see they were very sophisticated multiple processor computer circuits.

Horace said, "AMBROSE, scan around the room."

AMBROSE slowly swung the camera to aim around the room. As it got to one corner, the Doctor yelled, "Stop!".

Horace said, "AMBROSE, Stop there." The motion of the camera stopped. As they all stared at the monitor.

The Doctor said, "Look, that looks like a smaller and primitive version of the Time Portal. He is doing time research."

Horace asked, "Hilda, have you been able to attach to their Internet and get a data dump?".

Hilda answered, "We sure have. The Blue Doctor has a very good wi-fi system. As AMBROSE got close, we were able to hack into it. I got a very big data extract from that, the doctor's computer, and the Internet in their bubble. It will take time to make much out of it, but I got it all recorded and HOME BASE is returning the data".

Horace said I think we have done well for this test. Steven bring AMBROSE back. Steven said, "AMBROSE return to HOME BASE.".

The cameras showed AMBROSE rolling back to where he had entered that bubble. The return process was repeated and their HOME BASE and AMBROSE were back inside the Time Portal. Steven said, "AMBROSE what is your status?".

AMBROSE answered, "*I am well thank you, that was a fun trip!*".

Steven commented, "There is that AI personality coming through again.".

The Doctor said, "Team that was just as we hoped an amazing performance. Now let's see if we can determine where Blue Doctor was going when the accident happened.".

# CHANGING TIME

Over the period of a couple weeks, the team was very focused on a single project. That was to determine the life pattern of the Blue Doctor and try to save his life. All the systems worked flawlessly so they could all focus on this research not having to do any corrections.

Horace decided to call a team meeting. He was not required but Horace decided to invite the Doctor to attend. They met in the conference room.

Horace started the meeting, "From the individual feedback I have gotten from all of you, I believe we are getting very close to our attempt to contact Blue Doctor. I would like to get an update from everyone so that we might decide if we are ready."

"Steven, let's check on AMBROSE first?"

"Alright, AMBROSE is performing flawlessly and no changes in programming have been required. We gave him a physical check-over to be sure that everything is "Beautiful", as he said this morning. The AI keeps showing that personality. He got the statements from the Doctor which will be used to identify us and establish a believable link to Blue Doctor. AMBROSE is ready."

Horace then said, "Hilda, what have you been able to find from the data dumps?"

"Well, the world, in general, is not all that different from life in our bubble. There are certainly historical differences and the computer finds hundreds of human differences each day it searches. People who are here and are gone there. People who are here and never were there. People who died there and have never been here. All the possible permutations. Their history book records are totally different in many factual ways. But the general flow of society is not all that different.

As for Blue Doctor. He resides in Maine. At least the maps didn't change much. He was killed on the second Wednesday of August at 9:22 in the morning. I found a calendar on his computer. It had entries on the second Wednesday of each month for a meeting of the "Historical Time Ventures Club" at 10 A.M.

I did some research on the Club. It is a society formed to honor and maintain the historical legacy of the belief in time travel. Their founding charter says that they are the preservationists of the legacy started by the book, "The Time Machine" by H. G. Wells, published in 1895. That sci-fi work is credited with starting the belief that time travel is possible by using a machine to move around in time. I imagine the Blue Doctor as opened some other possibilities for them based on the theories he had at that point."

The Doctor spoke up, "Yes Hilda, I certainly imagine he has. We really don't understand if he took the trip that I did, but he would have the same theories I had at the time. I don't know what my experience may have done to him. Maybe we can determine that?".

Hilda said, "Yes Doctor, that might be possible. However, now we know where the Blue Doctor was going when the accident happened. My first question is should we try to change it?".

Horace said, "We still have no idea what the impact is of changing history since we have not been able to do that. If we go back to 2027 in that Bubble and somehow prevent the accident. The Blue Doctor lives and so does Michael McDow. That makes a change in the first fraction of a second after the incident. What could the longer-term changes be?".

The Doctor spoke up, "I have two very strong opinions about this. Unfortunately, they are opposites. If we go back and change something so the accident does not happen. My Doppelganger is saved. What will he be able to do in the years he has left after that? Maybe bring time travel into a permanent reality. Maybe he will find what we have about Time Bubbles? Maybe he will screw up the Quantum Physics of the universe and cause a massive time paradox.

That all could be bad or good. What things might Michael McDow the young law student do for the rest of his life? We have no way of knowing. He could be anything from a great scientist, legal mind, or another Son of Sam killer. Is this just too much power to wield in the world?

I am having the same feelings right now as Robert Oppenheimer when he saw the result of the Atomic Bomb and said, "I am become Death, the destroyer of worlds.". Certainly not in the same way but I fear we are wielding that power. Is it right for one person to have this power? I do want to make one statement to all of you. No matter what happens, this was my call and my responsibility. If we destroy the world, Dr. Mershon did it. If it somehow comes out great, then maybe Blue Doctor, did it? I just don't have an answer.

Right now, I am prepared to go with the plan, save the Blue Doctor and Michael. Then hope it is not the end of their world."

Horace then said, "OK, team you heard the man. Tomorrow at 7 A.M. we will start the mission for AMBROSE to meet Blue Doctor.".

Everyone seemed to agree.

The next morning, 7 A.M. seemed to come earlier. A beautiful bright sunny day. The entire team was assembled in the Time Portal room for this, "Historic" mission.

Horace led the team through the initial checkout and determined that everything was ready. AMBROSE said, "I am ready, let's go!" and he moved to the edge of the Time Portal. In a couple of minutes, the process had completed and AMBROSE's cameras were again showing Blue Doctor's house.

Horace commanded, "AMBROSE, approach the front door."

AMBROSE responded and the camera showed him approaching the front stairs and using his adjustable drive to climb up them in one easy motion. The camera showed the door and a doorbell button on the right.

Horace said, "AMBROSE push the button."

The camera showed AMBROSE's titanium finger reaching out and gently pressing the button. Through the speakers, they could hear the classic two-chime doorbell ring inside. In a minute, Blue Doctor walked up to the door and opened it. As soon as the door opened, he focused on AMBROSE. You could tell that he was shocked, but you could also see the scientist in him. NO real panic, just a deep curiosity, trying to determine what he was looking at.

# TIME BUBBLES

Before the Doctor could really react, AMBROSE began to explain.

*"Greetings Dr. Mershon, my name is AMBROSE. As you can tell I am an autonomous robot. I know you believe in time travel so I will tell you that I am here from the year 2037."*

*Pointing to the logo on his shirt he said, "I belong to a company called, Mershon Laboratories for Time Research (MLTR). The company is owned by you in the year 2037.*

*You instructed me to say two phrases. First, 'Something did happen to you on August 5, 1942.'. Second is the phrase, 'Time Bubbles'.".*

Blue Doctor stood quietly, deep in thought for a moment. Then he said in amazement, "It must be true!".

He opened the door and motioned for AMBROSE to come in. He walked over to a big recliner and sat down. Waving for AMBROSE to come closer.

Blue Doctor started to speak to AMBROSE, "So my company this MLTR has managed to create time travel and they sent you here to see me?"

"*Yes, Doctor that is the essence of it, but that is just the surface. There is much more to the story.*"

"Well, Robot! Get on with it!"

"*Yes Doctor, I will tell you what I have learned while working with Dr. Mershon and his team at MLTR. MLTR has over one hundred of the finest minds in several critical areas of science. All with backgrounds in the theory of Quantum physics and time. Their research has led to an understanding that we live in a time Reality. There are many of them all linked in some way. It appears that each one is like a Time Bubble. It has its own timeline and history. There are thousands of these Bubbles. It appears that they were spawned from each other. It seems that the adjacent Bubble may have a similar timeline to yours. At some Point of Divergence in time, the Bubbles are taken into their own timeline different from the Bubble they came from. So, with that in mind, I can tell you I came from a different bubble than we are currently in.*".

AMBROSE then said, "*HOME BASE Disconnect!*".

HOME BASE answered AMBROSE, "*Communication disconnected.*". Just as they received that message back in the control room, the camera displays and the audio went off. Horace asked, "Doctor, what the heck was that?"

The Doctor responded, "I had to tell AMBROSE to break the link to protect the top-secret information that he is going to share.".

Horace said, "Oh, I understand."

Back at Blue Doctor's house, AMBROSE continued, *"Dr. Mershon in our timeline took a mysterious trip back in time. He was doing some research onboard a 2025 Nuclear Submarine. The submarine was transported back to World War II near Guadalcanal in August of 1942. The submarine fought a Japanese fleet and destroyed it, along with two naval bases. Dr. Mershon has never told anyone about this because it was classified by the Navy. Even the team does not know these details. The Doctor was very curious about what your life did during the 7 days in 2025?".*

"You know, AMBROSE that was it, that time was strange for me in 2025. On August 1, 2025, I was told that I would be going on a submarine to do some research on how the new nuclear power plant affected the crew. The Navy flew me to the base at Pearl Harbor. The sub was to pick me up there. The pickup was delayed. Then suddenly on August 3rd, the Admiral in charge told me that the trip had been canceled because the submarine was reported missing in the Pacific near Bikini Atoll and they could not contact it. So, they flew me back home.

For nine days I was kind of in a mild coma, walking around in a fog like you get if you have a concussion. Then on the morning of August 12th, I had some kind of episode. Apparently, I snapped out of it suddenly. I explained it to the doctor as feeling like I was in two places at once or maybe being two people in one. They sedated me in the Hospital saying they thought I needed some rest to recover from whatever happened to me. Actually, thinking I was ready for the funny farm. They submitted me to several psychiatric exams trying to find the problem. Under hypnosis, they discovered that I had some strange memories of being involved in a submarine battle. However, I had never been on a submarine in my life. I felt like possibly I had time traveled. They never did explain it.".

AMBROSE continued, "*Well, our Doctor Mershon told me to explain to you that what you experienced was the meeting of two different Time Bubbles. Our Doctor started out in this Time Bubble. The mysterious radioactive force at Bikini Atoll transported him with the submarine USS Joseph Kane and the crew, back to 1942. They returned by going back through the radioactive force on*

*August 12th. At that instant, you, all the members of the crew, and the submarine itself changed places. Jumping between this Time Bubble to the one I am from. That had the effect of wiping out your memories because you were never in 1942 in a naval battle. Our Doctor was. The doctor described this as being a knife-edge cutting the film of history and splicing it back in a different connection. Your bubble had some significant historic changes made because of the actions of the Joseph Kane, but no one there knew about it. The crew and our Doctor, have the memories but our Time Bubble was not impacted. The Navy ordered them to never talk about the incident so no one there except the crew and Navy command knows about the story. Even if they did talk it would seem like a conspiracy theory.".*

"AMBROSE, that is an amazing story. Since I am kind of telling it to myself. I guess I have to believe it. Now that brings me to a question. Why did they send you here?"

*"Well Doctor, on August 12, 2027, at 9:22 in the morning, you are going to be killed in an automobile accident. It will be caused by a young man named Michael McDow. He will be driving a manual control vehicle and will lose control. Your autonomous car will not be able to react fast enough to avoid the collision. Unfortunately, both of you and he will be killed. We know that you belong to an*

*organization called, 'Time Venture Club' and that you will be heading for a meeting that day and time. We need you to skip that meeting.".*

Well AMBROSE, this all seems real and I appreciate the warning and will do as you ask. It is no big thing to miss one meeting.

*"That is good Doctor. We were hoping you would accept this story and keep yourself from being killed. Just one moment please."*

AMBROSE commanded, *"HOME BASE Reconnect!"*. AMBROSE heard the message, "Connection reestablished.".

Back in the Time Portal room, they heard the statement that they were reconnected and all of their camera monitors and audio from AMBROSE came back to life. AMBROSE said, *"MLTR go ahead."*.

Back at the control console, Doctor Mershon spoke. Through AMBROSE the voice resonated for the Blue Doctor to hear.

"Hello, Alfred this is me in 2035. I just wanted to do this as another first. Talking to yourself at different times. I am so glad you have accepted the story that AMBROSE brought you.

This will keep you alive at least for a few more days. I am sure you know we still have no idea what this change will do, but we will be following closely our technology allows us to watch your world and your Time Bubble. I know you are going to be fascinated by what you have learned today. Let me just assure you that getting hooked on this research is a very expensive and difficult road. You will serve yourself best to avoid it. However, I know a lot about you and imagine you may jump right into it. We will be watching. Best of luck.".

"Thank you, Alfred, for saving my life. Now that I have heard this, I am not sure what I will be doing, but I am glad you shared this with me. Thanks.".

At the console, Horace said, "AMBROSE return to HOME BASE.".

AMBROSE said, "*It is nice to have met you, Doctor, I must return now.*". AMBROSE then rolled to the door opened it and left. Returning to HOME BASE and back through the Time Portal. They left HOME BASE in place and had it launch a spread of rocket Drones so they could monitor that bubble.

The Blue Doctor just sat in his chair astounded by what had just happened. Still not understanding what had happened to him back in 2025. As he promised he skipped his meeting on August 12<sup>th</sup>. The team was watching.

# TIME GOES ON

The next day passed slowly. The whole team was focused on what impact it would have as soon as Blue Doctor changed history. They were all running the software to keep probing into the nearby Bubble which housed the Blue Doctor. No one had seen any historical changes from AMBROSE visiting him. That was to be expected because only this team and the Blue Doctor knew about it. The doctor was not running out to tell anyone in his Time Bubble.

Wednesday finally came. As they discovered before the time and date in these two Bubbles were in sync. The team assembled in the Time Portal room, watching the systems as the clock approached the critical time of 9:22 A.M.

As soon as the time passed, Horace focused the RealSim on the time and place in the other Bubble. It locked in and the image of the Doctor's house appeared again. The Virtual

Probe reading data from the Drones confirmed that the Blue Doctor was still alive and in the house.

Their Doctor sitting at the control console trying to lighten the mood said, "Well, I guess I lived!".

No one really knew if that was funny or not. No one could find any changes in their reality. At least not at the current time.

Hilda decided to start probing further in the future. She and Horace directed the RealSim to look ahead a year to 2028. The system was locked in and the Virtual Probe was activated. The Doctor's house was still there and a drone picture showed in the Time Portal. Looking a bit more run-down but standing.

They found some newspaper articles about the Doctor. Basically, accusing him of going insane. Apparently, he had grabbed onto some information AMBROSE had shared with him. The team didn't know what it was. However, the doctor started to run around to newspapers and TV talk shows talking about time travel and changing history. He had apparently jumped over the line from scientist to being taken as a weird old hermit with crazy ideas. Almost like they take conspiracy theorists. He had lost all credibility. Apparently, he had tried to get funding to start a research facility and was turned down cold. The investors thought he was mentally gone. According to one newspaper, there was an effort to have him committed to a mental institution. They had managed to have him arrested and sent to the mental hospital several times. They were attempting to have the city take his house and condemn it. Of course, some big builder was behind that, so he could steal the property cheap and build a high-rise apartment.

Hilda did some more searching to see what the story was with Michael McDow. She found that he had graduated from law school, passed the bar, and was running for election as a State Senator. People were very fond of his young progressive ideas. He was in favor of everything for the people and reducing the Government's hold on people's lives. There was a good chance he would be elected.

Back in MLTR, the team was reviewing these findings and evaluating what the next move should be.

Horace said, "Luckily for us, these changes only had a small impact. The whole thought scares me thinking about what damage we could do. Doctor Mershon what was your initial goal for this company?".

"Well, Horace it was to explain what had happened to me back in 2025. Since as you know all the Navy data is Top Secret, I was hoping that I could publish the result of this research to prove that time travel is real. Well, we have proved that. However, I still don't think I could publish it. All I can think of is the hundreds of dark purposes this could be used for.

I held a meeting with major investors. I, in simple terms, explained that we were at a junction where the impact of our work needed to be understood before we proceeded. I discussed with them what their original intent was for funding our research. Many of the ideas scared me to death. Even on a simple level like turning AMBROSE into a history-jumping assassin. He could pop into someplace in history and blow someone up and then leave. Not a trace of what happened, but history would be changed nonetheless. They had motivations for doing military changes which would bend the outcome of a war. They had ideas of popping into another country as soon as it was known they made military or political changes and then pop in to see the decision process. They expressed many more strange ideas. I told them that our research was dangerous and could not be released. That caused them to be very mad at me and upset. They will most likely seize the assets of the company and sell it all off. However, they now know there is nothing they will get to use coming from our research. I would now be afraid to let any of this out in the open.".

Horace said, "I agree Doctor, but that leaves us with nothing safe and constructive we can do with this knowledge and these software systems.".

"Horace, you are correct. I am thinking the only safe thing to do is shut it all down. Have our research added to the Navy Archives of the 2025 incident and secured forever. The investors will not be happy about that, but I just think it is far too dangerous.".

Steven spoke up, "I think the research my team has done with AMBROSE is usable and could be distributed?".

The Doctor said, "Sorry Steven, AMBROSE knows too much and there is no way to flush his AI brain. He would have to be destroyed.".

Horace said, "I hate to say it but I must agree Doctor. I don't want to be out of a job, but I think for the sake of all, that is the only possible plan.".

Hilda, "Spoke up. This has been tremendous. I hate to have wasted a couple years of my career for something I can't even talk about, but I think you are both right."

The Doctor said, "So that has to be it!".

In a couple days the Doctor held a final meeting. Thanked everyone for their efforts, gave them very nice bonus checks, and congratulated them on their success. Then he had the company's chief lawyer give a talk and hand out some fresh new very extensive non-disclosure forms for everyone to sign. They all knew that these two years would be lost in their life and they could not even be discussed. The

Doctor was already used to that idea since he had been hiding the story since 2025. But History went on safely.

**This is Randolph Ebb, signing off!**

Printed in Great Britain
by Amazon

41675907R00108